2 4 MAY 2000

LONG LOAN

This book is due for return not later than the last date
stamped above, unless recalled sooner.

PELICAN BOOKS

A753

A SOCIAL HISTORY OF
ENGLISH LAW

Alan Harding was born in Surrey in 1932, and from Guildford Grammar School he went as an Exhibitioner to read modern history at University College, Oxford. There legal history attracted him and after completing his first degree he worked for the degree of B. Litt. on an edition of a thirteenth-century plea-roll which is shortly to be published by the Selden Society. Out of two further years of research at Manchester University came an essay on the origins of the office of Justice of the Peace which won the Alexander Prize of the Royal Historical Society for 1959. He was appointed in 1961 to a lectureship in Medieval History at Edinburgh University, where his wife is a lecturer in Chemistry.

ALAN HARDING

A SOCIAL HISTORY OF
ENGLISH LAW

GLOUCESTER, MASS.

PETER SMITH

1973

To Marjorie

CONTENTS

Acknowledgements

I wish to thank Professor J. D. B. Mitchell, Mr M. R. Topping, and Mr D. A. Bullough of Edinburgh University for reading parts of this book in typescript. They are, of course, not responsible for the errors which remain.

INTRODUCTION:
LAW AND HISTORY

HISTORIANS long ago grasped the importance of law to history. They knew that medieval political theories were expressed in legal terms, and also the political conflicts of seventeenth-century England (see Chapter 10); yet they knew also that a country's law takes us far beyond its constitution, to every social activity important enough to seem worth regulating. It is a fact that legal records – deeds and records of litigation – comprise a very large part of the material for social history. Moreover, the legal evidence extends from men's everyday existence (the things they possessed, the work they were bound to do, and the way they died) to their most abstract thinking about morals and society: 'the history of jurisprudence is the history of civilization.' The nineteenth-century creators of modern historiography made it their ideal to take every period on its own terms, and believed that the study of history should encourage understanding of remote and strange cultures. It was no accident that these historians placed so much emphasis on law, or that one of the greatest of them was the lawyer, Frederick William Maitland (1850–1906), of whom G. M. Trevelyan said that he used law to open the mind of medieval man.[1]

Because law is the expression of social needs, a system of law is a description of the society for which it was made. It was through their study of Roman Law and feudal law, not directly of history, that sixteenth-century scholars first grasped the idea of different societies, each a distinctive organism. English lawyers, however, with the insularity of their nation, never looked beyond their own Common Law, which they believed was nearly perfect; it was on the level of revealed truth, and its social and historical origins needed no investigating. Coke buttressed this revelation with imaginary history (see Chapter 9), because real history would have confused it, and the working English lawyer has remained anti-historical ever since. While the historian goes to the past for evidence and prizes every bit he finds, the lawyer is after the single authority which will settle the case in hand. 'The lawyer must be orthodox,' wrote Maitland, 'otherwise he is no lawyer; an orthodox history seems to me a contradiction in terms.'[2]

For the daily work of the courts in applying legal rules real history may be unnecessary; but hardly when it comes to making and changing the law. For law is not, or ought not to be, the product of itself, but of past society (that is, history), and it is difficult to see how things can be changed without knowing how they came to be as they are. Further, and unexpectedly, the historical approach introduces the element of irreverence which keeps the law alive, for it shows by what absurd shifts and accidents much of the law has been arrived at; that a small part of it may be essential, but most is contingent. Maitland heaped devastating scorn on the oldest section of English law, the law of real property (see Chapter 14), and history may now suggest that even the criminal jury is not sacred (for its record is very uneven) and could be abandoned without catastrophe.

Perhaps the main practical value of legal history is simply to remind law that it exists for society and must constantly be reforming itself up to date with social change (that is, history). Law which forgets society is 'in danger of becoming an occult science, a black art, a labyrinth of which the clue has been lost'. The education of the English lawyer has been dangerously narrow, when it has existed at all, and the self-centred isolation of the inns of court has not encouraged social awareness or a feeling of social responsibility. In 1699 John Evelyn regretted that law students made 'such haste to precedents, customs and common-places'; for, through a study of ethics, Roman Law and history they might have penetrated 'into the grounds of natural justice and human prudence', and 'come to understand how governments have been settled, by conquest, transplantations, colonies or garrisons through all vicissitudes and revolutions . . .; how laws have been established, and for what reasons changed and altered; whence our holding by knight's service, and whether feudal laws have been derived from Saxon or Norman.' Evelyn's reproach still has some relevance.[3]

The lawyer's textbook looks more like a chemistry book than a history book: the law is divided up into a number of elements or rules, and when these are traced back to their origins through strings of cases the logical pattern remains dominant and the separate strands of development are not woven into coherent history. Maitland once said that the history of English law was not written because legal historiography was the handmaid of legal dogma. Since then, there have been some heroic attempts to describe the growth of English law in an historical way (see *Bibliography*), and beside them this book is small fry indeed. But it does at least try to be real history; to relate the development of the law as a whole, and forwards, to the development of English society, not to trace backwards a bundle of legal doctrines. If the result looks untidy to the lawyer, perhaps it is because history is untidy by nature; and if the law of past centuries is not described in the proper modern terms, perhaps this will be excused on the grounds that it was not modern law, nor even moving unerringly towards it. The layman who writes in general terms of recent law may inevitably seem irresponsible to the lawyer. But such a discussion of the relationship of law to society is what students of both history and law need and rarely get.

The concern of the book with the law as a prime historical factor explains its arrangement. Part One describes the development to 1642 of English law as a system of ideas. Part Two describes the human basis and actual working of the legal system in English life, the key chapters (9) and (10) showing how it was the product of society (Chapter 9: 'Law in the Making') and in return (Chapter 10: 'Law in English History') shaped the great seventeenth-century crisis of the constitution. Part Three carries the history of the law in relation to society down to the present day.

PART ONE

CHAPTER I

OLD ENGLISH LAW

THE beginnings of the Common Law are often placed in the twelfth century, but English society is of course much older, and as early as the seventh century the laws on which that society rested were remarkable for their vigour.

THE FIRST LAWS, THE FEUD AND 'PEACE'

In the year 597, missionaries from Rome arrived in Kent; and the local kings of England began to issue laws, as Bede said, 'in the Roman style', but in the English language:

The property of God and the Church is to be paid for with a twelve-fold compensation; a bishop's property with an eleven-fold compensation . . . a deacon's property with a six-fold compensation . . . the peace of the Church with a two-fold compensation. . . .

If the king calls his people to him, and anyone does them injury there, he is to pay a two-fold compensation and 50 shillings to the king. . . .

The breach of the king's protection, 50 shillings. . . .

The breach of a *ceorl's* protection: six shillings. . . .

If anyone kills a man, he is to pay as ordinary wergild 100 shillings. . . .

If hair-pulling occur, 50 *sceattas* [= 2½ Kentish shillings] are to be paid as compensation. . . .[1]

The reason for making this 'law' is clear enough. The foreign clergy, venturing into a rough and pagan society, had to be given an appropriate status and protection for the property they would acquire from noble patrons. There was a ready way of calculating worth and position: each level in that rigidly hierarchical society had its particular *wergild*, the sum of money which had to be paid as compensation to the

13

lord or the kin of a murdered man. So King Ethelbert wrote down the customary worth of his subjects, as well as the sums, proportional to the victim's wergild and the nature of the wrong, to be paid for injuries less than homicide; and he put the clergy at the top of the hierarchy of worth.

Ethelbert's decree is no more than a tariff of the compensation which has to be paid for violent attacks on other people. It says nothing of courts or judges, because there are none, save perhaps the community itself in its 'folk-moots'. The 'judicial system' can cope with nothing more subtle than the outright violence to which most private disputes would come. But Ethelbert is not really making law at all: he is writing down the custom of the people in all its weird and inflexible detail.

The tariff of compensation presupposes the existence of the blood-feud, a factor in the development of most societies (from it stems the theme of tragic necessity in both ancient Greek and German literature). This does not mean that the Anglo-Saxons were in the anarchical 'state of nature' imagined by Thomas Hobbes. There was a sort of 'peace in the feud'. Men knew that killing brought vengeance, that there was a large group of kinsmen, extending to sixth cousins, whose duty it was to avenge a murdered man. For lesser wrongs the victim himself could take revenge. The 'king' or 'kin-representative', and the Church with its notion of an avenging God, intervened first of all to see that the duty of vengeance was fulfilled.[2]

But sixth cousins include almost everyone in the community, who are thus related to both murderer and victim. Consequently there is always tension between the loyalty of the kin and their desire for a quiet life, and every effort will be made to end the feud by honourable compensation. In Iceland there were regular assemblies of the whole people at which the arbitration of disputes was the main business, but there seems to have been no comparable system in England. *Njal's Saga*, which describes the Icelandic practice, refers to a time four centuries after Ethelbert, but to a warrior society in a recently settled land. Ethelbert's laws suggest that Kentish society had passed beyond the stage of arbitration under the eye of the whole community: the detailed tariff implies that disputes are normally and almost automatically settled by payments or by the enslavement to the plaintiffs of the malefactors who cannot pay.[3]

A self-respecting Anglo-Saxon king would always try to bring order and tranquillity to his people, and in Ethelbert's laws there was already one principle by which kings could extend their influence. That was the principle of the *peace*. England was not a land of a single peace but of many, one belonging to each great lord and one to the church. Peace was something precious and almost tangible which went along with a priest or a lord, and which great lords could give to their followers to take with them: in that case peace was often called *protection*. There could be different values of peace. Long after the idea had grown up that the high roads and then the whole country were in some sense automatically within the king's peace, it remained more heinous to infringe the king's 'hand-given' peace, the peace which the king had explicitly declared. Just as one could injure a man himself, one could injure his peace, by committing a crime in his house, or in his presence, or against his protected servant; and there was a traditional compensation for the breach of his peace.[4]

THE KING ENTERS THE LAW

It took many centuries for the king's peace to swallow up all the rest. Yet Ethelbert himself possessed two rights which marked him out as the special guardian of the law. Firstly, whenever a freeman was killed, fifty shillings had to be paid to the king, in addition to the compensation to the victim's kin. Secondly, the king held assemblies of the whole people, and an injury committed in one of them involved double compensation to the victim and again a fine of fifty shillings to the king. The king's court was already acquiring special authority.

Some late-seventh-century Kentish laws set out the quite

elaborate procedure which had become customary for arbitration in the folk-moots. When a man had a claim against another, he took surety from him to submit to arbitration: in other words he forced someone to be responsible for the defendant's appearance. The defendant had then to do 'such right as the judges of the people of Kent should prescribe'. There was no attempt to sift evidence. The judges or dooms-men were merely guardians of a ritual performance, who at the most decided by which of a number of mechanical means the defendant should try to clear himself. Normally the defendant could avoid paying compensation only by bringing a set number of 'oath-helpers' to swear to the reliability of his oath that he was innocent.

In the majority of cases violence must have originated in disagreements over commercial transactions. Buying and selling were essential to the Anglo-Saxons as to any other society: so a great mass of customary rules appeared to prevent fraudulent selling. Here were special opportunities for the king to intervene and refine the procedure by his edict. Goods had to be bought in open market ('market overt', as the legal phrase still goes), and it was decreed that a man who bought in the great market at London had to have the transaction witnessed by 'two or three honest ceorls, or the king's town-reeve'. If he did not do this and the bartered goods were subsequently claimed as stolen property, the defendant had to produce 'at the king's hall' the man who had sold them to him, or else return them to the plaintiff.

The first surviving laws of Wessex, the kingdom to the west of Kent, are those of King Ine. The seriousness of the problem of keeping order is shown by Ine's classification of robber gangs. 'We call up to seven men "thieves",' says his law; 'from seven to thirty-five a "band"; above that it is an army.' An extension of the system of fines to the king is evident in Ine's law, another clause of which runs: 'if anyone within the boundaries of our kingdom commit robbery and rapine, he is to give back the plunder and give 60/– as a fine.' The king has to be compensated too, because he is wronged as guardian of the peace. The idea of compensation to the private plaintiff and the idea of compensation to the king are both present, but they do not lead to a distinction between 'civil' and 'criminal' cases, 'private' and 'public' law, for the same wrongs are very often subject to both payments at once.

King Alfred's laws, made between 871 and 899, declared that for treachery to a lord there could be no compensation and no mercy, 'because Almighty God adjudged none for those who scorned him, nor did Christ, the Son of God, adjudge any for him who gave him over to death; and he [Christ] charged [everyone] to love his lord as himself'. Treason is treachery to one's lord or patron, with whom one has sacred ties. High treason is already present in Alfred's laws: 'if anyone plots against the king's life, directly or by harbouring his exiles or his man, he is liable to forfeit his life and all that he owns.' The existence of these 'bootless' wrongs, not to be satisfied by compensation or *bot* – by the eleventh century they were house-breaking, arson, obvious theft, manifest murder and betrayal of a lord – may suggest that some real crimes were recognized. But they were punished by death rather as sins against the laws of God than as crimes against the king's laws.

LORDSHIP

Historians used to trace English democracy back to the forests of Germany from which the settlers had come, where the Germanic 'folk' was pictured sitting in parliaments under the shade of the great trees. However that may have been, the Anglo-Saxon conquest of England must have depended on leaders, who probably very soon became the landlords of the settled country. As two or three vast open fields, gradually fragmented by the English peasant's natural system of equal inheritance by the sons of the family into an increasing number of narrow strips, replaced the little enclosures of the Celts, the life of the village depended on communal arrangements. Probably village courts soon appeared, independent folk-moots at first, but known to us in the later Middle Ages as the hall-moots or manorial courts of the lords of the manors. The history of the manorial system, in which the normal unit of all cultivation was the lord's estate, often coincident with the village, has recently been traced to the morrow of the English invasions. The village headman soon became the lord's reeve and presided in a court where local custom was always strong, but the profits were taken by the lord.[5]

The profits from fines imposed in medieval courts were often more important than complete control over their procedure, and this fact makes it difficult for us to know whether the nobles had their own courts to deal with anything more than village matters in Anglo-Saxon England. They were certainly granted by the king the fines imposed for some quite serious wrongs, but were these fines taken in a court held by the lord himself or in a (king's) folk-moot? Perhaps the answer to this much-debated question lies in the realities of power and not in the technicalities of charters. The king could not grant away what he did not possess. He could not grant the power to do justice to criminals, because the criminals had first to be caught, and for a long time to come the resources at the king's personal disposal were quite inadequate to the policing of the countryside. Rather, by conceding the fines which should otherwise have come to him, the king encouraged the lords to exert their natural authority in the countryside. The seeds of a court were already present in the great lord's 'peace'.[6]

The ravages of the Norsemen, from c. 850 onwards, increased the power of the nobles in England, just as they stimulated the growth of feudal lordship in France (the word 'feudal' refers to the 'fee' of land – in Latin, *feodum* – which a retainer received and held on condition that he served his lord in war). Many of the cultivators, in the midst of their stricken fields, looked to the nobles for protection and for seed and implements to start again. In return for help they 'commended' themselves to the lords, became 'their men', and agreed to hold their land, which had been freehold, as the lords' tenants. Though there was no complete 'feudal system' as under the Anglo-Norman kings, some of these tenants were obliged to perform specific duties as a condition of holding their land and must have closely resembled feudal retainers.

The Anglo-Saxon kings encouraged the reorganization of society round the great nobles. The laws of Athelstan, king of England, made between 924 and 939, show concern about 'lordless men from whom no justice can be obtained'. It was the lordless, not the kinless, man who was the problem then, for the lords were obliged to give *borh* or surety that their men would appear in court and pay any compensation awarded. Indeed, throughout the Middle Ages the relationship of lord and man was regarded as a sort of kinship, never as purely mercenary. The lord must not protect a man from the law, but see that justice was done upon him, or else himself pay compensation to the plaintiff and a fine to the king.

But if neither lord nor kindred can bring him to court, the accused man is to be deemed an outlaw, and 'he who encounters him is to strike him down as a thief'. *Gerit caput lupinum* ('he bears the head of a wolf') and is hardly to be regarded as a man any more. Without a police force, the law is inevitably driven to give the obdurate criminal up, to be fair game to his enemies.

THE COURTS OF SHIRE AND HUNDRED

The seventh, eighth and ninth centuries were the centuries of the *heptarchy*, when several kings reigned in different parts of England at the same time. The Norse invasions in the second half of the ninth century destroyed the kingdoms one by one, till only Alfred was left in Wessex to lead the counter-attack and win his dynasty the right to be the first rulers of the whole country. Alfred left a remarkably able line of successors to reign from Winchester, but at the beginning of the eleventh century another Norse invasion coincided with the king known to posterity as the 'unready', and Canute the Dane and his sons came to rule in England. Canute, however, did not destroy but strengthened the government which he took over from the kings of Wessex. His laws were more elaborate than all their predecessors, and the last before a third band of Norsemen sailed in 1066 from their recently acquired home in France, bringing with them French institutions and more drastic changes.

The transformation by the king of Wessex of a number of tribal communities, each a mere section of a wider Germanic society, into a single and extensive kingdom, made necessary more sophisticated forms of administration and produced the first distinctively English institutions of government. Even before the Norsemen came, Wessex was divided into *shires*, each centred on a defensible town or an important royal estate, perhaps to facilitate the collection of the king's dues. In Wessex the shires were probably a natural growth. As the rest of England was reconquered from the Danes by Alfred's successors, the shire system was imposed upon it, and again the nuclei of the shires were the proliferating towns or *burhs*, some, like Northampton, the centres of Danish settlement, others, like Hertford, the fortresses built by the English to consolidate their advance.

The shires and boroughs, like other Anglo-Saxon communities, had their folk-moots, which were also in a special sense the king's courts, the king's officers presiding in them. There appeared in the tenth century a third unit with its moot, the *hundred*, intermediate between shire and town. The hundred, like the Wessex shire, was probably an old unit, perhaps an area of a hundred hides of land. Since the hide, like all units in a world of primitive technology, was not an exact measurement, but a notional equivalent, useful in a particular operation, the size and number of hundreds varied very much from shire to shire: in a medium-sized shire ten or a dozen hundreds would have been a fair number. The hide was reckoned to be the amount of land necessary to support a family, and to the king a hundred hides made up a convenient unit of government: it was probably imposed on the rest of England by the kings of Wessex at the same time as the shire.

The shire and hundred courts were, to start with, equal and parallel in jurisdiction: they were independent folk-moots, and not stages in a hierarchy of courts which would take appeals up to the king. The shire proved the more durable because the shire reeve was more useful than the hundred bailiff as an administrative official. But the hundred court was nearer to the Anglo-Saxon countryman and probably the more important court in his time. By the ordinance of King Edgar, made between 959 and 963, the shire court met twice a year and the borough court thrice, and the hundred court customarily met every four weeks.

THE LAW OF THE OLD ENGLISH STATE

The consistent aim of the Wessex dynasty was to do away with the blood-feud as the basis of private law. Alfred's laws forbade a plaintiff to attack an opponent in his home until he had besieged him for thirty days and sought justice from the king. Athelstan's laws provided that if anyone failed to answer a summons by a plaintiff to three successive borough courts it was for the leading men of the borough (not the plaintiff) to ride to him 'and take all that he owns and put him under surety'. Already one of its essential elements, delay, was entering legal procedure; delay, while the peaceful settlement that civil law seeks was arrived at, if possible 'out of court'. Private or 'civil' law arbitrates between the parties, and on the other hand a criminal offence is one for which the state will allow no settlement, even if the wronged person desires it. From Canute's reign we have the earliest record of a civil law-suit, settled by the shire-court of Herefordshire.[7]

The mitigation of the disastrous effects of 'self-help' was attained by the extension of the idea of the king's peace and the responsibility of all, not just of the parties to a quarrel, to see that it was observed. Athelstan thought of his laws as 'enacting a peace' and ordered his bishops, aldermen and reeves over all his dominions to observe it. Canute's laws imposed a fine on anyone who came across a thief and did not raise the hue and cry, and upon anyone who refused to ride in pursuit of the thief. Yet there was still no assumption of a single and general and permanent peace which a crime automatically broke. For a long time after the Norman Conquest peace 'died with the king' and had to be proclaimed anew by his successor, licence reigning in the interlude.

The eleventh-century kings tried to keep order by putting the whole community in the place of the kin, responsible for a man's behaviour. According to Canute, everyone over twelve years of age who wanted the rights of a free man in legal proceedings had to be in a hundred and a tithing. The *tithing* was a group of ten men, who were automatically obliged to stand surety or give pledge for one of their number: thus the system was called by the Normans the 'frankpledge system'. The tithing eventually became a new territorial division coinciding with the village, and its head, the tithing-man, became the village constable. Its origins must be connected with those of the hundred. The hundred may originally have been an area obliged to produce so many men for the *fyrd*, the Anglo-Saxon militia, and throughout the middle ages men were required to maintain weapons both for service in war and to keep the peace at home. Thus from the beginning the tithing was probably a sub-unit of the police. As early as the reign of Athelstan, the men of London organized a voluntary 'peace-guild', and resolved 'that we always are to reckon ten men together – and the senior is to have charge of the nine ... and afterwards a hundred of them together, and one hundred-man'; and they were to turn out as required to ride along the trail of stolen cattle.

The opinion of neighbours always prevailed, and a trial was a test of character: the question was, 'can the oath of the defendant be relied upon?'. Notoriety in England, as in many primitive societies, was for long as good a reason for condemning a man as proof of a particular crime: a man 'regarded with suspicion by all the people', said Canute, was to be put under surety by the king's reeve to answer any charges brought against him, and if he had no surety he was to be slain and to lie in unconsecrated ground.

Lords were still required to be responsible for their retainers, but the creation of the new administrative areas and
moots of the tenth century kept the folk system alive alongside the aristocratic one. The shire and hundred moots were
also the king's courts, and justice never fell into the hands of
the nobles in England as it did in France. But the legacy of
the folk system was not entirely beneficial. The king's aldermen in the shire courts and his bailiffs in the hundred courts
were not judges in our sense, capable of applying general
principles to specific cases. They were rather the mere presidents of moots where the customary law was 'found' by the
leading men of the area. Such law was necessarily enshrined
in simple, unsophisticated and unrelated maxims, which had
to provide specifically for every likely situation.

The law extended little by little into 'private' matters,
even reinforcing the mutual responsibilities of members of
the family. At a marriage, the bridegroom was to announce
what he granted to his bride 'if she should live longer than
he'; that is, what dower she should have. Perhaps this was an
example of the general tendency of law, posited by Sir Henry
Maine, to advance from the protection of status within
communities to the enforcement of contracts between individuals.

Towards the end, the Anglo-Saxons knew several sorts of
contract. When a man was summoned to appear in court, or
an agreement was made to pay compensation which a man
could not immediately raise; or when a couple were be-
trothed (at a 'wedding'); then a contract would be made by
the surrender of a *wed* (which the Normans called a *gage*) as
security for performance. The *wed* may once have been
valuable, but soon became a token only. More serious was
the surety which had to be found in a legal action, for the
surety (the 'pledge' of Anglo-Norman times) was a man – a
hostage, bound 'body for body' to the accused, as the man
who goes bail in modern criminal cases is still deemed to be.
Gage and pledge played an essential part in the development
of the concept of liability for contract.

The law was at its most mechanical in the actual trial of

the accused. Primitive law is so complicated because the issues are too serious to be left to the discretion of judges, indeed of any human person. Law is 'unchangeable' custom; verdicts are for God who searches the hearts of men. The oath was really an appeal to God, since a perjured oath was expected to bring its own punishment. But increasing reliance was placed upon the ordeal, as a less equivocal way of discovering the verdict of heaven. The more notorious a criminal, the greater was his ordeal. He must fast, go to Mass and swear to his innocence; then he holds the hot iron (if the burn festers, he is guilty); or is lowered into water (he is guilty if he floats, for the water rejects him); or, if he is a clerk, swallows the sacred morsel which has been adjured to choke the guilty man.

Occasionally a more modern attitude creeps in. One of Canute's laws says that 'it does not seem right to us that any man should make good his claim to goods where there is a witness and where it can be shown that there has been fraud'. Several stages of legal reasoning existed side by side in pre-Conquest law. Beside the barbarity of Canute's decree that the oft-convicted man should have his eyes 'put out and his nose and ears and upper lip cut off, or his scalp removed' must be set the same king's astonishingly modern statements on criminal liability. 'In many a deed,' he said, 'when a man acts under compulsion, he is then the more entitled to clemency in that he did what he did out of necessity; and if anyone acts unintentionally, he is not entirely like one who does it intentionally.' Even though these ideas were taken (by Archbishop Wulfstan, who composed Canute's laws) from the penitentials of the Church, where quite sophisticated psychology was applied to prescribing penances for sins, it is obvious that the 'tariff' mentality was losing its strength.[8]

CHARTERS AND LAND-TENURE

The laws of the Anglo-Saxon kings were all in the vernacular, and in substance they showed no signs of Roman influence. Some of the law of the late empire did, however, appear in

England in the terms of the Latin charters (introduced by the seventh-century missionaries from Rome) by which the king granted lands to churchmen and eventually to laymen.

A charter was a form of conveyance. *Conveyancing* is the activity of the legal profession concerned with the framing of the deeds by which property is 'conveyed' from one person to another. It is of the greatest importance for the substance of the law, since it states the various conditions on which property is held, and by so doing classifies the sort of property which *can* be held, and which the courts may be called upon to protect against encroachment. For some of the most important sorts of property are not physical objects, obvious in themselves, but rights which have to be defined. Land cannot be owned like money or a motor-car, which a man can take around with him and, if he wants to, destroy; nor can it be stolen. Ownership is only the most extensive of rights over land, which range downwards through leaseholds of various lengths of time, to such 'easements' as the right of a man to cross his neighbour's land to get to his own. These and several other rights over the same piece of land, which will have to be mentioned later, can exist concurrently in different hands. It is by no means easy to demarcate the various rights that are needed in practice.

The Anglo-Saxons had no systematic theory of rights in land and we do not know how the majority of land, the *folk-land*, was normally held or conveyed. It used to be thought that land was at first owned by families, not by individuals, and therefore could not be freely sold or 'alienated' by the head of the family for the time being: only a royal charter or 'land-boc' could give the right of alienation, turning the folk-land into 'book-land'. But it has recently been argued that folk-land must have been conveyed often enough by a simple ceremony without a 'writing': the charter was not needed to alienate land, but rather to give the existing owner rights of Roman conception, not known in folk-land, to dispose of the property by will, or to permanently alter its value by freeing the slaves upon it, or even to tie it up for the future.

For it was apparently even possible for a testator to entail book-land, that is to determine how it should descend long after his death. If one of the prescribed line of heirs alienated the property, this was a matter for the king in his witan as well as the heir's kinsmen, for the king had 'booked' the land and his great men witnessed the transaction.[9]

If that was the meaning of book-land, it was a mature form of ownership which had no immediate future. For a long time after the introduction of Norman feudalism land could not be devised by will, and entails protected by law did not exist again till the reign of Edward I (1272–1307).

The rights in land which did have a future were those connected with feudalism (in a rather loose sense of that word); franchises, in other words governmental and judicial functions delegated to landlords; and leases on condition of service. In Worcestershire, in the tenth century, Bishop Oswald was giving 'loans' of land which terminated on the death of the grandson of the grantee. Possibly this was a form of 'subinfeudation': perhaps Oswald, like the Anglo-Norman baron, granted the land on condition of military service in order to recruit the soldiers which the king required from him. These, however, were local arrangements, and there was no 'feudal system'.

The Anglo-Saxons were 'ahead' of the Normans, in so far as military service was regarded as a public obligation, incumbent on all who were able to perform it, and was not the result of private bargains between the king and each of his barons. But in consequence there was no coherent system of rights in land. Land-books came from the king as the source of political power: he (and his successors) would see that their terms were observed. It was left to the Normans to bring the idea that all land as such was held ultimately of the king, one which made possible a comprehensive system of tenures defined by the conditions (of military or other service) on which the land was held.

THE FOUNDATIONS OF THE COMMON LAW

How far did the Anglo-Saxons lay down the guiding-lines of

English law? The ideas of the king's peace and of the responsibility of local communities turned out to be vital. Here Henry
II built upon ancient foundations. And, though it is the
accepted view that the Normans brought the jury with them
from France, it is difficult to believe that this supposed
'cornerstone of English liberty' was not a natural product of
Anglo-Saxon communal responsibility. The jury of Henry
II's reign was a group of twelve neighbours, who *knew* the
facts of a situation, and did not decide what they were after
hearing evidence. But as early as 962 or 963 King Edgar
decreed that all buying and selling was to be witnessed by
thirty-six persons in a large borough and twelve in a small,
and these would perhaps give judgment in case of dispute.
From a code of Ethelred, possibly made in 997, comes the
famous instance of the 'twelve leading thegns', who were to
appear in the court of the wapentake (the hundred of the
Danelaw) and 'swear on the relics which are put into their
hands that they will accuse no innocent man, nor conceal
any guilty one'. Again, there was a strong duodecimal element in the calculation of the number of oath-helpers needed
by an accused man (the number was adjusted to the gravity of
his offence).[10]

From the jury and two other institutions, which began
but were not of legal importance in Anglo-Saxon times, the
office of *sheriff* and the *writ*, Henry II was to construct the
distinctive procedures of the common law. The shire courts
were at first presided over by the great regional officers of the
king called *aldermen* (the bishops of the regions sat with the
aldermen, since there was no separation of ecclesiastical and
secular matters and there were no separate church courts).
The alderman, however, tended to become the hereditary
nobleman of an area containing several shires, especially
after the accession of Canute, when the alderman took the
cognate Danish name of 'Earl'. By 988, we begin to hear of
a shire-man or shire-reeve who acts as the deputy of the
alderman in each shire.

Though he was technically the alderman's deputy, the
sheriff was one of the growing number of royal bailiffs or

27

reeves who were administering the king's estates all over the realm. Of all the bailiffs, the one at shire level became the most important, and for centuries the axis of government ran from the king to his sheriffs. Perhaps the sheriff was so important because the leading men of the shires comprised the natural local communities: till very recent times all politics and most of the important law-suits began amongst them. After the Conquest the law-finders in the shire-court ceased entirely to be wise men drawn from the people. They were an aristocracy composed of the landowners of the shire.

It is hard to imagine that England would have acquired the most precocious administration in the medieval west without the extraordinary vitality and toughness which the sheriff's office proved to have. And justice and administration were indistinguishable in the middle ages. It was not simply that the burgeoning race of irresponsible local 'civil servants' could be checked only by sending judges to hear complaints against them. Judicial procedure developed only from the actual business of policing, for which the sheriff was responsible. When the sheriff was told to do justice in a particular case, then arose the question 'what is justice in this situation?' and finally 'what is justice whenever this situation arises?'

The link between king and sheriff was provided by the most original of all Anglo-Saxon inventions, the writ. Why was it so original, when it was just a 'writing', a written order? Because nowhere else in medieval Europe was there such a tradition of austerely succinct and practical letters, without which efficient bureaucracy is impossible; letters which could therefore be sent in their hundreds to more or less illiterate lay officials. In early medieval Europe, Latin was the only intellectually respectable language to write. So the clergy learnt to write Latin and laymen remained illiterate. In England, however, there had been 'official' use of the vernacular since Ethelbert's laws; and the decay of Latin learning accompanying the attacks of the Norsemen may have compelled the writing of letters in English, which were certainly passing between lords and their servants in King

Alfred's time. Along with Latin, the letter jettisoned the elaborate formality seen in the charters of the period.

In fact, Latin charters of the old type were eventually replaced by 'writ-charters', and these make up almost all the pre-Conquest writs which survived, preserved in the 'cartu laries' of the monasteries to which they brought new property. The writ-charter shows us the writ's advantages. It was usually addressed to the sheriff for proclamation in the shire-court, where any disputes about the property would have to be heard; and it omitted, for instance, the tremendous and space-consuming anathema clauses of the old charter, which enumerated all the supernatural punishments awaiting anyone who did not respect the provisions of the grant. Instead of a long string of witnesses, a seal authenticated the document. Almost the only purely formal aspect of the writ was its simple beginning: 'King Harold sends friendly greetings to ... and I inform you that. ...' It was all so much cheaper than the old charter, because it was so much smaller – a piece of parchment only 8 ins. by 4 ins. might be sufficient for a writ.[11]

The writ as an instrument of government was a discovery which did not take place till well on in the tenth century. Though the writ-charters continued to be produced in the scriptoria of the monasteries who were the usual beneficiaries, the making of governmental writs became the side-line of the clergy ('clerics' or 'clerks') of the king's chapel. Out of the king's chapel would grow the chancery, though we do not hear of a chief secretary to the king with the title of chancellor until after the Conquest.

The Norman conquerors could not be expected to use English. Soon after the Conquest writs were couched again in Latin. Yet they retained their essential conciseness. The institutions of Anglo-Norman government and law, apart from the system of tenures, were inherited from the Saxon kingdom. The achievement of the French invaders was to find new uses for old tools.[12]

CHAPTER 2

THE COMMON LAW TAKES SHAPE

SCHOLARS still argue whether the medieval government of England owed most to the Anglo-Saxons, or to ideas which the Normans brought with them in 1066.[1] Fortunately, the historian of the law can leave the more difficult aspects of this question to one side. Although the origin of the jury remains controversial, no one doubts that the Normans inherited the writ and the sheriff from their English predecessors; and, on the other hand, it is obvious that only the vigour and ingenuity of the Norman and Angevin kings, and the interests of the Norman warrior-aristocracy, formed the Common Law from these three elements. The genius of the Common Law, imposed from above, was very different from that of the popular Germanic law in pre-Conquest England, however many details were common to both. Like the tenth-century system of regional government, the Common Law was an improvisation in the face of political changes.

FEUDAL TENURES

In 1066, William stood with his friends and followers over a conquered country: the whole land was for him to share out. The astonishing project to write down a detailed description of its resources, which produced Domesday Book (1086), reflects a dominance, a sense of possession in King William, that no English king had ever had. Yet the Normans were newcomers in a hostile land, and William's first requirement was a stable army of knights supported by incomes from land. Though the Conqueror, always eager to show himself the legitimate heir of Edward the Confessor, decreed that his followers should hold their property on the same terms as their predecessors 'in the time of King Edward', there was neither the time nor the means, in the early days, to find out how much military service each estate had owed according to Anglo-Saxon rules. Rather, William demanded an arbitrary number of knights from each of the Norman beneficiaries, *in return for* a grant of land.

The holding of land was then the result of a private contract and conditional on a service, the nature of which defined the holding or 'tenure'. Though the practical difference between the Anglo-Saxon and the Norman army can certainly be exaggerated, the legal difference between them is fundamental. The normal feudal tenure was the knight's fee, held on condition of service as a knight in the king's army; and each of the greater landowners – the earls, bishops and richer abbeys – might hold sixty or more fees, scattered throughout the country. To raise the force which his holding obliged him to provide for the king, the *tenant-in-chief* might maintain warriors in his household: more often, he did what the king had done to him – he gave land to a follower in return for knight-service. The process could be carried several stages, so that a 'feudal ladder' was built up.[2]

With the whole country divided by 1086 between some 1,500 tenants-in-chief (those who held immediately of the king), and with feudal sub-tenants abounding, it was natural for men to think that every occupant of land must have a tenure, defined by some form of service. We should perhaps distinguish between the social importance of tenure, which can be exaggerated, and its fertility as a legal concept. The feudal ceremony of homage and feoffment became a normal way of conveying land for many purposes. As well as warriors, the lords needed labourers to work the fields they retained 'in demesne', and tenants to pay rent in money or in kind. Everyone had to have his land and his tenure, but the services required varied as much as the social and economic activities of medieval people.

For instance, all sorts of services could be implied by

serjeanty-tenure (serjeant and servant are at root the same word). The serjeant might perform military duties rather less exhalted than those of a knight (this type of sergeant has survived), or personal and domestic services to the king, some of them strange ones, like holding the king's head when he was sea-sick crossing the channel. The medieval lawyer placed all the non-military holdings of the surviving free peasantry into the category of *socage tenure*. The socage tenant paid rent in money, kind or labour, and suit (*soc*) to the lord's manorial court. The better sort of socage tenant was some-times said to hold *in fee-farm*, because he held a fee as per-petual and heritable as the knight's came to be, but paid a rent or 'farm' for it. In Scotland, tenure by 'feu-farm' is still the normal 'freehold' tenure: in England, however, the creation of new fee-farms was barred (as we shall see) by the Statute of *Quia Emptores* (1290), and the fixed rents of earlier socage tenants became nominal through centuries of in-flation and were forgotten. Socage-tenure is now, therefore the technical classification of freehold in England, for all land is still said to be 'held' from the Queen.

A knowledge of tenures is essential to an understanding of English law, because they were by far the most important forms of property, and the source of the majority of the dis-putes which the common law was developed to settle. The power and wealth of the Anglo-Norman noble and knight were built up from tenures and 'the incidents of tenure'. The incidents flowing from tenants to their lord included not only the services – military or in the form of rent – for which they had been enfeoffed, but also the *reliefs*, paid by sons to be allowed to succeed to their fathers' fees, and the *aids* exactable by the lord at certain expensive moments in his life, such as the marriage of his eldest daughter. Other valuable incidents were the lord's right to occupy the lands of the heirs of his deceased tenants until they reached their majority (the right of *wardship*), and to sell these wards in *marriage*. The rights of wardship and marriage could them-selves be bought and sold and were regarded as lucrative investments; and the exploitation of the wardships of their tenants-in-chief was revived on a tremendous scale by the Tudors, when many other aspects of feudalism had become obsolete.[3]

A lord naturally reoccupied the lands of a tenant who left no heirs to succeed. This incident of *escheat* was enjoyed also by the lord whose tenant was convicted of felony, a fact which suggests that felony was at first disloyalty, though the description later comprised many crimes unconnected with feudalism. More profit arose from the tenants' obligations to attend the lords' courts of honour, manor and hundred (where that public court had fallen into private hands), for many fines would be taken at them.

The same incidents which were profitable rights coming from the tenants to their lord were burdensome obligations from that lord to his overlord. In this great network of rights and duties there were many points where collisions of interest habitually occurred. Everyone was naturally anxious to enforce the services due to him, and to minimize his duties. On the other hand, the feudal bond was reckoned to be a two-way business, the feudal superior having an equal obligation to be 'a good lord' to his dependents, who were otherwise entitled to *defy* him and renounce their due service. Private war was, in fact, the final sanction of the rules of feudal society, but private war was an aspect of feudalism which the Norman kings had determined to leave behind them in Normandy. Law would have to replace private war, as a solution for feudal wrongs.

There was another fundamental conflict between military feudalism and the needs of a settled society. The lord granted a knight's fee in return for a knight's – a warrior's – service: there was no reason why he should allow the beneficiary's son to continue in the property, and if the son was a minor or an idiot there were good reasons why he should not. But the tenant – and every lord but the King was himself a tenant of an overlord – naturally wanted to build up his family estates and know that they would descend to his heirs. In the event, it became the regular practice for the heir to receive his father's land on paying a relief and repeating the ceremony of homage which had constituted the feudal bond between his father and the overlord. This practice was very common within half a century of the Conquest, though when it hardened into the theory that a fee was heritable is a matter not quite settled. The inheritableness of the knight's fee was accompanied by the rule of primogeniture: that the estate should pass undivided to the eldest son. The fee which supported all sorts of service to the overlord could not be allowed to disintegrate. From this consideration followed also the prohibition of the devising of land by will.[4]

One consequence of feudal inheritance was that the knightly tenant's right in the land was as durable as his lord's. Then who owned the land, lord or tenant? The answer was that they both owned rights in the land, but different ones. These rights, like the incidents of tenure, were regarded in a particularly concrete way: they were the *things* which the early *actions* of the Common Law would be concerned to defend or recover. Feudalism was a complex of property rights loosely controlled by the king – particularly complicated in England because of the survival of the fragmented tenurial pattern of pre-Conquest times – and the 'typical baron . . . was an habitual litigant and a speculative gambler, expert in offering the King future payment for some present good. Land and office; wardship and marriage; franchise and litigation; these were the fields of endeavour in which fortunes might be sought, won and all too easily lost.'[5]

The knight's fee became inheritable, but there was a transitional period when the grasping lord could probably deprive an heir of his customary right with impunity, or demand an outrageous relief for succession. Here was a direction in which a national English law had to modify the rough habits of military feudalism if it was to fashion a settled society. Such was the confusion of public and private matters in the Anglo-Norman polity that these feudal problems of smooth succession, fair reliefs, and fair treatment of wards inspired not only some of the earliest procedures of English private law, but also – to regulate relations between king and tenants-in-chief – the great charters of Henry I and King

John, which limited the power of the king and in some way foreshadowed a national constitution.

THE KING'S COURTS BECOME SUPREME

The barons from Normandy and other parts of France who came with the Conqueror were used to a situation where even the highest criminal justice and such public offices as the *vicomte*'s had been appropriated by feudatories along with their fees. So the hundred-courts in England continued after the Conquest to fall into private hands, and the sheriffdoms – and thus the shire-courts – showed signs of becoming the heritable property of the magnates. It is significant that the equivalent that the Normans found for shire was county (latin: *comitatus*), and for sheriff, *vicomte* (l. *vicecomes*).

The Anglo-Norman kings managed to stop the trend towards the private ownership of counties. The new instrument of government, the Exchequer, which appeared in the reign of the determined king Henry I (1099–1135), and before which the sheriffs were summoned twice a year to account for the king's revenues, did much to bring the local officials under control. It was Henry I also who sent out a writ ordering that the shire- and hundred-courts – *his* courts – should be held as they had been held in the time of Edward the Confessor, 'and not otherwise'.[6] Furthermore, pleas concerning land were to be heard in the county-court, when they concerned the vassals of two separate lords (and thus two rival seignorial courts). The shire-court was very soon meeting not twice a year, but once a month, and so became a much more important court than the hundred. It did so, no longer as an omnicompetent folk-moot, but as a cog in the new machine of royal justice.

In 1072, the bishops ceased to sit in the shire-court, for William I issued an ordinance setting up separate ecclesiastical courts, conforming to the ideas of the church reformers he had known in France.[7] The mutual encroachments of the secular and ecclesiastical jurisdictions were to cause endless conflict in medieval England, not only between

35

Henry II and Thomas Becket. But, had the Conqueror's ordinance not been issued, the Common Law might not have grown up in virtual independence of the swiftly developing Roman–Canon Law.

Another change which was more fundamental than appears at first sight was the introduction by the Normans of honorial courts. It was reasonable that, in a society founded on land-tenure, each lord should be able to hold a court to decide the disputes over land which arose between his tenants – the court of the *honour*, as the scattered complex of the great baronial estate was called. We might be excused for thinking that the possession of this type of court by every great lord, in addition to his manor and possibly appropriated hundred-courts, must have placed justice firmly in private hands. But many honour-courts were inefficient, or moribund from the start. More important, the king too was a 'private lord', the greatest of them all; and he also had an 'honour-court', the *curia regis*, where his tenants-in-chief had to gather for the hearing of pleas between them. Appeals could be carried through the honour-courts, spaced up the feudal ladder, to arrive ultimately at the *curia regis*, for it was part of the ethos of feudalism that a tenant, denied justice in his lord's court, could seek a remedy from his lord's lord.

'Feudalism' is an imprecise word, and the 'system' itself was ambiguous in its effects. There was nothing inevitable about the 'feudal anarchy' which had fallen upon France, and seemed to be spreading to England during the reign of the insecure King Stephen (1135–54). Everything depended on which level in the feudal hierarchy was most able to exploit its rights and minimize its obligations. In England it was the line of kings, partly because of their Anglo-Saxon inheritance, partly because of their own native vigour and intelligence. No medieval English king was 'anti-feudal' in his policy. He just made the most of his 'legal rights', as every medieval lord was bent on doing, and his victory was the victory of his feudal court over the courts of the lesser lords.

The victory was due not to arbitrary suppression of the lesser courts but to the greater effectiveness of the legal procedures which the king's court offered. In the course of the twelfth century, the king, his few trusted friends and the professional clerks who were the permanent element in that court laid the foundations of a national administration. The earliest aspect of this administration to appear, after the Chancery or secretariat, was the financial one: by 1130, 'the king's court at the exchequer' (*curia regis ad scaccarium*) was summoning the sheriffs to Westminster, auditing the accounts with the aid of counters and chequer-board, and enrolling the results on the first great series of English public records, the Pipe Rolls.[8]

The name of the group of men who did this is significant – 'the king's court at the exchequer'. The 'national administration' was run throughout the middle ages by the king's cronies, who did any job that was given to them. There were no departments; only the king's court at the exchequer, or the king's court organizing a military campaign, or the king's court dispensing justice. All the various skills of the king's household servants were concentrated on each sphere of activity. The writs issued by the chancellor under the great seal of England were essential to the collection of revenues as they were to the enforcement of judicial decisions. Some 300 writs are mentioned in the first extant pipe roll.

Conversely, all the meetings in which the administration was supervised were judicial in form, and not merely because much time was spent in hearing complaints against officials. Feudalism was both a network of property rights and the main source of the king's income, and fines imposed by judges were another important part of the king's revenues. Furthermore, the ritualistic procedures which we associate with courts of law were the only means which people knew for testing or 'trying' anything. A sheriff presenting his accounts must have been not unlike a prisoner at the bar. The early pipe rolls are not in fact 'national accounts' but the records of judicial hearings of taxation disputes. Justice and administration were indivisible.

Increasing judicial activity was therefore an integral part of the growth of the royal administration. The most recent account of medieval English government credits Henry I rather than Henry II, and his minister, Bishop Roger of Salisbury, with the civilizing of the rough Anglo-Norman lords; and believes that Roger virtually created the English judiciary in close connexion with the Exchequer. On the death of the Conqueror in 1087, his realms were divided amongst his sons, but Henry I reconquered Normandy in 1106 and thereafter the King of England had to spend much of his time abroad. The administration of England had to be capable of running on its own, or at least under the direction of a viceroy, known as the *justiciar*. Roger of Salisbury, the first of a great line of justiciars of England, presided in the court at the Exchequer and employed a number of itinerant deputies to do justice throughout England, who were called 'justiciars of all England' because their jurisdiction was not limited as was the 'county officials'.[9]

THE SWORN INQUEST IN CRIMINAL LAW

Two streams of administrative activity can be distinguished, which gradually combined to produce the earliest forms of action of the Common Law; firstly, official inquiries by means of the jury into the property rights of the king or one or another of his vassals, and secondly, arbitrary commands, transmitted through the sheriff by means of 'executive' writs, for the surrender of disputed lands to the king or an aggrieved person.

The official inquiries or inquests, of which the Domesday proceedings were the greatest example, were probably introduced by the Normans from the Continent, where they had been extensively used by the Carolingian emperors. It was not the use in a dispute of the knowledge of a group of neighbours which was new to England, but the summoning of such juries by the king for his own purposes, rather than – for instance – by an accused man to support his oath in a folk-moot. The inquest, not the jury, was the Norman innovation. Even the inquest may have owed something to English practice, for attention has lately been drawn to the many cases of disputed possession which the Domesday juries had to decide before the survey could be drawn up, in which they acted more as supporters of the parties than as the king's agents. In the Domesday procedure there may be discernible a transitional stage between 'Anglo-Saxon oath-helping group' and 'Norman inquest'.[10]

The inquests of the Norman kings were held before the sheriff or special commissioners, as occasion demanded, and the suitors of the shire-court were often used as jurors. For instance, in 1127, Henry I ordered the sheriff of London to ask 'the men of the shire' whether the canons of St Paul's held certain property and should therefore be taxed upon it. This was an inquest for the king's benefit, but an increasing number were in the interests of parties in private disputes.[11] It is important to notice that every inquest had to be authorized by the king, and such authorization was normally in the form of a writ to the sheriff ordering the assembling of a jury. The most effective procedures were the king's monopoly.

The inquest method was first made permanent and general in the king's effort to keep the peace and suppress crime. Just after the Conquest, we get the impression that many a Frenchman died violently on dark nights. A decree was made that the hundreds near the spot where any man was found slain by an unknown hand should be liable to a very heavy fine – unless a jury 'made presentment of Englishry', that is, brought in a verdict that the dead man was an Englishman. Juries of the neighbourhood must have assembled almost automatically for this purpose. At first they probably consisted of the ancient 'lawmen' of the popular courts, who were gradually replaced by sworn groups of neighbours (*juratores*) summoned by the sheriff for the occasion.[12]

It now seems that Henry II (1154–89) was only confirming the methods of Henry I when he placed the *presenting jury* in the centre of his scheme for apprehending criminals; the scheme which is known as the 'Assize of Clarendon' of 1166. (*Assize*, by the way, comes from the same root and means the same thing as *session*, and could also denote, as here, the decree made at the session.) Henry II ordered that the

39

sheriffs of every county should call before them twelve men from every hundred, and the priest, reeve and four men from every village, and demand from them on oath the names of all persons suspected to have been murderers or thieves since the king's coronation. The 'presentments' were to be taken before justices sent to the counties from the king's household, and the justices were to put suspected persons whom the sheriff had been able to arrest to the ordeal.[13]

The presenting or 'grand' jury – which existed in modified form until the present century – was thus a device for catching criminals, not for their trial, which remained mostly Anglo-Saxon in nature. Indeed, the Assize of Clarendon in principle did no more than reinforce the inclination, visible in the laws of Canute, to take simple notoriety as adequate grounds for trying a man. Perhaps the main originality of the assize was its general application of the jury-method; its insistence that there were to be no local exceptions. The assize was to hold 'as long as the king pleased', and the sheriff could enter 'even the honour of Wallingford' to arrest an accused person. The ordinance was to be the Common Law of the land.

The assize says that the juries were to present 'robbers and murderers', and in fact all they were generally able to do was to point out the notorious criminal; they could not enumerate the multitude of separate crimes perpetrated in the countryside. The individual whose kinsman had been murdered or goods stolen and wanted some redress had still to resort to the primitive method of personal accusation known as the 'Appeal'.

Leaving the criminal Appeal aside for discussion on a later page, we must mention here that when we first know anything definite about this procedure, from the earliest surviving rolls of the royal justices in the 1190s, trial was by battle between accuser and accused. Trial by battle, used in the Appeal and in 'civil' disputes about land-ownership, had been the only procedural innovation introduced by the Normans.[14] A method of trial so barbaric and capricious might appear likely to have given way quickly before the jury verdict; but the extension of the jury from the business of inquiry to making decisions on guilt or civil liability seems in fact to have been a difficult step for the medieval mind. It was in 'civil' disputes about land, where there was no first presenting jury, that a proper verdict-giving or 'petty' jury appeared earliest.

THE ORIGINAL WRIT AND THE FIRST
FORMS OF ACTION

To understand this event, we must turn to the second element we mentioned, beside the development of the inquest, namely, the increasing use of arbitrary writs by the king, ordering the surrender of disputed property.[15] The Norman kings and their successors, the Angevins (1154–1399), were generally energetic and ruthless personalities, ready to order the redress of any apparent injustice as soon as it reached their ears. The hearing of a dispute over the ownership of land belonged to the lord of the disputing parties. But when a man was deprived of his occupation or *seisin* of land by the violence or silent encroachment of another – when, as the lawyers said, he was 'disseised' – it was a matter of urgency that he should be restored, before any issue of ownership was tried. That issue would probably raise complicated historical questions concerning the descent of the land through genera-tions, and while these were being discussed, the disseisor would be consolidating his position, or the disseised man would resort to 'self-help', gathering his friends to force his way back. If thieving was the everyday vice of the labouring population, disseisin was the crime of the upper classes, and a national scourge for centuries, until land ceased to be the only foundation of power and standing.

The majority of early writs were orders to the sheriffs to give possession to purchasers of land, orders which were read out in the shire-court and thus constituted title-deeds as well. By the twelfth century the single document had split into two: a charter as the title-deed, and a separate order to give seisin; and it was the second ('executive') writ which gave rise to judicial procedures for restoring dispossessed tenants.

When a dispute arose, the parties would plead with equal eloquence for the king's support, so we find him ordering the sheriff that such and such a man shall be put back into occupation if he has been *unjustly* disseised. This meant that the sheriff had to hold a judicial inquiry before he could act, and he had no alternative to relying on the knowledge of a jury of neighbours.

It was the ingenuity and determination of Henry II which created a permanent procedure from the improvisations of his predecessors. Henry succeeded in 1154 to the liabilities of King Stephen and his 'anarchy', and set about to liquidate them. The disseisins of the anarchy were beyond remedy, but Henry would not have the private wars for property continuing into his reign. A great attack upon disseisins appears to have been launched in 1166. Henry was planning to send out a group of justices through the shires to try criminals, and it looks as though he ordered presentment before them of all unjust disseisins committed since his coronation (the limitation of time which was also placed on criminal presentments by the 'Assize of Clarendon'). The attack on disseisins in 1166 seems therefore to have been a criminal investigation, which came to an end when the justices finished their circuit. The fact serves to emphasize a general point about the development of English law. The motive behind its creation – the creation of all of it, 'civil' and 'criminal' – was the administrative one of keeping order. Ever since the Conquest the king's grants of land had often been accompanied by grants of peace and protection, so that to seize the land was automatically to break the peace.

Henry II's predecessors had arbitrarily restored disseised persons. Henry II punished those declared guilty of disseisin by a jury. In Henry's later years we find a third stage – individual plaintiffs ask to be restored if a jury decides that they have been disseised unjustly. There appeared a stereotyped form of writ ordering the sheriff to send the defendant and a jury before the king's justices to try the issue:

The king to the sheriff, greeting. *N* has complained to me that *R* has disseised him unjustly and without judgment of his free holding at X since my last crossing to Normandy. So I command you that if N gives you security that he will prosecute the case, you shall cause the tenement to be restored and to remain in peace till T [a session of the court]. In the meantime make twelve free and lawful men of the neighbourhood view the land, and record their names. Summon them by good summoners that at T they be in the presence of me or my justices to make recognition about this matter. Put R under gage and safe pledges to attend and hear the recognition. And bring there the summoners and this writ. . . .

In this way was invented the most important of the 'petty assizes', the assize of *Novel Disseisin*. The procedure or 'action', and each separate application of it, came in this instance to be called an assize, and judges were sent out 'to hear assizes'.

The judges did not go just to hear assizes of novel disseisin. The development of the first 'form of action' was so important because the method could be adapted to many different occasions of civil dispute. The essence of it was the isolation of some relatively simple issue, less than the ultimate question of ownership, and the calling of a *jury of recognition* to decide that issue. As new issues were seen to be commonly recurring ones, the Chancery would frame new forms of writ, ordering the sheriffs to call juries to answer these questions before the king's judges. What the plaintiff had to do was to buy the writ appropriate to his situation.[16]

In Henry II's reign three other petty assizes were created, the most important of which was *Mort D'Ancestor*. The writ in this case demanded an answer to the question, 'did M, the ancestor of N (the plaintiff), die seized in demesne and as of fee of Z (the property in dispute), and is N his nearest heir?' If the answer was 'yes' to the threefold question, N was restored to his ancestor's land. The situation which required this remedy is sufficiently indicated by the order to the justices in 1176 to apply the assize when 'the lord of a fee refuses to give seisin to the heir of a deceased tenant': the common law of inheritance had triumphed over the conflicting needs of military feudalism.

The petty or 'possessory' assizes remedied immediate

injustice, leaving open the ultimate question of the right to the land. The disseisor was wrong to enter without a prior judgment of a court, but it might have been that he was asserting an ancient and justifiable claim. Though reversing disseisins could be considered part of the king's duty as keeper of the peace, decisions of right were known to be the business of the feudal courts. But, from the morrow of the Conquest, the king often sent sharp reminders to his subjects to 'do right' in particular cases, sometimes stipulating what the right thing was which should be done.

In the reign of Henry I a threat was added to the king's order: 'do right . . . and, unless you do it quickly, I order your lord to do it, and, if he does not, my sheriff shall, so that I may hear no further complaint.' Then the king began to grant the privilege to certain persons that they should not be sued for their property except by the king's writ. Finally, as part of his policy of protecting seisin – for persistent litigation in the local courts, even unsuccessful litigation, could be a way of harassing an enemy – Henry II seems to have generalized this practice to the momentous rule: 'no one is to be compelled to defend his free tenement in his lord's court unless the plaintiff has the king's writ.'

The *writ of right*, though it argued a great constitutional point (that even the lord's courts acted only on royal authority), made little difference to the actual exercise of justice: it merely ordered a man to do what he should have done already. Beside it grew another writ, however, named *Praecipe* from its key-word, 'Order . . .', which brought questions of right, along with questions of seisin, into the king's court. Henry II began to direct this writ, not at the alleged malefactor or his lord, but along what was becoming the normal channel for initiating litigation – to the sheriff, who was told to order the wrongdoer to restore the property, and in case of refusal to summon him in due form before the justices to show his reasons. The addressing of the writ to the sheriff suggests that the preliminary order ('restore the property or else . . .') was becoming mere form, and that the initiating of a judicial process was now the important thing. Because it began an action in a royal court, the writ, or rather the sheriff's order, was supposed to be addressed only to tenants-in-chief, for it was the right of the lords themselves to hear the actions of their vassals. But the interests of the king's peace sometimes broke through that restriction.

'The writ of right, Praecipe' was not concerned only with questions of right to land. In fact, like the petty assize, it was a process capable of application to many situations. Its two most important offspring were the *writ of entry* and the *writ of debt*. The writ of entry recovered property in a case where the defendant had entered with apparent justification but in fact through a tenant of the plaintiff who had not been entitled to sell, or by way of a lease which had since expired. The writ of debt instructed the sheriff to order a debtor to return the money owing to a creditor: 'and if he does not, then summon . . . .'

RIGHT AND SEISIN

Perhaps the most important concept of the early common law was the distinction between 'right', recoverable by writs of right, and 'seisin', recoverable by Novel Disseisin. What did the distinction amount to?

As in the lower feudal courts, so in the king's courts, cases of right were at first tried by battle between champions (soon professionals) acting for the parties. Henry II, recognizing the haphazard character of battle, allowed it to be replaced by the decision of a jury, if the defendant so desired: the ordinance which permitted this seems to have been made at Windsor in 1179 and was known as 'the grand assize' (it should be contrasted with the petty assizes concerned with seisin, and distinguished from the 'grand' or presenting jury of criminal law). Even in the lords' courts tenants could thenceforth refuse to accept battle on a mere allegation that their land was not their own; whereupon the plaintiffs were compelled to take the case to the king's court, for only the king could grant the privilege of jury trial.

But how could the location of 'right' to property be

decided by a jury or any other rational method? What indeed was this 'right', which had been inferred from orders 'to do right'? How can the abstraction which we call 'ownership' be distinguished from the fact of occupation by a lessee or a man who has thrust his way in illegally? Only a sophisticated system of paper conveyancing – of deeds and perhaps the registration of titles – can separate the two things with absolute security. In medieval England, however, land was not conveyed by that fallible and forgeable piece of parchment, the charter, which was useful only as presumptive evidence of the transaction and a record of its terms: conveyance was by the ceremony (necessary over and above homage) of 'livery of seisin', the actual placing of the grantee in possession; and seisin might unfortunately be established in other ways, such as the actual use of the ground, perhaps no more than the picking of apples from the trees. The method of *enfeoffment* was determined by the convenience of a rough military aristocracy, not the requirements of a legal system, which found it difficult to distinguish the results of enfeoffment from those of unauthorized occupation.

But all title to land in England was based upon this seisin, 'the beatitude of seisin' as Maitland called it, and the most solemn action concerning land ownership, the action on a writ of right, determined simply whether plaintiff or defendant had the *better* right, by asking which could prove the older seisin by himself or an ancestor. A system of law grew up by asking practical and historical questions, not questions of legal philosophy. In Novel Disseisin the jury had to decide whether A had enjoyed recent seisin of Blackacre and lost it to B. If its answer was 'yes', A recovered complete control over the property, unless and until E came along with a writ of right, and a jury found (for instance) that E's ancestor (C) had been in seisin, and that the property had descended in regular fashion to D, E's father, and then to E himself, this being a longer and more genuine descent than A could allege. The difference between Novel Disseisin and the action of Right was a matter of how far back you had to go to prove your case, and so of the complexity and cumbersome-ness of the pleading. The whole point of Novel Disseisin was its simplicity and immediacy, so the disseisin alleged had to be novel, the allegation brought while the event was fresh in people's minds.

But the seisin recovered soon came to be recognized as something more than mere possession. Some legitimate occupiers did not have it. The lord who had leased away his land for a period of years was the man who brought an action of Novel Disseisin if his tenant was ejected (this had to be so, because the writ talked about a 'free tenement' and the military aristocracy would not regard a lease as such): the lord was recovering some sort of title, but not possession, for he had granted that away. Between Novel Disseisin and the action of Right there were actions of intermediate weight and complexity, like Mort D'Ancestor, where the writ asked not one but three historical questions, or like the writs of entry. Seisin was a *right to possession* which grew stronger with time. But in Right as in Novel Disseisin there was a time-limit beyond which a defendant could not reasonably be expected to prove his title; and so the difference between the titles they established was a relative one. The first limitation of time placed on Novel Disseisin was the accession of Henry II, only twelve years before the assize was apparently created: no one could allege a disseisin before that date. In actions of Right, 1135 was the first date of 'prescription' (no written deed was needed to prove your right if you could show peaceful possession back to that date), and subsequent statutes moved it on so as to keep it about a century behind the times. The differences between the periods of limitation and prescription disappeared along with the forms of action in the nineteenth century, but it is still the case that an action for land must be brought within twelve years of losing possession, if title is not be be altogether extinguished.

THE KING'S JUSTICES

The new procedures of Henry II depended upon the sending

of justices from the king's household into the counties, to hear the inquests. The use of itinerant justices goes back to the commissioners who travelled through England on a number of circuits to compile Domesday Book. There seem already in Henry I's reign to have been circuits or *eyres* (the word is derived from Latin *iter*, a journey) and articles of inquiry like the later 'articles of the eyre'. From 1166 such justices were used constantly, though the number in any one group, the intervals of years at which they toured the counties and the minutest details of their itineraries were modified by the king through writs and never became completely a matter of routine.

When they arrived in the county the justices sat in the shire-court, and at first they were probably regarded as no more than presidents of that ancient assembly of the community. The justices were, however, commissioned to inspect the administration of the county, as well as to hear legal pleas, and they found it necessary to treat the sheriff and his subordinates with scant respect; so that they very early assumed the majesty of judges. The county-court's role had altered. It was no longer a popular assembly of the inhabitants of the shire so much as a unit in the king's government, the place where the sheriff carried out the king's orders; where, soon, the representatives of the shire in parliament would be elected and the statutes made in parliament read out. To the king the county-court *was* the county, and the crystallization of the county in its court was essential to the appearance of a representative assembly at the national level: representatives are produced only by groups with some sense of corporateness and a common mind which can be represented, and this could not possibly be the common mind of everyone within the county boundaries. Naturally, a few knights assumed the right to represent the shire to the king who was also their overlord, and to run the shire's affairs between the visits of the justices.

The shire-court, long after it had ceased to be of much importance as a court of justice in its own right, was essential to the machine of royal justice. Since juries could not normally be expected to trek to the king's central courts, cases begun before the king were adjourned whenever a jury verdict was found necessary, to the next visit of justices to the county concerned. Because the execution of justice depended so much upon the knowledge of the neighbourhood, and so little as yet on the expertise of professional judges, the county-court was bound to remain important; and the Angevin kings recognized the fact by appointing county *coroners* 'to keep the pleas of the crown'.[17]

On the other hand, it was an essential part of Henry II's work that the decision of pleas of the crown was removed from the sheriff's competence. Such pleas were to be held only before the justices in the king's household or sent out by the king, and the coroner's function was to record the accusations and preliminary pleadings which took place between eyres, so that cases could proceed when the justices arrived; as well as to list any rights which fell due to the king, such as the chattels of those outlawed in the shire-court. The coroners also viewed the bodies of those found dead, because a corpse was the commonest beginning of an indictment for homicide. The appointment of this local official was, then, a corollary of the monopolization of the king's pleas by the small group of royal justices.

The Eyre meant that innumerable local variations in practice were replaced by a single system, in which general principles could arise. The king might have achieved a similar result by closely directing the proceedings of the sheriffs' and the feudal magnates' courts through a barrage of writs. But men alone, not writs – only the itinerant justices – could provide the real link between the judicial and administrative headquarters and the shires. Writs to local officials had to be returned by those officials, endorsed with a note of the action which had been taken: the justices' report on the conduct of the king's servants in the localities was more impartial than the returns – and much less favourable.

The justices who went into the counties were the same group of men who heard the cases brought into the presence of the king himself, a fact which made for even greater

49

uniformity of practice. In the nature of things there was a court of justice wherever the king was, for long intervals might separate eyre from eyre; and it was the business of a medieval king to be accessible to all who sought him out as the fount of justice. Naturally also, the king called in his more experienced servants to cooperate with him in giving judgment. The very fact of the Eyre presupposes the existence of a body of men in the *curia regis* who were expert in judicial work, though we hear little about them till 1178, when Henry II detailed five members of his household, two clerks and three laymen, to remain with the king wherever he went, to hear the complaints of all free men.[18]

The instructions were exact in one respect: when the king went abroad – and in the twelfth century he was more often away than at home – the justices went as well, to do other jobs for their master. Then the free men had to resort for justice to the Exchequer, which had continued to act as a general court of law after Roger of Salisbury's fall in 1139, and possessed a duplicate of the great seal, used by the justiciar of England to govern in the king's absence. This court at the Exchequer became known as *the* Bench, the law-court *par excellence* (the benches on which the lawmen sat having been the principal material feature of every court since Saxon times). Above all, it was stationary at Westminster, using the abbey's out-buildings as a store, and it made Westminster the cradle of English law.[19]

In 1204, King John lost Normandy to the King of France, and the ruthless money-raising required by his efforts to recover the province was one of the causes of the baronial revolt of 1215. The loss of Normandy meant also that the king was more often in England, and John, whose greatest fault was the typically Angevin one that he governed too much, was extremely conscientious in sitting in judgment in the revived court *coram rege* ('with the king'), virtually abolishing the Bench.[20] Yet, for the litigant, the Exchequer court possessed that great advantage of a certain location, caused by the fact that the paraphernalia of accounting and storing money had become too bulky to be continually on the move; and in Magna Carta (article 17) the king was forced to grant that 'common pleas shall not follow our court, but be held in some fixed place'. John's son, Henry III (1216–72), was a mere boy at the time of his accession, and during his minority there was no court 'with the king'. From 1234, however, there are plea-rolls for two central courts. The 'King's Bench' and 'Common Pleas' started on their parallel course, to last till the age of Mr Gladstone.

The pleas heard in King's Bench were indistinguishable in form from those heard in Common Pleas. The existence of two courts where there should have been only one was 'an accident of politics'; and it was simply the special interest of a case to the king which brought it into the court before him. By 'common pleas' Magna Carta meant no more than ordinary pleas between commoners. Convenience produced a rough sharing of business. Thus, civil actions were usually left to the common bench, while Appeals of Felony were generally heard before the king. To the Eyre was left the hearing and settlement of criminal presentments, as well as the clearance of many civil actions. For convenience's sake the itinerant justices performed all the functions of the court with the king, which in the early days stood adjourned while they were on circuit. By the same token, the Eyre had no special functions: the King's Bench, following the king on ceaseless journeys, was indistinguishable from a normal eyre except by the king's presence.

LEGAL RECORDS AND CONTRACTS

To bring a judgment of the county court, which still decided minor cases, into Common Pleas for reconsideration, there issued a writ to order the recording of the county proceedings. The conclusion of a case emerged mechanically from the appropriate procedure and only a recorded mistake in procedure could invalidate it. The special writ of *recordari* was necessary in the instance of the county, because that court was not normally 'a court of record'. The writ ordered not the writing down of an account of the earlier trial, but rather an oral report by four knights of the shire, for 'record' meant just the authoritative testimony of the court. Writing was, however, soon accepted as an aid to memory, in the same way that a charter was a useful record of a grant but did not constitute it. 'Courts of record' did slowly become synonymous with courts which kept records. The king's 'central' justices were probably already keeping *plea-rolls* at the end of Henry II's reign, and there survive from 1194 the first specimens of a majestic series extending over the centuries.[21]

Very likely the plea-rolls were begun for a fiscal purpose: as early as Henry I's reign the justices may have sent notes to the Exchequer of judicial writs and jury verdicts for which plaintiffs had to pay, and of the fines imposed at the end of every case. At about the same time as the plea-rolls came into existence, and for the same fiscal reasons, began the enrolling (in the *patent-* and *close*-rolls) of copies of the king's writs-patent, granting privileges and licences, and writs-close, containing administrative orders. The patent-, close- and plea-rolls soon far exceeded their early fiscal purpose. The former, the 'chancery-rolls', satisfied the natural passion of a civil service to have files to look up, and incidentally constitute a godsend for the medieval historian, who finds in them a record of day-to-day government unrivalled for their time.[22] The plea-rolls allowed the procedures of law to become much more elaborate, to be adjourned from month to month for the obtaining of jury verdicts and the presence of recalcitrant parties and new witnesses; and eventually appeals to a higher court against judgment in a lower; all without the thread of the dispute being lost. The ink of records was the life-blood of the new law, as folk memory had been of the old.

Domesday Book stands at the dividing lines between the oral and the record procedure. The facts were collected largely by the oral testimony of juries, which was especially necessary when the ownership of land was in dispute, but they were written down into a book which founded a different sort of authority. 'We have called the book "the Book of

Judgment" ['Domesday'],' wrote the king's treasurer in Henry II's day, 'because its decisions, like those of the last judgment, are unalterable.' Because it satisfied the passion for reference and authority, Domesday Book had many successors. Because of this passion, new records were usually based in some degree on other records, earlier in time, or contemporary ones at a different level of detail, in the way that a record of a plea enshrined a writ. It is one of the frightening characteristics of documents to seemingly multiply by their own volition.[23]

So, for a number of reasons, it was well in litigation if you based your plea on a record and did not trust to a jury's inclinations and fallible memory. A record, of course, had to be a record of something, perhaps a private grant or agreement, but, far better, a previous settlement in a court: the old sense of 'record' as a solemn statement by an authoritative person or body here coalesced with the realization of the usefulness of written memoranda. The force of any writing was itself dependent on its being the product of a legal procedure: an action led to a record, and the record might be the basis of a further action. Some of the first easily enforceable documents were the records of decisions in real or fictional actions at law. The fictional plea may have been used first in the case of debt. The creditor brought an action for debt, arranging (presumably as a condition of the original loan) that the debtor should not contest the plea. Judgment was then given for the creditor, who could enforce it when he pleased, by getting a writ of execution issued on the basis of the record.

An action might end not with a judgment but with an agreed settlement (it needed the licence of the justices), which was embodied in a *final concord* or *fine*. Collusive, that is fictional, actions terminated in this way constituted a particularly safe means of conveying property. The final concord was usually in the form of a tripartite indenture: this method, evolved from the Anglo-Saxon *chirograph*, was given official recognition in 1195 and lasted in constant use till 1833. The agreement (that *A* surrendered the property in dispute to *B*)

was written out three times on a single piece of parchment,
the three pieces then being separated by a jagged ('indented')
cut. Each party to the 'dispute' took a copy, and the royal
officials kept the third, the bottom or 'foot of the fine'; and
the authenticity of any part of it could be tested by fitting it
to the others.

The effectiveness of the fine was dependent on an authority
or 'record' even more fundamental than the court's: the
king's. The king's record merges into his political action. Law
here is what the king will enforce, and a vassal's ability to do
with his land as he wishes depends on the supreme overlord's
concurrence, just as in Anglo-Saxon times it depended on the
king's 'book'. In a settlement by fine, the donor surrendered
the land before the witness of the court (including for this
purpose other distinguished men besides the judges), and the
king regranted it to the donee with all the force of 'seisin
under the king's ban'. Livery was executed by the king's
officers; and the transaction might be recorded not only in
the rolls of the king's grants by charter but also, in the form
of instructions to the executing officers, on the patent- or
close-rolls. It was perhaps in this way that the practice arose
of making private charters 'of record' by copying them on
the back of pipe-rolls, plea-rolls and chancery-rolls: when
the close-rolls were terminated in 1903, deeds were all that
was being entered upon them.[24]

The contracts enshrined in charters and fines were the only
sorts of contracts enforceable in the king's courts: those made
privately from Anglo-Saxon times by unrecorded ceremonies
like the handing over of sticks or 'earnest money' were not
recognized. Charters 'conveying' land were not enforceable
unless there was actual 'livery of seisin'. Such livery was also
essential to give effect to a fine, but the fine had the advantage
of barring the claim of a third party which was not made
within a year and a day. And whatever the legal force of the
document, the conditions upon which land was conveyed
needed to be written down; besides which the incorporeal
rights going with land (see below, p. 96), the things which
bulked largest in most grants, could not be 'delivered' in any

meaningful way, and were eventually regarded as passing by charter. Of particular importance in a deed was the warranty clause, by which the grantor contracted to defend the grantee's title if it was attacked by a third party, and, if the case was lost, to provide the grantee with another and equivalent property.

The fine was enforceable by a special executive writ. Early in the thirteenth century there emerged a new 'original' writ (that is one originating a court action) to enforce a charter or fine. In *praecipe* form and known as the *writ of covenant*, it began a procedure which in fact often had a fine only at its culmination: it was the collusive action which produced more often than it followed a written covenant. The writ represented a significant advance in ideas, for it was the first 'praecipe' which did not require the return of a physical object, but rather commanded performance.

THE GREAT CHARTER, DUE PROCESS
AND THE RULE OF LAW

A charter, like a fine, would often be drawn up to settle a real dispute, and this was true of the great charter which ends the period now being considered. Magna Carta was a worthy climax of the first stage of growth of English law, for in it the barons took up the laws of Henry II as part of their 'programme', and asked for more of them; for a stationary court of common pleas on the one hand, and, on the other, for more frequent visits of the justices to the counties to hear petty assizes (chapters 17, 18). They went on to turn the king's law against the king, forcing John to concede, in the very terms of the writ of Novel Disseisin, that he would restore all those whom he had disseised without judgment (chapters 39, 52). John had been expert at entangling uncooperative barons in the newly sophisticated forms of agreement: he had compelled them to seal charters conceding their own disinheritance should they omit to fulfil certain obligations to the king. In the 'security clause' of Magna Carta John was hoist with his own petard. He was made to concede that, if he failed to observe any of the provisions of the charter, twenty-five elected barons might seize his castles, land and possessions.

Fear of agreements made under compulsion is apparent also in the provisions against fines and amercements imposed by the king upon offenders. A 'fine' as we understand the word is also derived from 'final concord'. The man found guilty of an offence was in the king's mercy, and could be 'amerced' to any sum: but he would normally be allowed to make a reasonable agreement or 'fine' with the king. John did not observe the normal practice. He took unreasonable ('outrageous') sums, in fact as much as he could get.

The barons' answer in 1215 is sometimes described as an appeal to custom, and it is true that there had long been some customary *amounts* – for feudal reliefs, for instance – customs which the Angevins had sometimes chosen to ignore. But custom had little more to offer in the way of protection, for in government and law the whole twelfth century showed nothing but 'a rapidly changing, organic body of precedent and expedient'.[25] The barons must have known this, and they relied rather on an appeal to reasonableness, on demands for amercements proportional to the crimes, and the reasonable ways of doing things which had grown from twelfth-century experiments.

'*Lex*' in that century seems to have meant the law of an institution's working; men talked of 'the law of the exchequer'. It is in Magna Carta that we first hear of something more – a 'community of the realm' and a *lex terrae*, which apparently signified the processes of law available to all free men. In the famous 39th article of Magna Carta it was reasonable processes of trial the barons were granted, trial 'by the law of the realm and the judgment of their peers'; or, as it was happily transmuted in the fifth and fourteenth amendments of the constitution of the United States, that no one should 'be deprived of life, liberty or property without due process of law'.

In 1215 the due processes which the king had invented prevailed over the king. Perhaps the Common Law could only have been created by kings prepared to act ruthlessly, even 'lawlessly', and to put people in and out of seisin as they thought fit; kings who exalted their own will to the extent of giving anger and spite (*ira et malevolentia*) as reasons for their fiercer commands.[26] But by 1215 due processes of law had been evolved. The barons liked them, and were determined that the king, too, should abide by them, and that his power to alter and supplement them on his own should be circumscribed.

Magna Carta reflects the nature of the Common Law. The Charter may be called a treaty between king and barons, but medieval diplomacy was itself a matter of pleading in courts – it meant, for the King of England, pleading in the Papal court and the court of the King of France, his feudal overlord. In 1215, the barons sued for justice in the court of John's overlord, the Pope, by a process which began with their solemn defiance (*diffidatio*) of John, their withdrawal of fidelity from a bad lord, and ended with a grant of liberties sanctioned by a very common legal procedure. For, if the security clause seems to imitate John's own tyrannical devices, it also authorizes something very like the legal process called 'distraint', the king's or a private claimant's seizure of a man's property, within well-known limitations, to force him (in his 'distress') to appear in court or fulfil some obligation. The Common Law was first and foremost a collection of processes for settling common disputes, processes determined by the writs which began them. The first abstract principles of law emerged as judges had to decide whether the writs obtained were appropriate to the disputes; and from the earliest days plaintiffs were often told that their choice had been wrong. At that point there was almost unlimited possibility of growth for a legal profession, which should advise the parties, rationalize the existing processes into an abstract system of principles, and exercise its ingenuity on the devising of new processes.

Before the writ there had to come, of course, the simple complaint of injustice, the petition to Chancery for a writ. If the plaintiff was poor, or there was no time to get to Chancery and back before the justices in eyre left the county, the requirement of a writ might be waived and the complaint heard directly. Such complaints or petitions eventually came to be written down as *bills*, approximating in form to the equivalent writs. The petition or bill was to become an alternative way of beginning litigation – and then of beginning legislation in the High Court of Parliament – as procedurally fruitful as the writ itself. The Great Charter can reasonably be called the first English statute, for it was preceded by the first common petition or bill – the Articles of the Barons.[27]

CHAPTER 3

ALL SORTS OF JUSTICES:
THE CRIMINAL LAW TO 1642

THE EYRE

THE thirteenth century was the hey-day of the eyre, which visited every county at least once a decade. Each journey of the justices, judges of the central courts supplemented by a few experienced administrators, was a great venture, requiring careful planning and much energy. The story that in 1233 the whole population of Cornwall fled to the woods to escape the itinerant justices gives a wrong impression of the nature of the eyre. True, a single village might be fined a dozen times for failing to raise hue and cry when crimes were committed, or for burying dead (and stinking) bodies before the coroner arrived to view them. At the end of their month's session in Shropshire in 1256, the justices spent a day or two compiling a list of the fines imposed, which still survives in the eyre-roll at the Public Record Office. It adds up to 1,100 marks (£750), perhaps a fortieth of the whole yearly income of the king at that time, and as a consolidated figure was entered on the 'national' pipe-roll. But the fines and damages were assessed by local juries, not fixed arbitrarily by the justices, and the average was half a mark (6s. 8d.). The judges were more interested in accounting for the last half-penny of the chattels, forfeit to the king, of a man outlawed in the shire-court twenty years before, than in ruinous impositions at the time. Everyone knew what to expect. The eyre was a marvel of thoroughness and reliability, and for that reason attracted ever more private litigation. Those who suffered most from the justices were the grasping local officials.[1]

At the beginning of the eyre, while the presenting juries were away collecting answers to the list of questions (the 'articles of the eyre') given to them on the opening day, the justices heard the civil pleas. When the juries returned with their true answers (*veredicta*), the hearing of the crown pleas could begin. The eyre-roll contains the replies of the juries to questions about infringements of the king's rights and the misdeeds of officials, a body of questions built up gradually upon some that had been written down in 1194. We learn that a hundred-bailiff has imprisoned men without cause and demanded money for their release; or that a lord has jurisdiction over a hundred, holding it from the king at a given rent. To present the normal run of crown pleas, which had arisen since the last eyre and had to be considered in this one, the homicides and findings of corpses and the first stages of Appeals of Felony, the juries must have called in aid the coroners' records.

In the Shropshire session of 1256, the juries found that since the county had been last visited in 1245 there had been 183 cases of homicide, 61 of accidental death (by drowning, falling from trees, running over by carts, burying in chalk-pits, and even – in the case of a child – the bites of that dangerous medieval creature, the pig), 3 of suicide and 2 of robbery. There is something very odd about this. If there were 183 homicides, we may be sure that there were hundreds and hundreds of cases of robbery. The fact is that the juries could not keep up with the passing misdeeds which left no solid evidence behind: they recorded bodies, not crimes. The village constable and the hue and cry, the sheriff and his *posse comitatus*, rarely caught even killers; and the juries attributed many a corpse to 'unknown malefactors'. On thirty-seven occasions only were people said to be suspected of the crimes, often apparently because they had fled. Some of these suspects did not appear in court and were outlawed; those in three cases said they were clergy and were handed over to the bishop (but not before a verdict of guilty had been found against them); and those in eight cases asked for trial by jury.

For jury-trial had been extended from private cases to questions of criminal guilt. The Papal council of 1215 banned the ordeal from Christendom as a relic of pagan times. When the news of that decision arrived, England was in the midst of the civil war which had broken out again between John and his barons and continued into the reign of his son. The normal administration of justice was restored in 1218, and the justices found the gaols full of criminals whom they could not try – unless they allowed the accused to 'put themselves upon their country' (a jury of neighbours), on the general question of guilt or innocence; and that was the solution adopted. Trial by his neighbours seems to have been a justifiable risk for the suspected person, although it had been another local jury which declared him suspect: only two of the eight Shropshire cases of jury-trial for homicide resulted in hangings.

If only two actual deeds of robbery were presented, a considerable number of people were indicted (*indictati*) as notorious thieves. In ten instances the accused appeared and put themselves upon the country: six cases resulted in hangings. Though the listing of notorious thieves, rather than of separate crimes, was clearly due to the practical limitations of the presenting juries, some medieval jurists do seem to have assessed criminal guilt in terms of the length of a criminal's career, and there was no attempt to analyse individual criminal acts. Thus, the different types of crime were not very clearly distinguished in thirteenth-century England, nor was there much theory about criminal liability, the circumstances necessary to constitute the different sorts of criminal guilt, or which might be regarded as lessening it.

THE FELONIES

In the thirteenth century, we must admit that there was not even a very clear distinction between criminal acts and civil wrongs. The petty assizes, though they were brought by private individuals to secure redress for themselves, were instituted as part of the king's campaign to enforce his peace;

and a defendant against whom judgment was given always had to pay an amercement to the king as well as damages to the plaintiff. Initiation by writs, bought from the chancery by private persons, did tend to mark off some actions as 'civil' ones (the *jurate et assise* of the eyre-roll): on the other hand, the misdeeds presented by the grand juries under the Assize of Clarendon could be regarded as specially criminal (they were included in the 'crown pleas' of the eyre-roll). Procedural distinctions were thus producing rough conceptual ones.

Before Henry II's work there was, however, a single procedure, presumably evolved from the Anglo-Saxon way of settling disputes, for bringing into court all wrongs, whether civil or criminal according to later ideas: the Appeal of the person wronged.[2] This action was not made redundant by Henry II, for there remained many civil injuries not covered by the petty assizes; and we have seen also that separate criminal wrongs were beyond the scope of the presentment system. In these misleadingly named 'criminal Appeals', which are to be found in both sections of the eyre-roll, criminal law and civil law remained merged. There are hundreds upon hundreds of these Appeals in the plea-rolls of the thirteenth century. It looks as though this was the only form of litigation in the king's court which was understood by the ordinary countryman, below the level of those who knew about the chancery and could send for writs. Instead of getting a writ, the 'appellor' began his action orally in the county-court, from which it was referred to the eyre.

Perhaps it was the Appeal which first compelled the judges to make an explicit distinction between criminal and civil matters. Was it right or advisable, they asked, that a man should be placed in peril of his life (a 'criminal punishment') in an action brought by a private person, perhaps maliciously and usually for some pecuniary advantage? The appellor, the law begins to say, must allege a crime and offer to fight the accused person to prove it, and he cannot get pecuniary damages. The Appeal was to be a criminal indictment, if an indictment of unusual form.

The judges insisted that the appellor should allege a crime, and it was part of the ancient ritual of the Appeal that the two sides should affirm and deny the allegation in precise terms and unvarying form, any departure from which was fatal: here, then, conventional descriptions and definitions of crimes began to emerge. To give an instance: in the Shropshire eyre, William Tuppe appealed John son of William that when he, the appellor, was within the peace of the lord king in a certain wood at nine o'clock on the morning of St Martin's day, John came and assaulted him with a Welsh knife and made a wound in his left elbow seven inches long and three wide, and another in his right elbow three inches long and one wide; and then in robbery took away seven of the appellor's black pigs. And this, says William, John did wickedly and feloniously, and he offers to prove it on his body.

One of the allegations which the appellor made – and had to make – was that John had committed a *felony*. Felony was a vivid but imprecise word, signifying something 'cruel, fierce, wicked, base'. At law, felonies could be recognized by their consequences: the felon's condemnation to lose life or limb, and to forfeit his land to his lord. By the thirteenth century, felonies had become more or less commensurate with the 'bootless' crimes of Canute and the deeds which the presenting juries of the Assize of Clarendon had to list. Before going on to examine the various felonies in more detail, we should say that the imprecise moral attitude in the word felony perhaps helped to develop a concept of criminal liability. Felony implied a certain venom, malice, premeditation, in the felon.

The idea that 'malice aforethought' was necessary in felony had to compete with what seems an utterly contradictory principle, that a man was responsible for any effect which could be traced to him, however deviously, and whether or not it was intended. The first of the felonies, homicide, was said to be constituted by doing anything by which the victim was 'further from life and nearer to death'. This primitive logic went far beyond the bounds of rationality. If a cart ran over a man, or a tree fell upon him, his death was said to be by misadventure; yet the cart or the tree was regarded as his 'bane', in some mysterious way responsible, and had to be exorcized, so to speak, by being 'given to God' – it was a *deodand*, which was to be sold for the benefit of the poor. But it is unfair to stress the irrational aspects of an attitude which had the merit of cutting through many problems plaguing the sophisticated law of today. The words of a medieval chief justice, 'the thought of man shall not be tried, for the devil himself knoweth not the thought of man', contain, as Maitland pointed out, a kernel of uncomfortable truth for a law still struggling to appreciate 'the psychical element in guilt and innocence'.

Thirteenth-century logic therefore required that when one of the Shropshire juries in 1256 found that William son of Robert, an eight years old boy, had shot an arrow into the air, causing a man's death accidentally (*per infortunium* – the same term as was used of death by deodand), the boy should be outlawed and his village amerced for not arresting him. But, since there was no malice in such actions, it was difficult to regard them as felonies. In practice, they were referred to the king, who granted a pardon; and, according to c. 9 of the Statute of Gloucester (1278), juries were always to declare whether homicide was by felony or by misadventure. Only killing in self-defence (which may at one time have included a man's obligatory vengeance – killing 'for his honour' – in a feud), or killing a criminal in flight, were absolutely justifiable, and allowed the slayers to be acquitted. At the other extreme, felonious homicide, 'by malice aforethought', would bear no punishment but death.

Akin to homicide was suicide (*felo de se*), a term applied at first only to the self-killing of a criminal fearing a worse fate: its scope grew steadily, in step with the tendency, profitable to the crown, to declare forfeit the goods of anyone who died by violence. Wounding or imprisoning another man could constitute an appealable felony, but the injured man had the alternative of securing damages by the new civil action of *trespass*, and the judges encouraged him to take it. This made a great difference to the tone of the law. Instead of the old tradition of exacting blood for blood, quite serious assaults became the subject of financial calculations, and the effectiveness of the criminal law might have been permanently lessened if such offences had not also been included in the class of 'criminal trespasses' which must be described later.

Robbery was an open crime, often perhaps an act of retaliation, while *larceny* or theft was a secret and (therefore) much more dishonourable deed. In the thirteenth century a further distinction was growing up between petty larceny and the capital felony of grand larceny, according to whether the sum stolen amounted to one shilling. The petty thief might lose an ear or a thumb, but saved his life.

Rape, arson and *treason* made up the main list of felonies. Treason in the thirteenth century still meant treachery to one's lord rather than to the king. Though 'imagining the death of the king' was a special felony by 1214, high treason was not a very frequent charge, for its political usefulness had not yet been discovered – in fact, did not exist while the whole of the law was for the king to use as he pleased. There were one or two special crimes – forgery of a lord's seal was one, and minting false coin another – which were later brought under the concept of treason. Since the idea of felony had been extended from treachery to most serious crimes, it was beginning to be felt that treason was in a class of its own, even worse than felony; and particularly horrible punishments were being devised for it.

Accessories after the fact of a felony – those who harboured the fleeing criminals – were treated as on a par with the principal malefactors. Accessories before the fact were a more difficult problem. It was a corollary of the idea that a man was responsible for the harm he most remotely or accidentally caused, that a man who planned or attempted a crime which never happened bore no guilt at all. If he planned a murder which someone else committed for him, he was as responsible as the slayer. But he could not be tried for merely plotting the murder: he could be arraigned only when it had been proved, by the conviction of the 'principal', that a murder had occurred.

BREACH OF THE PEACE AND MISDEMEANOUR

The idea of felony, of the intrinsically horrible act which demanded a horrible punishment, enforced by all the resources of the king, was fundamental to thirteenth-century criminal law. But there was an alternative basis, and one which greatly extended the range of crime; namely, the idea that many misdeeds, particularly violent ones, although trivial in themselves, disturbed the peace which belonged to the king.

The greater crime of felony was taken to include this lesser one of breach of the peace, which an appellor usually alleged for good measure. Appeals of felony were often quashed by the judges, sometimes because the appellor had not conformed to the ritualistic procedure, at other times because the injuries alleged were thought to be too trivial to constitute a felony. But the accused man did not escape unscathed when the Appeal was quashed, for the justices nevertheless commanded a jury, 'for the sake of the king's peace', to say what had happened. If a verdict of 'guilty' was returned at this stage, the criminal was imprisoned till he made fine with the king, but was not treated as a felon. He had, as the jury sometimes said, committed a trespass (*transgressionem*) against the king's peace; one of those lesser crimes which would come to be known as *misdemeanours*, when the name of trespass was appropriated to the parallel civil action.

In the thirteenth century, no one thought of trespasses as a new class of crimes below felonies, but there already existed a large collection of miscellaneous offences which would fit into such a category. These were mostly administrative crimes – the misdeeds of officials and infringements by others of official regulations, like the assizes fixing prices for bread and ale. They were offences defined, in the first place, by the articles of the eyre. In the later middle ages, the power to create new trespasses by statute was of vital importance to government.

The direct complaints of the injured persons, as much as

the indictments of the grand jury, were the channels by which the tale of these trespasses reached the king's ear. In the later years of the thirteenth century these complaints began to be written down, and were then called 'bills'.[3] The complaints made to the justices were not confined to administrative trespasses, but included private matters, the assaults on persons and the ravaging of other people's land, which were endemic in medieval town and country. These offences were grouped into the reasonably coherent class of 'criminal trespasses' when they became, in the fourteenth century, the preoccupation of the justices of the peace and the allegations were required to be approved by a grand jury.

THE BREAKDOWN OF THE EYRE

In the 1290s, the eyre system broke down under an ever-increasing burden of work, of which complaints of trespass were a significant part. The king had tried to keep the whole judicial enterprise in the hands of a few judges drawn from his most intimate councillors. The sessions in the counties got longer and longer, the visits of the eyre rarer, till no one could tell when the justices would come again.[4]

New ways had to be found to deal with the rising tide of disorder. Luckily there were parts of the judicial system capable of development, since the eyre had been that system's hub, not its sole component. When there was no eyre, and outside the terms when the central courts were sitting, the judges had gone out at intervals of a year or so to hear the very numerous petty assizes: they had travelled in pairs, on rather more than the eyre's two circuits, and associated a few knights of each shire with them in their work. Commissions had also been sent to 'deliver' gaols; that is, to try the people arrested on suspicion or caught after indictment in the eyre. Commissions of *gaol delivery* were normally given to the existing justices of assize, to whom statutes of 1285 and 1340 (Westminster II, c. 30; 14 Edward 3, Stat. 1, c. 16) added power to conclude cases begun in the central courts and brought to the point where the verdict of a local jury was necessary. This last form of jurisdiction was called *nisi prius*, because the cases were adjourned to another meeting of King's Bench or Common Pleas, 'unless before' that meeting (*nisi prius*) the justices of assize should have visited the counties concerned.

There had also long been issued, in particular emergencies, or at the urgent petition of individuals, commissions of *oyer and terminer*, ordering justices to 'hear and conclude' specific matters, perhaps single civil pleas, or an epidemic of a certain type of crime which had broken out over a whole area. The stereotyped commissions of this sort which developed in the thirteenth century were concerned mainly with trespasses, which the eyre had too little time for.[5] A new era began in 1305, when there was announced, not another general eyre, but a countrywide commission of oyer and terminer, to deal, now, with felons of the deepest dye, who roamed through the counties, trailing their clubs or 'bastons'.

The commissioners of *trailbaston*, like the justices of assize, were a speedier and more flexible answer than the eyre to a crisis in public order, since they had a limited range of pleas to settle, moved in smaller parties on more circuits, finished their tasks quicker, and could go more often. Further, the partial commissions we have just mentioned were to be eventually combined in the powers of a single group of justices to produce something like an eyre once more: in fact the modern judges of assize derive their functions from just this combination of commissions. Yet the disappearance of the eyre was a disaster. In place of one majestic and irresistible tribunal, competent to deal with every injustice, and where every grievance might find a remedy, there was a collection of limited commissions, at whose approach fear was too often unmixed with hope of redress.

'KEEPERS OF THE PEACE' AND LOCAL RIVALRIES

There is an element still to be mentioned in the unsatisfactory structure which replaced the eyre: the local magistrates or justices of the peace. The appearance of this new justice was part of a general administrative, not merely judicial, revolution at the end of Edward I's reign. As government increased in scope, or at least in pretensions, it could no longer be kept in the hands of a few intimates of the king. On occasions of emergency throughout the century, it was necessary to appoint local lieutenants of the king to police troubled areas and defend coasts and borders against invasion. These lieutenants were called keepers of the peace (*custodes pacis*), and their function was at first purely military, even when their use was extended from the borders to all the inland counties during the baronial rebellion of 1263–5.[6]

The first jurisdiction which collected around the *custodes pacis* was thus one of military discipline. At first conferred by virtual commissions of oyer and terminer, these disciplinary powers were given to all military officers later in the middle ages by the *ordinances of war*, issued at the beginning of major campaigns, which were the ancestors of the later *articles of war* and the modern Army Act under which courts martial are held. The Edwardian *custodes* and the later lords-lieutenants were empowered to deal judicially with rebels as well as their own men; and the Tudor provost-marshal – the chief of military police – turned his efforts to the correction of rogues and vagabonds in general, thus inspiring the appointment by local magistrates of their own provost-marshals with certain summary powers. The activities of the provost-marshals – and they lasted till George II's reign – may have been the 'marshal law' to which the early Stuart parliaments objected, and were the nearest England has come to true 'martial law', in the sense of a summary process applied by soldiers to the civilian population in times of urgency.[7]

Edward I's reign was more orderly than his father's, and it was to assist the sheriff in routine matters of policing that the king twice – in 1277 and 1287 – appointed keepers of the peace in each county. 'Keepers of the peace', staying permanently in their shires and with force at their command, were obvious authorities for an aggrieved person to appeal to. They were almost certainly recording breaches of the peace, before they were instructed in 1287 to write down all infringements of the Statute of Winchester, which two years earlier had ordered the maintenance of watchmen in every town and village, the shutting of the town gates at night, the cutting down of undergrowth along the main roads where robbers could lurk, and the provision by every citizen of equipment with which he must join the 'hue and cry' after peace-breakers.

It was a natural step from recording presentments of crime to determining the cases, but the judges at Westminster were reluctant to admit local gentlemen to the status of justices, and with good reason.[8] The justices of the peace are often described as the mainstay of English government. Yet the justice was never primarily the king's servant. He was the local 'boss', whose power was measured by the extent of his land and tenantry. The justices were hardly 'chosen' by the king, for they chose themselves. They were the only possible wielders of the functions which were progressively given to them, by statutes which should be regarded as defining rather than bestowing authority in their localities: that authority was unlimited, indivisible, and based until very recent times on physical force. When we talk of the eyre and the royal justices in the thirteenth century, we must remember that the disputes of the peasantry, the bye-laws necessary for fruitful agriculture, the substance of everyday life, were still matters for the landlord and were transacted in his manorial court. The 'local-government' functions of the J.P.s were part of the immemorial continuity of social life and the justices were the landlords in another guise.

It was not the appointment of local justices alone which changed the situation, but their appointment combined with the disappearance of the eyre, the link between king and counties, which had quartered the land to see how the king's subjects were governed by their natural masters. The justice of the peace, left unrestrained to use his office for his own aggrandizement, was now the representative of the Common Law to the majority of the population, and as a consequence the whole judicial system was brought into disrepute.

The hero of late medieval story is the rebel who sets up his own good law against the bad law in authority. 'You who are indicted . . . come with me to the green forest of Belere-gard . . . for the common law is too uncertain'; so ran one song.[9] It was difficult enough for the king to tell the difference between the justices and the outlaws, for both maintained their armed gangs. From the J.P.s odium and contempt spread to the higher justices, usually J.P.s in their own localities, and in 1332 a judge of the King's Bench was even ambushed on the high road and held to ransom. The anarchy of late medieval England, culminating in the Wars of the Roses (c. 1455–71), stemmed partly from this devaluation of the law. Methods of aggrandizement by the abuse of judicial powers in the counties were applied to the politics of the king's court, where vindictive state trials became the accepted means of destroying dynastic rivals.

THE JUSTICE OF THE PEACE

Edward II (1307–27) was the first king to issue frequent commissions to keepers of the peace, and it is significant that his reign marks the beginning of almost two centuries of intermittent anarchy. By additions to the terms of their writs of commission, the keepers acquired power to call juries and receive presentments of felony and trespass, to arrest those who were indicted and also those they suspected of crime. The commons in parliament – not surprisingly, since they were the gentry and leading burgesses who enjoyed the commission of the peace – repeatedly petitioned on behalf of the keepers: it has been suggested by Professor Putnam that advocacy of local justices was the first conscious policy the commons ever had.[10]

Perhaps because they were the men on whom the king relied to fight the hundred years war with France, the keepers slowly prevailed over the prejudices against them in high places. A statute of 1361 (34 Edward 3, c. 1) made them justices, by authorizing them to try the criminals they arrested. Seven years later they were made responsible for the enforcement of the wage regulations inspired by the shortage of labour after the Black Death. This is an early indication of the special part the J.P.s were to have in the regulation of the country's economic life, in conjunction with the government's device of making undesirable economic practices into offences by statute.

The sixteenth-century expert on the J.P.'s office, William Lambard, estimated that to 133 statutes passed to regulate the justices' powers before 1485, Henry VII (1485–1509) and Henry VIII (1509–47) added 60, Edward VI (1547–53) and Mary (1553–8) 39 and Elizabeth I (1558–1603) 77. The Tudor justices enforced laws against Roman Catholic recusants, regulations laying down the clothes people might wear and the price they should pay for them, the running of ale-houses and the employment of the poor. But the real basis of the justices' power remained their duty to suppress riots, from which flowed their right to arrest anyone they considered to be disturbing the peace and bind him over to keep the peace in future.

In the middle ages all local government was carried on by authority of the king's writs of commission (letters-patent). In times of emergency commissions might not be issued at all, or, as in the Wars of the Roses, they might be multiplied as each faction, temporarily controlling the Chancery, used them as weapons of war against its enemies. The J.P.s differed from the itinerant justices in that they resided in their counties, and continued to act till a new commission changed the lists, perhaps merely by adding the names of young aristocrats who had just come of age. So, from the single shire keeper of the thirteenth century, the numbers of J.P.s had by 1565 'come commonly to thirty or forty in every shire, either by increase of riches, learning or activity in policy and government'.[11] Every person of consequence in the county now expected to be made a J.P. almost as a matter of inheritance. In the fifteenth century high ecclesiastics were included in the commission, and from the early seventeenth century an increasing number of the wealthier country parsons sat along with the squires.

72

By the sixteenth century, the county list was headed by a few of the great officers of the king's court. The judges of assize were in the commissions of the peace for the shires of their circuit. To be distinguished from the king's councillors, the 'honorary justices' who appeared in all the commissions, are the regional nobles who appeared for a block of counties because their power throughout them was very real: they probably did little of the magistrate's routine work, but used their functions to the fullest advantage in struggles with their equals for predominance. Finally came two dozen or so average gentlemen of the shire, who did the staple work of local government.[12]

Early in the fourteenth century, the most important man in the commission of the peace was sometimes called 'chief justice', but this office was superseded after 1368 by that of *custos rotulorum*, the keeper of the justices' records. Already by 1368 there were *clerks of the peace* who actually made the records and were nominated by the *custodes rotulorum*. In the later sixteenth century the *custos* was usually the lord-lieutenant of the county. The latter dignitary is often said to have been a Tudor invention, but was rather a reincarnation of the single keeper of the peace of the thirteenth century, responsible for the policing and defence of the shire in times of internal riot or threat of invasion from without. The office of lieutenant, the man who 'held the place' of the king in his shire, fell naturally to the richest landlords in the locality, and the J.P.s acted as his subordinates.[13]

THE SIXTEENTH-CENTURY PATTERN OF JUSTICE

By statutes of 1351 and later, the general sessions of peace were held four times a year, at Hilary, Easter, Midsummer and Michaelmas, and were therefore known as quarter-sessions. At quarter-sessions there was much time-taking legal formality, so in the second half of the sixteenth century we begin to find the justices in quarter-sessions referring matters to special gatherings of the justices in particular neighbourhoods. These 'petty sessions' gradually created new administrative districts, resenting interference from the J.P.s in the rest of the county; and the lord-lieutenant appointed a deputy-lieutenant from each of these half a dozen or so divisions. These were new units to control for the nobleman bent on local predominance, as well as for the Puritans aiming to spread their godly discipline through the organs of government: in Elizabeth's reign it was not unknown for a divisional meeting to include prayer and preaching.[14]

It was during the 'personal rule' of Charles I (1625–49) that 'petty sessions' hardened into a monthly meeting of the justices and officers of the division, chiefly to execute the Poor Laws. The by then continual supervision of the Privy Council, and the 'book of orders' it issued to the J.P.s in 1631, were the pressures which moulded the new institution.

The sixteenth-century justices rarely concluded cases of the more serious felonies or inflicted the severer punishments, but left them to the justices of assize, *nisi prius* and gaol delivery, who visited the counties twice a year. The J.P.s spent their time enforcing economic regulations.[15] The judges of assize tried to fulfil at least some of the supervisory functions of the old eyre. They advised the government on the appointment of J.P.s, transmitted to the latter the government's policy on such problems as religious dissent, and received frequent orders from the Privy Council to deal with particular cases of jury-packing and other abuses by the local justices. They heard a few appeals against the orders of quarter-sessions, and their order book was very like the J.P.s' in content. All the J.P.s were supposed to be present at the assizes, the more important sitting on the bench with the judges.

Behind the assizes was the court of King's Bench, which, in the disorder of the fourteenth century, sometimes went on eyre itself, displacing the J.P.s. But, after 1400, it rarely left Westminster, and the considerable body of criminal cases which it continued to hear were brought before it by writs of *terminari*, *certiorari* and *error*.[16] The first ordered the subordinate justices to send undetermined indictments to the King's

Bench; the second could command even the record of a concluded case to be transferred to the Bench for reconsideration, where the case was a difficult one; and the third was the only method of appeal open to a condemned person – a primitive and clumsy one, since it could not obtain a re-trial, but only the quashing of the judgment on the grounds of some technical mistake in the record, and the writ of error had to be obtained from the Crown which had won the case. It should be remembered that there was a two-way traffic between King's Bench and the lower courts, some cases being sent down for trial at *nisi prius*.

There was also in the sixteenth century the *Court of Star Chamber*. This special court was one aspect of the efforts of the Tudor dynasty to curb the crimes of their 'overmighty subjects'; 'to bridle such stout noblemen or gentlemen which would offer wrong by force to any manner men and cannot be content to demand or defend the right by order of law.' It is true that it heard most of its cases on the petition of private persons, and that they included complaints of libels: but libels, as yet inadequately covered by the ordinary law-courts, were particularly likely to lead to breaches of the peace. Star Chamber also helped to keep order by punishing perjury, jury-packing, contempt of court and conspiracies to pervert justice in any of the king's courts.[17]

Some implication of riot or lesser breach of the peace was necessary to bring a case to Star Chamber, as it had been to bring trespasses into the ordinary courts, though once again it was usually a fiction and known to be so by the judges. We cannot take at their face value even such complaints as that of Richard Joyfull in 1500 that Robert Warcoppe and 'other riotous and misruled people, to the number of 53 persons and more . . . with force and arms, that is to say with bows, arrows, bills, swords and bucklers' attacked him 'in God's peace and yours . . . to the great peril of your said beseecher and to worst example of others like offending. . . .'

In the sixteenth century, civil cases at the suit of the injured party, and criminal indictments, prosecuted by the Crown, were clearly distinguished in the Common Law courts. But

Star Chamber, by punishing enormous trespasses on private petitions and informations, continued, for reasons of expediency, to merge the two categories.

METHODS OF PROSECUTION

In the last part of this chapter, which traces the development of ideas of criminal liability up to 1642, we can separate the new methods of accusation and the newly-defined crimes into two classes: those which evolved in the 'normal' workings of the ordinary courts, and those which were specially related to the political troubles of the period.

It was common practice by c. 1360 for the justices of the peace to accept private accusations by petition, which they then submitted to the grand jury. If the jury decided that they were 'true bills', trial proceeded as if they were old-style presentments, and this procedure became the strict meaning of the term 'indictment'. It was not really new in the 1350s. In societies where policing was primitive, governments necessarily relied on the efforts of private persons in the detection of crime; and many of the presentments of the thirteenth century were certainly procured by the victims. In addition to this we know that, although the idea was established that a man should not obtain damages by a criminal prosecution, there remained a procedure – the Appeal – for the private accusation of felony, and that private complaints (bills) of trespass against the peace were listened to. After some hesitation, the fourteenth-century J.P.s, whose business was mainly trespass, were excluded from hearing civil suits. It was natural that the fact of private initiative should then be officially recognized in criminal accusations.

There was still no way in which the government could itself initiate criminal proceedings: it could only encourage popular action. To cope with the political troubles of the later middle ages, the crown began to use more direct methods. It ordered arrest and trial on the *information* of private persons, without getting a grand jury to confirm the

76

charges. The information was a further development of the complaint of trespass. In the eyres at the end of the thirteenth century, complainants by bills had the idea of saying, in addition to the allegations of trespass against the peace, that they prosecuted the cases for the king's rather than their own benefit, or 'as much for the king as for themselves'. The practice was encouraged by the provision, in statutes creating new offences, of penalties which should go partly to the informer. In early Stuart times an average county might have as many as twelve professional informers working in cooperation with the clerk of the peace, each bringing twenty or so prosecutions to quarter-session, and some directing rudimentary detective agencies. Trial in these cases followed the normal pleading of a civil action. Yet – and this was the chief importance of the information – it provided the model for direct prosecution by the king, through his attorney in the relevant court. The king's attorney was soon presenting far more articles of information than were private individuals. Informations were most used in the court of Star Chamber, against 'enormous trespasses', and were one of the grievances which led the Stuart parliament to abolish that court; but the common informer continued to operate, often under the stimulus of statutory rewards, and before 1951 found his happiest hunting ground amongst infringements of Sunday observance laws.[18]

It is clear, then, that the bill or petition had as great a scope in criminal as in civil procedure: and that the importance of the presentment has been rather exaggerated. Indictment was a combination of bill and presentment, and public prosecution by the attorney-general is descended from private bills of trespass.[19]

A rather more dubious proceeding than information, though it had ancient roots, was trial upon 'record'. It was in part an extension of the old principle that notoriety was adequate to accuse a man – and even to condemn him. J.P.s sometimes had authority to arrest on suspicion – though this was one of the powers which they were entrusted with only reluctantly and lost from time to time; and when they intervened to stop a riot, the rioters were obviously prosecuted simply on the justices' word. Now the justices' witness of riot was the authoritative 'record' of the court discussed earlier, and the analogous king's witness of rebellion was no less than incontrovertible, so that it was found politically convenient to condemn rebels on the king's record in the court of the Constable of England (see below, p. 164). The families of the noble victims of this doctrine that notoriety to the king equalled condemnation, naturally claimed that it was contrary to law; and it was certainly dangerous. The practice was, indeed, turned against the Crown, which found its ministers, from the end of the fourteenth century right on to the eighteenth, being impeached by parliament on the same basis of 'notorious crimes'.[20]

THE STATUTORY DEFINITION OF POLITICAL CRIMES

The first group of crimes to be discussed, of those newly defined in this period, are the ones which seem the peculiar products of the troubled times, when we may say that 'political' offences were first isolated.

Treason was defined by a statute of 1352 (25 Edward 3, Stat. 5, c. 2). It was a great statute, for it went some way to preventing the interpretation of the offence for political purposes, just as king or judges might choose. The issue for contemporaries was not, however, the political abuse of the idea of treason, but profit – if a man was convicted of treason, the king took his goods, but if of felony, his lord. The 1352 definition is rather old-fashioned, because the political undertones seem hardly to have been recognized, and the feudal criterion predominates: treason is declared to be compassing or imagining the death of the king; raping the king's wife or unmarried daughter, or the heir-apparent's wife; levying war against 'our said lord the king' and giving the king's enemies 'aid and comfort in the realm or elsewhere'; counterfeiting the great or privy seals, or the king's money; bringing false money into the realm; and killing the chancellor, treasurer or any of the king's judges in the performance of their offices. In these cases, the traitor was to forfeit his goods to the king. There were distinguished from them certain 'petty treasons', again characterized by treachery to one's natural lord, in which the forfeiture was to go to the immediate overlord, as in ordinary felonies: they were the slaying of a bishop, of a master by his servant, and a wife's slaying of her husband – 'her baron'.[21]

Although the definition of 1352 was moderate, it marked off treachery against the lord who was the king, and therefore by later reasoning treachery against the state, as particularly 'high' treason; and the distinction was confirmed by the horrible punishments reserved for the crime,[22] and the fact that a man could not escape by benefit of clergy: an Arch-bishop of York was beheaded for it in 1405. There was now a concept inviting political use, and in emergencies its scope was frequently enlarged. High treason was one of the few medieval crimes extended by judicial 'construction'. Yet the influence of the statute of 1352 remained, and no additions to it were permanent. The trial of Roger Casement turned on the interpretation of its clauses.

Part of the impressiveness of the Statute of Treasons con-sisted in the fact that it was one of the very few statutory definitions of crime in the Middle Ages. The outline of many crimes against the state, such as riot and sedition, had to be worked out in the courts, particularly in Star Chamber under the guise of 'enormous trespasses'.

But the growing habit of ganging together, and abusing the processes of justice to gain advantage over one's local rivals, did lead quite early to the statutory definition of two other crimes, *conspiracy* and *champerty*. 'Conspirators,' said an ordinance of 1305, 'be they that do . . . bind themselves by Oath, Covenant or other Alliance, that every of them shall aid . . . the others falsely and maliciously to indict . . . or falsely to move or maintain pleas . . . and such as retain men in the country with liveries or Fees for to maintain their malicious enterprises . . . Champertors be they that move Pleas and Suits, and sue them at their proper costs, for to have part of the land in variance, or part of the gains.'[23]

79

Conspiracy, as far as the statute of 1305 was concerned, was an offence connected with the abuse of legal procedure and was not very clearly distinguished from the crime of 'maintaining' legal actions in order to score off an enemy; which again was intimately connected both with champerty and with *livery*, the offence of keeping a large force of retainers and dressing them in uniforms for nefarious purposes. Until Tudor times statutes against the evils of livery and maintenance were frequent, and *maintenance* is still occasionally met with in the courts.[24] The crime of conspiracy, in the wider sense of joining together to plan an unlawful act (or even in some cases a lawful one), had a much more important future.

Measures against *libel* in the middle ages were largely political, since (following the attitude of the ancient Germanic courts) it was construed as a personal insult, which might be pursued in the civil courts as slander where the injured person was of small worth, but was to be regarded as a serious crime when directed against the nobility.[25] The political importance of the defamation, not the fact of its dissemination in writing, first distinguished libel from *slander*. The idea of criminal libel is discernible in a statute of 1275 (Westminster 1, c. 34), soon after the barons' rebellion led by Simon de Montfort, which enacted punishments for anyone guilty of *scandalum magnatum*, *viz*. publishing false news or scandal tending to produce discord between the king and his barons. The statute was confirmed in the 1380s (2 Richard 2, Stat. 1, c. 5; 12 R 2, c. 11), when Richard II was at odds with his magnates, and the council was then given discretion to punish offenders.

Another confirmation of 1559 (1 Elizabeth 1, c. 6) included new clauses on 'seditious words'; and libel against the crown had sometimes been regarded as 'constructive treason' even before Queen Mary declared it treason to say 'or hold opinion' that Philip of Spain did not, jointly with his wife, 'enjoy the style, honour and kingly name of this realm' (1 and 2 Philip and Mary, c. 10). Though the political potential of the printing press was quickly realized, seditious libels from

80

that source were checked by proclamations requiring a licence from the Privy Council or a bishop before a book could
be produced at all. Libel or slander, as a misdemeanour, was
dealt with chiefly by the court of Star Chamber, where
private complaints of the offence were admitted. It may be
that these complaints had to be entertained both because
they led to breaches of the peace and as a deterrent to
malicious accusations, to which Star Chamber was particularly vulnerable.[26]

It was no defence to show that a libel was true – 'it is not
the matter but the manner which is punishable: for libelling
against a common strumpet is as great an offence as against
an honest woman and perhaps more dangerous to the breach
of the peace.'[27] But by 1635 truth was beginning to be taken
as a justification for defamatory words but not writings, and
the substantive distinction between libel and slander may
have started in this way. Slander, in the sense of a lesser libel,
carried as punishment 'pillory, whipping, loss of ears . . .
wearing papers, confusion in public places'.

PARDONS, CLERGY AND THE CLASSIFICATION OF CRIMES

The process of defining crimes was slow and uneven. For
purposes of government and to elicit indictments, it was
sufficient to make vigorous rather than precise announcements about the activities which would be punished. The
few ordinances, like Edward I's about conspirators, which
were more exact in expression, purported only to mark off
(not to create) classes of crime which everybody should have
known to be crimes beforehand. Where there was no statutory definition, we find, in the proceedings before the justices
of the peace in the fourteenth and fifteenth centuries, similar
acts being presented in a number of colourful guises: *riot*, for
instance, appears also as 'making an affray', 'insurrection',
and 'raising the commons with warlike array and the ringing
of bells'.[28] As long as emphasis was on the verdict of the jury
and not on careful trial embracing legal analysis of the deed

as well as the fact of it, there could be only slow progress beyond the rough delineation of felonies.

In the case of the more ordinary felonies and misdemeanours, to which we now pass, it seems to have been the presenting juries themselves who did most towards a useful classification. The exclusion of the justices of the peace from hearing civil pleas automatically established the existence of the class of offences known today as *misdemeanours*, for the justices continued to punish, 'at the king's suit' only, many accusations of trespass against the peace. Between felony and trespass the frontier was not quite settled: in the sixteenth century it was apparently still up to the appellant or informant whether a larceny, or even a rape, was treated as a felony or as a misdemeanour, the choice being indicated by whether the indictment said that the accused had done the deed 'feloniously'.

After the word 'feloniously' (in a misdemeanour the corresponding phrase was 'against the peace'), the crimes might be described in a number of ways, controlled only by the aim of the presenting juries to give a better idea of the relative gravity of the offences than the rigid categories of the lawyers allowed. Though the only punishment for grand larceny was death, a pardon (easily purchased) or benefit of clergy might deflect that retribution, and juries were determined so to emphasize serious crimes that no pardons would be issued. The J.P.s who often heard these matters were of the class which provided the members of parliament, and no doubt had a hand in the legislation which eventually recognized the distinctions which the juries made.

Thus, in 1547, horse-stealing, larceny from a church and housebreaking to the dread of the inmates were made non-clergyable (1 Edward 6, c. 12). In that purely practical description, 'housebreaking to the dread of the inmates', lawyers found the clue for a definition of *burglary*. Presenting juries had often used that ancient term, of grim but vague import, saying of the burglar that he had broken into a house and feloniously stolen, or feloniously broken and stolen (or feloniously broken and feloniously stolen), adding on occasion the words 'by night' somewhere in the charge. Where did the essence of burglary lie and how was it to be distinguished from the 'breach of close' which was a familiar trespass? It was at length decided that simple breach of close (intruding upon somebody's land) could not be a felony, even if violence was used. In burglary there had to be the element of terrorizing the Englishman in what Coke called 'his castle or fortress'. Breaking into a house by day was the felony of burglary when accompanied by larceny; but at night the mere intent to commit a felony – and it was easy to presume intent to steal – was sufficient to turn housebreaking into burglary.

It seems to have been the professional judges in the central courts who isolated *robbery*, that is larceny with violence, as a separate crime, by declaring it in 1348 to be a capital offence even though the criminal got away with less than one shilling, or even with nothing at all. The juries alone gave attention to the *receiving* of stolen goods – perhaps they saw their own among the receiver's loot. They were unsuccessful in their attempts to assimilate receiving to larceny, and not till 1691 (3 William and Mary, c. 9) did a statute place receivers in the class of accessories. The juries in only a few counties had become accustomed by the fifteenth century to talk of planned homicide as 'murder'. More important was the habit of mentioning evidence of premeditation in homicide, particularly slaying in ambush. In reply to repeated petitions the king in 1390 (13 Richard 2, Stat. 2, c. 1) conceded that the grave charges of 'murder, slaying in ambush, in assault, or of malice aforethought' should not be answerable by general pardons, i.e. pardons which did not specify these particular crimes.

FORMS OF PUNISHMENT

The purpose of the punishments inflicted during the period was retribution and perhaps deterrence. Correction and reform were hardly to be thought of when prisons consisted at best of cramped dungeons in the castles of the shire-towns and of a few magnates with 'liberties'. Criminals had to be punished and gaols delivered as quickly as possible. Though even in the thirteenth century imprisonment was used along with fines as punishment for certain shocking offences – a poacher got three years, and a serjeant-at-law who deceived the king's court 'one year at least' – a man was normally kept in prison after trial only till he made fine with the king. The few special prisons in London were not primarily houses of correction. The gate-tower of Newgate, on the south of which, wrote Stow in the sixteenth century, was 'a street called the Old Bayly', or 'court of the chamberlain of this city', at first housed mainly *approvers* waiting to win their freedom by appealing and convicting their accomplices in battle.[29]

It was the only predominantly criminal prison. In the Fleet prison (by Fleet Street) lay defaulting debtors and others who had failed to submit to the processes of law. One purpose of imprisonment was to make a man see reason, by the 'restraint of his liberty as of the great expenses which he must there sustain'. People could be amazingly obdurate. The Fleet, and the City of London's own two debtors' prisons, the Poultry and Vintry 'compters', and its more general prison called 'the Clink' in Southwark, were as full of old lags as any modern penitentiary. In the late sixteenth century the population of the Fleet was swelled by Roman Catholics who had failed to pay their recusancy fines. The Fleet was an ancient prison, connected in some way with the rise of Westminster as a centre of justice, and the Warden of the Fleet was also Keeper of the Palace of Westminster. Courts tended to acquire their own prisons, several of which, such as the *Marshalsea* of King's Bench, were in Southwark, as great a place for prisons as for theatres in the sixteenth century.[30]

The penitential discipline of the church may have done something to produce a theory of punishment, and it was perhaps to allow time for repentance that the Conqueror abolished the death penalty, substituting castration and the tearing out of the criminal's eyes. Humanity for its own sake was not a Norman virtue, and the death penalty was soon restored. The devising of retribution, the choice of the method of execution or the limb to be severed, seems to have been a matter for cruel ingenuity, local resources and perhaps a rough idea of appropriateness. On the coast a criminal might be thrown from a cliff, or tied to a stake below high-water mark. Appropriateness may be seen in the statute of 1589 which decreed the loss of ears for seditious words, and of the right hand for seditious writings. The purpose here was not retaliation ('an eye for an eye'), but to leave signs of a man's guilt and its consequences as unmistakable as they were dishonourable.

The marks of punishment were dishonourable, because the punishment of crime always presupposed some code of behaviour. The quantity of moral horror inspired by a crime roughly determined the severity of punishment, and this in turn helped to mark off some crimes – like treason – from the rest. The puritanism of the late sixteenth century brought to the fore the moral element in criminal justice. The puritan J.P. thought it as necessary to mete out the humiliation of the stocks or the ducking-stool for small moral lapses as to execute traitors and murderers. As part of his duty to keep down the poor rates, he had to discover the fathers of bastards and compel them to contribute to the children's maintenance, ordering the mothers to be whipped for good measure. The new device of binding people to be of good behaviour, employable – in contrast to binding over to keep the peace – against actions only *tending* to a breach of the peace, allowed the J.P. to correct a variety of novel offences.[31]

The first imprisonment with corrective intentions was probably the confinement of 'poor and idle persons of the city' in the house of Bridewell, presented to London in 1553 by the pious protestant King Edward VI. In 1576 (18 Elizabeth 1, c. 3), the justices of the peace in quarter-sessions were required to set up Houses of Correction in the counties, not only to punish vagrants and set to work 'such as be already grown up in idleness', but also 'to the intent youth may be accustomed and brought up in labour and work, and then not like to grow to be idle rogues'.

The effectiveness of the medieval criminal law is difficult to gauge, but one is struck by the infrequency with which criminals were brought into court, or, once there, convicted and hanged. No doubt more were hanged by commissions of oyer and terminer confined to crimes than by the justices in eyre, and more still by the justices of gaol delivery, whose victims were by definition always to hand. Nevertheless, one of the main effects of the criminal law must have been to drive bands of outlaws on to the roads of England.

Perhaps, however, we are asking questions inappropriate to the age. The majority of the criminal population was anonymous and fugitive anyway, and the king's ordinances and commissions were not intended to correct individual offenders, still less separate crimes. Throughout the centuries the peace was kept – and the treasury filled – by imposing punishments on entire communities for the real or anticipated offences of their members. With a similar disregard for detail, a general pardon could be purchased to excuse a man the consequences of any and every crime he might have committed. The objective – to control the behaviour of the people *as a whole* – was achieved, and it was rather the failure of the king to curb the political crimes of his overmighty subjects, of the nobility and gentry, which gives to the fifteenth century its appearance of chaos, and his relative success an air of progress to the Tudor age.

Historically, the criminal law can be defined no more exactly than as that part of government concerned with keeping order; and before the era of the welfare state that was practically the whole of government. Keeping public order involved, rather than excluded, the remedying of private grievances made known by petition and information. Because it was co-terminous with government, criminal jurisdiction made the J.P. a viceroy in his own little realm. Only because they attributed a moral purpose to government and 'the godly magistrate' or governor, did the puritans begin to introduce a reforming intent into criminal punishment.

CHAPTER 4

PRIVATE LAW TO 1642

THE private law of the thirteenth century tried at the same time to modify and to bolster up the rules of feudalism. Feudalism had many aspects, and its military functions could be allowed to decay while its profits were enhanced. From scutage, the commutation of military service to a money payment, and from the aids a vassal paid to his lord, grew a system of national taxation. Only the king could impose such national taxes; but the great lords were as determined as he was to hold on to their due reliefs, escheats and wardships, which were threatened by two processes – continual subinfeudation, often in such a way that the feoffor retained no land himself but only the 'seignory' and thus had nothing to escheat or fall to his lord in wardship; and excessive gifts of property into the 'dead hand' (mortmain) of undying ecclesiastical communities, from which escheats and reliefs could never arise.

THE BEGINNING OF ENTAIL

By the Statute of *Mortmain* (1279), Edward I forbade the clergy to acquire further land, whether by purchase, 'art or cunning'. In 1290, the Statute of *Quia Emptores* banned the creation of new perpetual fees by subinfeudation: henceforth the purchaser of land must take the place of the seller in the feudal ladder and assume all his feudal obligations to superior lords.[1] Edward I had unintentionally petrified feudalism. In order to preserve the financial value of old social bonds, he had deprived feudalism of its power to form new ones. A man could no longer be bound to a lord by a grant of land.

Preservation of the profits of feudalism remained the royal policy, and the Tudors actually extended them. They set up a Court of Wards, to market wardships to the highest bidders; and granted out the lands of the dissolved monasteries by tenure *in capite*, claiming that *all* the property of the recipient, as a tenant-in-chief, was thenceforth liable for wardship. But in the sixteenth century few were prepared to buy on strict feudal terms, so that much monastic property had eventually to be released to be held not directly of the king, but 'as of his manor of East Greenwich', a fiction which made the tenure one of socage.[2]

A subsidiary clause of *Quia Emptores* proved of great importance. It said that, provided the purchaser was substituted for the vendor in the feudal hierarchy, a man could dispose of his land or any part of it just as he liked. This freedom of alienation conflicted not only with the overlord's natural wish to choose his own tenants, but also with the feudal principle of primogeniture, by which the estates which a man received from his forefathers should have passed undiminished to his eldest son. Here feudalism was giving way to the permanent desire of men to dispose of their own as they think fit, often to endow their daughters and younger sons.

But something like the feudal ideal of the inheritance remaining undivided through generations proved very tenacious. A man hopes to preserve the political and social power of his name and line by arranging that the lands on which this power is based shall continue intact after his death; and, if he gives part of the inheritance to a younger son, he will try to prevent that son or one of his descendants from disposing of it equally freely. Between the desire for free alienation and the instinct to tie up lands in enduring family settlements, so limiting the freedom of future generations, only an uneasy compromise can ever be reached. More usual has been a running fight between the curious tricks devised by the conveyancers and pleaders for destroying or 'barring' existing *entails* (the legal form of the family settlements), and the no less bewildering methods for creating new and better entails devised by the same conveyancers for the same generation of clients.

Quia Emptores provided a new definition of the fee, suitable to its new alienability. The statute spoke of land granted 'in fee simple' (*in feodo simpliciter*), and 'fee simple' became the name of the basic form of tenure to which was attributed these characteristics: that it could be freely alienated by the tenant for the time being or, failing such alienation, would descend perpetually through a line of heirs. But in 1285 the king had already conceded ways of limiting its freedom, in the chapter, *De Donis Conditionalibus* ('Of Conditional Gifts'), which heads the second Statute of Westminster. The law of entail which the barons desired grew up around gifts, not wills, because the rule remained in force that a lord could not divert the normal succession of his lands by a will or *devise* taking effect after his death: if he wanted to settle those lands on others than his next heir, he must give them up in his own lifetime. Referring especially to gifts of land by parents to newly-married couples 'and the heirs of their bodies', the statute said that henceforth the intention of the donors was to be respected. The intention was that the land should endow a new line; and the land must therefore descend through the heirs of the couple, or, if those heirs failed, revert to the donor or his heirs, or 'remain' to some other person named in the donor's form of gift (*forma doni*). Writs of *formedon* were provided for use against the tenant-in-tail who alienated the property.

For the effect of *De Donis* was to create another sort of tenure, between the uninheritable tenancy for life and the inheritable and freely alienable fee-simple; a fee but a 'cut-down' one – a *fee-tail* (from French *tailler*, to cut). It also spread interests in land far into the future. The land law was used to delving into the past. All title to land was based upon seisin, and the purpose of the land actions was to recover a seisin which the plaintiff or his ancestors had once enjoyed. Therefore, so it was argued, the person who claimed by a writ of formedon must be asserting a right to seisin, the essential link between a man and his property; but he could not do it on the basis of previous seisin by himself or his ancestor. For the right to seisin was created by the gift – not just one right to immediate seisin, but several successive rights to seisin *in the future*. Since it was protected by forms of action, this right to future seisin had to be recognized as a new type of interest in property, and was denominated the interested party's *estate* (or 'standing') in the lands concerned.

Each of the estates was regarded as existing from the time of the gift, though it might not bear fruit for generations. The most important of them for the moment were the *estate tail*, which would be inherited by the donee's descendants in turn, and the estate in fee simple which had always to round off the envisaged succession, giving back the completest form of ownership to the last remainderman or (on reversion) to the donor's heir in the direct line. The effect of *De Donis* was therefore to create a new framework of land-endowment: the theory of tenures allowed for the simultaneous endowment, the theory of estates for the successive endowment, of a number of people with the same property. The new abstraction, the future estate, and the logic built upon it, immensely enriched the Common Law, and by modern times had far outstripped tenure in importance.[3]

The conveyancers quickly developed ways of breaking entails, for the benefit of tenants-in-tail who wanted to alienate the land which came to them. The conveyancers' cleverest invention was the *common recovery*. It was known that a tenant for life or a term of years sometimes fraudulently conveyed away the fee simple of the land he occupied, by means of a collusive action: the purchaser claimed the land in court, and the tenant made only a gesture of defence, so that the purchaser 'recovered' the land by a legal judgment. The judges not unnaturally discouraged the practice by allowing the real owner to 'pray to be received' in such a case and 'falsify' the recovery. But they did not discourage a special kind of collusive recovery to break entails, perfected by the time of *Taltarum's Case* (1472). The breaking of the entail was achieved by an action on the part of the purchaser (*A*) against the tenant-in-tail (*B*), who did not 'vouch to warranty' (call in support) the true donor, but alleged that he had bought the property from *C*, 'a man of straw' and later often the crier of the court, who would fail to defend the action. According to the rules of warranty, *A* would be awarded the fee simple and *B* lands from *C* equal to those he had 'lost' – but the second award was of course unenforceable either by *B*, who would not want to enforce it, or by *B*'s heir, who certainly would.

The judges may have encouraged the breaking of entails because they and the king were beginning to see the political danger of huge blocks of property which could be built up and kept intact through the centuries. Queen Elizabeth in particular seems to have favoured free alienation, perhaps regarding as a healthy thing the vigorous land market stimulated not long before by a flood of monastic property. But on behalf of prospective donors, conveyancers continued to search for the philosopher's stone of their profession, the perpetual and unbreakable entail, which they thought they found in the 'contingent remainder' (for instance, a gift 'to *A* for life with remainder to his right heirs', which is contingent on *A* leaving heirs). The contingent remainder promised a perpetual entail because, under it, not a tenant-in-tail but a tenant for life was in possession, and any recovery against him could be falsified. In the crucial *Shelley's Case* (1579), the judges disallowed this ingenious device, which indeed involved logical oddities: it envisaged the creation of an estate belonging to no one, and if there were no heirs it would produce that monstrosity, an abeyance of seisin, when there was no one to succeed.

LEASEHOLD AND COPYHOLD

With the growth of entail and the doctrine of estates the fee was seen to be not an absolute concept, nor utterly contrasted to seisin. Seisin meanwhile was growing more like a species of ownership, less like straightforward possession actually remembered by the jury in an assize of Novel Disseisin, for the date of limitation of that action was allowed to fall further and further behind. Technical and abstract things, right and seisin lost their importance to another pair of ideas of land tenure, ones more appropriate to later medieval England, where land still dominated the economic aspect of life but that aspect was becoming more diversified. These ideas were of land tenure as the endowment and unifying thread of a family dynasty, and land tenure as an economic investment.

Entail was the product of the first, the *lease* the expression of the second. The temporary renting of land to the man with money and labour to spare by the man who wants a safe income from his property without losing ownership must in fact be a practice much older than entail, though little evidence of its early use survives. There must always have been some prosperous yeomen eager to farm extra land for a set term from lords whose own farm-management was unprofitable. Lately, the fact has been revealed that there was continual selling and leasing of land by charter within the peasantry – many of them villeins – who in theory could neither own land nor have seals to make charters. The solitary widow would naturally lease some of her land, the father with numerous sons take up leases.[4]

The later Middle Ages was a good time for the English peasantry, because the Black Death of 1349, by reducing the labour force, raised the level of wages and persuaded the landlords to lease out their land on a greater scale. By the end of the sixteenth century, a good deal of the country was cultivated through farming leases, commonly of twenty-one years. When the lease fell in, it would be renewed to the same person on the payment of another entry fine, which, like the purchase price in a sale of the freehold, was calculated as a multiple of the annual income from the property. Twenty times the annual income was a normal price for freehold in the earlier sixteenth century and five times was a common entry fine in a lease. The twenty-one-year term was a compromise between the leaseholder's desire for reasonable security and the landlord's anxiety to keep up with the inflation of the time by raising the entry fine at frequent intervals.[5]

The value of leases depended to a large extent on the protection which the law provided for them. The judges at first would not regard as a 'free tenement' a form of tenure so different from the aristocratic fee: the leaseholder for a term of years was not permitted to use the assize of Novel Disseisin if he was ejected within the term. A tenant for life was not denied in this way, perhaps because it was remembered that even the knight's fee had once been granted for life only.

A form of the civil action of trespass soon gave the ejected 'termor' damages, but it was not decided until the very end of the fifteenth century that it would also recover him his tenancy. The decision had unimagined consequences, for Trespass was a simpler and swifter action than the assizes of Henry II, and the termor was suddenly better placed in law than the freeholder. By the invoking of fiction, *ejectment* – as the trespassory action to recover leasehold was called – was actually made to replace the old assizes as the normal way of claiming freehold. Suppose a piece of land was held by *A* but claimed by *B*. Then *B* would grant a lease of the property to a friend (*C*) who would allege ejectment by *D*, another collusive party. To avoid losing his land by recovery, *A* (who was all the time in occupation) would have to enter the case and dispute *B*'s right to grant the lease. In the seventeenth century, the lessee (*C*) and ejector (*D*) ceased to be actual people and became mere names – Fairclaim and Shamtitle, or most often John Doe and Richard Roe – behind which the real parties could make use of the most expeditious method of trying the issue of the freehold.

The increased economic importance of the peasant farmer was also reflected in greater legal security for the tenant-at-will, the villein who occupied land on the sufferance of a lord. At all levels feudal arrangements were giving way; the ties of service – the villein's like the knight's – to a tenurial relationship which was part economic, part legal. The villein's unfreedom was at root economic. Originally the villein could not leave his land and the tight-knit manorial community simply because it meant starvation to do so. Henry II's assizes added a legal mark of villeinage: the villein's land was not his own but his lord's, and so a villein was a man who could not himself bring actions at Common Law if his land was taken from him. Villeinage nevertheless resided in the tenure and only secondarily in the tenant. When the lords found it convenient to commute villein-services into money rents, distinguishable villein status faded away and the last and tardy instance of it was heard of in 1618.

After the commutation of the villein's services came the legal protection of his tenure, called *copyhold*. Villein-tenure was regulated by manorial custom, and the manorial courts with the lord's goodwill had often imitated for the villein's benefit the legal processes which protected the freeman at Common Law. The king in particular provided processes for the use of the villeins on his own domains, and the peasants of other lords found that they could obtain the privileges of royal villeins by showing from Domesday Book that the manors they inhabited had once been within the king's 'ancient demesne' though they were no longer.[6] The peasants of the fourteenth century knew that there was available to them a legal system separate from but hardly less useful than the Common Law of freemen, and were conscious of the importance of legal records. In the Peasants' Revolt the object of some of the rebellious mobs was the destruction of the lords' court-rolls which proved their villeinage; but the customs recorded in the rolls would often protect the villein, who held his land – so it came to be said – 'by copy of court-roll'.

By soon after the middle of the sixteenth century the copyholder was allowed to employ the freeman's action of trespass against a stranger who entered his land, for a plaintiff in that action was required only to have had possession, not a 'free tenement'. But he could get no more than damages that way, and in any case could not sue his own lord, so that it was left to the lord chancellor to restrain landlords in particular instances from expelling their tenants-at-will. Finally, towards 1600, the tenant-at-will was allowed the freeholder's action of ejectment, against his lord as well as against strangers. 'Now Copyholders,' said Chief Justice Coke, 'stand upon a sure ground, now they weigh not their lords' displeasure, they shake not at every blast of wind, they eat, drink and sleep securely.' Since their tenures were usually inheritable, they were indeed better off than the lessees for life or term of years descended from generations of freemen, who were at the mercy of the 'improving' landlord when their leases fell in, and went to swell the pauper class of Tudor England. As the dominant factor in society, medieval status had given way to hard economic bargaining, in which the law was an umpire of enormous power.

TRESPASS AND TORT

The economic value of possession (more important than seisin, when everyone sued by *ejectment*) could be undermined in many ways, and the law had to do more than put one man out and another in. It had to safeguard the *natural rights* and *easements* giving a man access, and the right to lead water supplies, across a neighbour's land, and giving his property protection against being physically undermined from an adjacent tenement. The villein and his lord had an equal need to take logs for their houses and hearths from the woods surrounding the open fields, to pasture their pigs on the waste ground and their cattle in the common meadow. The importance of common rights were reflected in the complicated legal theories about them, and in the hardship and protests evoked by centuries of enclosure.

All these rights, though 'incorporeal', could be regarded in varying degrees as 'things' and recovered by the possessory assizes; rights of common, gradually made more definite in quantity, could be recovered by Novel Disseisin, and the easements which were incapable of exact definition, by the assize of Nuisance. The jury in a case of nuisance was required to say whether, for instance, the defendant had made a ditch or a hedge across the track from the plaintiff's holding to the common pasture, or constructed a pond which kept water from the plaintiff's land or overflowed on to it, to the harm

(*ad nocumentum*) of the plaintiff's holding. If the answer was
'yes', the defendant would be ordered to undo the nuisance
as well as pay damages. Unfortunately, like all the petty
assizes, Nuisance talked of the plaintiff's 'free tenement' and
required him to have seisin. Again the villein or lessee turned
to the action of trespass, which would at least give him damages and was adaptable to almost any situation.

It is time to describe this *action of trespass*, which by the end
of the thirteenth century was the most commonly used
procedure and the growing-point of private law. It developed
very differently from the assizes: it was distinguished not by
being adapted to a single and fairly narrow situation, but by
the plaintiff's allegation that the wrong – whatever it was –
had been committed 'against the king's peace' and 'with
force and arms'. We have seen that, in the thirteenth century,
the Appeal was ossified by the regulations of lawyers into the
hazardous and cumbersome Appeal of Felony. But the
peasants who knew no other way to obtain justice went on
complaining of injuries committed upon them 'against the
peace'. These complaints divided into two streams, one
leading to the indictable trespasses or 'misdemeanours'
brought before the justices of the peace, the other, of complaints which asked for damages, to the civil action of trespass, which by the second quarter of the thirteenth century
could be initiated by a writ.[7]

The peremptory phrases of the writ, ordering the defendant to appear 'to explain why' (*ostensurus quare*) he had
committed the wrong; the allegation of violence and breach
of the peace; the swift procedure and the resort to outlawry
if the defendant did not appear – all this suggested that a
crime had been committed: but the action was a civil one,
and the suggestions of crime were only labels attached by the
plaintiff to bring the case before the most effective court. Like
all labels, they were attachable to any packet – any temporary invasion of a person's property and the destruction or
carrying away of his crops, and all personal assaults which
did not amount to felony. At a bound the civil law took into
account the whole great residue of miscellaneous injuries,

which the painstaking formulation of individually appropriate writs would not have covered in generations.

Of course, the method depended on a fiction. At first the plaintiffs felt that they must give plausibility to the allegation of breach of the peace by telling a long story of violence. But the required allegation was soon reduced to the stereotyped phrases, 'with force and arms and against the king's peace', and everyone knew that their purpose was jurisdictional, not descriptive. The idea of trespass left behind in English law a whole conceptual division between crime on the one side and cases arising from contract on the other: this was the group of *torts* or civil 'wrongs', acts wrong in themselves and not as breaches of a prior agreement, but subject to damages to the injured man rather than criminal punishment.

Two elements were equally essential to the growth of civil trespass, firstly the idea of breach of the peace, and secondly the desire for damages in money. Damages, and not any 'specific relief' like the undoing of a nuisance, were all the plaintiff could obtain in an action of trespass, but in many situations this limitation was no disadvantage – indeed, for personal injury specific relief is often impossible.

As actions multiplied, lawyers – particularly those with a knowledge of Roman Law – tried to group them into a few simple classes, a task not easily accomplished within that untidy but effective improvisation, the law of England. The first grouping was not into contractual and tortious actions (the *ex contractu* and *ex delicto* of Roman Law), for contract was slow to be recognized as a separate concept, but into the equally Roman categories of *real* and *personal* actions. The thing (*res*) which gave the real actions their name was land, and by that standard the thirteenth-century assizes were clearly 'real actions'. On the other hand, the trespassory action for assault was clearly personal: no land need be involved. Between these strongholds was disputed territory. Paradoxically, in the thirteenth century the dispossessed leaseholder could gain no more than damages by an action of trespass, whereas rights ('incorporeal things') merely attaching to the ownership of a piece of land (e.g. the right to

hold a market) could be recovered by the assize of Nuisance.
A useful rule was to label those actions as personal where only
damages were recovered, and they will be found to coincide
more or less exactly with the class of torts.

Anomalies remained when attention was turned from the
actions to the property they recovered. Land was *real
property*, the rights going with it *incorporeal things*, the rest of
a man's possessions his *chattels*. Lawyers balked at calling
leasehold a chattel, though the only action that protected it
was a personal one; so they invented the monstrous term
chattels real. The name had practical consequences, for chattels, but not land, could be disposed of by will; and, even
when leases could be recovered by ejectment, they retained
the advantage of being devisable. In order to enjoy this
power, a lord would sometimes grant his land to a friend in
fee simple and take it back on a 999 years' lease at a pepper-
corn rent.

The new personal actions were the procedures with a
future. They both adapted themselves by fiction to matters
of land (ejectment was a personal action which, as we have
seen, p. 94, became a way of asserting title to land) and took
in the subtler problems of social and commercial intercourse.
There were, indeed, writs of the old type providing a certain
safeguard for mobile wealth. Because a specific sum of money
owed by a debtor or misapplied by a bailiff could be regarded
as all the time the property of the creditor or the bailiff's lord,
'praecipe' writs would compel repayment or call the bailiff
to account. The writ of *detinue* secured the return of a chattel
'bailed', that is deposited with someone for a limited period
and understood purpose, as a man might lend a neighbour
his spade, and unlawfully detained.

Detinue was even more useful when it threw out, in the
fifteenth century, a new branch, *detinue sur trover*, to recover
a chattel which the defendant had 'found' (French *trouver* =
'to find'), i.e. obtained otherwise than by the plaintiff's
bailment (but not by stealing – no civil action ever became
established for reclaiming stolen goods from the thief). But
Detinue would still only restore the object itself or the exact

value placed upon it – it would not allow for the general damage to the plaintiff's interests. So it was the action which replaced detinue, the variety of the action of 'trespass on the case' known as 'trover and conversion', which became the almost universal remedy for interference with chattels.

THE ACTION ON THE CASE, NEGLIGENCE AND FRAUD

Remedy for damage incurred in many everyday transactions, and protection for new varieties of contract, were at length provided by this action of *trespass on the case*. A modification of the old action of trespass, in which the allegation of damage 'by force and arms' was replaced by a clause (introduced by the word *cum*, 'whereas . . .') describing some special situation in which the defendant had treated the plaintiff unfairly ,'the action on the case' came to embrace most of the torts important in the modern world. Strict trespass was more useful than the assizes, because it required in the plaintiff only possession, not seisin, of any tenement involved in the dispute. Trespass on the case did not even require the plaintiff's possession of the land or goods at the time of the injury. The usefulness of the new methods allowed them to displace the old property actions like the assize of Nuisance. By the sixteenth century, 'the action on the case for trover and conversion' was replacing 'detinue sur trover' and encroaching on the territory of the form of strict trespass concerned with the seizure of someone else's crops (*de bonis asportatis*), for it could obtain damages at large (not just the object's price) and lay for goods which had come into the defendant's hands by means, such as purchase from a thief, which did not constitute direct violation of the plaintiff's possession.

The origin of 'case' used to be found in the 24th clause of Edward I's second Statute of Westminster (1285), which authorized the chancery clerks to make new writs in situations similar (*in consimili casu*) to ones already provided for. But probably *negligence, deceit* and most of the other categories

of case were created not by the invention of new writs but by
the stricter classification of old ones – of the writs of trespass
by which every sort of injury had been brought to court under
pretext that they were violent breaches of the peace. 'Case'
would then have been created by the slow acceptance of
allegations of private wrong for their own sake, without
pretext of violence, provided that the writs precisely described the special nature of the case; and that process was not
completed till near the end of Edward III's reign (1377).[8]
It is difficult, in fact, to see how such wide categories of
wrong as negligence or deceit, so different from the specific
acts like disseisin remedied by the older writs, could have
appeared at all in English law, if writ had just been added to
writ with the progressive recognition of new issues of substance. The truth is that the unity of early-thirteenth-century
trespass was formal (the allegation of violent breach of the
peace) not substantive: every kind of injury could be brought
within its scope, and the lawyers, when they felt the need for
substantive landmarks, were compelled to divide up the
wilderness into very broad areas. This was an important
moment in the growth of concepts of civil liability.

Let us follow the history of negligence. A man who lent his
spade to a neighbour, or left his horse with a smith to be
shod, was able quite early to sue for damage to his property
while out of his possession, if to the formal allegation of trespass he added a '*cum*-clause' explaining the circumstances.
Since 'force and arms' were obviously implausible he might
emphasize the wrong by saying that the deed had been done
'maliciously' (borrowing a term from criminal liability), or
perhaps 'negligently'. The word *negligence* may have been
applied first to a nuisance caused by a man's complete
omission to do something, failure to clean a ditch, perhaps, so
flooding a neighbour's land.

The law found it difficult to divide negligence from accident in the damage caused by trespassers and bailees. In a
case of 1466 (*Hull* v. *Orynge*), the defendant to an action of
trespass said that he had entered his neighbour's property
only to collect clippings which accidentally fell on the wrong

side of the hedge he was cutting.[9] The remarkable discussion in court tended to the view that civil liability was not like criminal liability, where malice aforethought was necessary to convict of felony. In a civil wrong, as in the homicide of more primitive times, it was felt that a man should be liable for unintentional damage if he 'by any means could have prevented it'. Or, as it was written a century later: 'felony must be done with felonious intent; yet in trespass, which tends only to give damages according to hurt or loss it is not so, and therefore, if a lunatic hurt a man, he shall be answerable in trespass . . . .' Throughout this period absolute inevitability was the only safe excuse in trespass and in more modern times the first reductions in the standards of liability were due to changes in ideas of what is inevitable.

Trespass on the case covered a whole world of humble transactions with the smiths, innkeepers, carriers and so on, whose services were indispensable to society. And not just commercial transactions: 'If a man play with another at dice,' a legal authority, Fitzherbert, wrote in 1534, 'and he hath false dice with which he playeth and gets the other's money, he who loseth his money may have his action on the case for the deceit.' *Deceit* was a very old tort – as old as trespass, to which it was assimilated – and it was most important in another field which Fitzherbert mentions: 'If a man do sell unto another man a horse and warrant him to be sound and good and the horse be lame or diseased that he cannot work, he shall have an action on the case against him. . . . But . . . if he sell the horse without such warranty, it is at the other's peril and his eyes ought to be his judges in that case.'[10]

CASE AS A REMEDY FOR BREACH OF CONTRACT

The idea of deceit or fraud, even more frequently than negligence, implies a contract which has not been kept. A smith, it was said, 'undertook' (*assumpsit*) to shoe a horse, or an innkeeper to provide hospitality. Thus began a new form of trespass on the case, called 'assumpsit', in which the '*cum*-clause' of the writ alleged an unfulfilled undertaking. In a

PRIVATE LAW TO 1642

case of 1369 of a horse cured 'so negligently' by a horse-doctor that it died, the plaintiff admitted freely that there was no written deed and therefore the action of covenant would not lie. He was avowedly suing in a new form of Case, and the new action prevailed.

For a time it was possible to reconcile 'assumpsit' with ideas of tort: the surgeon who killed when he undertook to cure, or the man whose failure to roof a house as promised led to damage by rain, had committed positive wrongs. But was that man liable whose undertaking was followed by no results at all? It was here that the idea of deceit was so valuable, for a man who pocketed another's money and then refused to hand over the promised goods could very properly be called deceitful. A much greater step was needed to the doctrine stated in the early sixteenth century, that 'if he to whom the promise is made have a charge by reason of the promise . . . he shall have an action . . . though he that made the promise had no worldly profit of it'.

The emergence of a proper idea of contract is seen best in the law of sale. Striking a bargain and selling a commodity is one of the commonest of social acts: but difficulties arise if the money and the goods do not change hands simultaneously. The courts of the merchants had long enforced contracts of sale marked by the transfer of 'earnest-money', but the Common Law was far behind. If the goods were transferred and the price withheld, the vendor could bring an action of debt at Common Law: if the money passed, but not the goods, the buyer could sue by detinue. This was to apply to the situation the rigid concepts of property law, and only in the fifteenth century did the idea begin to creep into the Common Law courts that a bargain was a contract, created by the agreement of the parties and merely 'executed' by delivery; a contract demanding good faith in such matters as promptitude of delivery and the condition of the goods.[11] The change came so slowly because it was the realization of the very idea of contract in the strict sense of a binding agreement based on mutual consent which was growing: the 'contracts' enforced by such actions as covenant had been promises made *as a result of* agreements and owed their force not to the mutual consent of the parties but to the individual obligations formally undertaken and officially recorded.

The mechanism of sale made its particular contribution to the idea of contract by shifting attention from the end of the matter, the tortious deceit or negligence, to the preliminary agreement; for in sale the 'assumpsit' was not an abstraction but a very real act of bargaining. Negligence, deceit and sale had played their parts in the development of the idea of contract. Debt is also relevant to the story, because a man already indebted (*indebitatus*) might undertake to pay his debt at a specific date and be liable to an action of assumpsit if he did not. Ordinary debt was a matter for the Court of Common Pleas: assumpsit, as a trespass, was triable in the Court of King's Bench. So King's Bench, to win litigation from its rival, began to presume an assumpsit in all debts and turned *indebitatus assumpsit* into an alternative to the creditor's old proprietary action – an alternative with the extra attraction for the creditor that it did not permit the antiquated defence, surviving in Debt, of 'wager of law' (compurgation). The decision in *Slade's Case* (1602) confirmed the result of the manoeuvres of King's Bench, and by so doing added contract to real property and tort as an irreducible concept of private law.

John Slade alleged in King's Bench that Humphrey Morley had 'assumed and faithfully promised that he would pay John £16 at the Feast of St John the Baptist . . . in consideration that John . . . had bargained and sold to Humphrey' a quantity of wheat. 'Humphrey Morley, little regarding such promise, and intending to deceive and defraud John Slade of the said £16, has not paid or in any way satisfied John for the same, although John has often asked Humphrey to do so, and altogether refuses so to do. John says that he has consequently suffered damage to the value of £40.'[12]

The jury in Slade's case found that there had been no explicit assumpsit to pay at that time, and the defendant maintained that the action should have been the ordinary one for debt. But the case was adjourned to the court of Exchequer Chamber, where all the judges of England considered difficult cases, and it was there decided that 'Every contract executory imports in itself an assumpsit, for when one agrees to pay money or deliver anything, thereby he assumes or promises to pay or deliver it; and therefore when one sells any goods to another and agrees to deliver them at a day to come, and the other in consideration thereof agrees to pay such money at such a day, both parties may have an action of debt or an action of the case on assumpsit. . . .'

From the presumption of the secondary *assumpsit* to fulfil the bargain it was only a step to the presumption of a primary contract where none had been explicitly made. So, in 1610 (*Warbrook* v. *Griffin*), an innkeeper recovered payment for his services though no price had been agreed upon with his guest. A large field of implied contracts now became enforceable. If a jury in *assumpsit* thought a debt existed a defendant would be bound to pay, and the result was not always just. Executors, in particular, found themselves liable to *assumpsit* for testators' debts of which they knew nothing.

The modern idea of contract is not an obvious one, so history seems to show, but is the result of the fortuitous convergence of several processes. The initial step was the attribution of an 'assumpsit'. There might have remained different actions – Covenant, Debt and Detinue – to enforce different sorts of contract, but in fact all were brought together in the action on the case. The origins of the modern action are recalled by 'the doctrine of consideration'. The law was now ready to enforce promises other than those formally recorded; but there had to be some evidence that a contract really existed. It becomes the rule that the *consideration* or inducement must be shown, in return for which the unfulfilled promise was made. The plaintiff's statement of the consideration can be seen in the passage from *Slade's Case*. The doctrine that 'the nude pact' is unenforceable indeed goes back to classical Roman law, but it was the realities of debt and sale which engraved on the English mind the notion of the *quid pro quo* in contract – that a man rarely does 'something for nothing'. A wide range of possible considerations had to be recognized by the law: in a bargain a promise had to be taken as the consideration for a promise; and in a grant of land by charter, when that too was incorporated in a single law of contract, a consideration was simply assumed according to the maxim, 'a seal imports consideration'. The origins of contract in an *assumpsit* – the undertaking of one man to another – also meant that the Common Law adhered for centuries to the doctrine of 'privity of contract', which confined the right to sue upon an agreement to the actual contractors, and denied an action to any third party who might have suffered from its breach.

After all the juristic extrapolation necessary to make the action of trespass on the case an effective sanction for contracts, we may mention the more straightforward adapting of that action to the problem of *defamation*, when the Reformation had undermined the jurisdiction of the ecclesiastical courts in the matter. We have seen that the Common Law first treated defamation, called 'libel', as a political offence. It now permitted a civil action on the case for less serious instances of defamatory words or writings (both as yet called *slander*), provided that actual pecuniary loss could be proved (a normal requirement in tort), or (a less defensible limitation, which still survives) that there had been imputed to the plaintiff a serious crime or an infamous disease.

THE MORTGAGE AND THE USE

Perhaps because of the antiquity of the real actions, the Common Law did not so easily adapt itself to problems arising from the entry of the commercial spirit into land. The fact is demonstrated by the history of the *mortgage*. A man often had nothing but his land to offer as security (or 'gage') for a loan, while, for the merchant with capital, land was almost the only outlet for investment. When the profits from the land pledged were used to pay off the debt, the gage was said to be 'living'; but, when the creditor got the profits in addition to the repayment of the debt, they constituted disguised interest, and the gage was 'dead' (*mort*), usurious and sinful. Such, nevertheless, was the pressure for investment, which is pointless without interest, that the mortgage had to be accepted by the law. And such became the legal security of the mortgage that in the twelfth century Jewish moneylenders – town birds with no wish to change their feathers and reside on the land – often sold pledged estates in blocks to the wealthier monasteries, especially when the debts seemed unlikely to be paid; and through this medium a thriving land market grew up.[13]

In the sixteenth century, or perhaps a little earlier, appeared the classical mortgage, which gave the creditor the fee-simple, subject to the condition that he would reconvey it to the debtor if the latter paid on time, but (by 1600, at least) left the debtor in actual possession. This was to be the classical form for the very important reason that the lord chancellor, with whose law of Equity the rest of this chapter is principally concerned, intervened to control it. He softened the Common Law's insistence on automatic forfeiture by allowing the defaulting debtor to redeem his land when he could (this was called 'equity of redemption'), while giving the insistent creditor a process of 'foreclosure'.[14]

The *use* was another ancient device. As early as Domesday Book people can be seen conveying land to others to be held *to the use* (*ad opus*), i.e. for the benefit, of themselves, the donors, or of third parties. The method was employed by those who wanted to endow Franciscan friars, debarred from owning property – and by men contemplating treason or felony who wished to safeguard their family lands from forfeiture. It must be understood that the donor granted away the fee-simple, retaining for himself or another beneficiary (called the *cestui que use*) a form of property (the 'use') unknown to feudal law. Lawyers nevertheless came to recognize the value of this new interest in land and to imply a use passing to the purchaser as soon as a real bargain was made (ownership did not pass till the ceremony of delivering seisin); or remaining with the donor, in any transaction where the donees (therefore presumed to be 'feoffees to use' – merely trustees of the land) had not paid for the property, and there seemed to be no other consideration for which the donor might have surrendered it absolutely. The rule in the second case allowed a donor to delay his settlement of the uses he wished to place on the property (or, to put it differently, the disposal of his own use) until long after he had enfeoffed the land away, perhaps until he made his will.

Suppose that a man holding from the king by knight-service conveys his lands to a number of feoffees to his own use. The donor now has no fee from which a creditor can levy debts and when he dies his heir will not have to pay a relief: nor will the land be 'wasted' by wardship, for the joint feoffees will not all die before the heir comes of age and can in any case add to their own numbers. Yet the donor's interest in the land remained no less valuable than a fee, and it could be disposed of more easily: like real property it could be entailed, but unlike real property it could also be devised by will.

THE STATUTES OF USES, ENROLLMENTS AND WILLS

To the king, therefore, the use meant fraudulent evasion of feudal dues, and at last, in 1535, Henry VIII forced through parliament the Statute of Uses, embodying the brilliantly simple provision that the legal estate (the ownership at Common Law) would thenceforth be regarded as residing in the *cestui que use* and not in the feoffees: the use would be 'executed'.[15] The drafting of statutes is unfortunately an unbiddable thing, and brilliance there may be a fatal error. Some of the problems attendant on the Statute of 1535 were seen at once. The uses implied by lawyers in certain situations would now be legal estates. Thus, in a bargain and sale of land, not a use but a legal estate would pass at the bargain, doing away with the necessity of a subsequent livery of seisin. Land itself now lay in grant and not in livery, and – here was one problem – the grant might be part of a secret arrangement. The essential publicity of conveyancing had to be bolstered up by attaching to the Statute of Uses a Statute of Enrollments, requiring the registration of land sales. But the use, once conceived, was not to be eliminated easily, and the fact was that King Henry's statute had made it (if a pun will be excused) more useful still: instead of a passage having been deleted from the logic of conveyancing, a new theorem had been introduced – 'by creating a use in the old way, a legal estate can be passed in a new way'.

The Statute of Enrollments spoke only of freehold transactions. It was found to be possible, without registration, for *A* to bargain to give a lease to *B*, so that *B* received a use and thus (by the Statute of Uses) the leasehold proper without even needing to enter upon the land. A deed 'releasing' to *B* the fee-simple at the end of his lease was yet another transaction not accounted for in the Statute of Enrollments and in the seventeenth century would very often be made the day after the sale of the lease. By the device of 'lease and release' the freehold had been conveyed without the necessity of registration or the entry of the purchaser. To cap it all, if he had a family settlement in view, *A* could declare uses on the release which would again become legal estates: for example, he might, as he felt his end draw near, release the fee simple to *B*, a brother, to the use of *B*'s son for life, with remainder to the son's son.

More than just an attack on uses, the statute of 1535 was an attack on the power conferred by the use to devise lands; avowedly because 'such persons as be visited with sickness in their extreme agonies and pains . . . being provoked by greedy and covetous persons lying in wait about them, do dispose indiscreetly and unadvisedly their lands and inheritances'. But a return to a rigid feudal ban on the devising of land was more than even Henry VIII could achieve. Tudor wills usually contained lengthy provision for the endowment of daughters when they should marry – on condition that they married with the approval of the feoffees to their use, or the executors of the will, or the noble overseers whom testators prudently nominated to settle disputes about inheritance.

The abolition of the power of devise was an indirect cause of the rebellion known as the Pilgrimage of Grace (1536), and by the Statute of Wills of 1540 that power was restored with the condition that a man who took land by devise must pay the feudal dues of a normal heir. An entail could now be most conveniently arranged in a man's will, and the Statute of Wills, along with the use, meant that a father need not give up his land in his lifetime for the benefit of his children. Moreover, the statement of the Statute of Wills that a man could now devise land 'at his free will and pleasure' was interpreted to permit certain forms of gift by devise which would have infringed the rules of entail had they been made during the donor's lifetime.[16] The effect of the Henrician statutes was to recognize and expedite, rather than to reverse, a revolution in the methods of land dealing.

CHANCERY, THE TRUST AND THE FAMILY SETTLEMENT

The earliest experiments with family settlements were possible in the late thirteenth and fourteenth centuries, when the king looked with favour on the arrangements of specific members of the nobility. The general manipulation of uses became possible when the lord chancellor, probably sometime after 1409, showed his willingness to enforce the intentions of such settlements. The ordinary courts of Common Law provided no remedy if a person enfeoffed to someone else's use treated his tenure as a fee-simple with which he could do what he liked. But the chancellor was prepared to concern himself with any breach of good faith and equity, and in the fifteenth century we find him attributing contractual obligations where the Common Law would not: for instance, compelling the conveyance of land according to a defendant's promise; and singling out for quashing, from the number of contracts which were formally valid, those that had been obtained by fraud. (Since the Common Law would enforce rigidly a covenant under seal, we find petitions to the chancellor expressed in such pathetic words as 'your said beseecher cannot make any bar in the law, for that it is his deed, which shall be deemed his folly'.) The chancellor made his own considerable contribution to the idea of contract, by focusing attention on the importance of the purpose in an agreement.

As for uses, though granting land to use was not unlike bailment of a chattel for safe-keeping, which could be recovered by detinue, the Common Lawyers would not see the analogy. In the 1460s a judge told a defendant who pleaded in answer to a suit of trespass that he was only exercising his rights as *cestui que use*: 'There in the Chancery a man shall have remedy according to conscience upon the intent of such a feoffment. But here by the course of the common law in the Common Pleas or King's Bench it is otherwise.' One of the most important rules enunciated by the chancellor to facilitate uses was that of 'notice', which declared that the burden of the use could be conveyed by the feoffees to use along with the land (the burden, with the land, would normally descend to the feoffees' heirs), provided that there was no consideration in the conveyance (i.e. it did not pretend to be a sale), or, when it was a sale for value, that notice was given to the purchaser that the use existed.

An enfeoffment to use was the creation of a *trust*, as can be clearly seen where the duties imposed on the feoffees to whom the land was *confided* were active, such as the collecting and employment of the profits to pay the debts of the *cestui que use*. In addition to its private functions, the *trust* was to be, as Maitland said, 'a most powerful instrument of social experimentation', for it opened up the possibility of granting permanent endowments for an enormous range of charitable ventures at a time when charity alone provided most of those services now considered the responsibility of the state. A case in chancery from the reign of Edward IV (1461–83) shows how far the idea of the trust had then advanced. Richard Meredyk had enfeoffed John Hugh and David Kemp of certain property to the use of himself and his wife, Elyn. In his will, Richard had said that after Elyn's death the land was to be sold and the money used for certain charities, to the welfare of the souls of Elyn and his two previous wives. 'And thereupon, in presence of credible persons, yet living, he declared by his mouth the said Deeds of Charity, that is to say: that the said money should be disposed to the finding of a priest by a year in the church of St Martin's in the Field. . . . To the Marriage of five Poor Maidens, and To the Amending of the Highway in the Lane behind the Mews, and then he died.' But Hugh and Kemp sold the reversion of the land, 'Converting the said sum unto their proper Use, contrary to all truth and conscience'. Elyn therefore asks 'That your Lordship would grant several writs of Subpoena to be directed to John and David, commanding them, at a certain date by you to be limited, [to appear] to be examined by your Lordship of and upon the premises, that they may be ruled to do . . . therein according to the said Will, at the reverence of God and in the way of charity.'[17]

The property entrusted might be in the form of goods or money or land, the profits of the latter being much the most valuable as well as the most secure endowment before the time when money could be invested in shares. Whatever the nature of the trust, the chancellor's means of enforcing it were *in personam*, not *in rem* – he could subpoena and impose indefinite imprisonment on a recalcitrant person but not interfere directly with the property. Like Star Chamber, Chancery was precluded by the jealousy of the Common Lawyers from deciding questions of freehold and had therefore to emphasize the alternative basis of civil jurisdiction, the grave personal fault of the defendant: which in this case was the affront to conscience, rather than – as in tort – the breach of the peace. Obviously the concept of the trust as a personal responsibility was thereby enhanced. After 1535 only the use executed by the Statute was generally called a use, and 'trust' was able to become the distinctive term for those charitable arrangements which Chancery exempted from the provisions of the Statute, and then for all uses which remained enforceable.

The last great service of the chancellor was to open the way for the classic family settlement. A use was entailable exactly like a Common Law fee – no, more easily, for the existence of feoffees to use meant that there would never be the 'abeyance of seisin' which was the objection to contingent remainders.

There was a system of 'equitable estates', protected by Chancery, corresponding to the 'legal estates' dealt with by the Common Law. Conveyancers began to advise their clients that with the help of a trust they could frustrate the known methods of breaking entails. According to their instructions, Lord *A* would convey land to feoffees to the use of his son, *B*, for life, with remainders in turn to *B*'s sons. The trust avoided the contingent remainder which would have existed if *B* (who might leave no son) had been given a life-tenancy of the fee directly, and since he *was* only a life-tenant the Common Law would prevent *B* from working the common recovery method of alienation (see p. 91, above). At this point human nature completed the near foolproof entail which the law abhorred. *B*'s heir-apparent, *C*, the tenant-in-tail, could break the entail with his father's cooperation and he was usually prepared to do so in order to create a new settlement, giving himself (*C*) an income in his father's lifetime but also reducing his estate to an inalienable life-estate (the form was a grant to *B* for life, remainder to *C* for life, remainder to *B*'s sons). Repeated each generation, this device prevented there from ever being a 'tenant-in-tail in possession' who could break the entail in order to alienate. This 'strict settlement' was not perfected till well on in the seventeenth century, though it was having perceptible effects by 1600.[18]

FROM FEUDALISM TO COMMERCE: PRIVATE LAW AND SOCIETY

We might characterize the period from 1216 to 1642 as one in which private law steadily moved its grounds from 'feudal' status to 'commercial' contract according to Sir Henry Maine's pattern. The characterization is misleading because there was always a strong contractual strain in the feudal relationship between lord and man. But the statutes of Edward I were the last which could be devoted to protecting the rights of each class of subjects separately, rights assumed to be determined by their place in a feudal hierarchy. The indentures which sealed the ties of later medieval 'bastard feudalism' do present newly commercial features. Monetary considerations and written conditions replaced enfeoffment and loyalty; the stable relationships based upon land give way before flexible but also ephemeral commercial arrangements. The medieval communities built upon land and status were breaking up at the manorial level also, under the effects of the leasing of the demesne in some places and enclosure for sheep farming in others.

The movement from status to contract is seen clearly in the decline of the old property actions and the changes in the relative importance of the various courts of law. An active court no longer went automatically with lordship. Instead of a continuous hierarchy of feudal courts, there were now basically two laws, the Common Law of the king's courts for the gentlemen and the somewhat less formal and uniform body of rules enforced in market, fair and manor, for the benefit of pedlar and peasant. The procedure of the country courts seems very often to have been borrowed from the king's courts – trespass against the peace of the king could be matched in a manor court by 'trespass against the peace of the lord abbot' – but may also have contributed something to the Common Law in the way of more equitable methods of decision.[19] Juries of neighbours came to be used extensively in the courts-leet of the greater landlords, the fusions of the old franchisal, honorial and manorial jurisdictions, which until the eighteenth century performed a vast amount of local administrative and civil business, especially small conveyancing transactions. The important point to be made is that courts were now created by functions to be performed, not by right, and the main function of private law at both levels was to facilitate men's natural arrangements in regard to their families or trades.

The old communal courts of shire and hundred stood half-way between the king's central courts and the private courts, for if he kept within the statutory limit of 40s. cases the sheriff could enforce informal promises unregarded by the Common Law. In the courts of manor and fair there were no writs to perpetuate rigid forms of action, and an equitable jurisdiction could coexist with such forms as there were. Copyholders were employing the use and the mortgage, and even disposing of land by will in fifteenth-century manors. The lord's steward, called by Coke a 'chancellor in his court' of the manor, protected such transactions and exercised an equity of redemption in the case of mortgages.[20]

The period from c. 1350 to c. 1550 may be called 'the age of equity', if it is understood that the whole of private law – and not just the chancellor's court – made a fresh beginning. A whole legal system was being reconstructed in the way that legal systems usually are, by continual experiment in the arbitration of the disputes arising from new social arrangements. The narrow habits of King's Bench and Common Pleas should not blind us to the fact that the judicial system as a whole was still in a state of flux and formation. To keep the peace in the sixteenth century, the king's Council and Chancery continued to experiment with that most primitive of legal commissions, the oyer and terminer, to order the arbitration of local disputes, brought to the king's notice by simple petition or 'bill'.

PART TWO

CHAPTER 5

THE OLD PROCEDURE

SINCE procedures were the beginning of English law and remained central to it, in this chapter we must watch more closely the movement of cases through the Common Law courts. To the next chapter will be left the 'new procedure' of Chancery and the 'conciliar courts'.

INITIAL AND MESNE PROCESS

The pattern of a model action turns out to be the result of centuries of experiment. The initial processes were concerned with choosing the proper tribunal and compelling the defendant to appear at the right time. They contained elements older than the court-hearing itself, which had been introduced to divert the customary processes of the Anglo-Saxons from their fatal course. The fundamental right to fight back against the man who harmed you was softened even in Alfred's time by the rule that you must first sit outside his house for thirty days and seek justice of the king, while the right of self-help remained in the carefully regulated power of the individual to distrain for services and debts.[1]

The initial process could be manipulated to unexpected ends, just as much as the court hearing. The poor man unable to afford a writ might revenge himself by obtaining the presentment of his enemy or force him to come to terms under threat of an Appeal. The usual consideration, however, was to get one's case into an effective court with the least trouble, and this it was which spun an extraordinary web of legal make-believe round the *bill of Middlesex*.[2] Justices in eyre or King's Bench would sometimes waive the requirement of a writ and listen to immediate bills of trespass, but they would do this only in the county where the wrong had been committed. When the eyres came to an end, the privilege of complaint was thus confined to victims of injuries within Middlesex. After the complaint or bill, writs of attachment and arrest were sent to the Sheriff of Middlesex, and if that did not succeed the plaintiff could sue out a writ of *latitat* to some other county where the defendant was said to 'lurk', ordering him to be sent to the prison of the King's Bench. Once in the King's Bench prison, the defendant could be sued by any sort of action the plaintiff chose, for the court was eager to widen its jurisdiction. Nevertheless, by 1542 King's Bench was losing litigation quickly to Star Chamber, and therefore it allowed the whole procedure by bill of Middlesex before the issuing of the *latitat* to become a fiction. Now there was one simple form of writ in King's Bench (*latitat* itself) to begin such actions as debt, detinue, covenant and account *wherever they occurred* – though in substance they were properly matters for Common Pleas – and a writ which ordered the arrest of the defendant as summarily as Star Chamber could. To cap it all, the plaintiff in King's Bench did not risk the reversal by *writ of error* of a decision in his favour.

We have now passed from the strictly initial process to the *mesne* process, the intermediate procedure to compel a reluctant defendant's appearance, or by which either party might legitimately delay the hearing of the case. Very often, the sheriff would not be able to find an alleged criminal in the first place, and the man would be publicly summoned or 'exacted' at five successive meetings of the shire-court and outlawed at the fifth. The criminal might have fled to sanctuary in a local church where he could abjure the realm before a coroner: he must then leave by the nearest port and under Henry VIII would be branded, so that if he ever returned he could be recognized and instantly hanged. Some liberties such as that of St Martin's in the Fields, which were abolished at the Reformation with other clerical abuses, gave much greater protection to the criminal, who became a sort of registered inhabitant within them.

In early days, failure to appear in a private action was

treated as a breach of contract between the parties, since the hearing was in the nature of agreed arbitration. This was one contract which the law soon found it expedient to enforce: the writ in one of Henry II's petty assizes instructed the sheriff to take from the parties the pledges of appearance which they would before have given to each other. The defendant was then faced with a number of possible reactions between default and pleading his case in person. For a certain number of appointed hearings, he – and the plaintiff also – could send excuses (called *essoins* – the most common was sickness) which entailed adjournments of the case. Essoining was very often just procedural tactics, at its most scandalous in 'fourcher', the alternate casting of essoins by co-defendants.[3]

The law's reaction to default varied according to the nature of the case. A criminal could not be condemned in his absence – but then outlawry was hardly a better fate than condemnation. A similar attitude governed the procedure in torts. Since the trespasser offended the king as well as the plaintiff, on a first default he would be required to find two sureties for appearance and on a second he would be outlawed: but the case was not decided for the plaintiff. In the later Middle Ages, outlawry, in a mitigated form not involving summary execution or escheat of lands, was extended to many private actions. On a first default in a land case, however, it was the land in question (not the man) which was 'taken into the king's hand', to be given to the plaintiff if the defendant did not put in an appearance within fifteen days. Such apparently arid procedural rules as these made an immense difference to the efficiency and consequent fate of the various actions. Novel Disseisin was popular with plaintiffs because it permitted no essoining by defendants. Writs of trespass triumphed because they were backed by the threat of outlawry.

THE LAW'S DELAYS

Litigation was a long-term project, requiring persistence and much travel. Richard of Anstey's unemotional account, preserved in the Public Record Office, of his five-year action to recover lands left to him by his uncle, against a daughter of that uncle's annulled marriage, is one of the odysseys of English history. Richard began in the summer of 1158 by sending to the king in Normandy for a writ. The hearing before the justiciar back in England had to be adjourned to the courts of the church when the matter was discovered to turn on the allegedly annulled marriage, but two years of pleading in the English ecclesiastical courts proved fruitless, and in 1161 Richard appealed to Rome. The Pope referred the case back to judges-delegate in England before he gave confirmation of the annulment to Richard's messengers in Rome late in 1162. Armed with this decision, Richard went in pursuit of the king, who was always on the move, and he was able to write that at Woodstock in July 1163 'at last by the grace of God and of the king, my uncle's lands were adjudged to me'. Richard was not a great man, but his accounts of the cost of one law-suit in terms of gifts to the right people, expenses of messengers and advisers, and horses worked to death, reads like the budget of a military campaign.[4]

Richard of Anstey's case admittedly involved two jurisdictions – the lay and the ecclesiastical – and many tribunals, but so did most cases: his experience was that of litigants through the ages. The king's reference of a particular issue in the case to the church courts, and the Pope's reference back to local judges-delegate, was later paralleled every day by Common Law commissions of oyer and terminer and *nisi prius*. Three developments did however soften the lot of litigants. In the first place, *judicial* writs (the name distinguishes them from the *original* writs beginning actions) began to be issued directly by the courts to begin each new stage of proceedings and 'keep things moving' – examples are the writs of *capias* and *latitat* to arrest reluctant defendants. Secondly, Magna Carta confirmed the tendency to make the Court of Common Pleas stationary in a known place. Thirdly, the stabilization of the *law terms* allowed the litigant to pin down the court in time as well as place.

Parliamentary, university, school, law, and – earliest of all – exchequer terms, have all been determined by the distribution of the festivals and saints' days of the church; both positively, because the king's great courts were liturgical occasions appropriately held at the greater feasts; and negatively, because the church forbade oath-taking on holy days, and legal proceedings had therefore to avoid any clusters of festivals. An additional 'close-season' was high summer, when fear of the plague and the requirements of the harvest kept lawyers out of London; and on into October, preoccupied with quarter-sessions in the counties. The Court of Chancery alone – this was one of its advantages – was always open. Four law terms resulted, beginning after Michaelmas in the autumn, after the feast of St Hilary in January, after Easter, and after Trinity in summer; and their unequal lengths were measured by the number of *return-days* they contained. These 'return-days' were in fact groups of four days at about weekly intervals on which new litigation had to be commenced and to which the old was adjourned. Another way of distinguishing an expeditious from a dilatory form of action was by the customary number of return-days for which it could be spun out: the system did not apply at all in equity proceedings or bills of Middlesex.[5]

A litigant's miserable existence was measured out in return-days. Richard of Anstey essoined once and put in an appearance seventeen times at the Archbishop of Canterbury's court before appealing to Rome. If the 'plea-rolls' of the king's courts were originally required to record not pleading but the writs for which the plaintiff must pay, they were soon necessary to follow the continuance of cases through adjournments, reference to *nisi prius*, essoining and all the rest.

PLEADING

Suppose that the parties are now in court and the hearing can begin. This stage, too, is a formalized battle between the parties: '*Smith* v. *Jones*' or '*Rex* v. *Jones*'. Until comparatively recent times the ammunition in the battle was not so much witnesses and evidence as statements and counter-statements made alternately by the contenders until a clear disagreement on the facts was reached on which a jury could decide (the pattern of the argument was 'Yes, but, . . . Yes, but, . . . Yes, but, . . . NO!'), or an issue of law for the judges to determine. In a civil case, of course, refusal to plead was equivalent to default. On the other hand, an arrested criminal who refused to plead was subjected, on the strength of a Statute of 1275 which spoke only of his incarceration in a '*prison forte et dure*', to the horrible '*peine forte et dure*', slow pressing to death by weights placed on his chest as he lay naked in a dungeon. Such a death was not execution, nor did it imply conviction, so brave men sometimes accepted it to ensure that their chattels should not escheat to the crown and leave their families in poverty.

The merits of oral pleading were publicity and formality, great protections for the defendant, who was never faced by the unexpected. Pleading should also have been a speedy way of isolating the real issues. Like so much Common Law procedure, however, it ceased to be a means and became an end in itself; or (as in the common recovery mechanism for breaking entails) a means to ends quite unconnected with the apparent dispute.

The first move in civil pleading was the plaintiff's 'count' or 'tale', delivered in 'law-French', in which it was necessary to keep strictly to the terms of the original writ (which would have been 'returned' into court). It might run like this: 'This sheweth unto you John Smith by his attorney who is here [the attorney is actually speaking] that David Jones who is there by his attorney wrongfully deforces him of the manor of Blackacre with the appurtenances . . . [all the rights going with the manor are exactly described]; and wrongfully for this, that they are his right and heritage of which William Smith, his ancestor, was seized in his demesne as of fee and of right in time of peace in the time of king Richard, cousin of the king who now is (whom God preserve), taking the profits . . . [exactly enumerated]; and from William Smith the right descended . . . [descent in detail] . . . to John Smith who now demands. And that such is the right of John Smith, he has suit [a group of followers who support his claim] and good proof.'

The defendant (if he does not want to admit responsibility) must make a denial 'word for word' of 'tort and force and the right of John Smith who is there, entirely and completely, and the seisin of his ancestor, William Smith . . .'; and he must offer to prove his denial as the court shall decide. But defendants began to do more – to argue, and 'lay exceptions' to certain details of the plaintiff's case. The earliest exceptions were probably to the original writ which had been chosen, on the grounds that it was the wrong writ for the case or was phrased wrongly. Exceptions might also allege that the case had already been decided elsewhere – once again the importance of legal records is underlined – or point out that the plaintiff was a villein who could not sue at all.[6]

Some of these exceptions raised preliminary but very important questions of fact suggested by the original writ. In Mort D'Ancestor three such questions arose: the defendant could object that the plaintiff's ancestor had not possessed a free tenement (he might have been a leaseholder), or been seised in demesne (he might in fact have leased out the land to the defendant), or that the plaintiff was not the next heir. If these exceptions were successfully answered by the plaintiff's 'replication', the defendant would have to go further into the merits of the case, either by 'traversing' (denying) the plaintiff's facts or by 'confession and avoidance' (acknowledging some of them but advancing others which altered their significance). He usually preferred to pick holes in the plaintiff's case by pleading rather than to accept the verdict of the jury on the 'general issue' (in an assize of Novel Disseisin, 'did A disseise B?'). The defeat of the plaintiff on one point of fact or law was sufficient to 'non-suit' him; and indeed many of the judges' complex rules against 'surplusage' and 'duplicity', 'argumentative' pleadings and 'negatives pregnant with affirmatives' were designed to bring the case quickly to one single issue, however technical and distant from the real matter at stake. To the same end were directed the excessively rigid rules of 'estoppel', which prevented a man from raising at a later stage any point which he had avowedly or tacitly conceded in his earlier pleading.

Clearly the alternatives facing a defendant were complicated, and often he began by asking for an adjournment while he talked the matter over with counsel and prepared an elaborate case. Returning to the pleading in court, we may arrive at a *demurrer* (from French: '*demeurer*'), when the parties cease to dispute the facts and agree to 'rest' upon the court's judgment of some point of law arising from them. The 'joinder of issue' might of course be not 'in demurrer' but on the facts of the case, when the verdict of a jury would be necessary before judgment.

THE JURY AND THE SEPARATION OF EVIDENCE AND VERDICT

The findings of the jury were the seeds of the trial as we know it today (almost the only judicial duels after Henry II's time were between approvers). The jury listened to no evidence in court, for it was called in only when pleading had arrived at a special issue of fact or the defendant asked for a decision on the general issue; and then it was expected to *know* the facts in dispute, rather than to *decide* upon them. The very simplicity of the jury as a method of settling cases often caused to be left to it both the functions of a group of witnesses providing facts and of a judge deciding questions of law. A number of different institutions seem to merge into each other: the twelve Anglo-Saxon oath-helpers, the 'jury' (its very name means 'sworn') which in some early instances seems to have been nominated jointly by the parties from their supporters, the 'suit' of supporters necessary in every claim, and sworn witnesses of the modern type. An early jury was sometimes composed of sworn groups from a number of villages, which provided the court with material for its decision: 'The eight men of Wormley being sworn say. . . . The eight men of Enfield say upon oath that they believe that the mare was Hamo's and foaled to him, for everybody says so. . . .'[7] Juries in the later middle ages were said to be 'elected, *tried* and sworn', for the defendant could challenge and exclude up to thirty-five jurymen whom he believed hostile, and the rules disqualifying jurors were very like the canonist rules disqualifying witnesses.

In practice the jury would usually not know the facts directly and would have to go to a man's house and ask him what he knew. For the man to take the initiative in offering evidence to the jury might be illegal 'maintenance', and against this fear only the chancellor's *subpoena* was effective in making witnesses come forward. But coroners, as part of their duty of recording the preliminaries of accusations, examined persons who could give information. A Statute of 1554 (1 and 2 Philip and Mary, c. 13) made examination of criminals and the recording of it incumbent on coroners and J.P.s. A contemporary description of an Elizabethan criminal trial shows that the preliminary depositions were already being used as evidence in the trial, and that sworn witnesses for the prosecution carried on an altercation with the prisoner till the judges had heard enough.[8]

The treatment of evidence was rudimentary: the criminal had no notice of those witnesses who would appear against him, and he was not allowed to arrange for any on his own behalf. The last condition was slowly modified in Elizabeth's reign, but at first the prisoner's witnesses could not be sworn: so much was sworn inquisition a prerogative of the crown, and criminal trial a contest in which there was no reason to concede advantages to the other side. In any event, criminal trial was essentially still by jury and not by witnesses, as Chief Justice Coke often said, perhaps in dislike of the Crown's use of examination and bullied witnesses in political trials.

The chancellor's *subpoena* was the only way of enforcing the appearance of civil witnesses before 1563. Nevertheless, throughout the middle ages witnesses to deeds and commercial transactions had appeared to sit with the jury when those deeds were in dispute. Here the witnesses were taking over some of the jury's original functions and forcing the jury into something like its modern position. Counsel became interested towards the end of the Middle Ages in assembling evidence to convince the jurymen: that is, in the modern way of presenting a case.[9] The change began in Chancery, for the chancellor, like the Roman Law judge, worked in his court without a jury, deciding issues on the evidence of deeds and witnesses. So, unlike his Common Law brethren, he had to evolve 'rules of evidence', to decide the relative weight of the different sorts of evidence and assess the reliability of witnesses. Only at this point, when it begins to be weighed in the balance, does a statement cease to be a verdict and become a piece of evidence at all.

As written evidence there were deeds and records of previous cases. The latter were particularly important when cases were adjourned from one court to another far distant. The first exhibits were objects dropped by killers who had fled: they were entrusted to the tithing-man for production before the justices.

As well as constituting evidence of facts and a decision on the evidence, the verdict of a medieval jury might involve decisions of law, today the business of the judge alone. This was so if a defendant simply denied the charge and the case was decided on the general issue, for the jury's decision that the defendant had, for instance, perpetrated disseisin required knowledge of what seisin was as well as of the facts of the matter. But in the thirteenth century we see the king's judges interfering to question the legal as well as factual basis of verdicts, and the jury gradually settled down to a middle position of being neither witnesses, nor judges of law, but judges of fact. The *assisa* of twelve sworn neighbours answering the question posed by the original writ was the essence of the procedure in the twelfth-century assizes, and little room was left for debate. In trespass, however, the defendant was simply commanded to defend himself from the complaint. There, a jury verdict arose out of the pleading, to decide the fact on which issue was joined. The jury in an action of

trespass was the true ancestor of the modern civil jury. From
c. 1470 we have a description of a civil trial where the jury is
presented with evidence from both sides in open court.

Thereafter the usefulness of the jury depended not on its
knowledge but on its unanimity. The value of the ordeal, trial
by battle and even wager of law, which provided evidence
and judgment at one and the same time, had been their
finality, and the jury was expected to provide the same super-
human certainty. By 1350 judges were prepared to shut up a
jury or carry it around in carts until it would agree.

THE JUDGES TAKE CONTROL

After the verdict comes the judgment proper: the judges'
statement of the result of the trial and their order regarding
execution (the sentence in a criminal case).

Once again, something – here, the judgment – which seems
an obvious and essential part of the legal process turns out to
be the result of experiment in the arrangement of a number
of possible elements. In the old English moot, the person most
like a judge was the lawman or doomsman, but his judgment
came before the verdict by ordeal, the form of which it determined. The form of the ordeal was at that time the subject of
legal expertise, for on conviction punishment was automatic
and hardly needed anyone's authority. When trial by jury
became the almost universal conclusion of a hearing there
was no room for a judge even to decide the manner of trial,
but by then the king had become a new and irresistible force
in legal procedure, determined to have the last word in every
case through his commissioners presiding in the court. The
function of the judge as the executive officer of the king is
reflected in the terse words of the judgments in the early
plea-rolls: 'The jurors say that the aforesaid Ralf disseised
the aforesaid Margaret of the aforesaid tenement, as the writ
says. Therefore Margaret shall recover her seisin and Ralf
and the others be in mercy.'

A judgment was thus an order, for which legal reasons
(the modern 'judgment') were not yet given, since there was

little substantive law to consider; and there was no essential difference between a judgment, an 'injunction' ordering a defendant to refrain from some wrongful interference, and an 'interlocutory' decision in the middle of process. The value of them all was the compelling nature of the judge's pronouncement, derived partly from the representative character of the Germanic law-man but mostly from the power of the Angevin king. The importance of the judge, as judge rather than as royal henchman, grew with the elaboration of the game of pleading, in which he was the referee; and, since it was in the central courts that pleading became most extensive, it was the king's commissioners there, and not in eyre or assizes, who seem to us the essential judges. The king's great hall at Westminster, which stands to this day, was the cradle of the Common Law.

The original judge was the justiciar, whose office had grown in step with the exchequer, the regent when the king was abroad, the director of the administration when the king was at home. After the young Henry III quarrelled with his justiciar, Hubert de Burgh, the office was cut down to that of chief justice of King's Bench. The judge was thus descended from the justiciar, and his glamour was the glamour of the king shining through his *alter ego*. With such power behind them, the king's judges could set about winning for themselves a key position in the judicial process. The finality of the jury's decision was reduced by the division of evidence from verdict: the judges achieved their modern power of direction over witnesses and jurymen separately, and reserved questions of law to themselves. Yet it is surprising that the English judges did not do more to encourage trial by witnesses. For in Roman and Canon Law the practice and the ideal of the judge were entirely bound up with the examination of witnesses. The judge was the seeker after truth, and his pride was to develop better methods of interrogation and rules of evidence, to become more expert in estimating the truthfulness of witnesses: these functions alone he could not delegate. The business of the continental judgment was to explain why some witnesses had been preferred to others in reaching a conclusion.[10] When the ordeal was abolished in the early thirteenth century, English judges can be seen for a time examining juries on the basis of their verdicts. The surprising fact is that the sixteenth century criminal trial described by Sir Thomas Smith shows so little advance on this. True there were witnesses who argued with the prisoner till the judge 'hath heard them say enough'; but the handling of witnesses was undisciplined in the extreme, and the jury still was and still is there to decide upon the truth.

It is a crucial fact in English legal history that the small twelfth-century committee of the *curia regis* just could not provide enough trained men to direct trials in the Roman fashion. Because it was taking on such immense responsibilities so early, English law had to conserve its small force of competent judges by the use of pleading to narrow down issues, and the use of jury-verdicts in place of the examination of witnesses. Had the king of England been able to dispose in the twelfth century of the huge force of trained lawyers in the French king's *Parlement* at the end of the Middle Ages, the jury might have disappeared from England – as it did from France – and the Roman type of trial might have become established before a numerous body of examining judges each sitting separately in his own chamber. English kings got used to making do with a small and inexpensive bench of justices, the jury became an ineradicable if subordinate part of the English trial, and a Roman Law conquest of England in the manner of the *Reception* which occurred on the Continent at the time of the Renaissance became quite unlikely.[11] Only in some special fields of business – the court of Admiralty is an example – did apparently foreign modes of trial appear. And perhaps also at the level of the J.P., to whom statutes of 1496 (11 Henry 7, c. 3) and later permitted summary determination of petty offences without jury – there were plenty of justices of the peace with the leisure and inclination to behave in their own little realms in the fashion of the inexorable inquisition.

The judges' control of evidence and juries was therefore confined to occasional questioning of the basis of verdicts, somewhat illogically linked with an insistence on unanimous verdicts. The judicial bullying of juries which was a conspicuous element of English legal history for several centuries was not caused by a despotic hatred of a 'pillar of English liberties' but by exasperation at an unsatisfactory yet indispensable tool. It was reasonable that the judges should not be satisfied with a jury's statement that it 'rather thought' something was so, or that it believed something because 'everybody says so'. Not so innocent was the occasional sixteenth-century practice in political trials of punishing in Star Chamber jurors who had acquitted men at Common Law when the matter 'was held to have been sufficiently proved'.

JUDICIAL REFEREEING AND LEGAL ARGUMENT

At length, a distinction between issues of fact and issues of law emerged from the practical divisions of responsibility between judge and jury, and the English judgment became principally concerned with the law. This was neither a self-evident nor (as we shall see) a clean division, but was rather a sensible compromise in the struggle of judge and jury to shift unwelcome jobs on to each other. If the judges did not have time to examine witnesses, most juries did not have the knowledge to decide that an act was technically (say) disseisin; and they ran the risk of attaint if they decided wrongly. They played safe. After listening to some particularly wordy and casuistical pleading by counsel, the jury might take several hours to consider the matter and then return a 'special verdict', stating the facts as it saw them and leaving the judges to decide their legal import.[12] In 1285 the king expressly ordered that jurors should not be compelled to say whether there had been a disseisin in law provided they told the truth. Counsel, who naturally felt happier arguing disputable law rather than intractable fact, encouraged special verdicts by actually drafting them for the jury, or used the pleading move known as *demurrer* to take agreed facts to the point of judicial consideration.

So in some cases the demurrer was in effect a verdict by

agreement of the parties, which allowed the judges to decide a case without a jury. But the medieval litigant would not have seen it in this light. He was not admitting facts so much as asserting their irrelevance to the situation, as he 'demanded judgment' on his opponent's bad pleading. The medieval judgment decided a case on some mistake or technicality far more often than by reviewing the whole situation like its modern successor. The first questions which the judges had to decide were questions of procedure.

The writ was the procedural element which gave the judges their great opportunity: 'then said Gilbert of Preston, "Dionise, you cannot have your reasonable share without G, because he is your parcener [he also has a claim to a share in the inheritance]. And, since G is not named in the writ, this court decides that A [the defendant] may go home, and that D is in mercy and must get a better writ if she wishes to plead."'[13] Although Dionise's mistake was probably just a convenient technicality to the defendant, a real point of justice was involved, for G might have lost his share in a legal hearing of which he was ignorant. The judges had a real judicial function to perform in the vigilant criticism of original writs, which – it is important to remember – they had had no part in issuing. The vital 'separation of powers' between the judges and the chancery as a writ-issuing department invited the judges to make judicial criticism of the form of writs. From deciding on the goodness of the writ, the judges advanced to the refereeing of the pleading contest; and now they could go beyond the non-suiting of the plaintiff to an award against the defendant, if he was unable to match move with move. The judges' punishment of attorneys for 'speaking foolishly' (*stultiloquium*) and their decisions on the validity of intermediate pleas might elicit strong protests from counsel.[14]

The reporters of these early cases seem to have been interested in the theoretical problems which arose by the way and the judges' *dicta* upon them, not in the actual outcome of pleading, and a judgment – just like counsel's ingenious arguments – sometimes explored all sorts of possible lines of pleading which parties might have followed, oblivious of their growing remoteness from the matter in hand. The law of the professional lawyer was comprised of rules derived from judges' *dicta*, which were collected in court and served up from the later years of Henry III in treatises like *Brevia Placitata* ('Writs Pleaded') and *Casus Placitorum* ('Examples of Pleading'). The first judge whose *dicta* have left an indelible impression on English law was Chief Justice William Bereford, who flourished at the beginning of the fourteenth century. He it was who first said, three centuries before Coke, that law was built on reason, but there is a certain bravado about his attempts to exalt his sense of natural justice over the rigid forms of action determined by the Chancery's writs. Bereford might snarl at an attorney, 'get to your business: you plead about one point, they about another, so that you never get near to settling anything'; but, when he rejected a writ as not falling within the terms of the Statute of *In Consimili Casu*, he was forced to go to the Chancery and apologize, saying 'Blessed be he who made that statute, make the writ out and we will maintain it'.[15]

On the occasion of Bereford's humiliation, Chancery was not, however, relying on its own authority but on the authority of statute. More often it was the judges who were able to increase their standing by playing off Statute against Chancery (from time to time interposing their own ideas of natural justice); just as they had become supreme in the judicial process itself by dividing witnesses from jury and directing each separately. The judges as royal councillors could claim as intimate a knowledge as the chancellor of the purpose of statutes: 'at the present moment you are in the Court of Common Pleas,' Bereford told one party; 'when you are in the chancery you may avail yourself of chancery's ordinances . . . this ordinance was never statute law.' The Chancery's control of the original writ, though opening up a new jurisdiction for the chancellor, was losing its creative position in English law generally, both to statute and to the 'judicial writs' which the judges themselves could issue once a case had been initiated by original writ or bill.

The judges' scope for classifying wrongful acts and adapting penalties to them was perhaps greatest in criminal cases, where there were no writs to provide definitions. 'They have acquitted you of the deed, and we acquit you,' said Chief Justice Thorpe in 1348; 'and I would tell you that . . . in many cases one man may kill another without liability, as where robbers come to kill a man or burgle his house, he may safely kill them if he cannot arrest them.' The judges did their work with the aid of a mental 'ready-reckoner', full of not very sophisticated 'rules of judgment' and notions of liability which were common to the whole legal profession. 'The will is here to be taken for the deed' was a little tag often produced by judges to justify the condemnation of attempted murderers.[16]

In civil cases judgments moved further and further away from simple defects in the writs, and the judges' sense of justice needed to become progressively more subtle to draw lines between wrongful acts. 'And if a smith undertook to cure my horse, and the horse is harmed by his negligence or failure to cure in a reasonable time, it is just that he should be liable': so said Cavendish, the Chief Justice of King's Bench, in 1374. 'But if he does all he can and applies himself with all due diligence to the cure, it is not right that he should be guilty therefore, though there is no cure, for there is a big difference between the two cases.' Everyone could have opinions about the validity of the writ, and counsel joined with judges to bandy about the maxims which were their common property. Judges and the counsel from whose ranks the judges were appointed cooperated to produce efficient pleading, which was biased towards the isolation of issues of law and was a medium for experiment in the formulation of judgments. Hypothetical cases were advanced. Chief Justice Hengham said in 1305: 'This is not a writ of right nor a writ of wrong; for of a truth we do not know what writ it is . . . but I tell you that one of these apprentices has made the purchase to find out what judgment we shall give. . . .'[17]

Pleading, which had begun amongst the ritual of procedure, led gradually on to the modern judgment from legal reasoning. Emphasis shifted from discussion of special issues of pleading, past the verdict on matters of fact, to the final and increasingly discursive review of the relevant substantive law. A statute of 1585 (27 Eliz. 1, c. 5) distinguished special demurrers, alleging technical defects in pleading, from general demurrers which gave the whole case into the judges' consideration; and commanded judges to decide 'according to the very right of the cause and matter in law' if a technical flaw was not insisted upon.

No wonder, then, that after a morning in court fifteenth-century judges retired to spend 'the rest of the day in studying the laws, reading Holy Scripture, and otherwise in contemplation', while parties consulted with counsel. From such contemplation would come forth the great leisurely pronouncements of a Coke, to mould the constitution of the whole kingdom by the power of legal reasoning. Dr Bonham, a graduate in medicine of Cambridge, sued the Royal College of Physicians for wrongful imprisonment, and the college pleaded a statute and letters-patent of Henry VIII allowing it to imprison any who practised in London without its authority. In Trinity term, 1609, Coke delivered his judgment:

... it is an old rule, that a man ought to take care that he do not commit his soul to a young divine, his body to a young physician, and his goods or other estate to a young lawyer ... for in these cannot be the privity, discretion, and profound learning which is in the aged: and he denied that the College of Physicians is to be compared to the university, for ... *Cantabrigia est academia nostra nobilissima* ... but he said, when he names Cambridge, he doth not exclude Oxford, but placeth them in equal rank: but he would always name Cambridge first, for that was his mother. ... The said president and college cannot commit any physician ... for ... they shall [then] be judges *in propria causa*, and shall be summoners, sheriffs, judges, and parties also: which is absurd, for if the King grant to one by his letters-patent under the Great Seal, that he may hold plea, although he be party ... the grant is void, though that it be confirmed by Parliament ... for it is said by Herle in 8 Ed. 3, 30, Tregore's Case, that if any statutes are made against law and right [they are void] and so are these, which makes any judge in his own cause ... and so he concluded that judgment shall be entered for the plaintiff, which was done accordingly.[18]

Perhaps Coke's decisions were no greater in their constitutional importance than, for instance, Justiciar Raleigh's, which reversed King Henry III's peremptory outlawry of Hubert de Burgh. The difference was that Raleigh insisted upon proper procedure, while Coke had moved to statements of abstract principle, now regarded as the essence of the judge's business.

FINAL PROCESS AND APPEAL

The plaintiff, we hope, has lived long enough to see judgment. Perhaps a record of a *nisi prius* verdict in his favour comes back from the county, and is reviewed on 'the day of judgment' at Westminster, only for the case to be adjourned yet again because the judges do not like the verdict and want to force a reasonable compromise. But let us assume that the judges are kind and no more than reduce the outrageous damages assessed by the jury. The plaintiff must now pay the clerks to enter judgment and give him yet another writ – for execution. Final process has only just begun.

If he had been disseised, the successful plaintiff would simply get an order to the sheriff to put him back in his tenement; but in personal actions he was confronted by a choice. He could have a writ of *fieri facias* to levy damages from the defendant's property; or of *elegit*, if he 'chose' to occupy half the defendant's land, or of *capias ad satisfaciendum*, ordering the defendant's imprisonment till the debt has been paid. The last method – it almost looks like a revival of the old English judicial slavery – was made generally available only after 1352, though in 1285 masters were permitted to imprison defalcating servants without trial. This effective weapon of the courts at Westminster did much to reduce the local courts to insignificance, for these could only command distraint of the defendant's chattels (which the plaintiff was then not allowed to sell). If he paid the plaintiff promptly, the defendant could escape imprisonment on a final *capias*, but he still had to surrender to the warden of the Fleet Prison and give bail for the amercement which all defeated parties owed to the king.

The defendant might counter-attack: it was seemingly impossible in English law to bring a campaign of litigation to a decisive end. The sort of procedure which took up most of the profession's time was concerned with justifying or reversing writs of outlawry which the defendants said (for instance) had spelt their names wrongly. The defendant might sometimes bring an action for conspiracy against an indicting jury, and he could challenge a jury's verdict in a civil case by attainting the jurymen. Attaint, however, involved getting twelve defendants into court at once, and persuading another jury of twenty-four knights to 'slander and deface' these 'honest yeomen their neighbours' by saying they had perjured themselves.[19] The procedure might have been appropriate when jurymen were in effect witnesses, but clearly a new method of reversal was needed when they had to give judgment according to their limited intelligence on the evidence of others.

It was found in the equally antiquated practice of alleging error in the record, which was made in a roundabout way to check injustice in the trial of the case. A court of appeal could not review the pleas of the disgruntled litigant rejected at the earlier hearing, for such pleas were not recorded. A clause in the second Statute of Westminster (1285) allowed that litigant to put in a *bill of exceptions*, which the trial judges were obliged to seal and attend to acknowledge in the higher court: this simultaneously made the relevant matter of record and alleged error in the original record for excluding it. So a judgment of the Justices of Assize might be quashed in King's Bench on the grounds that they had 'proceeded without trying the exception in due course of law'. Writs of error, obtainable in Chancery and usually returnable in King's Bench, brought up the records for scrutiny.

There should also be mentioned the right of the convicted criminal to protest, just before sentence was passed upon him.

Though he is still given the opportunity, there is nothing the prisoner can now effectively answer to deflect the penalty, but it was once the case that he could escape by proving an error in the indictment or claiming to be a clergyman and not subject to the jurisdiction of the Common Law courts. That the opportunity to protest comes so late is the result of the struggle between church and state over benefit of clergy: medieval kings reluctantly admitted the privilege of clerics to be tried in their own courts, but took a verdict from a lay jury (which put moral pressure on the church courts) before listening to the claim of 'clergy' and surrendering the accused to the bishop's officer. The test of the convicted man's claim was his ability to read 'the neck verse' from Psalm 51: 'Have mercy upon me, O God, according to thy loving kindness; according to the multitude of thy tender mercies blot out my transgressions.'

It was also theoretically possible for a condemned criminal to get a writ of error: but the Crown was not disposed to give a second chance to its own victims. The criminal was hustled away to execution, and for centuries it was virtually an axiom that criminal judgments could not be reviewed.

CHAPTER 6

THE NEW PROCEDURE
AND NEW COURTS

In the later Middle Ages procedure underwent two main changes: first, the appearance of written pleading and the peculiar judicial methods of Chancery; and second, the growth of new tribunals, using these methods, which we may group together under the name of 'the conciliar courts'.

PAPER PLEADING AND INTERROGATION

In a modern civil case the pleading of claims takes place by the exchange of papers between solicitors in advance of the trial in court, which can be confined to the hearing of evidence and legal argument. Something of this method of proceeding already appears in the report of a case of 1460 in the Court of Common Pleas. Counsel refused to plead suspicious matter on a client's behalf. The litigant thereupon got a clerk of the court to make a 'paper' of the plea and persuaded a serjeant-at-law (a barrister) to put it in officially to another of the clerks, who entered it on the plea-roll. And there it looks just like other entries.[1]

There are considerable similarities between English paper pleading and the Roman Law practices which, in the second half of the fifteenth century, were sweeping away the oral procedure of the customary courts of Germany. In England, as in the rest of Europe, an opening for the revival or *Reception* of Roman Law had long existed through the ecclesiastical courts, where Canon Law was built on the legacy of Imperial Rome. When Richard of Anstey says that he went from church-court to church-court in the 1160s 'armed for pleading' (*munitus placitandi*), he must mean 'provided with written material', and his case shows four stages of written proceedings: the *libellus* (the plaintiff's 'bill' of complaint), the defendant's *answer*, the plaintiff's *replication*, and the defendant's *rejoinder*.[2]

The English Court of Admiralty was apparently using Roman-style written procedure – along with Roman substantive law – by the end of the fourteenth century. There is record of a case held 'at Lostwithiel near to the flow of the sea on the 28th day of the month of March at the first hour and the first tide in the 14th year of the reign of King Richard II', in which each party repeatedly prayed a copy of the 'said replication' of the other 'and a day to plead further'; and the case went to proof after 'the party of the said John Curteys then and there handed to the court a quadruplication expressed in writing. . . .' A special commission was then sent to hear witnesses suggested by the parties. These 'having been sworn and carefully examined and questioned', their evidence was recorded at length; 'and then . . . the said John Curteys . . . appeared and . . . presented to the [main] court a transmission of the depositions of the witnesses produced and examined on his behalf before the said Sub-Admiral.'[3] Thus Richard II's Court of Admiralty was already using, in addition to written pleadings, the lengthy written depositions of witnesses which are one of the most prominent features of early proceedings in Chancery.

But the English bill, though reminiscent of the Roman *libellus*, was probably no more to begin with than the scribbled drafts of the poor man's oral complaint. Soon the defendant would also have his answer ready in writing, as in a case of 1482 in Common Pleas: 'and he further says that he is not learned in the law and he drew out from his pocket a certain written bill in pauper's form in English in these words: "John Pecock in proper person seith that to the takyng of this enquest the juge owht not procede. . . ." He asks that that bill and the writing therein with what he said before be received as his plea. . . .'[4]

Even in the thirteenth century the clerks sometimes asked

to have a written copy of a complicated oral plea.[5] The rolls of the king's court had grown from brief memoranda of the actions into true *plea*-rolls, giving the gist of each statement, and such was the authority of the record that pleading became directed to producing a particular result in the roll. The judges and clerks jealously guarded the rolls from vulgar eyes, but (in order to keep business moving at all) they were forced to permit the parties' attorneys to put in amendments to their pleas. For both judges and clerks necessity opened up unforeseen advantages. The former discovered that a good deal of business could be sent straight down to 'Hell', the clerks' office below Westminster Hall, for written pleadings to be copied immediately on to the roll. The latter found that they virtually controlled the judicial process and its profits.[6]

English written pleading thus shows all the signs of having developed organically from English oral pleading, which remained in content as insular as could be, and very unlike pleading in the ecclesiastical courts. But the interrogatories and depositions of Chancery suggest Roman influence not only because they were written but also because they were part and parcel of an 'inquisitorial' procedure which is supposed to have been intrinsically Roman. In Chancery, said Sir Thomas Smith, 'the usual and proper form of pleading of England is not used, but the form of pleading by writing which is used in other countries according to the Civil Law; and the trial is not by twelve men, but by the examination of witnesses as in other courts of the Civil Law.'[7]

The *interrogatory* was a numbered list of questions 'to be administered to witnesses to be produced on the part and behalf' of one or other of the parties, questions of very wide scope, such as 'Did not Mr Coke often declare or discover that he had a greater kindness for the defendant than for any other person whatsoever? Was there not an entire friendship and familiarity between them? Declare what you know or believe.'[8] The depositions of the witnesses followed the interrogatory, item by item. The chancellor does seem here to have been fulfilling the main function of the Roman Law judge – to seek after the truth by the skilful examination of witnesses.

But we may feel that he did not need to copy foreign methods, when we find that in 1415 the Commons petitioned the king against the preoccupation of the Common Law judges with examinations 'according to the Civil Law and the law of holy church in subversion of your common law'. The petition shows that interrogation was a Common Law practice before it was a Chancery one, while we can discount the Commons' allusions to 'Civil Law' and 'holy church' as rhetorical flourishes: examination in England had several purely English characteristics. Enquiries ordered by the king, were, we saw, one of the roots of Common Law procedure, and from Chancery issued the writs initiating them and to Chancery returned the answers.[9]

English legal procedure has always had a local component, and the English procedure by interrogation was therefore very different from the Roman. The Civil Law judge's professional function was to question witnesses in court, rather like modern counsel. After an initial period of mainly live examination at Westminster, the chancellor, in the middle years of the fifteenth century, adopted the essentially English method of commissioning knights of the shire by writ of *dedimus potestatem* to do the work locally. The depositions obtained could then only be returned in writing.[10]

THE RISE OF THE COURT OF CHANCERY

There was one great difference between a Chancery commission to examine witnesses and a Common Law hearing at *nisi prius* – the commissioners questioned individuals with special knowledge, not a group of jurymen representing a community. It could have been a growing idea of witness-trial which opened the way for Chancery as a court (and not vice versa), for Chancery as a writing-office was well-equipped for examining witnesses; equipped not so much to record the evidence as to produce the writs of subpoena compelling the appearance of parties and witnesses by threat of a stated penalty for default, and the new style of commissions to take evidence and settle disputes by arbitration. The chancellor could also order the 'discovery' of documents relevant to a dispute. Perhaps he first interfered judicially to enforce agreements proved by witnesses or informal writings but for which there were no charters or fines such as the Common Law would recognize.[11]

This ability to decree the most important steps in a case was derived from a discretionary power delegated to Chancery by the king's council, as well as from purely technical resources. With the king remained the ultimate duty of government, the keeping of the peace, but all except the greatest problems he left to his permanent council. When the central Common Law courts broke away from it in the reign of Henry III, the council retained responsibility for the enforcement as opposed to the adjudication of law. By 1400 there were numerous complaints of the council's interference with the Common Law by writs under the privy seal. Many of the petitions which were brought to the king in council, particularly at Parliament time, when special machinery was provided for their reception, concerned routine disputes which might be referred to the judges, or uncommon problems of moderate urgency which might be left to an expert in judicial remedies – an expert who was to hand in the chancellor, the most regular attender in council. Chancery as a court of law was the creation of the council, and equity can best be defined as the power of the council, administered by the chancellor, to see that the law was enforced fairly and effectively, and thus sometimes to supplement the rules of the Common Law according to the dictates of natural justice.

The political importance of the chancellor after the disappearance of the justiciar – still reflected in the fact that he changes with governments – also caused many problems to be left to him. Thomas Becket in Henry II's reign, Robert Burnell in Edward I's, Cardinal Wolsey and Sir Thomas More in Henry VIII's were the greatest men of their time under the king and often the most expert in the whole field of government and law. The chancellors of those days were busy administrators who would stand no academic nonsense: Lord Chancellor Ellesmere in the reign of James I ordered that the Warden of the Fleet should lay hold on an equity pleader who had drawn a replication of 120 pages where 16 would have done, 'and shall bring him unto Westminster Hall . . . and there and then shall cut a hole in the midst of the same engrossed replication . . . and put the said Richard's head through the same hole . . . and shall show him at the bar of every of the three courts within the Hall.' In late Tudor and early Stuart chancellors like Sir Nicholas Bacon (who established that peers, like commoners, could be committed for contempt of court) and his yet more famous son, determination to curb the injustices of the overmighty may have been accompanied by a middle-class envy of the old nobility.

The administrative nature of the chancellor's work made the appearance of a separate *court* of equity slow, and the dating of the process is a matter of dispute. Reference to a Court of Chancery deciding equitably as early as Edward I's reign seems to be to the king's council, including the Common Law judges, meeting under the chancellor's presidency. Since equity was simply a way of working the Common Law, there was never any special training for Chancery lawyers, who were only Common Law barristers practising in Chancery. The best we can say is that a separate court of equity came into being at the moment (necessarily unrecorded) when the chancellor felt that in some matters he need no longer take the advice of his fellow-councillors. Some differences between the Common Law and the law of Chancery were recognized by *c.* 1450, because then the chancellor was taking account of grievances strange to the Common Law, such as ones concerning uses; which he did by granting, according to principles of his own formulation, subpoenas to summon defendants and witnesses. In 1482 the judges were still objecting to the calling of witnesses to prove a case against the Common-Law heir of a trustee: 'if a descent can be disproved by two witnesses in Chancery it follows that one may disprove twenty descents, which is against reason and

conscience . . . It is a lesser evil to cause him, who allows his
feoffee to die, still seised of his land, to lose this land, than by
testimonies in Chancery to cause many persons to lose their
inheritances.' To which the chancellor replied that it was
'the usual course in the Chancery to grant *Subpoena* . . . on
feoffment of trust where the heir of the feoffee is in by descent
or otherwise, for we find record in the Chancery of such
cases.'[12]

But even if Chancery was establishing its own peculiar
jurisdiction, its earliest judicial business was almost certainly
'Common Law business'. By *injunctions* the chancellor would
stay a trial at Common Law while deeds were discovered and
witnesses examined; and 'quiet' or protect a tenant from
interference till his Common Law case was decided, preventing his immediate ejection if the case went against him. He
would relieve a petitioner against one who 'with great rigour
and malice has vexed and daily vexes your said beseecher
with divers feigned actions and unlawful imprisonment'; and
sometimes, by writ of *supersedeas* to the sheriff, safeguard a
litigant in Chancery from arrest by order of another court.
But only reluctantly would he interfere in Common Law
proceedings to the extent of ordering a party to cease his suit
in another court: as in 1482, when a plaintiff in an action of
trespass was forbidden under penalty of £100 to proceed to
judgment in King's Bench, though he had already got a
verdict at *nisi prius*. Finally, Chancery would supplement the
Common Law's resources by ordering local inquiries or
arbitration 'for the sake of the peace'.[13]

Chancery's characteristic jurisdiction consisted more in
this procedural control than in court hearings: the actual
adjudication of disputes unsuitable for Common Law trial
were sent to arbitration by commissions of oyer and terminer.
Chancery, even judicially, was a central office rather than a
court, and, although by the fifteenth century it enjoyed the
immense asset of a clerical staff 150 strong, the chancellor
was for long its only judge. In Elizabeth's reign the judicial
action of Chancery was becoming more procedural still in
commercial matters, and many Chancery suits were begun

just to obtain commissions of arbitration to cut through the custom-ridden technicalities of trade.

Much of this may seem to have been gratuitous encroachment on the province of the Common Lawyers, but the latter were in fact compelled to admit that equity was necessary to the execution of law in a fashion tolerable to litigants. Indeed, equity and other Chancery concepts came from the Common Law, and not all Common Lawyers were so fascinated by legal technicalities as to be prepared to surrender equitable discretion; one of them proclaimed in 1464 that 'The law of the Chancery is the common law of the land'.[14] Chancery even took over the Common Law doctrine of consideration in contract, a field in which its advantages were its wide powers to order specific performance as well as damages, and particularly to subpoena and imprison, sanctions against the defendant's person which were more effective than the Common Law's antiquated process of distraint against the defendant's property.

THE SUBSTANCE OF EQUITY

Every bill in Chancery was for the discovery, by means of the subpoena, of some fact relevant to fair and equal judgment between persons. Some of the facts so discovered would alter the course of proceedings in a Common Law court; but naturally most subpoenas were made returnable in Chancery, and action on the new evidence was decreed there. It was at this point that the office turned into a court.

In some cases Chancery's order would be automatically decisive, as when it was for the production of a purse, lost by the petitioner, or for the surrender of deeds; neither of which could be recovered by the Common Law action of Detinue unless the plaintiff knew the precise contents of the purse or the muniment-chest.[15] But often the defendant would embark upon legal argument. If Chancery was going to pronounce judgment itself, as well as to stop judgments in other courts, it had to formulate principles of its own and argue that there were considerations of fairness or equity higher than strict law. The petitioners determined what problems the chancellor tackled. Generally speaking, he interfered less and less to protect the poor against the overmighty (other conciliar courts were provided to do that), and more to relieve hardship caused by bad faith, or simple mistake or accident: this way led to the chancellor's modification of Common Law judgments enforcing contracts without regard to the fraud or unintended evil which would result, or the ruinous penalties they contained. The development of 'equity of redemption' for the benefit of mortgagors was directed to the same prevention of the harsh exploiting of legal agreements.

To be distinguished from the hardship intrinsic in the Common Law's rejection of 'pretence of conscience' were situations which the Common Law had never considered – *all* of which, so the theory ran, it could not possibly consider in their infinite variety. The chancellor would thus order specific performance of a contract, adjudicate on the validity of a will (here poaching upon ecclesiastical preserves), protect the interests of a married woman, and enforce a trust (by the last item, gaining a jurisdiction in matters of title to land). The third stream of Chancery jurisdiction, arbitration through local commissions, dealt with many issues which today would not reach a court of law at all, and settled mercantile disputes, in which the chancellor may first have learnt to think in terms of 'equity' (mercantile cases were again delegated from the council, concerned with them because they involved treaty rights and international questions).

Since there was no jury, the chancellor's judgments were of fact as well as law: thus, Chancellor Francis Bacon was 'of opinion that the said assignment having been made so near unto the said marriage and without any real or valuable consideration and having been also secret for so long a time, was fraudulent and ought not in any sort to prejudice the plaintiff in his purchase, and he accordingly . . . ordered and decreed that the plaintiff should and might for and during so many of the said sixty years as were yet unexpired and to come [enjoy the property, and the defendants should not interfere] by force or colour of the verdict or judgment at Common Law.'[16]

The use of subpoenas and injunctions to create a new body of law did arouse the resentment of Common Lawyers, and the judges were led into a contemptuous and damaging rejection of any exercise of equitable discretion for themselves. As a way of initiating an action, the subpoena had the great advantage over the writ that it was valid everywhere (not in a single specified county) and did not commit the plaintiff to a narrow line of attack which he might not have fully understood when he started on it. But of course it was sometimes unfair to the defendant to be summoned by a missive, rather too easily procured, which did not set out what it was he would have to deny (in practice, he must usually have known well enough), and it was on this 'injustice' that the Common Lawyers took their stand.[17] In the rise of the Court of Chancery, and of the conciliar courts still to be described, English law harvested for a second time the fruits of procedural experiment, but the Common Lawyers would have no part in them. The Common Law and Equity were to be different things.

The story of Chancery was not glorious for very long. The chancellor became more of a judge as he lost his predominance in the new Tudor Privy Council to the secretaries of state: and the Masters in Chancery, led by the master of the rolls, became something like the chancellor's puisne justices. The Court of Chancery found its own place in the south-west corner of Westminster Hall. The old cycle repeated itself: subtle and flexible procedural devices were solidified by habit into the mysterious and tedious 'course' of a new court.[18]

PRIVY COUNCIL AND STAR CHAMBER

Chancery was only the first of a number of courts to break away from the council which were a factor of great importance in English history from the accession of the Tudors to the Great Rebellion. The family rivalries which broadened into the Wars of the Roses had originated within the aristocratic group of councillors which ruled England during Henry VI's minority, so it says much for the intelligence of the Yorkist King Edward IV that, instead of dispensing with a council (as historians once believed), he began the creation of the body of dedicated administrators, largely aloof from aristocratic politics, which was to make the Tudors so strong. In contrast to Henry VI's small but explosive oligarchy, Henry VII's council was a large and heterogeneous group of forty to fifty bishops, canon lawyers, peers, knights, judges and serjeants-at-law, united by nothing but their usefulness to a king who directed council meetings in his own person.[19]

After the accession in 1509 of Henry VIII, a king more careless of administrative detail, the presidency of the council (not yet a formal office) passed to Cardinal Wolsey, who was in effect his own 'privy council', and then to Thomas Cromwell, the king's agent in the political attack on the church of Rome, who founded a true privy council before his downfall in 1540. The way for these changes was prepared by the relegation of the ancient administrative 'courses' of Chancery and Exchequer to a formal role, in the face of new household departments; by the very appearance of this departmentalism and specialization, which had been foreign to the Middle Ages; by the triumph, in the person of Thomas Cromwell, of the secretary of state over the medieval chancellor, last truly represented by Wolsey; and by the decline of seals and writs, as instruments of administration, before the Privy Council's informal, caustic letters, pouring out from its almost daily meetings to chide and galvanize the local agents of the Crown. Henry VII's council contracted in size to form the Privy Council of Elizabeth, less than twenty strong, where William Cecil, lord treasurer and master of the Court of Wards, presided over half a dozen regular attenders, heads of departments like the secretaries (there were now at least two), the comptroller of the household, the treasurer of the chamber and the chancellor of the exchequer. Of the judges only the lord chief justice was left a member.[20]

The petitions of those who felt they had any sort of grievance were naturally attracted to the most powerful institution in the land under the Queen. In Elizabeth's reign the
council made efforts – their frequency shows their ineffective-
ness – to divert the stream of petitions to the ordinary courts.
In 1582, 'considering what multitude of matters concerning
private causes and actions between party and party were
daily brought unto the Council Board, wherewith their lordships were greatly troubled and her Majesty's special services
oftentimes interrupted,' the Privy Council decided that
'henceforth no private causes . . . which may receive order
and redress in any of her Majesty's ordinary courts shall
be received . . . unless they shall concern the preservation
of her Majesty's peace or shall be of some public consequence. . . .'[21]

It would, however, act as a clearing-house, referring a case
to its proper court, or arranging for arbitration locally and
seeing that decisions there were enforced. Grievances brought
to the Council were 'rather ended by overruling an obstinate
person who is made to acknowledge his fault, or else the
parties are remitted to some court of justice or equity, or
recommended by some letters to some justices in the country
to compound the differences either by consent of the parties
or by direction'. In all this, the Privy Council was acting as
the ultimate court of equity which it had always been. To
deny that the Privy Council was a court at all is to confine the
term over-narrowly to a tribunal where formal pleading took
place. If Chancery was a court, so was the Privy Council. It
ordered preliminary examination in treason cases, and
summoned before it persons suspected of crimes against the
state, whom it could imprison for long periods without trial.
After hearing the reports of lawyers whom it had appointed
to investigate quarrels between the city and the university of
Oxford, it imposed its own solution 'according to right and
equity'. It secured the appointment of commissions under
the great seal, composed predominantly of privy councillors,
to determine treasons; and in 1587 it took upon itself the final
responsibility for the execution of Mary, Queen of Scots.[22]

It is true, though, that matters requiring pleading were reserved for special meetings of the Privy Council, which became recognized as a separate court; so that Stow, after describing the other courts in Elizabeth's Palace of Westminster, could write:

> Then there is also the Star Chamber where in the term time every week once at the least . . . the lord chancellor and the lords and other of the Privy Council and the chief justices of England, from 9 of the clock till it be 11 do sit. . . . There be plaints heard of riots, routs and other misdemeanours which, if they be found by the King's Council, the party offender shall be censured by these persons (which speak one after another) and he shall be both fined and commanded to prison.[23]

The majority of Star Chamber business was the hearing of private petitions. One immediately asks why another court was needed for this purpose over and above Chancery. Star Chamber began as a court of equity with a jurisdiction almost indistinguishable from Chancery's, hearing cases turning on unwritten contracts and uses, and enforcing Common Law decisions. The mystery deepens when we discover that Star Chamber was dominated by the chancellor – indeed, was securely established as a court by Chancellor Wolsey – and that early Star Chamber petitions were addressed to the chancellor. There was, however, a certain distinctive tone – it cannot be put more positively – to Star Chamber's jurisdiction. Though Star Chamber and Chancery dealt with similar situations in similar ways, Star Chamber's purpose was to keep the peace, Chancery's the pursuit of equity; or perhaps – since Star Chamber also acted on private petition – we should say that the one pursued equity for conscience's sake, the other because lack of it caused disorder. The distinction was something like that between Common Pleas and King's Bench business in the Middle Ages, the relative interest of individual cases to the government.[24]

Petitioners in Star Chamber, while asking for remedy as in Chancery 'for the love of God and in the way of charity', emphasized the fear and force used against them, and related horrible cruelties and dreadful threats: 'Where is that whoreson the priest? If I had him I would hew him in small gobbets to sell him at the market ere I went.' Or they brought to the Council disputes with men 'of great power and alliance' which would not get a fair hearing locally, because the petitioners were 'not of power nor acquainted in that country to defend their right and title'.[25]

As always, the government relied on private complaints to bring crimes to its notice, but as crimes it certainly treated them. The Council found that it could deter the enormous trespasses of the overmighty by its heavy fines and humiliating punishments, though medieval statutes had debarred it from imposing penalties of life or limb or landed property, and confined matters of freehold, treason and felony to the Common Law courts. When it had the idea of sentencing men to be given to Sir John Hawkins, 'to work in chains as galley slaves, and, for a time at least, on a low diet', it was discovering the idea of imprisonment with hard labour.[26] Star Chamber became the most effective weapon of government, so that Wolsey could write to Henry VIII that he would teach the magnates 'the new law of the Star Chamber, that they should beware how from henceforth they shall redress matters with their [own] hands'. Appropriate to its governmental role was its punishment of dishonest lawyers and of contempt of other courts, and adjudication of disputes between public bodies – the Merchant Adventurers and the Merchants of the Staple, the City of Exeter and the City of London. It was Star Chamber's job especially to enforce legislation against disorder, and statutes would sometimes announce that redress could be had there on complaint of the offences defined.[27]

There was a cutting edge to Star Chamber procedure (in general like Chancery's) which reflected its high responsibilities. A defendant was often questioned in Star Chamber itself, so that his heart would be cast down by 'those chief personages of England, one after another handling him . . . with such gravity, with such reason and remonstrance'. Use was sometimes made of the Roman Law procedure known as 'ore tenus, upon the confession of the party in writing under his hand', which, though 'he again must freely confess in open court', Coke thought was somehow not 'the fairest way'.[28]

It was in the 'sentence' (another Roman Law term), often indeed sententious, that the solemn tone of the court is most obvious, for the councillors spoke in turn in ascending order of seniority. In 1605, the attorney-general prosecuted the publisher of a libel against John Whitgift, the late Archbishop of Canterbury. The first councillors, in few words, assigned a fine of £1,000, together with 'imprisonment, to wear papers on the pillory . . . and [have] his ears nailed'. Lord Zouche, speaking ninth, 'loves brevity' and agreed with his predecessors. Lord Salisbury, as befitted King James's chief minister and the son of Elizabeth's, launched into a justification of his master's policies and an eulogy on that Queen who had been 'by her government memorable, by her death happy, and the wonder of her sex'. Nineteenth and last came Lord Chancellor Ellesmere: 'And the law of the Lydians was to punish the libeller by torture and death. . . . King Edgar and Canute cut out the tongue. . . . Vowell versus Chief Justice Fitz-James (1526–39), his ears cut off. . . . Now it is a libelling time.'[29]

By King James's reign the inevitable 'procedural deceleration' was turning Star Chamber into just another court. The loss of its advantages to the individual petitioner, as much as any positive tyranny exercised through its processes, prepared the way for the destruction of Star Chamber in 1641.[30]

THE COURTS OF REQUESTS AND THE REGIONAL COUNCILS

Another conciliar court which shared Star Chamber's fate (though it lapsed rather than was formally abolished) was the Court of Requests, 'the poor man's court of equity'. Poverty was the main reason for presenting bills in the king's courts rather than purchasing writs, and the king always felt a special duty to give justice to the poor. In 1483, under Richard III, there was already a second clerk of the council with responsibility for 'the custody, registration and expedition of bills, requests and supplications of poor persons'.[31] Councillors were told off for the actual hearing of poor men's cases: churchmen – particularly the almoner who distributed the king's alms – seem to have been regarded as appropriate. The Court of Requests and Star Chamber appeared at about the same time and to begin with were only slightly different aspects of the same institution. Wolsey gave the court a fixed location in the White Hall at Westminster. When the council contracted into Privy Council, the judges of Requests ceased to be councillors and were reduced in number to two 'ordinary masters of requests', supplemented from 1562 by two 'extraordinary masters'.

The jurisdiction of Requests diverged from Star Chamber's to cover essentially private matters, which it treated as questions of equity and conscience, and this was the real cause of its downfall. Like Chancery it seemed to poach upon the fields of the Common Law. The great masters of requests, like David Lewis and Julius Caesar, all indeed began as Masters in Chancery. With the faults of Chancery, Requests did not have Chancery's procedural strength and usefulness as a supplement to Common Law, or its fertility in producing new legal concepts: it was just a court, and to the Common Lawyer's way of thinking a pernicious and unnecessary one.

The court's early expeditiousness contributed to this situation by attracting plaintiffs who were anything but poor. Since its judges were usually competent civil lawyers, a variety of mercantile cases came to it, and matrimonial disputes which would earlier have gone to the church. A woman who had separated from her husband because of his 'vile and inhuman' treatment of her could go to Requests to ask 'for her sufficient maintenance and that of her infant'. There is no doubt, however, that Requests did something to protect the small tenant-farmer and possibly to protect the lesser artisans of the towns, at a time of social upheaval, when enclosing landlords were ignoring manorial customs and imposing arbitrary fines and forfeitures, and when guilds were becoming more monopolistic.[32]

Medieval kings, at least from William the Conqueror, had provided for the defence of the realm by giving large domains and special powers to nobles of the Welsh and Scottish borders or 'marches'. The bishops of Durham, the earls of Chester and the dukes of Lancaster thus acquired 'palatinates' in which their rights in some respects – including the enforcement of Common Law procedure – were almost equivalent to the king's. Fortunately for the king, the Duchy of Lancaster and the Palatinate of Chester eventually merged with the royal estates, and Chester was made the seat of one of the three justices to whom the administration of law in conquered Wales was committed. The Wardens of the Scottish and Welsh marches (the most durable examples of the thirteenth-century military keepers of the peace) were brought under control only by the appointment of special councils for those areas in Edward IV's reign – just when Star Chamber was beginning to impose order elsewhere.

The Council in the North, with headquarters at York, was reorganized by Thomas Cromwell after the northern rebellion known as the Pilgrimage of Grace (1536). Its fifteen or so members were made up of the northern peers and knights, ecclesiastics and lawyers. Its sixteenth-century presidents were such people as Robert Holgate, Archbishop of York, and the earl of Huntingdon, whose long rule helped to restore the situation after the formidable rebellion of the Northern Earls in 1569. Thomas Cromwell again strengthened the council in the Marches of Wales, as did statutes of 1536 and 1543 which united England and Wales administratively and 'shired' the estates of the great marcher-barons. But it was the sheer persistence of Rowland Lee, bishop of Coventry, lord president of the Council in the Marches from 1534, who brought a measure of order to the region. The problems facing the borders are clear in a statute of 1601, which made it felony in the northern counties for 'men of name . . . friended and allied with great robbers' to take 'a certain rate of money, corn, cattle or other consideration, commonly there called by the name of black mail' for protection from the aforesaid robbers.[33]

The powers of the regional councils were not delegated by the Privy Council, though they were supervised from Westminster: in fact, they included Common Law jurisdiction by oyer and terminer which the Privy Council did not have. The development of the jurisdiction of these other councils was rather parallel to that of the Privy Council, the same general responsibility for order leading to the same functions in equity. To many an aggrieved person it was a better remedy to get a local magistrate to bind an oppressor to keep the peace, than to trek to London for a judgment; better still to be able to apply to a substitute Privy Council. In regulations of 1484 (here there is another striking coincidence with the beginning of Star Chamber and Requests), the holding of quarterly sessions 'to hear, examine and order all bills of complaint' was placed before the suppression of riots amongst the duties of the Council in the North. Perhaps the frequency of ecclesiastical presidents also helped to give the regional councils their equitable jurisdiction. The characteristic conciliar pattern of judicial development was repeated.[34]

There were yet other local examples of the process: the courts of the lord warden of the Cinque Ports and of the Palatinate of Durham, and the council of the Duchy of Lancaster, the vast patrimony which continued to be administered separately when its owner became king of England in 1399. The history of this council, which sat as the equitable 'Court of Duchy Chamber' in the palace of Westminster, is highly suggestive, because it seems in many ways to have anticipated the changes in the king's council, though it was itself only one of many councils which formed round the magnates in the fourteenth century. In its use, to keep order, of writs of privy seal, arbitration and commissions of oyer and terminer, it behaved just like the 'national' conciliar courts. Was the truth in fact the other way round? Was the king's law still learning its tricks from local and baronial practice, mediated in this case through the Duchy of Lancaster?[35]

A rather different example of the local court of equity was the Court of Requests established by the city of London in the

reign of Henry VIII and confirmed by statute in 1604 'for
the further relief' of the 'poor debtors' with whom London
abounded. This was to be the model for the local courts 'for
small claims' which sprang up spontaneously in the late
seventeenth and eighteenth centuries, after the central
Court of Requests had vanished.

STATUTORY AND ADMINISTRATIVE COURTS

Under Edward IV conciliar courts developed naturally
under the pressure of petitions. The Tudors, on the other
hand, began to feel the power of statute, as a means of
exploiting the conciliar apparatus. Both the fertility of
council and statute, and the intractableness of the problem
of law enforcement, are needed to explain the Tudors'
extraordinary series of judicial projects, the interest of which
is not lessened by their ultimate impermanence. The first of
the schemes was embodied in an act of 1487, which, because
someone later endorsed it with the words '*pro camera stellata*',
was long thought to have been the origin of Star Chamber.
No such act was necessary to create that court, and in the
event it seems to have been another tribunal which was set
up, consisting of the chancellor, treasurer, keeper of the privy
seal, a bishop, magnate and the two chief justices; its purpose
to try cases of livery, maintenance and a few other named
offences.[36]

One main purpose of the schemes of 1487 and later was to
give to the council and other specially equipped bodies, in
conjunction with the justices of the peace, the same power to
enforce statutes against disorder which in 1362 had been assigned to Chancery. 'Better it were' that statutes 'never had
been made unless they should be put in due and perfect
execution', said a draft of *c.* 1534 (never enacted) for the
appointment of six 'conservators of the commonweal' to
enforce all 'penal and popular' statutes passed since the
accession of Henry VII. 'Penal and popular' statutes were
those which invited private prosecution by information and
provided a penalty to be awarded to the informant. Because

of embracery (the corruption of juries) 'nothing or little may be found by inquiry', ran the statute of 1487; so effective law enforcement had to rely on private bills. The criminal side of conciliar jurisdiction was no less criminal for using the procedure of Chancery. Another stillborn scheme of 1535 or 1536 proposed to give a court like that of the 1487 statute the hearing of charges of official corruption.[37]

Statutory systems of courts found their chief scope in the field of government finance. The Exchequer – always a court for pleas which could be alleged to involve the king's financial rights – developed an equitable jurisdiction by subpoena at the same time as Chancery did (the exchequer had a copy of the great seal for its own use). Administered by the chancellor (or chief clerk) of the exchequer, this court of equity was not merged in Chancery till 1842. But at the end of the fifteenth century, when the privy council's letters were beginning to rival the administrative 'course' of Chancery, it was quite certain that the wellnigh incredible 'course of the exchequer', swathed in red tape and crippled by caution, would be by-passed by new financial departments.

The Privy Council, leaving to the exchequer the collection of the now unimportant sheriffs' revenues, supervised new financial agents. Control was exercised through yet more conciliar courts. For a few years after 1500 there was a committee of the council – 'the council learned in the law' – sitting as a court to collect feudal dues and fines from the enforcement of penal statutes. Henry VIII created a Court of General Surveyors in 1542 to administer the majority of crown lands, vacant bishoprics and feudal profits. An act of 1536 set up 'a certain court commonly to be called the Court of Augmentations of the Revenue of the King's Crown', to take responsibility for the great accession of property resulting from the dissolution of the monasteries. This was to have a chancellor as president, disposing of a great seal and a privy seal, and an attorney 'learned in the laws of the land'; it was to be a court of record; and it was to follow 'such process and precepts with reasonable pains to be therein limited as be now commonly used in the court of the King's Duchy

159

Chamber of Lancaster being at Westminster . . .' In 1540 was formally established a Court of Wards and Liveries, to deal with the dues accruing to the Crown from feudal succession, and the Court of First Fruits and Tenths, the province of which was the ecclesiastical revenues newly diverted to the King by his 'reformation'.[38]

The counter-attack of the exchequer on the new financial courts succeeded more quickly but less completely than did the Common Lawyers' on the conciliar courts proper. In 1554 all but the Court of Wards were absorbed into the exchequer, but traces of them survived in such exchequer offices as the seven auditorships of the land revenue.

THE CHURCH COURTS AND THE HIGH COMMISSION

The Reformation made necessary new courts to deal with those matters of substance which in the Middle Ages had belonged to the jurisdiction of the church. These matters were of two sorts: first, the misdemeanours and disputes of the clergy; and second, the misdemeanours and disputes of the laity, either against the clergy (for instance, non-payment of tithes or riotous behaviour in church), or sinful in themselves (heresy, not attending church at all, adultery and fornication, ill-treatment of wife or children, the fraudulent execution of a man's last will and testament, perjury, defamation). The disciplinary responsibility of the church for the morals of the laity was particularly important in the case of marriage: the bishop could not of course dissolve a proper marriage, but he had much scope to decide that a marriage had never been valid and to compel the separation of the couple 'from bed and board' (sometimes called *divortium*).[39]

The lowest of the church courts was the archdeacon's; above that the bishop's or 'consistory' court, presided over by the bishop's 'official', usually his chancellor. At the top were the courts of the archbishops of Canterbury and York. Each archbishop had an ordinary metropolitan court, known in the case of Canterbury as the Court of Arches (presided over by the Dean of Arches), since it met in London

at the church of St Mary de Arcubus at Bow; a court of
appeal and equity, called the Court of Audience; and a
'prerogative court' exercising the jurisdiction over the
proving of wills which the archbishops claimed whenever
the property bequeathed lay in two or more dioceses (as the
property of all important testators would do). Probate
jurisdiction remained the exclusive and immensely important
preserve of the church courts till 1857, and the registers of
wills proved in the prerogative Court of Canterbury (now
kept in Somerset House) are historical records of great value.
The control of the Church over wills, concerned principally
with movable goods, was a cause of the division between the
laws of real and personal property; for, while the deceased's
land passed to his heir, the goods passed to those responsible
to the church courts for executing the will.

The business of the ecclesiastical courts which depended
on private complaint declined sharply after about 1490,
probably in face of the extra remedies provided by the king's
conciliar courts. The disciplinary jurisdiction left to the
church became merely irksome to the laity, and was one of
the causes of the Reformation. But the freedom of the people
from religious direction was not the intention of any reformer,
and the courts remained to act in matters of doctrine much
as they had under Catholic sovereigns – to vex the puritan
critics of the reformed (not yet 'Anglican') church, who
themselves, as J.P.s, were often enthusiastically exercising a
'godly discipline'.[40]

What Henry VIII did destroy was the right of appeal to
the Pope, as incompatible with his supremacy in state and
church. But some ecclesiastical court of appeal above the
co-equal authorities of York and Canterbury there had to
be, and for private cases this was provided by a High Court
of Delegates, appointed by royal commission from the ranks
of the ecclesiastical lawyers whenever a case arose. It seems
almost inevitable, however, in view of the impetus of conciliar
control in the sixteenth century, that the Privy Council should
straight away have intervened judicially in many spiritual
matters. The council was the agent of the royal supremacy,

and the agent – almost another manifestation – of the council was the Court of High Commission.

Religion was, after all, the great disturbing force of the time. Even in Henry VIII's reign the council took a hand against 'foolish prophets' who 'talked of the scripture', and sent one 'to the coal house at Windsor' where he 'came to himself'. The Council in the North, round about 1544, was told to instruct the people in the laws 'touching the abolishing of the usurped and pretended power of the bishop of Rome, whose abuses they shall so beat into their heads by continual inculcation as they may smell the same . . .' Finally, in 1559, the archbishop of Canterbury, the bishop of London, several councillors, masters of requests, serjeants-at-law and doctors of (civil) law received the first of the special commissions to punish 'notorious and manifest advoutries, fornications and ecclesiastical crimes and offences within this our realm, according to your wisdoms, consciences and discretions'.[41] There were some dramatic trials before the High Commission, such as that of the presbyterian leader, Thomas Cartwright, and his associates in 1591–2, but more important is the fact that the secular state was taking responsibility for matrimonial and other matters once the preserve of the church, and treating them as it did any other legal problem. The powerful Sir Walter Hungerford spent three years in the Fleet prison in the 1570s for refusing to support his wife, from whom he had tried to get a divorce on the grounds of her adultery with the notorious 'wild Darell'.

THE COURT OF CHIVALRY

In August 1348, before any of the conciliar courts we have so far mentioned had a separate existence, a court kept by the Constable of England and his associate, the Marshal, is found ordering the arrest of a French prisoner-of-war who had betrayed the trust of his captors. The new court, variously known in its long existence (not yet terminated) as *Curia Militaris*, the High Court of Chivalry, the Court of Honour, the Court of the Constable and Marshal, and in the end as

the Earl Marshal's Court, received its jurisdiction by delega-
tion from the king's council of cases which were outside the
Common Law because (i) they arose from events outside the
realm, or (ii) the parties were aliens.[42] The Admiral acquired
his parallel jurisdiction over cases at sea between merchants
at about the same time, and it seems probable that we must
now include his court amongst the offshoots of the council.

Most of the constable's legal business was a by-product
of foreign wars, or more specifically of 'the business
side of medieval warfare'. The court was not a 'court-
martial' in the modern sense: *Curia Militaris* meant 'the
court of the knights', and it heard disputes about the contracts between captain and trooper, by which medieval
expeditionary forces were mainly assembled, and about the
ransoming of prisoners, a thriving business of importance to
the national economy in the later Middle Ages.[43] The increase
of cases of the second type after the outbreak of the Hundred
Years War in *c.* 1339 may have been the reason for the
court's origin. But more and more the court became concerned with claims and counter-claims to *arms*, in the sense
of the armorial or heraldic devices which, though originating
in the practices of warfare, were soon reckoned to be a social
necessity for a truly gentle family. The right to bear arms lay
in the grant of the king alone, made through the heralds of
what was to become the College of Arms, but it could be
asserted and confirmed in the Court of Chivalry on the basis
of use since time immemorial, just as right to land could be
asserted at Common Law. In 1467, the idea appears that
arms and the Court of Chivalry had begun with the Conqueror, from which followed the theoretical requirement
that the possession of arms must **be** proved back to 1066. In
consequence, the Court of Chivalry was the scene of immensely complex heraldic disputes like *Scrope* v. *Grosvenor*
(1385–90), their records replete with invaluable social and
genealogical information along with a good deal of myth.

Long after the criminal Appeal was moribund as a procedure in other courts, the Court of Chivalry enjoyed a
criminal jurisdiction over Appeals of treason and murder

committed outside the realm (for which, of course, there was no other form of prosecution), and even heard Appeals of treason within the realm. In 1398, the duke of Hereford brought against the duke of Norfolk in the Court of Chivalry the Appeal, alleging treasonable schemes against Richard II, which led eventually to Hereford's accession to the throne as Henry IV; and there, in 1631, Donald, lord Reay, appealed a Scottish courtier of plotting on board ship near Elsinore to put the marquis of Hamilton on the throne of Scotland. It was in the Court of Chivalry, too, that armed rebellion within the realm was tried on the *king's record*, for the international rules of war were reckoned to apply as soon as banners were raised or cannon fired.[44] This was the limit of the court's power. When it began to encroach upon the Common Law jurisdiction over Appeals of felony within the realm, the Commons complained to the king; for in front of the lord high constable there was no judgment by peers according to Magna Carta.

In 1485, war within the realm came to an end, and indentures ceased to be much used for the raising of expeditionary armies. For over a century the Court of Chivalry was virtually inoperative. After the execution of the duke of Buckingham in 1521, the office of constable was in abeyance, and the earl marshal was left to exercise a minor jurisdiction over matters of precedence, the proper ceremonial at gentlemen's funerals, and other heraldic questions, through his control of the College of Arms. The court was revived by the concern of James I at the growing fashion of duelling, and his theory that a Court of Chivalry must be able to give remedy for scandalous words (provocative of duels), which usually amounted to saying that the injured party was 'unchivalrous', 'not a gentleman'. In 1622, the Privy Council, at the king's request, gave the opinion that the earl marshal could hold the Court of Chivalry on his own, and that dignitary was therefore ordered to 'restore and settle' the ancient procedure of the court.

The revived court was therefore much concerned with punishing insults; or worse, what amounted to the subversion of the natural order, the claim of an inferior being like the mayor of Exeter, a merchant, to be 'at all times and in any place as good a man' as his social superior, Sir Popham Southcote, knight. The proceedings are very important for social history, for only a gentleman could institute them, and there was much discussion as to what a gentleman was. Was it enough to be a knight, if, like Sir Popham, you were also a soap-maker? The coincidence of another historical process added to the court's importance after its revival: it was the only court which could deal with Appeals of murders committed in the new colonies.[45]

The court sat in the ancient Painted Chamber at Westminster – the walls of which Henry III had adorned with almost all the war scenes in the whole Bible – or in the earl marshal's castle at Arundel. Trial would involve the usual commissions of interrogation, appointed to meet in some well-known hostelry in the locality of the dispute, and interlocutory hearings in the chambers of the earl marshal's professional *surrogate* in Doctor's Commons. A more notable part of the sentence than the monetary penalties, or the imprisonment which could be used only to punish contempt of court orders, was the customary requirement that the defeated party should admit his fault, ask his opponent's forgiveness and do something very like penance. One man, accused of assuming the title of gentleman unwarrantably, had to publicly confess his disrespect 'to the gentry laws and officers of arms of this kingdom'.

The Court of Chivalry was destroyed in January 1641 by the resolution of the Long Parliament that it could not meet without a lord high constable, and that its assumption of jurisdiction over scandalous words was unwarranted. Longer than any other court it had suffered from the fear and resentment of the Common Lawyers. A great series of medieval treason trials in the court, such as Archbishop Scrope's in 1405 and those of Edward IV's opponents before John Tiptoft, earl of Worcester and lord high constable, in the 1460s, might once have given plausibility to the charge that it was an instrument of tyranny. Since in Tiptoft's character savagery was combined with the culture of the Italian renaissance, it was possible to paint the Court of Chivalry as an inquisition, where free-born Englishmen suffered the cruelties of the '*lawe padowe*', the Roman Law taught best of all at Padua. It does seem that Tiptoft, who had lived in Padua, introduced a particularly summary method of trial in cases of treason.

But the Court of Chivalry and the other conciliar courts developed gradually and organically from far back in the mid-fourteenth century and can have owed little to any sudden infusion of Roman Law at a 'Reception' in the late fifteenth or early sixteenth. Since they dealt much with foreigners, the church courts, Admiralty and the Court of Chivalry made a good deal of use of Roman procedures and terminology; but these were common-sense ways of proceeding, with purely English parallels. The two essential changes in the late medieval courts – in England as elsewhere – were towards more written proceedings and more rational ways of discovering the true facts. In England the changes began in the Common Law courts but were carried through in the new conciliar courts, with their youthful zest for efficiency and dependence on the petition, a natural beginning for written proceedings. Men of the fifteenth century seem to have been unsure whether or not the law of chivalry was Roman Law, but they were sure that it was 'the law of the land and the law of our Lord the King'. They also knew that it required 'more than ordinary understanding' to judge chivalry cases.[46] There was the rub. Law had entered a more professional stage and initiative had passed to new men. More writing and interrogation meant far more legal officials, even when much was delegated to local gentlemen: its large secretariat may have given Chancery its judicial opportunity. Those with some training as civilians were better able to cope with the new methods and had perforce to fill the gap left by the canonists at the Reformation. They seemed to threaten the business – and so the incomes – of the Common Lawyers.

CHAPTER 7

THE LEGAL PROFESSION

GENTLEMEN, ADMINISTRATORS AND LAWYERS

ADMINISTRATORS, not lawyers, framed the earliest writs
and laid down the basic processes of the law. They came from
two sources: the Church, and the gentlemen who counselled
the magnates. Both these groups served king and lords as
administrators before they did so as justices and attorneys.
Churchmen staffed the royal administration because they
were literate. This has been orthodox history much longer
than the realization that even in the twelfth century there
were plenty of literate laymen. Illogically, the country
gentleman has been regarded as 'a rather bellicose Sir Roger
de Coverley' at home, yet in Parliament as a shrewd politician 'who for a generation of scholars seems to have lost
his rusticity on the way to Westminster'. The truth is that
the magnates, needing businesslike stewards as much as
warriors, trained the gentry for their centuries-long position
as the real administrators of England. The earl of Lancaster
would retain a lesser lord to come when summoned, with a
knight in attendance, '*pur counseiller*', to give counsel. Laymen like these continued to administer the magnates'
patrimonies for the king when they escheated to him. Men
who were the *de facto* rulers of the countryside moved easily
from private to public service, and knights and squires began
to appear even in the king's council.[1]

The national system, part judicial, part administrative,
developed by Henry I and Henry II for the repression of
crime, could not have worked without drawing on the land-
holders for coroners and jurymen. Nor could it have worked
if some at least of these men had not had administrative
experience. It is possible that the king went further, definitely

167

choosing to give essential functions to 'gentlemen-amateurs' out of a wish to economize in the number of clerical and semi-professional judges in his courts. As law grew more complicated, the administrative expertise of the gentry became legal expertise, and legal counsel became the service which the magnates wanted most. Law came to be a profession of the lesser gentleman with ability and ambition, the only career beside that of arms in which he could honourably engage. It was then only a matter of time before laymen ousted the clerics from the Bench.

The lawyers of England are by this time, the thirteenth century, 'worldly men, not men of the sterile caste; they marry and found families, some of which become as noble as any in the land; but they are in their way learned, cultivated men, linguists, logicians, tenacious disputants, true lovers of the nice case and the moot point. They are gregarious, clubable men, grouping themselves in hospices which become schools of law, multiplying manuscripts, arguing, learning and teaching, the great mediators between life and logic, a reasoning, reasonable element in the English nation.'[2]

THE EARLIEST JUDGES

The judges were a committee of the king's councillors: the justices of King's Bench long continued to take the council oath and the king occasionally sat with them as late as 1465. Because they began from this committee, each of the three great Common Law courts was presided over not by one but by a group of three or four *puisne* (pronounced 'puny') justices under a chief justice (in Exchequer they were 'barons' and the 'chief baron'). Yet by Henry III's reign the central courts were clearly something separate from the council. Specialization was taking place, and the judges were no longer all-purpose councillors drawn from the great ecclesiastical dignitaries. By the thirteenth century, benefices were the rewards rather than the qualifications of judges, who could obtain them without being even deacons: they were in the lowest orders.

Professional training appeared in the shape of apprentice-ship to some judge of the previous generation. The writer of the greatest medieval treatise on English law was Henry of Bracton, appointed a justice in eyre in 1245 and later a puisne justice of King's Bench. He also became chancellor of Exeter cathedral. He idolized and may at some time have been clerk both to William Raleigh, rector of Bratton Fleming (Bracton's probable birthplace), treasurer of Exeter, and bishop of Winchester, as well as the foremost of the king's judges; and the great judge, Martin of Pateshull, archdeacon of Norfolk and dean of St Paul's, whose clerk Raleigh had certainly been.[3]

The extensive training of a judge can be seen even better in the career of Ralph of Hengham, who was a judge's clerk before 1268, a justice of assize by 1270, a puisne justice in eyre in 1271 and a judge of Common Pleas in 1273–4. He was then transferred to the chief justiceship of the King's Bench. The number of clerkships in which such men could get a start was increasing, for the courts were acquiring a permanent staff. By the fifteenth century, these clerks (clerks in the modern sense) were no longer drawn from the pool of 'king's clerks' (still proper clerics) but from a newly prominent group of 'king's esquires'; or, where the appointments were not the king's but the chief justice's, from the 'swarming ranks of the students in the inns of court'.[4]

Much earlier still, churchmen had ceased to predominate among the judges of King's Bench, and after 1327 there seems to be record of only one clerical appointment. In the second half of the thirteenth century the legal responsibilities and needs of laymen had called into existence a numerous pro-fessional class beneath the judges. Lawrence del Brok, made a judge of Common Pleas in 1268, and Gilbert of Thornton, promoted direct to the chief justiceship of King's Bench in 1290 to replace the discredited Hengham, seem to have been the first in their respective courts to rise through the ranks of the gentlemen-lawyers, but that path rapidly became the usual one.[5]

THE LAY ATTORNEYS

The body of the legal profession was made up of *attorneys*. In Anglo-Saxon times even bishops appeared in court personally to put their cases, but, as courts and pleas multiplied in the Norman period, personal appearance on all occasions became impracticable. In the twelfth century, a party's place was often taken by a *responsalis* ('answerer'), the principal's friend or bailiff, who looked after all the necessary procedural moves. In the thirteenth century, 'responsalis' became 'attorney', but remained usually an unprofessional agent of the principal, appointed for a single case – a wife could fill the role. Professionalization perhaps began with monks who regularly represented their litigious communities in court. Then, some men would have no suitable friend or relation and had to employ clerks of the courts (who would have to be there throughout the lengthy process anyway) or servants of the sheriffs (more familiar to parties from 'the provinces'). Gradually, therefore, a pool of experienced attorneys grew up in each county, men who acquired business by first of all acting as sureties for litigants. The judges got to know these people, expected them to act professionally and punished them for 'speaking foolishly'.[6]

For a time there was a natural prejudice against the commercial exploitation of plaintiffs' necessity. Henry III ordered the closing of law schools. In 1292, however, Edward I found himself compelled to provide for the training of attorneys in King's Bench:

concerning attorneys and apprentices the lord King enjoined Mettingham [the Chief Justice] and his fellows to provide and ordain at their discretion a certain number, from every county, of the better, worthier and more promising students . . . and that those so chosen should follow the court and take part in its business, and no others.[7]

Though Edward I thought that 140 attorneys and apprentices was the ideal number for King's Bench, the actual number in the 1290s was nearer 30. But the profession was growing fast under the stimulus of the growing complication of procedure, and of pleading in a language, 'law-French', which ordinary men understood less and less. The attorney took over the business of buying the writs and other necessary documents. So that he could get court orders enrolled and obtain judicial writs (the writs necessary in the course of an action which the court could issue without recourse to Chancery), the attorney was grudgingly allowed access to the records of the court. The legal profession displaced the old clerical officials from many tasks. It was alleged in the early seventeenth century that the majority of cases were decided between the attorneys without the judges' knowledge; and the framing of all judicial writs and their entry in the rolls had fallen into the attorneys' hands by that date. The written pleadings, still framed by the clerks in the fifteenth century, were also drawn up by the attorneys in the seventeenth, though until the very end the clerks demanded the fees.

When, in the fourteenth century, the professional standards of the barristers came to be guarded by the Inns of Court, the 'common attorneys' who were not also barristers (i.e. who did not take part in the oral pleading in court) were not required to attend an inn and became inferior in status, and around 1600 they began to be officially excluded from the inns. Lacking this control, untrained attorneys multiplied in proportion to the numbers of middle-class litigants. The Parliament of 1402 complained of 'falsifications, deceits and disinheritances' caused by the excess of attorneys, many of them clerics and bailiffs 'little or entirely unlearned in the law and some of tender age'. The checks then imposed through the courts seem to have had some effect, because numbers remained fairly constant from *c*. 1400 to *c*. 1600. Then there was another sharp increase, the 313 attorneys of Common Pleas in 1578 becoming 1,383 by 1633.

A measure of order was preserved amongst the attorneys by the rule that each of them must practice in only one of the central courts, of which he was regarded as in some sense an official. The attorneys had much more in common with the clerks of the court than with the barristers. Both attorneys and clerks owed allegiance to a court, not to an Inn of Court, and were trained by apprenticeship. The clerks were in fact increasingly appointed from persons trained as attorneys. In 'Hell' and, for less formal business, in the church of the London parish where the chief justice resided, the clerks and attorneys of Common Pleas practised their own special mystery. A church like St Bartholomew's, Smithfield, was a convenient place for 'the clerks with the rolls and writs of the Common Bench and the attorneys' to 'come together after the noon meal' during term. Towards 1500, however, the court officials were settling into chambers in or near the Inns of Court, where the barristers and serjeants lived.

SERJEANTS-AT-LAW AND BARRISTERS

The unversed litigant needed someone to say the right thing for him during pleading even more than he needed an attorney to go through the procedural moves. Some of the new profession specialized in the techniques of essoining, some in pleading. The pleader stood beside the litigant prompting him, but not replacing him – the litigant had to take the pleader's words as his own. The professional pleader, like the attorney, was for long a suspect figure, especially in the manor-courts, and in 1297 he was banned from the Exchequer. Nevertheless, by 1235 there were several 'advocates or counters' (Latin: *narratores*) in Common Pleas, and in 1275 there is a reference to a 'serjeant-counter'. The victory of the term *serjeant* for the pleader (by 1310, *serjeant-at-law*) suggests that he had become the permanent and necessary servant of the great men of the realm, who were also great litigants. In the 1270s a rank of 'king's serjeant' was already appearing within the group of serjeants-at-law. The twenty or so 1 .1 in the larger group were the *counsel* of their masters on every legal question – sometimes actually members of their permanent councils – but they were also available to be 'retained' by anyone with a case to argue in Common Pleas. [8]

The serjeants were the people who specialized in the substance of legal disputes, and in Henry III's reign it was they who kept the clerical judges on their metal. The particularly brilliant group of advocates who flourished between 1290 and 1310 lured some of the judges well out of their depth. By then, though, the king was recruiting the judges increasingly from the ranks of the serjeants. Of eighty-six advocates who became serjeants between 1400 and 1500, fifty-eight went on to be judges. The consequences of the fusion of the judiciary with the legal profession were immense. Being a judge became largely a matter of technical skill, not of government or politics. The common experience of judge and advocate led to a cooperation which expedited cases. At the same time, judges who could remember trying the same tricks themselves were healthily sceptical of meretricious brilliance in pleading. Success depended on quick and keen thinking, not – till the Renaissance at least – on showy oratory.

The serjeants worked mainly in Common Pleas, where they soon obtained a monopoly of the right to speak. For some time, mere attorneys continued to plead in King's Bench, though serjeants might be called in for difficult matters. The distinction here was in the quality of the work performed and the pay demanded: the serjeants were those who received regular retaining fees.[9] The serjeant-at-law of Chaucer's time was the prince of his profession, a man

who paid his calls
Wary and wise, for clients at St Paul's. . . .
He often had been Justice of Assize. . . .
His fame and learning and his high position
Had won him many a robe and many a fee.
There was no such conveyancer as he;
All was fee-simple to his strong digestion,
Not one conveyance could be called in question.
Though there was none so busy as was he
He was less busy than he seemed to be. . . .
He could dictate defences or draft deeds:
No one could pinch a comma from his screeds. . . .[10]

These powerful men, whose oath talked of loyalty to their clients, not of service to the court, were in the fifteenth century hardly more numerous than the judges. They were appointed by royal writ and installed with far greater splendour than were the judges; with such costly splendour indeed that many tried to evade the honour and in 1412 a £1,000 fine had to be imposed for refusal. About eight serjeants were usually created from the apprentices at one time, and they would together provide 'a feast and entertainment such as are held at the coronation of a king, which lasts seven days'. The new serjeants would give 'to each prince, duke and archbishop present at that solemnity, and to the chancellor and treasurer of England, a ring of the value of £1 6s. 8d. . . .' The king himself would sometimes attend. The coif (a close-fitting cap of white lawn) which the judges wore they wore as serjeants, and neither judge nor serjeant ever doffed his coif 'even in the presence of the king, even though he is talking to His Highness'.[11]

As Chaucer indicates, the serjeants consulted with their clients in St Paul's, where a stand against one of the pillars of the porch was allotted to each of them. When pleading became largely written, their business seemed likely to be lost to the clerks of the court who framed the pleas. But they succeeded in keeping the prerogative to sign special pleas, while they moved to the new techniques of examining witnesses and presenting evidence.

Around 1300, judges and serjeants were training up their successors by experience in court. The judges of the court often addressed remarks to the *apprentices*, who are mentioned in the writ of 1292. The presence of the apprentices may first have inspired the judges to make their decisions into general statements of law. The apprentices, for their part, were anything but overawed by the atmosphere of the court, and were not afraid to contradict the chancellor himself. What was said in that part of the court set aside for them and jocularly known as 'the crib' was sometimes thought worth recording in the Year Books.[12] After all, a man could remain an 'apprentice' for a lifetime if he did not become a serjeant, and he might have been earning his living for years as a common attorney.

At the Inns of Court, when these had become the centres of legal education, a student became a serjeant only after twenty years or so, by which time he would have married, obtained a private legal practice and held public office. When the profession of law became too esoteric for training by apprenticeship alone, the inns replaced the actual courts as at once the seminaries and the trade unions of the pleaders. But the students remained 'apprentices' till they were entitled to betake themselves to one of the two serjeants' inns, from which they and the judges would still often return to dine in their 'old college', their inn of court. It was from one of the activities of the inn that the senior apprentices, the advocates who were not serjeants, took their name of *barristers* (properly 'utter' or 'outer' barristers). They sat on the form or 'bar', in those outermost places reserved for senior students called upon to argue at the moots or mock courts.

The serjeants had always left some routine matters to the apprentices, even in Common Pleas, and in the other courts the barristers' business was increased by the concern of litigants to take their problems where an expensive serjeant was not essential. The greatest opportunities for the barrister were in the service of the Crown, for the king's serjeants disdained the emerging offices of solicitor-general and attorney-general. The disdain was misguided; after the middle of the sixteenth century, barristers were promoted regularly from those two offices to judgeships, only then taking the degree of serjeant as a matter of form.

SOLICITORS AND CONVEYANCERS

The barristers were products of the Inns of Court in London and did most of their work at Westminster. They relied upon the ordinary attorneys, who did not need to go to the inns and practised all over the country, to send them clients who wanted opinions on their claims and advocates to argue them in court.

The evolution of the intermediary between client and advocate, whom we call the *solicitor*, was a long one. From the earliest times a number of attorneys had often to act together to carry a case through to its conclusion. One would be needed to represent the party at the hearing in Westminster Hall, another to attend the trial at *nisi prius* in the county; and the litigant might appoint some more for safety's sake. In 1285, at a time when attorneys had normally to be appointed with great formality for each action separately, magnates with lands in many counties were conceded the privilege of having 'general attorneys' to follow the eyre and act in any cases which might arise. At Westminster each attorney was confined to a single court, though magnates became accustomed to conducting multiple litigation in several courts at once. Since there it was both unlawful and impracticable to have a single general attorney, persistent litigants tended to retain one legal adviser to engage and organize a staff of attorneys and serjeants. By 1300 cases are recorded where attorneys acted like modern solicitors in retaining and instructing counsel.

As, after 1400, the barristers gained a monopoly of audience in King's Bench equivalent to that achieved earlier by the serjeants in Common Pleas, attorneys had to seek a living at a variety of legal work outside the courts. The law was mostly about land, so the earliest type of attorney to be called a solicitor (the name appears in the second decade of the fifteenth century) was a kind of land agent who 'solicited' or instigated pleas to defend and increase his master's estates.

James Gresham, who figures prominently in the *Paston Letters*, was such a man. He sends writs for his master, Sir John Paston – 'item, the *certiorari* for my mistress your mother . . . item, I send you a *distringas* against Tudenham' – and, on the other side, a long list of writs out against Sir John. He works on the lord chancellor to obtain commissions of oyer and terminer consisting of men friendly to Paston to hear Paston's suits, and he keeps his master informed of the movements of the justices. He deals with judges and serjeants.

And against all the difficulties of communications, which do much to explain the appearance of such agents, Gresham kept Paston in Norfolk informed of the progress of his suits in London:

> As touching the friar he abideth in law upon our plea of profession, like as I sent you word by writing, which I sent you in a box with other stuff by a man of the Archdeacon of Richmond. I endorsed it thus: 'To William Plumstede, with my Lord of Winchester, or to John Paston'. . . . We should have amended our plea of profession, but then your counsel feareth he would take an issue that he is not professed. . . . The day of the assizes in Norfolk is die Veneris proximo post Festum Nativitatis. . . . As touching the suit against Osbern. . . . As touching Drew Barantyn. . . .[13]

Such men are hardly to be described in legal terms alone. They were the general business agents of the gentry, of whose business litigation was indeed so much. Gresham added the duties of news correspondent to the rest: 'This same Monday,' he wrote in August 1450, 'goeth my Lord Chancellor . . . into Kent to sit upon an *oier* and *determyner*. . . . And this same Wednesday was it told that Cherbourg is goon, and we have not now a foot of land in Normandy. . . .' A solicitor on the national scale was Thomas Cromwell, who rose from wool-dealing, money-lending, and a practice in Chancery and the conciliar courts, to the managing of Henry VIII's divorce case, and the drafting and guiding through Parliament of the statutes which made the English Reformation.

In the sixteenth century the solicitors became an important part of the attorneys' profession. The new humanist education of the gentry was less practical and legal, so that legal agents were in greater demand. In addition, the printing of law books in the first half of the century made a little profitable learning immediately available to young students, tempted thereby to cut short the years of practical training at an Inn of Court which led to advocacy. One last factor was the permanent settlement of many lawyers throughout the year in the region on the west side of the City of London where the Inns of Court still stand. The country solicitors were left to provide the London specialists with work, and became the actual clients of the city men: the rule was established that the barrister must sue the solicitor, not the litigant, for his fees. As a solicitor, the attorney remained, and still is, an essential officer of the court, for without him a litigant could not retain a barrister, nor the barrister find trade.

Like all middlemen, the solicitor was despised as a profiteer, and his social usefulness was slow to be recognized. All the antique prejudices against professional legal representation were turned against him. Lord Chancellor Egerton thought solicitors 'caterpillars of the commonwealth' against whom charges of maintenance would lie. 'Grasshoppers of Egypt . . . devourers of men's estates by contention, and prolonging suits to make them without end', was how another described this 'new sort of people called solicitors, unknown to the records of the law. . . .'[14]

Some students not intending to become barristers managed to avoid the fate of the attorneys who were thrust out of the inns by specializing in more respectable departments of the legal profession. These 'practitioners under the bar' were 'pleaders' (necessary again, now that barristers had forsaken the formalities of pleading for the presenting of evidence and arguing of matters of substance), 'equity draftsmen' and 'conveyancers'.

The drafting of deeds of conveyance was as old as the law. Anglo-Saxon charters were drafted by the beneficiaries, and great abbeys and the households of some bishops could afford *scriptoria* (writing shops) which would do the writing – not to mention the systematic forging – of charters for other churches as well as their own. The Chancery and these 'private' scriptoria provided a fair-sized pool of professional scribes moving between public and private service; and the clerks of the courts of law were an additional group favourably placed to secure conveyancing business. The machinery of the fine, the practice of enrolling deeds on the dorse of court rolls, and Henry VIII's Statute of Enrollment also gave the government clerks a large share in the profits of conveyancing though the attorney of the parties came to do the actual work.[15]

From *c.* 1350 there was a London company of scriveners with a monopoly of the writing of certain legal documents, but the scriveners did not write so well as the Chancery clerks and their influence on conveyancing was never great. In fact, they had at length to swear to draw 'no deed touching inheritance nor other deed of great charge . . . without good advice and confirmation of counsel'. A conveyancer needed to be expert in the law which determined the validity of his products, so the attorney was given and still retains a monopoly of legal drafting; and, anyway, the scriveners turned to more lucrative and sometimes doubtfully legal activities as investment brokers. Many of the 'attorneys' who took up conveyancing were little more reputable. Probably the parish clergy had always done some of the writing required by the transactions of the villeins. William Sheppard's conveyancing manual, *A Touchstone of Common Assurances* (1641), asserts the existence in every parish of 'an unlearned, and yet confident, pragmatical attorney . . . or a lawless scrivener, that . . . never read more law than is on the backside of Littleton; or an ignorant vicar, or it may be a blacksmith, carpenter or weaver . . . and yet as apt and able (if you will believe themselves) . . . to make a conveyance'.

THE STAFF OF THE COURTS AND THE CROWN'S LAW OFFICERS

The three *prothonotaries* or senior clerks of the court of Common Pleas were responsible for entering the pleadings on the rolls, gave opinions on technical matters and assessed costs. The office of *keeper of the writs*, sometimes called the principal clerkship of the court, was always held by a courtier from the fifteenth century, and was exercised by deputy: it carried responsibility for the records in current use, kept in St Bartholomew's, Smithfield. The two *chirographers* looked after 'the feet of fines', probably in the chapter-house of Westminster Abbey, but their offices, chiefly valuable for the fees, were farmed (i.e. rented out) by the seventeenth century. The twelve *filacers* (literally the 'filers' of writs) in theory made out the judicial writs and entered the steps of mesne process on the rolls (the attorneys actually did it, in the end); and the *exigenter* made out the writs beginning the process of outlawry. The *clerk of the treasury* ('the clerk of hell'), originally the personal servant of the chief justice, who was finally responsible for the official records of the court, looked after the completed plea-rolls. The wardenship of the Fleet Prison counted as an office of the court and was also held in serjeanty: it could thus 'come to a man by descent and inheritance in the manner of lands and tenements', and in Edward IV's reign was in fact held in tail by a woman. The *keeper of the hanaper* accounted for all the fees paid into the court. The clerical organization of King's Bench was similar to that of Common Pleas, except that there was one extra official of great importance – *the clerk of the crown and attorney of King's Bench:* he was responsible for the framing, reading and recording of criminal indictments in the court, functions now performed by the Crown Office of the Supreme Court of Judicature.[16]

Since public prosecution was for the most part modelled on the private suit, the king had to have his own legal representatives in the courts, and these constituted a middle group between the bulk of the legal profession and the judges and clerks. Attorneys employed by the king generally took over from the appellors and private informers the job of prosecuting criminals and presenting the case against them in court. The first official guardians of the king's interest in King's Bench had been the judges themselves, who were keeping a second set of plea-rolls in the thirteenth century (the *Rex* rolls) as memoranda of the cases which were being prosecuted for the king. By 1247, however, Lawrence del Brok was being retained by the king to act as his permanent attorney in King's Bench. Thenceforth the office was continuous, and the king's attorney had often to engage other attorneys to act in particular cases. He needed special facilities, such as access to *veredicta* presented to the court, and he took over the keeping of memoranda of the king's suits: his rolls, sometimes called the *Controlment Rolls*, included copies of indictments, lists of prisoners and confessions of approvers. Thus his full title became 'clerk of the crown and attorney of King's Bench' and his shorter name 'the coroner of England', since he looked after the king's interests in the central court as the ordinary coroner did in his county.[17]

Occasionally, of course, the king was concerned in one of the 'civil' actions begun by writ which were normally heard in Common Pleas. He would then engage a serjeant to plead his case. But by far the most frequent cases of interest to the king arose in the eyre on writs of *quo warranto*, which required the defendant to show 'by what right' he exercised a *franchise* – rights of justice or other privileges normally reserved to the king. When, by the Statute of Gloucester of 1278, Edward I demanded that *every* franchise-holder should appear in the eyre to prove his title (ideally by producing a charter of grant), he retained three serjeants to act for him. *King's serjeants* were appointed in each subsequent eyre, but when that court fell into disuse in the 1290s their number was reduced to one king's serjeant in Common Pleas. In 1315, however, the king retained four very distinguished serjeants, two of whom were raised to the bench of Common Pleas in 1320. The king's serjeants had also to operate in the courts of Exchequer, Chancery and Parliament, and from Edward II's reign were summoned to sessions of Parliament along with the judges. It was their duty, in addition to pleading for the king, to act free of charge for very poor suitors.

There was not much distinction at that time between a serjeant and an attorney, except that the former's fee was just twice the latter's. So, no *king's attorneys* were appointed in Common Pleas till 1315: the king's serjeants were sufficient. We then find king's attorneys working with king's serjeants on the same cases according to the division of functions developing in the profession as a whole. The king's attorney in Common Pleas was never the court's officer as the attorney of King's Bench was, perhaps because the king's interest was not so intrinsic in every case there, but in the fifteenth century he was able instead to become the *attorney-general*, with universal responsibility for prosecuting the king's suits and power to appoint deputies. A king's solicitor also existed by 1461, and from 1530 customarily succeeded to the attorney-generalship. The attorney-general and solicitor-general, uncommitted to judicial impartiality, their task rather to advance royal aims by litigation, were by the end of the sixteenth century important political figures.

It was natural, though, that the serjeants-at-law should scorn to move to these positions, which might be more powerful but were professionally inferior. On the other hand, mere attorneys and solicitors soon could not aspire to them, and the barristers were thus given their chance to ascend through the attorney-generalship and solicitor-generalship to the highest judgeships. Barristers began in the king's service as *king's counsel learned in the law*, retained to assist the attorney-general and solicitor-general when called upon. King's counsel ranked next below the serjeants, whom in modern times they were to oust from their preeminence in the profession of advocacy. They sat along with the judges and king's serjeants in Parliament, in due precedence upon the woolsacks, but by the end of the eighteenth century their duties for the crown were nominal only.

The king's serjeants were already half-way to being judges. Not only were they sent with the eyre to plead in *quo warranto* cases, but they served with the judges on special commissions into the counties, especially where the king's rights were concerned. The recorded judgments of the courts sound more and more like serjeants' arguments. So there came the momentous change by which the judges ceased to be drawn from the clerks of the court and a single legal career was established, leading an able student up through advocacy to the bench. The judges were drawn from the ranks of the serjeants, and more than half of them in the fifteenth century from the king's serjeants. After their promotion they often continued to live in one of the serjeants' inns. But the further development of the crown's legal service prevented the serjeants from obtaining a monopoly of the judiciary, and kept the career wide open to talent. The sixteenth-century attorney-general and solicitor-general were as prominent in the proceedings in court as the serjeants were.[18] From the middle of the sixteenth century to almost the present day, the holding of one of the two offices has been the quickest way to the chancellorship and the chief justiceships, the serjeants, as long as they lasted, being confined to the *puisne* justiceships.

COUNTRY LAWYERS

It would be a mistake to conclude that lawyers were mainly to be found in London. There were two poles to English legal activity, Westminster and the local community of shire, borough or manor. English private law was mainly about land; the solicitor began as a land agent; and law, if not order, permeated the countryside. The action of the sheriff of the county was essential to Common Law procedures, and the central courts were organized to deal with cases by their counties of origin: each clerk had an area allotted to him, from which to enroll the pleas. From time to time the judges and serjeants set off on horseback from Westminster into the uncertain weather, roads and hostelries of distant counties, the temper of whose inhabitants was often more uncertain still, to sort out the disputes arising from the clashes of local rivalries. With them for a change of air went clerks and attorneys of the Bench, one of whom would act by special commission as clerk of the assizes and take back the rolls of the circuit to keep in his London chambers.

The justices of the peace tried to imitate the lordly judges of Westminster. Quarter-sessions began with a lengthy 'charge' by the senior justice to the jurors – a sort of review of the moral state of the nation.

Our good Queen is the supreme executioner of all her laws. Between her Highness and you, in this part of the law, stand we that are justices of her peace. . . . And as it pleaseth her Highness to use us as the mouth of her laws in this behalf (for indeed we ought to be *lex loquens*, a speaking law), so also she appointeth you that be jurors in place of the eyes of the same law.[19]

But the influence from above should not be overestimated.

The English legal system was built on the gentleman-amateur justice, who merges, as we look back into feudal times, with the court owner. The judges at Westminster were themselves of this landowning class and usually had personal connexions with the regions where they heard assizes.

Many of the J.P.s would certainly have been to that 'gentlemen's university', the Inns of Court, and a few would have worked as local attorneys. The return of cases from Westminster to the counties for trial at *nisi prius* required the existence of a local profession, and magnates with scattered properties needed considerable legal staffs to defend their interests in local courts. John Estgate acted for Margaret Paston and others in both the borough-court of Norwich and the bishop's consistory court there. The staple work of the local attorney was conveyancing and rent-collecting for the aristocracy, and particularly the stewardship of the lord's manorial courts, or courts-baron, or courts-leet. Courts-leet existed where the twice-yearly great sessions of the hundreds held at the sheriff's 'tourn' had fallen into private hands and been merged with manor-courts: they dealt mostly with copyhold matters and public nuisances such as the obstruction of the rights of way by dung-heaps, but they could be made lucrative enough to others besides the steward. In 1455 a petition was presented to Parliament against the increase in the number of attorneys in the seignorial courts of Norfolk and Suffolk, 'which go to every fair, market and other places where congregation of people is and stir procure move and excite people to make untrue suits'. Even in the thirteenth century the counsel of a lawyer was not out of reach of a villein.[20]

A more worthy lawyer wishing to practise locally could hope to become the clerk of the commission of the peace for his county. Edmund Wykes, clerk of the peace for Somerset from *c.* 1611 to *c.* 1637, was a barrister and eventually became recorder of the town of Wells. He received quantities of petitions to the J.P.s, provided a rudimentary legal service to petitioners, and was an all-powerful executive officer. He received the records of preliminary examinations of criminals from the legally untrained private clerks maintained by each of the hundred or so county justices, and proceeded to frame indictments for submission to the grand jury, to record informations, and to issue warrants. The routine work was done by a permanent staff of half a dozen underclerks, comparable to the clerk's modern staff. These again were attorneys, who took the posts as a normal step in their professional careers. Sometimes they also acted as town clerks, for the local profession of the law merged into a municipal government service.[21]

The highest local recognition of a lawyer's distinction was to be made 'standing counsel' to a borough and then its *recorder*, with which would very often go appointment to the county commission of the peace and election to Parliament as one of the borough's two representatives. James Warnecombe of Ivington, who began his legal education at the Inner Temple in 1537, became standing counsel to Ludlow, Leominster and Hereford; recorder of Ludlow in 1551 and M.P. in 1554; a Herefordshire J.P. in 1554 and sheriff of the county in 1576; M.P. for Leominster in 1555; and mayor and M.P. at Hereford in 1571. Perhaps it was legal prolixity which earned him the nickname in Parliament of 'Warnecombe the weary'. Leominster was assiduous in sending gifts to Warnecombe in return for his legal counsel, which involved such work as obtaining new charters for the town.[22] The office of recorder had arisen because in the later Middle Ages boroughs had often been granted the right by charter to have their own J.P.s. The boroughs valued the right chiefly in its negative aspect, as removing them from the interference of the county magistrates, and were glad enough to pay a barrister to do the work of holding sessions.

THE SCHOOLS OF THE COMMON LAWYERS

John Stow wrote, at the end of Queen Elizabeth's reign, that in and about the city of London there was 'a whole university . . . of students, practicers or pleaders, and judges of the laws of this realm, not living of common stipends, as in other universities . . . but of their own private maintenance . . . for that the younger sort are either gentlemen or the sons of gentlemen, or of other most wealthy persons'. Stow goes on to name the colleges of the 'university': the four 'houses of court', the Inner Temple and the Middle Temple in Fleet Street, Lincoln's Inn 'in Chancery Lane by the old Temple' and Gray's Inn in Holborn (all still very much alive); nine 'houses of chancery' (now vanished); and three serjeants' inns (also gone). Sir John Fortescue, 130 years earlier, already knew of four *inns of court*, each containing at least 200 students, and of ten 'lesser inns . . . called Inns of Chancery', each with 100 students. The students of the Inns of Chancery were 'for the most part, young men, learning the originals and something of the elements of law, who, becoming proficient therein as they mature, are absorbed into . . . the Inns of Court'; which, according to a later author, 'received not the Gudgeons and Smelts but the Polypuses and Leviathans, the Behemoths and Gyants of the Law'.[23]

The origins of the Inns of Court must probably remain conjectural. The problem centres on their relationship to the Inns of Chancery. Was Lincoln's Inn, which seems to have been in existence in 1311, then one of the Inns of Chancery; and did the Inns of Court only slowly separate themselves from the common run of Chancery inns to become schools of advanced study? In support of this thesis is the fact that in early times the Chancery inns seem to have produced barristers and even serjeants: and that the connexion of specific Inns of Chancery with specific inns of court, which provided 'readers' for their satellite schools, was not finally established till Henry VIII's reign.[24]

The development of the Inns of Chancery is clearer. They were simply the hostels of the clerks of the royal Chancery, but they began in the fourteenth century to admit students to practise the clerical arts on the drafting of 'writs of course'. The drafting of writs was the factor common to the training of both the Chancery clerks and the lawyers. The oldest of these Chancery hostels (it can be detected in Edward I's reign), the inn kept by the master of the rolls in the building in Chancery Lane originally used to house converted Jews, was not destined to become a legal inn at all: it has grown into the Public Record Office. But by 1344 nearby Clifford's Inn was occupied by 'the apprentices of the bench'; and law students had crowded out the original inmates of the Inns of Chancery before Fortescue's time. These inns, it should be emphasized, were houses of Common Lawyers: they had nothing to do with Chancery as a court.[25]

The inns were at first held on lease by their occupants, and some of them took their names from the lessor (a bishop, perhaps, with a little-used London house), some from the leader of the clerks in the house, some from the locality. The Inner and Middle Temple grew from the church and inn of the Templars, the military order dissolved in 1312; Lincoln's Inn may have been deliberately founded by the Earl of Lincoln, one of Edward I's leading councillors, in 1292, when provision was made for the attorneys in King's Bench. As early as 1331 there were arrangements for the free access of the clerks of Chancery through the New Temple to the river, between sunrise and sunset, so that they could go by boat to Westminster, itself lacking suitable living accommodation. As Fortescue put it, the inns were situated between the courts, 'so that the students are able to attend them daily', and the city, 'richest . . . in all the necessaries of life' but 'where the tumult of the crowd could disturb the students' quiet'.

The impulses towards the formation of the inns were an inextricable mixture of those which had brought into being the medieval universities on the one hand and craft guilds on the other. They were not official schools, but the self-governing clubs of the apprentices whose training Edward I had assigned to the judges in the courts. Like the universities, they began as democratic organizations of the students, and they conferred a virtual degree (that of barrister); yet they were like guilds in that they soon controlled admission to the profession of advocate. Unlike the colleges of Oxford and Cambridge, they enjoyed no endowments from munificent 'founders'; but neither did they incur the restrictions applying to corporations, for they tied up what property they did acquire by means of that peculiarly English device, enfeoffment to trustees.[26]

The young Thomas More studied first at Oxford, then proceeded to New Inn (a Chancery inn) at the age of sixteen and to Lincoln's Inn at eighteen (in the year 1499). He was perhaps peculiar for the thoroughness of his education and the advanced age of his entry to the Inn of Court: some would go straight there at the age of fifteen or less. A man was usually admitted to an inn 'at the instance' of some existing member or officer who was a relation or county neighbour, and he would probably board in his sponsor's chambers. The occupants of chambers must sometimes have comprised a legal partnership or firm, but often the cramped accommodation was provided on a purely commercial basis, and one of the complaints against the prothonotaries and filacers who still entered the inns in the sixteenth century was that they let their chambers to ignorant persons. On entering Lincoln's Inn, Thomas More was 'pardoned [i.e. exempted from attendance during] four vacations'. The enforcement of residence in vacations was a very important stage in the growth of the inns, for they could not have survived on their income as hotels for lawyers in London only for the law terms. But what were they to do in vacations? It was at this point that they began to take up the education of lawyers, by means of mock courts (while the real ones were in recess) and of *readings*.[27]

After perhaps six years as a junior student and four as an utter barrister a student would be called upon to read a course of about sixteen lectures on statute-law throughout a 'learning vacation'. Readers gave two courses, five years apart, the first in the autumn and the second in lent, when the audience was larger; 'after which last reading they be named apprentices at the law, and ... these are, at the pleasure of the prince, to be advanced to the place of serjeants'. 'The apprentice' was now in fact a mature lawyer in a position of authority over his fellow-students.[28]

The inns were schools which preserved a national system of law quite different from the universal Roman Law taught in the universities. The crucial question is why the universities did not educate the English lawyer. Fortescue said it was because lawyers needed to be expert in English and a peculiar form of French, as well as in Latin, while at Oxford and Cambridge only Latin was used. But Fortescue was wrong in thinking that French composition was not taught at Oxford in his day: moreover conveyancing, the forms of mortgages and fines and so on, had been taught there since the thirteenth century. At Oxford many of the young men had once been trained who went on to write the lords' letters, keep their courts, and assist them in their public functions as coroners and sheriffs. Obviously it was the location of the courts at Westminster which took legal education out of the orbit of the universities and simultaneously away from the influence of Roman–Canon Law.[29]

Around the beginning of the sixteenth century a spell at Oxford or Cambridge, often instead of attendance at an Inn of Chancery, once more became the normal introduction to the study of law. Members of the Paston family had been going from Cambridge to the Inns of Court several decades before Thomas More went from Oxford to New Inn, or Edward Hall, the chronicler on whom Shakespeare relied considerably in his historical plays, passed from Eton to King's College, Cambridge, and thence (not long before 1521) to Gray's Inn. The entry of the aristocracy into the universities at this time does not mean that the upper classes were turning from the barbarities of feudal law to the humane studies introduced by the Renaissance. Sir Thomas Elyot in his *Book Named the Governor* (1531) might protest against the setting of children of fourteen or fifteen to peruse the 'fardels and trusses' of legal authors before they had studied true philosophy, but the very title of his work gives the show away: the purpose of education was still to give 'gentlemen's children . . . the knowledge of government and rule in the commonwealth', and law was obviously a large part of this knowledge.[30]

So the gentry did not turn away from the Inns. Rather the inns colonized the universities, which were made to provide the elementary vocational training for the administrative career which they had previously provided for the clerical career. Of course the change did have effects upon the law. The youthful eloquence of the moot, praised by Elyot as a 'figure of the ancient rhetoric', was elevated to a higher place in the gentleman-lawyer's accomplishments, creating the modern image of the great advocate.

THE STAFF OF THE CONCILIAR COURTS AND THE CIVIL LAWYERS

Second to the chancellor, who sometimes had to be content with the title of 'lord keeper of the great seal', was the *Master of the Rolls*, who in Elizabeth's reign was also a privy councillor and summoned to sit in the parliament chamber. The M.R. was crucial because he commanded (and indeed, until 1527, accommodated in his hostel in Chancery Lane) the *six clerks* who controlled procedure as the chancery equivalents of prothonotaries and attorneys combined. The subsidiary equity judges, who spent much time deciding intermediate issues on commission from the chancellor, were the twelve *Masters in Chancery*, the original senior clerks of chancery as a secretariat. The new courts were riddled with sinecurism as quickly as the old. The clerkship of the Council in Star Chamber was certainly a sinecure in the hands of Sir Francis Bacon after 1608, for he was already solicitor-general when he got it.[31]

Much of the business in the new courts was, of course, promoted by the king; and in Star Chamber cases prosecuted by the attorney-general had priority. Many other cases in that court were brought by 'common solicitors': these were attorneys attempting to make a living out of statutory penalties. The courts of Wards and of Augmentations, and the councils in the North and in the Marches of Wales, each had its own attorney and in some cases its own solicitor to act for the king, who were amongst the most senior officers of the court: '*the* attorney of the Court of Wards' (for instance) was a very different matter from an ordinary attorney acting there. In the Court of High Commission and in the Court of Chivalry, the equivalent officers were called, through Roman-Law influence, 'king's advocates', while in the Court of Admiralty the king's representative was the *proctor* (there is still a Queen's Proctor in the Probate, Divorce and Admiralty Division, to oppose collusive divorce actions). In the courts both of Admiralty and Chivalry there were civil lawyers who acted as ordinary attorneys or proctors, and the chief clerks of these two courts were called *registrars*.[32]

The most interesting question about the practitioners in the conciliar courts concerns their training. Were they Roman lawyers ('civil lawyers' or 'civilians'), or canon lawyers, or neither? We cannot gauge the knowledge of Roman–Canon Law possessed by the churchmen who filled the office of chancellor in the Middle Ages, but it is unlikely that it was often extensive. After 1340 anti-clericalism sometimes caused laymen like Sir Robert Bourchier to be appointed (the chancellor was still then the king's chief minister), and on the downfall of Wolsey in 1529 Henry VIII chose a Common Lawyer and the son of a Common Law judge, Sir Thomas More, after considering the archbishop of Canterbury and the Duke of Suffolk. From that time all the chancellors were Common Lawyers except Sir Christopher Hatton (1587–91), a courtier without legal experience, and Bishop Williams (1621–5). As the Masters in Chancery turned to legal business, they also were drawn predominantly from the ranks of the Common Lawyers. The shortage of civilians in Chancery is shown by the practice of referring technical mercantile points to juries of merchants or the chancellors of dioceses. Since Star Chamber's own professional resources were slight, pleadings there were also more and more referred to commissioners for assessment – but this time to Common Law judges or King's Counsel.

By Elizabeth's reign the Master of the Rolls was the most prominent lawyer likely to be a civilian. The career of one Master of the Rolls displays almost all the legal offices filled from the ranks of the civil lawyers. Though he was formally admitted to the Inner Temple in 1580, Sir Julius Caesar, born Julius Caesar Adelmare, graduated as a Doctor of Laws (civil and canon) at Paris in 1581 and as a Doctor of Civil Law at Oxford in 1584. In October 1581 he became a commissioner for piracy cases, in 1583 a commissary of the bishop of London, and in 1584 the judge of the Admiralty Court. His subsequent career reads: Master in Chancery, 1588; Master of Requests, 1591; Chancellor of the Exchequer, 1606; Master of the Rolls, 1614. It appears that the Courts of Admiralty and Requests and the ecclesiastical courts employed civilians as proctors or advocates as well as judges, and that such men might also find openings in certain sections of Exchequer and Chancery. The Court of Chivalry, in which Caesar could play no part since it was in abeyance till the end of his life, relied upon civilians too.[33]

Where were these civilians found and trained? Though it is noteworthy that Caesar was an Italian who spent some time in Paris, a very old tradition of civilian learning is just distinguishable from the Roman–Canon Law of the church, which at home in England was so battered in the Reformation that the church courts were forced to employ civilians. Doubtless the sort of student who learnt the art of composition and the forms of conveyancing from the same masters at thirteenth-century Oxford or Northampton mostly acquired an undifferentiated smattering of Canon–Civil–Common Law, useful in the service of both ecclesiastical and lay magnates. Just how like their 'Roman Law' was to Justinian's (say) one can only guess. At any rate the peasantry found the accusation a useful and plausible one in the later Middle Ages that civil lawyers employed by grasping landlords were driving out the good old customs of the countryside. If there was the beginning of a Reception of Roman Law in England, it must be looked for at the local level, where Common Law procedures were less well established.[34]

As it happened, the Common Law was already so developed (proving capable for good measure of evolving its own written pleading), that Common Lawyers were more useful to the magnates than the civil lawyers. Though there were English law students at Bologna in the fifteenth century,

Roman Law in England must by then have been a bastar-
dized thing, for it needed complete reconstruction in the
sixteenth century. In 1538 Henry VIII forbade the study of
Canon Law, founding instead professorships of Civil Law at
Oxford and Cambridge. A little earlier, in 1511, the civilians
– mostly practitioners in Admiralty – had formed themselves
into an Association of Doctors of Law. These red-robed
doctors, their ranks swelled by practitioners in the Court of
Arches, were incorporated in 1565 at 'Doctors' Commons'
(a sort of Inn of Court) on the south side of St Paul's church-
yard. They were a strange community: they included no
permanent judges, but any of them might be commissioned
to decide a particular case, returning next day to practise as
an advocate. They numbered only about forty, and after the
promise of a great revival of Civil Law in the sixteenth
century had been disappointed, their prospects were progressively restricted. To Dickens their work was to seem only
'a very pleasant, profitable little affair of private theatricals,
presented to an uncommonly select audience'.

CHAPTER 8

LAWYERS AND LAW BOOKS

WRITTEN LAWS

BOOKS were as essential to the growth of the legal profession as records were to the progress of individual cases; and, since the law was built on precedent decisions, law books consisted mainly of the records in a digested form. Even the statutes made by 'the High Court of Parliament' could be regarded as judicial decisions on what the law actually was, and collections of statutes made up one, if not the most important type of law book. To be authoritative, such decisions did not need to be written down or published. Writ-charters, however, were essentially notifications to all the king's subjects of the grants made by him, and were meant to be read out in the relevant shire-courts; and because some of the most far-reaching legislation of the Norman and Angevin periods was in charter form – Henry I's coronation charter and John's Magna Carta, for instance – 'copies' of statutes began to be sent to the sheriffs for publication. ('Copies' is not quite the right word, because, as in the case of Magna Carta, there was no one 'original' or 'authoritative' document.)

Not until 1299 were statute-rolls kept, and these last until 1468. Around 1300, too, odd memoranda of proceedings in Parliament began to crystallize into the *Rolls of Parliament*, which last till 1503: these contain a good deal of the statutes, since they follow through the processes of law-making from the presentation of the petition or bill. But from the end of the fifteenth century actual master-texts of the statutes, and sometimes drafts as well, survive as separate documents in the Lords' Record Office. The advent of printing made the publication of laws much easier, accompanied as it was by

the increasing use of the vernacular in literature generally
and statutes in particular (fourteenth-century statutes had
been in French, thirteenth-century ones in Latin). But
printing also allowed much Tudor government to be carried
on not by statute but by ephemeral *proclamations*, copies of
which are still being laboriously tracked down.

When the great edition of the *Statutes of the Realm* was
commenced in 1810, private compilations had to be used to
supplement the very incomplete official records. In Henry I's
reign, the Old English laws were collected together in such
monastic compilations as the *Textus Roffensis*. The author of
the *Quadripartitus* (*c.* 1114) tried to arrange these laws in a
logical rather than chronological order, in work which was
the first in Europe to be concerned with 'a body of territorial
law which was neither Roman nor Canon'. But it seems to
have been during the period which included Magna Carta
and the Statute of Merton (1236) that lawyers realized that
a great new body of law was coming into existence; and by
1300 many handbooks of statutes were circulating amongst
them, the first statute-roll being only a continuation of one
such book. Because the laws of England have never been
codified, the making of collections of statutes has continued
to the present day. Too often the government itself did not
know what laws were in force, and the fourteenth-century
Vetus Codex in the Public Record Office may have been a
much-needed official reference book of extracts from statutes.[1]

THE REGISTER OF WRITS AND OTHER FORMULARIES

In Henry III's reign statements of English legal practice
were compiled for transmission to the king's justiciar in
Ireland; and one of these documents was an early *register of
writs*. Some collections of writs must have been made for the
Chancery clerks, but most seem to have been for the use of
monasteries, continually involved in litigation, or for attorneys.
Consequently, the many manuscript registers, while growing
steadily in size, vary considerably in content. But in all of them
the writs appear in the same general order, which has much to

tell us about the logic of English legal development. The final corpus, 'The Register of Writs Original and Judicial, printed at London by William Rastell' in 1531 (it contained 700 pages, as against the 10–12 pages, and 50 or 60 writs, of the earliest thirteenth-century registers), was so much the structure of English law itself that in Maitland's words 'to ask for its date would be like asking for the date of one of our great cathedrals'.[2]

The register was the starting-point of more general works on procedure. One of these was the great treatise 'Concerning the Laws and Customs of the Kingdom of England', written not long before the death of Henry II, customarily attributed to Henry's justiciar, Ranulf Glanvill, and built on Henry's new writs, Praecipe, Novel Disseisin and the rest. Thus, an example of the writ of Novel Disseisin is followed by the note that 'In this species of recognition no "essoin" is permitted. For . . . it spares no person, neither one of full age, nor a minor, nor will it even await a warrantor . . .' For centuries, legal treatises continued to be produced which were no more than collections of writs with a few comments.[3]

The Register was just the most important legal example of a very common medieval type of handbook, the *formulary*, recalled today by the books of etiquette telling you how to write a formal letter to a duke or a bishop. Under the heading of legal formularies come several collections of conveyancing styles, and a thirteenth-century treatise on French orthography – 'the plural of nouns and verbs ending in *e* is formed by adding a letter *z* thereto: e.g. *amez, enseignez*' – which must have been invaluable to pleaders and reporters of pleading. As if to emphasize that legal forms were only a variety of the formal ways in which all life was conducted, one thirteenth-century conveyancing treatise contains a form for the appeal to a father's generosity by an Oxford student *numismate carenti* ('in want of coin').[4]

PLEA-ROLLS, YEAR BOOKS AND REPORTS

From guides to procedure we move naturally to records of actual cases. Generally speaking, the Common Law courts kept bulky 'plea-rolls', any one of which (for a single term) might amount to a hundred closely-written membranes, about 2 ft long and 8 ins. wide, sewn together at the top to form something like a modern calendar: while the new courts, the Duchy of Lancaster, Privy Council and Star Chamber, retained the written pleadings and depositions in their original form and kept registers of their *acts*, *orders* and *decrees*. The official records were of little use in legal education, however, for they were difficult of access and gave only the formal stages of procedure: bill, demurrer, joinder in demurrer, judgment.[5] They omitted the discussions between the justices and serjeants, the opinions beginning 'Suppose that . . .', or 'I do not think he will have an action, because . . .', by which the substantive law grew.

For legal argument we have to go to the *Year Books*. Perhaps no episode in the history of English law has provoked so much discussion as the making of the Year Books, which cover the period from 1283 to 1536. What was the purpose of these French reports of cases in the Common Law courts, each year's grouped into a volume of which there are many manuscripts, varying considerably in content? It is probable that they had a semi-official status like the registers of writs and the collections of statutes – or modern law reports. But the manuscripts of the Year Books vary too much for them to have been fully official; they must be the private notes of the apprentices sitting in the 'crib'. This theory is compatible with the rapid organization of law reporting on a commercial basis. The texts needed in medieval universities were provided by the obligatory depositing in the university chests of theses which could then be hired out in sections or *pecia* for copying. If some comparable system obtained in the legal university of England, some of the discrepancies in Year Book manuscripts would be explained by the mistakes which arise in mechanical copying. The books, which circulated very widely, were probably made up from separate pamphlets issued at the end of the law terms by barristers – who may have been the readers in the inns – for the use of the students in the learning-vacations.[6]

The Year Books reflect three centuries of change in legal outlook, a growing consciousness of principles and opinions in law. They begin as offshoots of thirteenth-century writ-manuals like *Brevia Placitata*: they are at first the marginal notes of court practice which keep the manuals up to date. If examples from the plea-rolls were cited in thirteenth-century treatises, they were thus illustrations subsidiary to general theses. But the multiplication of working lawyers, and of the plea-rolls themselves, soon replaced such leisurely picking and choosing by a hasty and undirected reporting of every big case for its own sake as it rushed by. There came to be recorded what the apprentices heard – the uninhibited and exciting argumentation of the serjeants, as much as the ritual which the parties and officials enacted. Then, the day-to-day legal journalism of that heroic age of pleading which began about the year 1290, gave way to a more academic attitude to pleading, based on study ranging back through the lengthening series of the Year Books themselves. These consequently became more authoritative, and fewer and more expert reporters seem to have been operating.

A further logical step led to the *abridgements*, collections (perhaps first compiled as students' exercises) of the reports for several years at a time, condensed and arranged by subject-matter. All previous abridgements, and the Year Books too, were superseded by the *Grand Abridgement* of a judge of Common Pleas, Sir Anthony Fitzherbert, printed in 1516, which used an enormous range of reports, including one great source, 'Bracton's Note Book', that was not rediscovered by modern historians till 1887. 'Fitzherbert' was the bible of generations of lawyers, and the mostly procedural captions of its sections, from 'Abatement' to 'Withernam', dominated legal terminology. In one of the greatest ventures of the early days of printing, the Year Books were systematically published by Pynson between 1493 and 1528 and Tottell in the mid-sixteenth century. But even as they began to be printed, the Year Books were superseded by the new sorts of textbook: their production became intermittent and ceased for ever in 1536. The abridgements share responsibility for their disappearance with the advent of paper pleadings, which changed the whole nature of the advocate's art and inspired formularies called *books of entries* for the use of the attorneys and clerks who entered pleadings. The Year Books were characteristic of an age of public and oral pleading which had come to an end.[7]

Next from the abridgements developed the *reports* in a reasonably modern sense, which filled the place of the Year Books. The reports were Year Books and abridgements rolled into one, for they combined recording with learned comment on individual cases. At first intended for personal use rather than publication, they were soon collected and published by some pupil of the alleged reporter.[8] There is evidence that the judges in Star Chamber made notes on the cases before them, as a modern judge has to, for assistance in giving judgment; and it may be that such judges' notes were at the core of the early reports. The great reports of James Dyer, chief justice of Common Pleas, running from 1537 to 1582, and particularly Edmund Plowden's *Commentaries* (1550–80), were, however, explicit works of learning.

The crown and glory of the reports were Coke's thirteen volumes, which began to appear in 1600 and have ever since been known just as 'the Reports'. Coke set out to present every previous authority bearing on the case he happened to be reporting, and thus made his work what it still is – the main entrance into the study of medieval case-law. But for his own day Coke was less a reporter than a layer-down of the law. He assembled medieval 'precedents' which he often but dimly understood, to justify in the heat of a fierce constitutional battle his idea of what the law should be: and *that* his own immense authority for ever after made it. Even Sir Francis Bacon, who did not get on well with Coke, was constrained to admit that without the Reports, 'though they may have errors, and some peremptory and extra-judicial resolutions more than are warranted . . . the law by this time had almost been like a ship without ballast, for that the cases of modern experience are fled from them that adjudged and ruled in former times'.[9]

Because the books of entries covered formal pleading, the reports were more concerned with legal reasoning than the Year Books had been. But when he threaded his way through page after page of the arguments leading to the decision in *Shelley's Case*, Coke was completing a more fundamental change of emphasis in the law from procedure to argument and judgment. The Year Books reveal no concept of the importance of decisions (though later generations of lawyers were interested in them on account of the precedents they were thought to contain). Nor were even Coke's reports based on a clear idea of case-law. Rather as Bracton had, Coke put cases to his own purposes, 'turning every judgment into a string of general propositions' in a way (said Lord Chancellor Sugden, 1781–1875) 'least calculated to transmit a faithful report'. Yet because he chose to appeal to so many decided cases, so many precedents, it is no exaggeration to say that Coke established case-law.

Coke reported on cases in the old courts of King's Bench, Common Pleas and Exchequer. By the end of the sixteenth century the new courts had their reporters as well. The law reports varied enormously in quality over the centuries, but the 176 volumes of the modern collected edition, *The English Reports*, covering all the courts for the period to 1864, comprise the greatest mass of source material for legal history.

TEXTBOOKS

General treatises grew out of the special types of English manual, but under the inspiration of Roman–Canon Law. Glanvill's trail-blazing work contains comment on the writs which owes much in style to the school of Anglo-Norman canonists which had appeared in his lifetime; and we know that Richard I's justiciar, William Longchamp (*d.* 1197), tried to write a single code which would summarize English, Roman and canonical procedure. Roman–Canon Law was at that time procedural enough for an English lawyer to be immediately at home in it; but almost certainly it gave to English law a newly theoretical and substantive bent. This is apparent in such little things as Glanvill's remark that all pleas 'are either criminal or civil' (a generalization probably untrue of the English law of his day).

There can be little doubt that the pre-eminent medieval work on English law, the treatise *On the Laws and Customs of England* written by Henry of Bracton, a judge of King's Bench, about the middle of the thirteenth century, owes its form to Roman legal thought. Bracton made a gallant attempt to separate the substance of law from the procedure. He showed in fact that, however elaborate its superstructure might be, English law rested upon principles, acknowledged or unacknowledged. Long Romanist chapters on the different types of property or person ('There is also another and second division of things, because some are corporeal and others incorporeal ... incorporeal things are such as rights, which cannot be seen or touched, as the right of ... leading water ...'), or his classification of crimes as felonies and trespasses, may not have fitted the English law of his time particularly well. But without them it is difficult to see how that law could have avoided disintegration.[10]

In Edward I's reign Bracton was summarized for students in two little books by Chief Justice Hengham and emulated on a rather less grand scale by 'Fleta'. But the Bractonian tradition was remarkably short-lived, probably because these Latin treatises were characteristic of a time when legal education was available only in hybrid Roman–English law schools at Oxford and Northampton. When legal training was provided in the courts and then in the Inns of Court, the treatises in demand were the more practical and procedural ones like the Edwardian *Fet Asaver* and *Britton* – which had the additional advantage of being, like the Year Books, in French, the Common Lawyers' vernacular.

The tradition of practical treatises, usually confined to some particular section of the law, was continued in the readings at the Inns of Court, the equivalent for the statutes of the abridgements and reports of cases; by works on the law-merchant; and especially by manuals of conveyancing and the land-law. The latter were represented by the anonymous *Old Tenures* (late fourteenth century); and by the *Tenures* of Thomas Littleton, a judge of Common Pleas who died in 1481, a 'thoroughly medieval book written in decadent colonial French' which was nevertheless the greatest treatise since Bracton's and could be described by Coke as 'the most perfect and absolute work that ever was written in any human science'. There were handbooks, too, on practice in assizes and in the sessions of the peace. Assizes were reported and abridged like Westminster cases, but the J.P.s relied rather on distillations of their senior colleagues' everyday experience in such works as William Lambard's *Eirenarcha*, published in 1581.[11]

In 1569, *Bracton* was printed and at last exercised its due influence, for it inspired another comprehensive work, Coke's four *Institutes*, the first of which appeared in 1628. These rested on an unrivalled if uncritical knowledge of medieval law – the first institute was a commentary on Littleton, the third on Pleas of the Crown – and were once more profusely illustrated by cases (the section on murder by the contemporary Overbury scandal). Yet, by an admixture of the new sense of judicial purpose fostered in the courts of council and equity, they transformed that medievalism into the triumphant and aggressive Common Law which was Parliament's chief ally against Charles I.

JURISPRUDENCE AND LEGAL HISTORY

Coke's work shows the influence of the sixteenth-century growth of jurisprudence, that part of law which Bracton defined as 'the knowledge of divine and human things, the science of what is just and unjust'. Jurisprudence is concerned with the place of law in society and merges into social and political theory: thus Bracton discussed the Roman Law maxim, 'the law is what the king wills' and concluded that while it was certainly for the king to make particular laws, kingship was rather the product of law. Law was for the medieval man a prerequisite of any society, and societies could be distinguished according to their laws. Sir John

Fortescue, Chief Justice of King's Bench, wrote a book *In praise of the laws of England* (1468–71), which argued in detail for their superiority over their French and Roman equivalents: it took the conventional form of instructions to a young prince (Edward, son of Henry VI) on how to rule justly. For Fortescue, England's law and constitution (a limited monarchy: *regnum politicum et regale*) were the best in the world.[12]

Chancellor More wrote about 'the manners, customs, laws and ordinances of the Utopians' (1515–16), seeming to suggest that society would be better for fewer laws – but he may have had no very serious purpose in writing that amusing work. Sir Thomas Smith, in his *De Republica Anglorum*, attempted to show how 'England standeth and is governed at this day' (28 March 1565), not 'in that sort as Plato made his commonwealth ... nor as Sir Thomas More his Utopia, being ... vain imaginations, phantasies of Philosophers to occupy the time ...': he incidentally gives the first real description of an English trial. The sociological attitude appears in England in Chancellor Francis Bacon's essays (as it had in France in the essays of another lawyer, Montaigne). For Bacon 'all civil laws' were derived from nature 'but as streams', yet they were none the less essential to a settled society: 'Revenge is a kind of wild justice, which the more man's nature runs to, the more ought law to weed it out ...'[13]

It was natural that this way of looking at society should be transferred to the international level, especially by civilians concerned with maritime cases. It was the sub-title, *jus inter gentes*, of a work by Richard Zouche, appointed Judge of the Admiralty Court in 1641, which suggested to Jeremy Bentham the term, *international law*. To Zouche, war between nations was like the feud to Bacon, a primitive sort of justice which must be controlled by law. John Selden (1584–1654), wrote to prove, against Hugo Grotius, his Dutch contemporary and the pioneer of international law, that Britain had dominion over the surrounding seas.

The rise of the Court of Chancery posed questions which evoked much of the early jurisprudence: what theoretical justification was there for this new court? In his two *Dialogues*

between a Doctor of Divinity and a Student of the Common Law
(1523–32), a barrister of the Inner Temple named Christopher St Germain used his exceptional grasp of Canon Law and legal philosophy to establish conscience as the basis of equity. He maintained that life in its infinite variety threw up many problems which could only be solved with perfect justice by a chancellor free to exercise discretion according to his conscience. Selden, on the other hand, thought settled law and conscientious discretion incompatible: 'Equity is a Roguish thing: for Law we have a measure, know what to trust to; Equity is according to the Conscience of him that is Chancellor' – and that, said Selden, varied as much as the length of a chancellor's foot.[14]

It is not much of an exaggeration to say that legal history was brought to birth by the Common Law jurists in a 'cold war' with the civilians. Selden produced an edition of 'Fleta' with an unfriendly introduction on the place of Roman Law in England. He also denigrated the ecclesiastical courts, maintaining that 'Marriage is nothing but a Civil Contract', and that 'There's no such Thing as Spiritual Jurisdiction'. Amongst the rest of the surprising amount of good history to come out of this period of turmoil were Selden's edition of Fortescue's *De Laudibus*; his history of the judicial duel; the *Judicial Origins* of the great antiquary, Sir William Dugdale; Lambard's somewhat earlier pioneering work on the Anglo-Saxon laws; and, in the next generation, the *History of the Common Law* by Chief Justice Sir Matthew Hale (the first general history of English law), and his more valuable *History of the Pleas of the Crown*. Partisan versions of the law, backed by suitably coloured history, were obvious weapons in constitutional struggles. Coke twisted history to prove against the Stuart monarchy that Parliament was a court supreme over the king's council and all its offshoots.[15]

In the sixteenth century, printing and the writing of law books had important effects on each other. To the new printing trade, law books were as reliable a source of income as cookery books today; while the work of Pynson, the Rastells and Tottell encouraged the writing of legal textbooks and disseminated legal ideas far more widely. In the careers of John Rastell, who married Thomas More's sister, and of his son, William Rastell, who edited More's works and in 1558 became a judge of the Queen's Bench, printing was especially combined with legal and political activity. By 1600, legal literature was sufficiently extensive for William Fulbeck to give a critical survey of it in his *Direction or Preparation to the Study of the Law*.[16]

Printing perpetuated a rather barbarous lawyer's language. A 1688 edition of Dyer records that at the Salisbury assizes of 1631 a prisoner condemned by the Chief Justice of Common Pleas, '*ject un Brickbat a le dit Justice que narrowly mist*', for which was '*son dexter manue ampute*' and the man himself '*immediatment hange in presence de Court*'. Though Latin remained the language of plea-rolls till 1731, law-French had got into the new Parliament and statute-rolls at the end of the thirteenth century and did not entirely disappear from them till the early eighteenth. Despite an artificial attempt in 1362 to make pleading in English, law-French has been the patois of the majority of generations of English lawyers. It had originally been perfectly normal French. Only as the links between the English and French aristocracies were progressively severed did law-French become crabbed and technical. And only as it died as a language were its most useful words, like *defy*, *mortgage* and *defer*, freed to enter and enrich the English tongue.[17]

The uncouth but vivid language of the Year Book pleadings probably contributed as much to English literature as the rhetoric of Coke or Bacon or the advocates of any later time. Legal idioms are embedded in the language of most great English writers. From the early Germanic and the feudal law came 'lay a wager', 'beyond the pale', 'for the sake of', 'pay homage to', 'in defiance of', and 'in danger of' (a corruption of 'in the *dominium* [power] of'). Pleading gave us 'to plead for', 'special pleading', 'lend colour to', 'at

issue', 'in rejoinder' and 'vouch for'. Idioms from procedure
are 'to put one's case', 'make common cause with', 'in the
last resort', 'put out of court' and 'have no record of'; and
other aspects of law produce 'have no right to', 'mother-in-
law', 'man's estate', 'a moot point', 'a new lease of life',
'self-defence' and possibly 'red tape'. The richness of allu-
sion in the language of Shakespeare and the Authorized
Version of the Bible is achieved to a significant extent by
exploiting the legal terms which were on everybody's lips.[18]

THE LAWYERS IN SOCIETY

The dignity of the lawyers was reflected in their uniform,
which began as the richest and most fashionable court dress
of the time, presented to the lawyers by the king or noble
clients. At first the judges affected green robes in summer and
red in winter, topped from the fifteenth century by the white
coif almost hidden by a dark skull-cap. In the latter half of
Henry VI's reign the royal colour of scarlet was adopted for
the judges' full dress. The Tudor period added a limp square
cap (the black cap donned for other solemn occasions besides
the pronouncing of a death sentence) and, for the chief
justice, the golden ss collar, probably in origin a mark of
favour conferred at large by the Lancastrian kings. The lord
chancellor adopted his stylish black silk gown with gold
facings towards the end of the sixteenth century. By the mid-
seventeenth century, barristers had assumed something close
to their modern dress of a black gown and white neck-bands –
the short wig came later. King's counsel, the attorney-general
and solicitor-general, and recorders, marked their superiority amongst the barristers by having their gowns of silk;
and in the eighteenth century king's counsel clung to the full-
bottomed wig, along with judges and serjeants, long after it
had given way to the shorter type in lay fashion.[19]
The way to the leading places in such a company was
naturally long and hard: the reluctance to assume the rank
of serjeant shows that considerable ambition was necessary
to stay the course. Ability too was needed, but it was most

profitably deployed in acquiring friends at court. Even a Francis Bacon had to have the earl of Essex to back him for the solicitor-generalship. Competition was so fierce because high legal office was perhaps the straightest path to wealth and the topmost ranks of society. From Edward II's time judges were regularly knighted, while in Richard II's reign and in Charles I's, being a barrister seems to have carried the rank of esquire. Of course, as the scope of law widened, so did the social range of litigants and their lawyers, and the local attorney was often no more dignified than a small tradesman.[20]

The greatest lawyers of late-medieval England were on a level with the foremost London merchants, in whose wills they are named as executors and whose daughters they married: lawyers' sons entered trade, and merchants' sons the law. The nobility for a time looked askance at both law and trade, and branded one of Richard II's judges as 'not a gentleman, because he was the king's justice'. In Edward IV's reign there seems to have been a change, law being one of the chief skills which began to take 'new men', ordinary knights, to the leading places in the king's council. In 1483, a descendant of Sir William Howard, one of Edward I's judges, became duke of Norfolk. A descendant of judge William Paston was created earl of Yarmouth in 1679, and Viscount Cobham is the representative of a line made illustrious by Thomas Littleton. For many of the new leaders, however, legal training was only a formal episode in a career based on other foundations. Those who reached the nobility had often completed by a well-placed marriage what legal talent had but begun generations before – not till after 1660 was legal talent sufficient of itself.[21]

But this very association of the law with the other factors changing society was its peculiar importance as a profession. It was the only one capable of acting as a bridge between the merchants and the nobility, between money and land. The marriage which completed the ascent of bourgeois lawyers might inject new wealth into an impoverished nobility and new efficiency into the management of great estates. And by way of legal fees the work of the lawyers for the aristocracy could bring the profits of the land into trade.

Already in the fifteenth century there were some very wealthy men amongst the lawyers. The richest Londoner in 1436 was the Warden of the Fleet Prison – if not a lawyer, at least one who lived on the products of law; and the Recorder had long been the most highly paid of the city's own officials. Popular rumour spread fantastic stories of lawyers' fortunes. Spencer of Althorp, a Northamptonshire sheep-farmer of no great lineage, was thought around 1600 'to have by him the most money of any person in the kingdom', a position achieved largely by a marriage to the daughter of the prodigiously successful Common Lawyer, Sir Robert Catlin. Nicholas Bacon, the reputed son of an East Anglian sheep-reeve, had an income between £4,000 and £5,000 a year in 1575, when he was lord keeper, and was spending a quarter of it on his estates. His younger son, Francis, starting with a mere two or three hundred a year, may have been getting £15,000 just before his fall. Much lower in the social scale we find Thomas Stampe of Lincoln's Inn, late recorder of Wallingford: his fortune when he made his will in 1612 was indeterminate, because he had invested £300 in the voyage of the *Joan of London*, not yet returned from the Guinea coast.[22]

THE COST AND REPUTATION OF THE LAWYERS

If the figures given here are understood to be only very approximate indications of the relative place of lawyers in society, it may be said that in the early seventeenth century some £170,000 was being paid yearly in (mainly legal) fees to the Exchequer, Chancery, King's Bench, and Common Pleas, as compared with the king's (or government's) income of £618,000. The lawyers received perhaps £2 million a year from all sources, or a quarter of the income of the landed classes of which they were a part: the national income was £25–30 million. The net income from law of a puisne judge of Common Pleas was about £2,000 a year, of a six-clerk in

Chancery about the same, of the chief clerk in King's Bench (to which there had recently been a decisive shift of business from Common Pleas) around £5,000. By comparison, the lord treasurer made perhaps £7,000 a year from his office, a secretary of state £2,000, while the income of a reasonably prosperous London merchant was £2,500, and of an average peer from his land, £6,000. But precision is impossible: the greatest legal incomes had a wide margin where fees merged into bribes, which in the case of the lord keeper may have reached astronomical figures.[23]

Moreover, there **was** something feverish and impermanent about legal fortunes as there was not about even mercantile wealth. Francis Bacon, though the son of a lord keeper, had to start again from scratch. Heavy debts on the one hand and money-lending on the other were a normal part of a great lawyer's business. Nor were such gold mines acquired without a high capital expenditure which only several years of exploitation would recoup. The reversions of legal offices, with the normal exception of the judgeships, were bought and sold like the rest, at prices calculated as multiples of the offices' yearly income and adjusted to the age of the existing incumbents. The seventh reversion of a filacer's office worth £120 a year could fetch £1,100 even though three of the first six reversions were for two lives. The sale of offices seems strange to us, though it was general in all the great European countries of the time. No sense of public responsibility had yet replaced the identification of office with property – particularly natural to a lawyer – from which buying and selling logically followed. It is not certain that sale on a commercial basis was worse in effect than the distribution of office by noble patronage or even by royal appointment. The attempt of Elizabeth and the early Stuarts to increase their patronage in the courts was made simply to swell their revenues, and resulted in the creation of superfluous clerkships, and to real scandals like the auctioning of the mastership of the rolls for £15,000 in 1639.[24]

As property which had been dearly bought, legal office had to be exploited in ways which seem to us corrupt. Fees had to be extorted at every step of process, since no official could afford to give up what he had calculated on receiving. Part of the damages awarded to plaintiffs went into the pockets of the court officials, as the 'rake-off' known as *damna clericorum* or 'damages clere', only abolished by Charles II. Each single fee was no more than a shilling or two, so it was in the clerks' interest to prevent process from reaching a swift conclusion; and what Chief Justice Hale described as 'the scambling and scuffling between the protonotaries, every one striving to get as many [attorneys] as he can to bring grist to his mill', contributed to the building up of a legal underworld described by Richard Burton as 'so many locusts . . . gowned vultures . . . thieves and seminaries of discord . . . common hungry pettifoggers'.[25]

It was the expectation of presents, as well as of fees, which led Solicitor-General Bacon to seek the clerkship of the Council in Star Chamber, valuing it at £2,000 a year, though its salary was £26 13s. 4d. In 1621 Lord Chancellor Bacon was ruined by the disclosure of the presents he had been receiving from litigants in Chancery, though these had been abnormal only in their size. The importance of these gratuities can easily be exaggerated. The giving of valuable presents to those in high places, the king not excluded, especially on New Year's Day, was a custom which long endured. The hope was to gain the favour of those with power to speed the bureaucratic wheels, rather than to secure false decisions. Of all government, the highly procedural Common Law was most susceptible to such greasing; and the chancellor in particular was regarded not as a judge, but (so to speak) as a machine-tender who would only work if you bought him a drink. In the country, the clerk of the peace, able to decide the agenda of sessions, was comparable to the chancellor and was equally 'corrupt'. On the other hand, the rarity of false judgments is shewn by the indignant punishment they received. It should be noticed that a judge's salary (only £188 a year in 1600) was quite inadequate without gratuities.[26]

The pursuit of profit certainly damaged the efficiency if

not the integrity of the law. When documents and procedures were paid for by length, delay was the lawyer's business. Vexatious litigation – the harassing of an enemy by interminable and inconclusive suits – took its point from the expense of the law. Were the lawyers worth the cost to society? To an appreciable extent they worked only for themselves. Each of the courts was a 'liberty' protecting its officials from arrest and offering them special facilities for their own suits. Disputes between lawyers over fees were common. It is impossible to estimate how many other actions and prosecutions were inspired by the lawyers. Gilbert Sherman, attorney at the Common Law and therefore able to engage in law-suits without charge to himself, was accused in Star Chamber of beginning suits against his neighbours and then accepting payment to leave them in peace.[27]

Hostility has always outweighed any sense of their social value in the popular attitude to lawyers. 'The first thing we do, let's kill all the lawyers', says Dick to Jack Cade in Shakespeare's *Henry VI*. The historical Cade, the great rebel, proclaimed in 1450 that 'the law servyth of nowght ellys in these days, but for to do wrong, for nothing is sped almost but false maters by colour of the law for mede, drede and favor'. One medieval judge was popularly reported to have held up an abbess's action 'until one day she brought with her the more good-looking nuns of her house'. The subtlety of the lawyer was hated more than his greed (or lust). The advocate is the fox in the fable of Reynard the Fox. Any wickedness can be clothed with legality. 'Convey' is the lawyer's word for 'steal'. Advocacy is essentially dishonest:

> In law what plea so tainted and corrupt
> But being seasoned with a gracious voice
> Obscures the show of evil.[28]

LAWYERS AND POLITICS

In 1372 the election of lawyers as knights of the shire in parliament was forbidden, on the grounds that they presented petitions concerned with their patrons' private interests rather than with the common good. Yet some 40 of the 262 members of the parliament of 1422 were lawyers. The number of lawyer-M.P.s was further increased as the country gentlemen worked their way into the borough constituencies in the fifteenth and sixteenth centuries. The Commons of 1593 included 60 barristers; and 197 members, or forty-three per cent of the House, had enjoyed a legal education.[29]

Lawyers were very useful in the organization of the business of the House. The power of the Commons was being constructed in the sixteenth century on the basis of the committee system. Before the middle of Elizabeth's reign it was the Lords, where the judges and other legal experts sat, which more often committed bills for scrutiny and modification. The lower House took up the practice in a more critical spirit. The lawyers in the Commons, elected members, not royal servants, played their part in the small committees whose very appointment indicated hostility to the government's legislation, and they were particularly valuable on committees concerning the all-important privileges of the House. Above all, the profession provided the majority of the Speakers of the Commons; and the Speaker was to be a key figure in the century of constitutional struggles ahead. More and Audley, Speakers in 1523 and 1529, were later lords chancellor; Puckering in 1584 and 1586 a later lord keeper. Wray (1571), who went on to be a distinguished judge, Snagge (1589) and Yelverton (1597) were serjeants, and Croke (1601) was recorder of London. Onslow (1566), Popham (1581) and Coke (1593) were solicitors-general at the time of their election. Part of the object of the Crown's two principal law-officers was to sit in Parliament and defend the government's legal policy, and consequently the Commons, fearing undue government influence, refused till after the Restoration to allow the attorney-general to be elected to its membership (judges were always barred).[30]

One of the great political facts of the sixteenth century was the rise of the gentleman-lawyer in society and in Parliament.

The number of the lawyers, wrote Thomas Wilson with some exaggeration in the last decade of the century,

is so great now that, to say the truth, they can scarcely live one by another, the practice being drawn into a few hands of those which are most renowned, and all the rest live by pettifogging, seeking means to set their neighbours at variance . . . they undo the country people and buy up all the lands that are to be sold. . . . Not to speak of the twelve chief judges and the multitude of serjeants . . . there is one at this day of a meaner degree, namely the Queen's Attorney – Edward Coke – who within these ten years, in my knowledge, was not able to dispend above £100 a year, and now . . . may dispend betwixt £12,000 and £14,000.

One interpretation of the Great Rebellion of 1642 sees it as the assertion of political supremacy by the middle class, which had recently gained economic supremacy. As applied to one social group, the lawyers, there seems to be something in this concept. There were seventy-five barristers in the Long Parliament which met in 1640 – all opposed to Charles I's idea of his prerogative.[31]

SIR EDWARD COKE

Not as a typical lawyer – he was hardly that – but because he more than anyone realized the potential of the lawyer's place in society, Sir Edward Coke may fittingly round off this chapter. Born in Norfolk, he was educated at Trinity College, Cambridge, Clifford's Inn and the Inner Temple, where he was called to the bar in 1578. 'Beginning on a good bottom left him by his father', he married 'a wife of extraordinary wealth' and rose swiftly, enjoying the patronage of Lord Burghley. He became recorder of Coventry, Norwich and London; M.P. for Aldeburgh in 1589, solicitor-general in 1592, and Speaker of the Commons in 1593; attorney-general in 1594 (in despite of Francis Bacon), and in 1606 chief justice of Common Pleas. He acquired many manors, and played a sufficiently skilful part in the affairs of the Virginia Company that when he became a nuisance to James I as a judge it was actually proposed to move him to a post of financial responsibility. He was conventionally pious, supporting charities and bestowing the benefices in his gift with great scrupulosity. Yet his domestic life was disastrous, and his second wife, Burghley's granddaughter, wrote after his death: 'we shall never see his like again, praises be to God'.[32]

The turning-point in Coke's career was when as judge he began to exalt the Common Law above the king's prerogative. On one occasion King James almost struck Coke in his anger, 'which the Lord Coke perceiving, fell flat on all four'.[33] The situation was complicated by the quarrels of Coke with the court of Chancery and with Francis Bacon, who suggested in 1613 the expedient by which his rival was 'promoted' to the less important chief justiceship of King's Bench. Three years later, Coke was dismissed altogether. Paradoxically, it was because he went on beyond the highest legal offices that Coke was unique as a lawyer. The deposed judge became the leader of the parliamentary opposition. After a gap of a quarter of a century and at the age of sixty he re-entered the Commons, helped to manage the impeachment of Bacon, spent several months in the Tower, and still in 1628 suggested the Petition of Right in which Parliament appealed to Magna Carta against Stuart tyranny. On his death in 1634 his manuscripts were seized and destroyed on royal orders.

For it was the idea of legal precedent, embodied in his writings, which Coke had made a principal weapon of Parliament. His speeches in the Commons in the 1590s show him to have been already much concerned with history and precedent. He interposed in a debate concerning the validity of the election of a member outlawed for debt, to announce his researches into the history of parliamentary privilege and contribute a precedent he had read (one would like to know where) 'of a Parliament holden before the Conquest by Edward, the son of Ethelred . . .' In his closing oration as Speaker in 1593, he not only 'desired leave to compare her Majesty to a bee', the Queen of a 'sweet Commonwealth of the little bees', but proclaimed that 'in the Heptarchy of the West Saxons . . . Parliament was summoned by the noble

Queen Ine in these words. . .' (Ine was a man, but perhaps
Coke thought the precedent of a Saxon queen was flattering
to Elizabeth). Since it had existed even in the seventh century, 'This High Court of Parliament (most high and mighty
Prince) is the greatest and most ancient court within your
realm'.[34]

CHAPTER 9

LAW IN THE MAKING

W E can now begin to see how English law came into existence.

LAW AND CUSTOM

Law is created by society, to fulfil its needs. It begins as
custom, those ways of behaving which, because they are
necessary for its survival, a group imposes on its members by
'moral pressure', and so become 'internalized' as duties.[1]
Medieval customary law was alive and growing. 'A custom,' wrote a thirteenth-century expert, 'can be called long
if it was introduced within ten or twenty years, very long if it
dates from thirty years, and ancient if it dates from forty
years.' Custom was not at all mysterious – just the way of
doing things accepted by a reasonable number of people as
the best. Each town and manor had its special customs and
often elaborate and written ones – the 'unwrittenness' of
custom was a myth invented later for political purposes. The
towns and the whole body of merchants had their own customs because trade in many different commodities and services required regulations which were specific and therefore
various.[2] In the matter of copyhold, custom showed itself as
an instrument of social revolution. It was also a national
symbol and a political weapon. In 1236 the barons refused to
alter the laws of England to conform with Canon Law, and
they attacked other ordinances of Henry III as importations
from Savoy: custom was the peculiar heritage of a country,
as it might be of a locality. The programme of Magna Carta
was custom, which the king might not touch because it was
older than monarchy. Here an idea was borrowed from the
pleading of an ancient seisin in a real action: if no charter

could be shown originating the customs maintained against John, it was because they had existed since before the days of writing, were *prescriptive, immemorial*. For the purposes of political controversy, custom was at the same time living and unchangeable.

In the sixteenth century the common lawyers exalted customary law almost to the position of perfect equity. The ideal of custom was summed up in these words:

> For the *Common Law of England* is nothing else but the *Common Custome* of the Realm. . . . And this *Customary Law* is the most perfect and most excellent, and without comparison the best, to make and preserve a Commonwealth. For the *written Laws* which are made either by the Edicts of Princes, or by Councils of Estates, are imposed upon the Subject before any Triall or Probation made, whether the same be fit and agreeable to the nature and disposition of the people. . . . [But English customary law is] so framed and fitted to the nature and disposition of this people, as we may properly say it is connatural to the Nation, so as it cannot possibly be ruled by any other Law. This Law therefore doth demonstrate the strength of wit and reason and self-sufficiency which hath been always in the People of this Land, which have made their own Laws out of their wisedome and experience (like a silk-worm that formeth all her web out of her self onely), not begging or borrowing a form of a Commonweal, either from *Rome* or from *Greece*, as all other Nations of *Europe* have done. . . .[3]

But the custom which was being praised so highly in politics was being relegated to a minor position in law. The landlords who were irked by its restrictions within the manor, and the Renaissance humanists harking back to the order and rationality (to their ideas) of classical Roman Law, combined to depreciate custom. The lawyer-landlords turned round the argument, used in the struggle over the constitution, that custom *was* immemorial, and required that all customs pleaded in court should be proved to have existed from 'a time whereof the memory of man runneth not to the contrary' – a thing not easily done. So were developed the modern tests of the validity of a custom: it must be shown (to the satisfaction of a jury) to have been in notorious, peaceable and continuous use since ancient times, and (to the satisfaction of a judge) to be fair, reasonable, specific (e.g. on the number of beasts which might be pastured), obligatory (more than a social habit), and not in conflict with statute-law or a general rule of Common Law. In *Simpson* v. *Wells* (1872), a customary right to keep a refreshment stall at a fair, claimed in defence to a charge of obstructing a footway, was disallowed on the grounds that the fair was not immemorial – not older, indeed, than Edward III. The great example of the issue of reasonableness was the *Tanistry Case* (1608). On that occasion, the English judges disallowed an Irish custom of succession which gave inheritance not to the the eldest son but to 'the oldest and worthiest' of the clan, partly because in practice (they thought) it led to 'the effusion of blood and much mischief' and let in the most ruthless.[4]

Customary law reflected social needs closely, but had practical disadvantages. It was too local and unsystematic for the nation which was emerging. Foreign merchants could not be expected to know all the local variations of custom; and the failure of the king's judges to grasp them is demonstrated by their use of juries to find out what the customary law was. Royal orders began very early to supplement customary procedure, and new boroughs helped in the standardization of substantive law by examining the customs of established boroughs and adopting the most attractive ones. Custom, selected and made of national force, became the Common Law.

PROCEDURE AS A SOURCE OF LAW

Basic factors in the human condition determine the elements of law. Human vulnerability requires forbearance from indiscriminate violence if society is to survive; a law of property and laws organizing labour and the exchange of goods and services are made necessary by man's limited natural resources. Procedures of enforcement are required by men's limited understanding and strength of will – just because they are sheltered by law from the harsh realities of the state of nature, some men are tempted to break the law – and such rules are made possible by men's approximate equality, which persuades each of them to compromise, or ultimately compels him to submit to a combination of his fellows.

The commutation of the feud was the first customary type of compromise, and the kin the first combination of men for legal purposes. The marches, with their 'protection rackets', and their 'love-days' for arbitration, remained at this stage until the Tudor period.[5] The borders were too far away from Westminster. But up to a certain limit the badness of communications was one of the natural factors creating the Common Law process, eliciting the devices of essoins, outlawry, commissions of oyer and terminer and *nisi prius*, and even the writ itself. Soon the legal jargon of Westminster was being talked in all the manors of England, and the first Common Law was a common custom of procedure.

Next, the lawyers escaped from the deadening grip of the 'original writs' produced by the administrators in Chancery. First, they tinkered about with the unyielding forms of action with the spanner of legal fiction. The make-believe of John Doe and Richard Roe was necessary if procedures were to keep up with social needs. 'Judicial writs' were a second means of extending procedure; and, in the later Middle Ages, of transforming it. It was then that the judges seized full control of procedure, and the result was the age of equity. The injunction; *latitat*, turned by King's Bench, with the help of fictions and a prison, into a potent 'original writ'; even the subpoena of the chancellor in his judicial capacity: these were its products. Judicial writs could be more peremptory and left much more to be decided by the judges in court. The original writ was outmoded.

Procedure developed the principles or substance of the law. The concepts of the law of property have been determined to a large extent by the nature and limitations of the old property actions. By providing stringent procedures for settling some issues and none for others, the lawyers selected amongst the ancient customs and changed their relative importance. Soon the available actions were regarded as defining substantive law, and it could be said that 'the remedy comes before the right'.[6] But the remedy was provided only because somebody asked for it. The plaintiff continually injected shots of real life into the small and complacent world of legal technique. The age of the judicial writ was also the age of the bill or petition, which pushed aside the original writ and demanded more efficient and equitable remedies. First, as the complaint of trespass, it created the commission of the peace; then it called into existence the conciliar courts; and it was a main inspiration of the 'High Court of Parliament'. Even in King's Bench the writ of latitat was the answer to the *bill* of Middlesex; and the criminal prosecution was based on the bill or 'information' of the attorney-general. The law is a dialogue between lawyer and plaintiff.

JUDGE-MADE LAW AND FOLLOWING PRECEDENTS

The judgment in a case determines under which rule of law or statute falls a particular act which has been admitted by the defendant or found by a jury (in *Hull* v. *Orynge* the hedge-clippings fell on the wrong side of the hedge – was it trespass?). There is no logical and unmistakable connexion between a definition in law and the action under consideration: someone must observe or judge that they match (the defendant keeps a dog-track at which there is a totalizator – is he guilty of organizing a 'game of chance' in the meaning of the statute of 1873?).[7] The layman needs to know what the law is in terms of practical consequences, not of abstract principles, and he can only be directed to the practice of the judges. This it is which must be consistent if law is to be certain; and the fact entails in some measure the system known in England as *stare decisis* – following precedent.

There must be rules as to which precedents bind a court. It has to follow the last relevant decision, not choosing arbitrarily between a number of precedents with a bias to the most ancient ones, as medieval judges inclined to do. The precedent decisions of superior courts naturally bind inferior ones – but here it must be said that the rules placing the courts in order have a very complicated history. Most difficult of all: how does the judge recognize the relevant precedent? Partly this is a matter of the quality of law reporting and the clarity of the earlier decisions. Still there is left a margin of free judgment about which previous case the present one most resembles, and the uncertainty and the freedom of choice is obviously greater as the novel elements in the case are more numerous. In a very novel situation the judge is tying the future as much as he is tied by the past. There is no virtue in denying that he is making an important type of law; but he is adding bricks to a building the architecture of which he cannot alter, as statute can.

The system of precedent was only beginning to coalesce in the Middle Ages. Scholastic philosophy had a faith in general definitions, and the Common Law a faith in technical terms, which obscured the advantages of reasoning by analogy from one set of circumstances to another. Decisions were seen as statements of the eternal principles of law (though, under the appearance of 'defining custom', judges could add to the stock of explicit principles as much as did statutes, which were regarded as merely the judicial decisions of the Court of Parliament). Of course the knowledge of earlier decisions was recognized as valuable. Chaucer's man of law did better than Bracton, knowing 'every judgment, case and crime / Recorded ever since King William's time'. Judges were afraid to confuse the students by deciding old situations in new ways. Bracton even saw the positive advantages of proceeding 'from like to like'. But earlier cases only showed what the custom was, and no single case made binding law. If clear principles were lacking, judges felt that 'reason, not examples' should be the guide. Before 1500 the appeal to examples from the past was apt to be looked on as a dangerous and rather unfair weapon, preventing a case from being decided on its merits. Precedents more often established bad things than good, such as the taxes which Parliament asked should not become precedents even as they granted them. ''Twill be recorded for a precedent, / And many an error by the same example / Will rush into the state.'[8]

The biggest obstacles to a strict rule of *stare decisis* were technical. Precedents – a whole Year Book even – could be invented, when the machinery of law reporting was primitive. Worse, the *ratio decidendi*, the legal reasons which had swayed the judges, could rarely be distinguished in the reports from the judges' inessential comment or *obiter dicta*, and the bearing of the earlier decisions was obscure. Counsel argued from imaginary situations or related anecdotes of cases they remembered personally. The later Year Books did, however, provide a more usable collection of precedents, cited respectably by court and term. There were also the first signs of the rules to determine the authority of one court's decisions in other courts, which were essential if precedents were not to conflict and each court evolve a law of its own (as Chancery had). In the fourteenth century, when they ceased to attend the council as a group, the judges began to meet in a room at Westminster called the Exchequer Chamber, to decide difficult cases referred to them by the regular courts. To Coke the decisions of the Court of Exchequer Chamber were like statutes. Naturally they had authority in the courts where the judges who consented to them normally sat; and they were individual decisions which had this binding force, not conflicting examples which could be 'reconciled' out of recognition.[9]

But the age of Plowden, Dyer and Coke was still far from the technique of binding precedent to which Exchequer Chamber pointed the way. Coke was suspicious of the 'farrago of authorities' often produced, which only 'lessened the weight of the argument', and he had reason to know, for it has been said of his own judgments that 'the longer the list of authorities reconciled, the greater the divergence from cases cited'.[10] The great change was nevertheless implicit in Coke's manner of working. Naturally, judges felt the power to make new law by setting precedents before they grasped the unexciting truth that existing precedents must, in logic, also circumscribe this power. Bacon's exhortation to men 'of great place' might have been Coke's motto: 'set it down to thyself, as well to create good precedents as to follow them.' Precedent as a way of advance in law depends upon the courage of judges to choose what is relevant in past cases and reject what is not. For the system of *stare decisis* to get started at all it was necessary to choose in a radical fashion amongst the great mass of medieval 'examples'. It does not matter that Coke's standard of choice was his own prejudices; that he created more precedents than he found.

Because of his unique position in history, Coke's decisions are not typical examples of judicial law-making: but they do demonstrate the interaction of legal judgments and social change. Coke shows a consistent bias against the regulation of trade, perhaps because he feared the royal prerogative which was the instrument of this regulation, but also because he was a member of a class which was grasping the opportunities of untrammelled economic enterprise. In the *Case of the Tailors of Ipswich* (1615) Coke held that a company could not, on the strength of a royal charter, restrain an unqualified person from working at a lawful trade, for 'the law abhors idleness, the mother of all evil . . . and especially in young men, who ought in their youth . . . to learn lawful sciences . . .' The most resounding enunciation of his economic doctrines had been in *Darcy* v. *Allen*, the *Case of Monopolies* (1602). Coke had there argued against the Queen's patent to Darcy, a groom of the privy chamber, for the sole making of playing-cards in England, on the basis of various odd precedents and of the chapter in Magna Carta (no. 39) saying that 'no free-man shall be . . . deprived of his . . . free customs'.[11]

Clearly, the 'sociology of judicial decisions', the investigation of the class interests and personal prejudices of judges, is of some importance. But there is nothing shocking about the social factors in judgments. When new situations come up for adjudication – and few civil cases are exactly like previous ones, or they would not be commenced – they can be brought into line with determined cases only by the exercise of opinions about the way society works and what is good for it. The facts of law are the facts of life, and judgment is action based on the observation of life as well as the rules of law. When he appeals to 'reason' or 'natural law', a judge is invoking his idea of society. His discretion, guided by the experience of his predecessors, makes of law what Coke called an 'artificial reason', an experimental social science which can advance.

LEGISLATION

As for what we would call legislation, it certainly happened throughout the Middle Ages, prevalent though the feeling was that only God could make real law (embodied in custom) leaving to kings the preserving and declaring of it. The Roman idea of legislation survived in the Old English codes, and in the unofficial compilations of laws which date from Henry I's reign. Henry I may, in this respect, be called the last of the English kings; but he was also the first of the Angevins in his use of the charter to 'confirm the customs and liberties' of his subjects. Such charters are too easily thought of as concessions: contemporaries thought of them – and historians speak of them – as the *acts* of the king. The king made the laws. Whether the enactment resembled 'a grant of lands, a proclamation of successful revolutionaries, a treaty of peace dictated by conquerors, a bargain between two contractors, or a writ to the judges', depended on its origin 'in a gift of the King, a fight against the King, an agreement with the King, or an order by the King'.[12]

The barons insisted that the king could issue some orders only with their concurrence, given in the name of 'the community of the realm'. They claimed that it was *their* customs of which the king was custodian, and Henry II therefore found it expedient to dress up his legislation as judgments given at sessions or *assizes* of his court. In the revolution of 1258 the barons further established that the chancellor could not create new original writs 'without the order of the king, and of his council, which shall be present'.[13] The main result of the thirteenth-century political struggles was to show that in the most important matters the king and barons must work as one, and thus to isolate a particularly solemn mode of legislation, arising where the king had a 'representative' council or 'parliament' around him; a change which did not destroy the king's power to legislate by ordinance or through, for example, a writ of commission to his judges. This solemn legislation acquired, in the second half of the thirteenth century, the name of *statute*.

A weighty body of opinion holds that the original function of Parliament, which took shape in Henry III's reign, was judicial – it was from the beginning 'The High Court of Parliament' – and that it originally comprised a body of councillors, meeting three times a year at known terms to hear the petitions of those denied justice in other places.[14] However, Parliament was soon meeting as and when the king chose, for he grasped the propaganda value of discussing and enacting great matters *in* a fully representative assembly. One of the most intriguing questions of English history is how those matters came eventually to be controlled *by* that assembly, even national and public legislation taking the form of the old 'private' petition.

Edward I set up elaborate machinery for receiving petitions at parliament time: Parliament acted a bit like a stationary eyre. But this special machinery for petitions (all addressed to the king) operated *at*, not *in*, Parliament, which was an event rather than an institution and as such incapable of being petitioned or petitioning. The petitioner did not get a remedy: he was only 'put in the way of getting one' from the ordinary courts or Chancery, while Parliament went on to discuss affairs of national importance. Just a few petitions were distinguished as 'common petitions', because they claimed to speak for public opinion and in the common interest, and these bills alone were sure to be brought to the king's notice, by way of the Clerk of the Parliaments and the king's council. The Commons as a body had little opportunity to approve or disown even the petitions put forward by individuals in the community's name: the objection to lawyers in Parliament was that they too readily claimed national significance for their clients' grievances. The Commons as a whole did advance just a few petitions, which may properly be called 'the Commons' petitions'. The statute in a reasonably modern sense perhaps originated in 1327, when the knights of the shire in Parliament 'asked that the substance of the commons' petitions and the council's answers should be put in writing under the great seal, so that the sheriffs might cause proclamation to be made accordingly'.[15]

This was not, however, the beginning of the modern legislative process. That happened when some petitioners in their own private interest began, towards 1400, to address their pleas to the Commons (not to the king), asking that House to intercede for them to the king. Their petitions were granted by the king in his council 'by the assent of the Commons', as important petitions had long been granted 'by the assent of the Lords'. The merging of the two streams – petitions submitted to the clerk of the parliaments for the advocacy of the Commons in the one case and the assent of the Lords in the other – produced the modern legislative practice by which bills can proceed from either house to the other; and even the king chose to send his legislation through these authoritative channels.[16]

Statutes made in Parliament finally overcame the medieval prejudice against explicit law-making. Petitioners were obviously asking for changes in the law, even in Edward I's time, and *Quia Emptores* (1290), granted at the urgent demand of the barons, was probably the first statute avowedly to change the rules of the Common Law. By using Parliament to curb the Church, Henry VIII and Thomas Cromwell showed that on earth there was no higher law than statute, the versatility of which was demonstrated by the sheer mass of Tudor legislation (the acts of Henry VIII's reign alone equalled the output of all the previous two-and-a-half centuries). The king was seen as the physician of his people, continually removing 'all fumes and smells which may offend or be prejudicial to their health'. Legislation took a further step in 1563 with the appearance of the first 'consolidating act', digesting 'into one sole law' a number of previous acts concerning artisans (5 Eliz., cap. 4).[17]

Private petitions or bills remained alongside national or government bills. Like actions at law, legislation may be public or private, private acts being those which confer special rights on individual persons (such acts are now rare) or on individual local authorities, rather than on all citizens or all authorities of that type.[18]

It was clear that there were many things that only a statute could do. It could destroy and remake fundamental rules of law and confer legal rights, where courts could only refine them or protect them. Some of this force it possessed as the ('judicial') decisions of the highest court, but by 1485 it was realized that repealing a statute was different from reversing a decision. A bad precedent never was law, an inconvenient statute was law which had to be destroyed. The power of statute was most evident in this ability to retrace its steps, to abrogate as well as make law. Statute-law reached a new stage of distinctiveness in the mid fourteenth century when Parliament affirmed that, whatever a simple ordinance might do, only a statute could unmake a statute. Legislation was much more than the king's order: it was a statement of the future customs of the land. 'Be it enacted that . . . the King for the time being . . . may set forth . . . his proclamations'; 'be it enacted that the justices of gaol delivery and the peace . . . shall from henceforth have full power and authority to . . .': this was the typical language of statute.[19]

A statute was not, therefore, an example of the king's command making law. Nor did it require, as many have thought, the existence in the state of a *sovereign* unlimited in power. For although statute-law was 'above' other forms of law to the extent that it could overrule them, it was so by choice of the users of the law: it was just another rule of law that, where Common Law and statute-law conflicted, the latter was to be taken as the law which was binding. A law qualified for this supremacy only if it was made according to the rules of legislation. The location of a sovereign power to legislate was not, therefore, a medieval problem. The burning issue then was whether properly speaking there could be any human legislator, or any besides God's earthly vicars, the Pope and the Emperor. Henry VIII solved that problem by deciding that England was an empire in itself; but he also knew that he 'never stood so high' as in his Parliament.

Medieval law-making was a conjunction of forces from above and from below, the balance of which, though threatened, was never upset. On the one hand government-inspired acts predominated over true petitions after the fifteenth century; it was held that a statute did not apply to the king unless it said so explicitly; a statute never lapsed through non-user, because the rule was that 'time does not run against the king'; and in the Tudor period printing and long preambles made the element of royal policy still clearer. On the other hand, the king found it convenient to use Parliament as the medium of legislation, and he appreciated the inconsistency of overriding in particular cases what he had agreed to generally. Though by the sixteenth century the king had become the dominant contractor and there was no one to make him keep his promises, a statute was still in a way a treaty, like Magna Carta. Nothing but common sense prevented the medieval and Tudor kings from dispensing with statutes too often. The Stuarts lacked that sense. The seventeenth-century struggle of king and Parliament was to some extent a struggle between the two parties in legislation, each fighting for the sovereign part.[20]

THE PLACE OF STATUTES IN THE LAW

Statute-law could only work within the existing framework of the Common Law and government: it did not make law in isolation. Though statute-law and the Common Law (a name here used to denote the procedures and rules developed empirically by the courts) are often contrasted, they are really interdependent. The great German jurist, Savigny, believed that legislation interfered with the proper, organic, growth of law; yet a certain amount of conscious engineering appears necessary if law is to have purpose. In any event, the judges were very soon forced to admit the power of statute: 'when the law is known and clear, though it be unequitable and inconvenient, the judges must determine as the law is, without regarding the unequitableness . . . if inconveniences necessarily follow . . . only the Parliament can cure them'.[21] Statute maintains in a serviceable state a law which (unlike precedent) it *may* alter as it likes, but finds impracticable to transform. The tone of statute-law is very far from that of a Roman Law code. Many late-medieval statutes created new misdemeanours; but the concept of trespass or misdemeanour was a Common Law product. Statutes were themselves the fruit of the Common Law process of complaint and judgment; of the petition which survives in the form of the statute, and the judicial hearing which survives in the formal inquiry preceding much subordinate legislation. Conversely, statutes might provide new forms of action, set up new courts (one of its chief functions in the hands of the Tudors), and confirm or diminish the jurisdiction of old courts such as Admiralty.

Statute was neither an independent, nor the earliest, form of legislation. But it came to control the other forms. The powers of rule-making it can now delegate to officials and bodies outside Parliament are the successors to the many independent modes of legislation in medieval England. The bye-laws of the manor, the regulations of the city companies and other corporations, the rules of the Common Law courts – all these were only slowly brought under the surveillance of Parliament. The judgment of any court made a sort of law, and every considerable medieval baron had a court. The assizes of the king's court were paralleled by Simon de Montfort's ordinance substituting primogeniture for ultimogeniture in his town of Leicester, and by Prince Edward's establishment at Chester of rules which anticipated his own statute of *Quia Emptores*. This local law-making of medieval England was first brought under the control of the king in his council, as powers to be granted and censored by charter and letters-patent. So, in 1575, for the sake of quiet between the university and city of Oxford, 'places necessary to be ordered always by the order and authority of the Privy Council', the government had certain orders written into 'the common book of the said University and city'.[22]

The orders of the king in council might themselves appear to have rivalled statute-law. The council's proclamations, bearing such titles as 'Articles agreed uppon by the Lordes and other of the Quenes Majisties pryvy Counsayle, for a reformation of . . . servantes in certayne abuses of apparell . . .', created many new offences and attached penalties to them. Government by proclamations and by commissions and grants of monopoly under letters-patent is said by one recent authority to have been increasing at the expense of statute in later Tudor and early Stuart times. Henry VIII's statute 'against deceitful stuffing and making of featherbeds' would, a century later, have taken the form of a patent to the upholsterer's company 'for the sole stuffing and making of featherbeds'. Orders in council continue to have a function in some of the fields, particularly the rules of corporations, which they controlled in the sixteenth century. Even then, however, they were a supplement to statute-law rather than its rival, for they coped with the details, not the principles, of social and economic life. The supremacy of statute over laws made by the king alone had been decided by the downfall of Richard II and was well understood in the sixteenth century. Statutes would sometimes confer on the king power to enforce their provisions by proclamation; and though the judges told Thomas Cromwell that 'proclamations . . . devised by the King and his Council . . . should be of as good effect as any law made by Parliament', it needed a statute (the Act of Proclamations of 1539) to give authority to their opinion. Like all conciliar jurisdiction, proclamations could not (in theory, at least) touch life or limb or freehold, and they had no force in the Common Law courts.[23]

The chief restraint upon statute was not a political but a logical one; not rival forms of legislation, but the fact that statutes had to be interpreted by judges. The most detailed statutes can only talk in abstract terms about classes of situation. Not surprisingly, the drafting of the earliest statutes gave rise to a host of judicial conundrums. A number of corrections and explanations had to be issued of the Statute of Gloucester (1278), and no one was sure whether *De Donis* allowed entailment beyond three lives. The essence of the problem did not become obvious at this early stage because the judges sat in the king's council and, as Hengham said on a famous occasion, had literally made the statutes which counsel presumed to interpret to them. In difficult cases, no legal pedantry stopped the king from explaining the intention of his statutes. It might indeed have happened that the king and then Parliament would have become accepted authorities on the meaning and application of legislation. There was good reason why this common-sense solution was not adopted. By the time that the judges accepted the fact that statutes came to them from outside, as authoritative orders which they must follow strictly, legislation had ceased to express the clear intention of any one man: it might be a compromise between several interests in Parliament which none had willed (or perhaps, as in the case of a modern finance act, even understood). Judges had, unaided, to give a consistent application to the *words* of statutes.[24]

The advent of printing and the great sixteenth-century improvement in Parliament's machinery for the exact drafting of legislation, by making the range of statute-law clear, paradoxically made interpretation more necessary and respectable, for judges could no longer tacitly ignore what seemed inconvenient. The Statute of Uses was a landmark in the handing down of detailed law to the judges. Soon afterwards followed the first work on the interpretation of statutes, *A Discourse upon Statutes*, written probably by the young Thomas Egerton, and using the interpretative methods of renaissance learning. The sensible, if not enormously helpful, 'golden rule' was formulated, that the judge should work from the *ratio legis*, or general purport of the statute, to be sought through the 'ordinary meaning' of the words in which it was framed. In their judgment in *Heydon's Case* (1584), the Barons of the Exchequer went further, to suggest that the judges should ask: ' 1st, What was the Common Law before the making of the Act; 2nd, What was the mischief and defect for which the Common Law did not provide'; 3rd, What was Parliament's remedy; and 4th, what was the 'true reason' of the remedy, which would assist the judges to fulfil Parliament's intent? Thus, almost accidentally, the judges, having long since ceased to be the makers, became the independent critics of the statute. The mere necessity came to seem a *power* to interpret statutes, then almost – in the hands of a Coke – to interpret them away. The Common Law courts gained and jealously guarded a monopoly of interpretation which gave them an important place in the constitution, between the legislature which designed the law and the executive which needed it.[25]

Interpretation might amount to a new form of judicial law-making, for the most common and unavoidable inadequacy of a statute is its failure to foresee *all* the contingencies for which it seeks to provide. Faced with *casus omissi* a court may have to decide, for instance, that broadcasting comes under the statutory rules governing the telegraph. Judges quite early felt the temptation to say that a statute had really meant to cover the case before them. By taking statutory definitions widely, they declared offences to amount to (say) *constructive* treason. But 'construction of law' meant no more than the 'construing' of a statute to cover what it did not explicitly mention. No intentional 'building up' of the law was involved, and, quite often judges have given an unduly narrow application to an act. For their 'control' of statute was in fact merely an instance of the confining effect on legislation of the Common Law framework. Parliament was presumed to be familiar with and to work within that framework, and the rule is that 'The general words of an Act are not to be so construed as to alter the previous policy of the law, unless no sense or meaning can be applied to those words consistently with the intention of preserving the existing policy untouched' (*Minet* v. *Leman:* 1855).[26]

THE LEGISLATORS AND THE USES OF STATUTE

Who made statute-law? The answer is 'the government', or 'the aristocracy', or 'the bourgeoisie' (the classes represented in Parliament) according to the pressures evident in the drafting of the acts. However much they might claim to represent the *communitas regni*, the medieval barons were often acting blatantly in the interests of a limited aristocracy of landowners. At Merton in 1236, for example, they obtained a provision allowing the lords of manors to take into their demesne-lands those areas of common which were 'in excess of the peasants' needs'. The fourteenth-century statutes to limit labourers' wages and to extend the powers of the J.P.s were to the advantage of the ordinary knights rather than of the barons. But the great struggles in the new legislature were between the conflicting interests of the knights and the burgesses, and of the different groups within the burgesses. An analysis by Professor Bindoff of the amendments written into the bill, preserved in the House of Lords Record Office, for that allegedly 'consolidating act', the Statute of Artificers of 1563, shows how much the final product owed to the work and will (exercised through repeated committals) of different groups in the Commons: the government's conservative, agrarian, bill became a statute for the promotion of industry and trade.[27]

Another social animus worked out in legislation was that of the secular landowners against the clergy. In 1401 the church was still capable of getting statutory support for the horrible practice of burning heretics, which England had previously escaped. But Mortmain had been in the interests of the laymen against the clergy; so were the fourteenth-century statutes of Praemunire (still unrepealed) and of Provisors, which sought to prevent papal interference with the landowners' rights of presentation to livings and imposed severe penalties on clergy who invoked the pope's authority; and so were the Reformation statutes which gave church property to the gentry and reduced the irksome powers of the church-courts.[28]

Statute was a social and a political weapon. Its facility for setting and removing penalties made it the easiest way of outlawing or encouraging and (with respect to individuals) of punishing or rewarding certain types of political as well as social behaviour. At the extreme, political expediency produced the *Bill of Attainder* or (later) *Of Pains and Penalties*, which condemned political victims retrospectively; and the *Bill of Indemnity* which excused such people as officials acting over-vigorously in an emergency from the penalties to which they would have been liable at Common Law. The law was the keenest weapon in the royal armoury, and, realizing the fact, the Tudors fostered a new type of politician, epitomized by Thomas Cromwell, who would tactfully guide the hand of the Commons in its framing and amending of bills. The relatively sudden discovery of the full possibilities of statute brought a rush of government schemes, most of them remaining unimplemented amongst Cromwell's papers. The constitution was altered by the statutory erection of new courts which were in effect new financial departments of the state.[29]

In the preface to the fourth part of his *Reports*, Coke, indeed, wrote of statutes as though they were wild things ignorant of their own strength, making impulsive alterations to the law which had afterwards to be reversed. But a glance at the indices to the bulky volumes of the *Statutes of the Realm* leaves an impression of a tradition of statutory law-making not much less conservative than custom; of an empirical and too-gradual adaptation of the old law to new conditions. Antique statutes were less often repealed than allowed to fall into oblivion as inappropriate to a changed society.

LEGAL CONCEPTS AND FUNDAMENTAL LAW

The law was rooted in the ideas about society held by the people at large and then refined by the lawyers. Without a few primary ideas – of justice, compensation, the king's peace – Henry II's assizes could not have been thought of. Law is a system of ideas like these – but its logic is all its own, advancing partly by deduction from existing principles, partly by induction from the needs of society. 'Law,' said Maitland, 'is where life and logic meet.' The apparently absurd rules of the old land law, or concerning uses, were a compromise between the demands of life and logic. The law providing for new circumstances could not easily escape using old terms. One can as well see a modern chancellor of the exchequer reconstructing the whole taxation system because of tax evasion, as imagine Henry VIII achieving the erasure of the idea of the trust because of its abuse. An idea which has once existed is ineradicable. A term once added to the logic of the law could be modified by succeeding terms but never destroyed.

Counsel use before the court the normal methods of argument and may bring in any material of logical relevance whether it be 'legal' or 'historical' or something else.[30] The advantage of the concepts which became established was their adaptability. The *due care* required to avoid a claim for negligence has to be rapidly adjustable in a world of dangerous machines, so it is assessed by the standards of that equally useful though indeterminate concept, the 'reasonable man'. The technical concepts of the law are those working distinctions necessary to any body of thought: the distinctions in English law between species of wrong (crime, tort, breach of contract); between types of property (land and chattels); between civil actions (real and personal); between levels of rights in land (seisin, lease, easement, tenure-in-tail, future interest); and between types of crime (felony and misdemeanour; burglary, larceny and the rest). Eventually, more abstract concepts still are attempted – rights and duties; obligation and liability.

Technical concepts easily cease to be a convenience and become live forces moulding the development of the law. So from the idea of the personal action it was reasoned that the benefit and liability of (say) an action of trespass died with the original plaintiff and transgressor: after one of these had died there could be no action. Never an exact expression of the law in practice, the rule was only swept away in modern times by the crop of industrial and road accidents. Reasoning in a void sometimes outstrips the law's empirical provision for social needs and produces concepts which (unless they are twisted into barbarities like 'chattels real') vastly oversimplify the problem. Sometimes only historians are misled. Whatever distinctions actually existed between civil and criminal actions, they did not until quite late prevent the king from taking amercements from the defeated parties in civil cases and offering rewards to informers who reported crimes; or the public from accepting it as perfectly natural that he should. The separation often made between *procedure* and *substance* in law does equal violence to history. Sometimes categories have simply proved too abstract to hold the products of expediency: so the late-medieval lawyer laboured vainly to decide whether the action of Debt was based on the concepts of property, contract or tort. The 'life' element in law was here in danger of being sacrificed to the logic. Matters were complicated further by the lawyers' pretence that some of the products of their logic were real *things*: in this way, claims for debts or damages enforceable in the Common Law courts were by the fifteenth century called '*choses* in action', those in Chancery, 'equities'.[31]

Behind the technical concepts were certain moral preconceptions and legal ideals, many of them very old and often borrowed from the Roman or Canonist systems. The sixteenth-century ideal of the 'commonweal' – what would now be called 'public policy' – is an originally Roman principle still invoked in the courts. The utilitarianism of Jeremy Bentham was anticipated by the canonist demand for 'suitability' in the laws. The sanctity of the family and of private property are feelings quite as ancient, and Chief Justice Hale once stated bluntly that christianity was part of the Common Law of England.[32]

The universality of Roman Law, the supposed antiquity and immutability of feudal custom, and the moral imperatives of christianity combined to create the medieval idea of a *natural law* behind all local ('municipal') codes. The Romans themselves had believed in a natural (moral) law which all men must instinctively recognize; and, beside that, in a law of mankind (*ius gentium*) which all men did in fact recognize, an observed common factor in the various local systems of law. Medieval scholars, haunted by the vision of a natural law, distinguished between actions wrong in themselves (*mala in se*) and actions wrong because some authority had prohibited them (*mala prohibita*). Where was this basic law to be found? For some sixteenth-century jurists its fullest expression was still Roman Law, 'writ with such gravity, that if Nature should herself prescribe particular means whereby mankind should observe her laws, I think she would admit the same'. This was the easier to believe because the medieval church had used Roman Law (somewhat modified into Canon Law) as her blueprint for the Christian society. Its rationality rather than its moral inspiration might, however, be regarded as the greatest virtue of Roman Law, especially at a time when the medieval church was in eclipse; and St Germain thought that reason, which was 'written in the heart of every man', might as well replace natural law altogether. The sixteenth-century judges began to interpret statutes by the light of 'common reason'.[33]

The emergence of the nation-state was roughly coincident with the Reformation, and in these new entities natural law had to perform another function: it ceased to be the universal morality behind the laws of all nations, and became instead the basic constitution of each one. It developed national variations. In England, the class structure seemed most important to those fifteenth-century writers who identified the natural law with the law of arms; while Henry VIII emphasized the sacredness of property, maintaining that English law was chiefly concerned with questions of 'meum and tuum'. The natural law of an individual nation acquired a new name: *fundamental law*. Because it carried all the moral force of the old natural law, the idea of 'fundamental law', 'fundamental rights' and 'fundamental government', which were supreme over the king, was a potent weapon in Parliament's hands. Fundamental law was seen as the main constitutional safeguard, of which Parliament was merely the agent, and it was sometimes identified with the whole of the Common Law.[34]

The law developed certain ideals and a moral terminology peculiar to itself – justice, impartiality, equity, good faith, due process, rights and obligations. Justice is the application of the social ideal of equality to the legal process, and consists in dealing equally between all parties and classes. The ideal of justice has been the particular inspiration of certain departments of law, often ones with an economic bearing: it gave rise to the canonist principle of the just price and to the law about what the civilians call *unjustifiable enrichment*, that is, profiting by fraud or mistake at another's expense. The rule of impartiality, derived from the ideal of justice, has as its own derivative the principle invoked by Coke in *Bonham's Case* that no one should be judge in his own case. Equity again is a particular application of the ideal of justice; this time the application of the spirit of justice to the many cases in which strict law, by its inflexibility, would cause hardship. It was this ideal of equity, not the technical processes of Chancery, that English law took from Greek philosophy and Canon Law by way of St Germain. Against a foreign concept of equity so vague as to be interchangeable with 'conscience' and 'reason', the Common Lawyers could advance their opposing ideals of rigour and consistency. They complained with some justification that 'pretence of conscience' could veil arbitrary injustice, and they held to due process as their standard. The term 'Common Law' was thus used in opposition to 'equity'; and, to emphasize the empirical development of the Common Law procedures, it could be opposed to 'statute-law' as well. Equity, Common Law and statute-law were separate ideals in danger of engaging in a three-cornered contest.[35]

If politics is the art of the possible in government, law is the art of the possible in public morality. The really influential ideals of law are social goods in a form modest enough to be enforceable by the means of law. Similarly, the moral distinctions used in law must not be too subtle for use. When it requires proof of *mens rea*, English law does not mean that a criminal must be shown to have acted with 'a wicked mind' – only to have acted consciously. *Responsibility*, the fitness of a man to answer for his actions in court, is the chief moral criterion invoked in criminal cases. Again, in private law, the standards of negligence – for a long time simply the failure to avoid what was not absolutely inevitable – have been applicable rather than ideal ones. Its restriction of society's high ideals within the bounds of the possible has naturally made law appear sometimes rather shabby. But this modesty of aim is surely preferable to strong contrasts between ideals and facts.

THE EUROPEAN BACKGROUND

In two senses the ideas of law are historical in origin. Firstly, they may be the products of a particular historical situation: 'the Common Law' and perhaps even 'custom' became current as political slogans. Secondly, lawyers and jurists, giving a lead to anthropologists, sometimes turned to the history of society for their remedies for present ills; as the chancellor in *Rex* v. *Pickering* (p. 154, above) invoked the methods of the Indians against libellers. Both roads take us back to Roman Law, the supreme example of a legal system which reflected, and in its turn shaped, the ideas of a whole civilization. The concepts of rights and duties, crime and civil injuries, relate not to narrow legal issues but to the place of man in society, and these and many other ideas – as opposed to procedures – the Common Law drew from the stream of jurisprudence which had sprung up in Rome.

The development of the Common Law has been described so far in this book as a purely autonomous process, and in one field – the growth of the conciliar courts – the influence of Roman Law has been expressly denied. But, of course, the ideas of the Common Law – as opposed, again, to its detailed procedures – could not escape the influence of what has been for 2,000 years the greatest body of law in the world. Even the procedures on which English law was built in the twelfth century may have been suggested by Roman practice, transmitted for the most part by the canonists. There is a fascinating similarity between the classical Roman formulary system and the English forms of action, and *Praecipe* in particular may have had Roman antecedents. But the actual transmission of Roman and canonist procedures to English law is difficult to demonstrate. Sometimes it was clearly only a case of the natural growth of law in Rome being repeated again in England. Roman Law is important just because it was the first great example of the crystallization of social processes into law, and its still unfinished course is the prime example of the historical interaction of law and society over the centuries.[36]

The year of the completion of the Emperor Justinian's code, 534 A.D., has a claim to be regarded as the greatest landmark in the history of law, and it is true to say that 'next to the Bible, no book has left a deeper mark upon the history of mankind than the *Corpus Juris Civilis*' (as the code was called). The criminal law of Rome was much less developed than her private law; and so 'civil law' (*jus civile*), which to the Roman meant all 'the law of the city', and to a medieval person meant secular Roman Law as distinct from Canon Law, at last became the name which distinguishes private law from the law of crimes. The barbarian kings of 'dark-age' Europe continued to issue codes of garbled Roman Law. That law survived, intermixed to a greater or lesser degree with Germanic and feudal law, and acquiring many local and customary variations. For a time the autocratic quality which had entered Roman Law in the imperial age was modified by contact with the *folk*. Then, the scientific study of Roman Law was reborn at Bologna under the teaching of Irnerius. Perhaps 'no later movement – not the Renaissance, not the Reformation – draws a stronger line across the annals of mankind than that which is drawn about the year 1100, when a human science [law] won a place beside theology'. The rebirth of Roman Law was at the same time the birth of the universities, along with new ways of teaching and the criticism of ancient texts. Half a century later the law of the church was codified on the Roman model by Gratian. This Canon Law was the most fruitful branch of the Roman tradition in the later Middle Ages, emphasizing the high social purpose of law; but in the hands of the pope and his agents it acquired once more a summary and despotic aspect, symbolized by the Inquisition.[37]

Roman Law has remained the great norm, which legal

reformers have often sought to restore in its original purity. In the early sixteenth and in the early nineteenth centuries, as in the twelfth, cultural renaissance was accompanied by a renovation of Roman Law: the first associated with the France of Jacques Cujas (*c.* 1522–90) and the geographical extension of Roman Law known as the Reception, the second with Napoleon's *Code Civil* of 1804 and the German jurist, Savigny (1779–1861). The necessary background to both reforms was intense historical investigation.

All this time, England had been retracing Rome's steps with variations appropriate to her own historical situation. By the sixteenth century, English law was strong enough to resist the Reception of the 'purified' Roman Law, while Scotland, whose medieval law was much as England's but less developed, slowly succumbed. In 1871, Sir Henry Maine believed that Roman Law was 'fast becoming the lingua franca of a universal jurisprudence' and would oust the Common Law from America and the colonies. This has not happened, and Roman Law and the Common Law are now hardly the same kind of things. Roman Law is a reservoir of juristic ideas applicable in any system of courts and procedures, particularly applicable perhaps in a system where judges have a great deal of discretion. A rule of Roman Law may still get a favourable reception in an English court.[38]

CHAPTER 10

LAW IN ENGLISH HISTORY

THIS chapter will try to justify the assertion in the introduction that the history of the law is the history of society and to a large extent also of politics and the constitution.

THE LAW AND LIBERTY

Law was the protector of men from arbitrary government. The individual defendant was safeguarded by the due process of the Common Law, and the 'constant course' of Star Chamber. In 1328, the Statute of Northampton declared that a royal command disturbing the course of the law should be ignored by the judges, and fifteenth-century judges swore not to delay justice even at the king's order. The security and courage of the judges were therefore essential to liberty. Judges were originally appointed 'during the king's pleasure' (*durante beneplacito*), and from time to time one of them (like Coke in 1616) was dismissed for inconvenient judgments. It was in a way a compliment that few officials apart from legal ones were dismissed by the Stuarts for political reasons: law was too important for legal offices to become property and their holders irresponsible. Legends arose of the courage of judges before angry kings – of how Chief Justice Raleigh reversed the irregular outlawing of Hubert de Burgh by Henry III, and Chief Justice Gascoigne imprisoned Prince Henry – later King Henry V – for contempt of court.[1]

Usually, the king had to resort to the same corrupt methods as his greater subjects to divert the course of justice, for he enjoyed few special advantages. Slowly the ordinary criminal was accorded reasonably equal terms in his contest with the Crown: proper, indeed excessively formal indictment, within a definite period from the alleged offence; freedom from giving evidence on oath, which might have compelled self-incrimination; and (as early as the thirteenth century) security from re-arrest for a crime of which he was once acquitted (*autrefois acquit*). After 1552 at least two witnesses were required to convict a man of treason (5 & 6 Ed. 6, c. 11). On the other hand the sixteenth-century Privy Council authorized torture, and the Court of High Commission used the *ex officio* oath to compel the unorthodox to condemn themselves out of their own mouths. The criminal trials of that period look brutal and one-sided to us – the prisoner was allowed no copy of the indictment, no counsel, no witnesses on his behalf – but there was a certain logic in this: it was the Crown which had to make a case and prove guilt, and if the prisoner needed advocates he should find them in the judges.[2]

Individual liberty was threatened as much by tyrannical officials or intolerant society as by the king. To a Parliament which condemned men unheard by acts of attainder the rule of law seems to have meant as little as to a modern 'people's court'. Some feared that the parliamentary lawyers were out to destroy the king's prerogative to become 'more absolute Governors than any legal prince in Christendom'.[3] The royal prerogative might fail against Parliament, but it was an effective protection against the petty injustices of local officials. The writ of *habeas corpus* which ordered the giving up of a prisoner was a medieval 'prerogative' writ, put under the control of King's Bench only in the sixteenth century, and turned against an arbitrary monarch in the seventeenth.

No less important were the prerogative writs of *certiorari*, *prohibition* and *mandamus*, for they were the means of restraining courts and other public bodies against which the individual is powerless, and the root of what is now called 'administrative law'. A normal action for damages was the remedy against the individual official, whose misdeeds fill the medieval plea-rolls: there was a large 'administrative' element from the beginning of English law. But some special means was needed to curb the organization which overstepped its authority. The writs of certiorari and prohibition

A SOCIAL HISTORY OF ENGLISH LAW

were evolved in the Middle Ages to quash the judicial decisions of the J.P.s and the church courts respectively, when they seemed to have exceeded their jurisdiction, and in the mid seventeenth century the method was extended to the administrative acts of the J.P.s, particularly in connexion with the poor law. Mandamus, a weapon which Coke appears to have seized for the King's Bench from the Privy Council, was used to restore freemen deprived of their borough franchise, and then any official arbitrarily deprived of his office by a corporate body – it was the office-holder's 'writ of right'.[4]

THE LAW AND INEQUALITY

The law emphasized class distinctions, and to a great extent was the custom of the aristocracy. The villein was marked out by legal disabilities: since he could not own land, he could not use the real actions. The Common Law was the law of freemen – or rather, of freeholders. In a system worked by the corruption of juries and the 'grace' of officials the rich had an overwhelming advantage. 'Law,' said Langland in *Piers Plowman*, 'is so lordly, and loth to make end without presents.' In the sixteenth-century Chancery, peers could give evidence on their honour, and a lady objected successfully against impertinent interrogatories. Chancellor Hatton, indeed, asserted that 'law is the inheritance of all men' and developed special procedures for poor suitors. The scheme of *c.* 1534 for 'conservators of the commonweal' would have provided a sort of legal aid, and even costs for acquitted defendants. But the cost of the law remained one of the chief grievances of the poor.[5]

Justice might be described as the morality of class relationships; but it was in the control of the gentry. In the Court of Chivalry men were forced to confess their sins against 'the gentry laws'. As J.P.s the gentry put down the riots of their labourers, and as M.P.s they passed the statutes which allowed them to do so. A J.P. was sworn to 'do equal right to poor and rich', but at the end of the sixteenth century he was

244

defined as 'a living creature that for half-a-dozen chickens will dispense with a whole dozen of penal statutes'. Mr J. P. Dawson believes that the main peculiarity of English legal history was the king's unusual reliance (for purposes of economy) on amateur justices and the courts of the local communities: thus it was that the Englishman established his freedom and learnt his well-known respect for the law which he administered. In fact, it may be doubted whether the respect was not a form of social subservience to justices who promoted nothing so much as the dominance of their class.[6]

In many ways, the law, which was primarily a law of land, served the purpose and set the tone of the upper classes. In Henry VIII's reign there was a proposal to restrict the right of entail to the nobility, whose land was their foundation. A man's 'honour' was the collection of feudal services due to him, and he was 'out of countenance' if he was displaced from his *contenementum*, his piece of land and his position in society. Only the purchase of land could make an aristocrat of a merchant. Amongst the social phenomenon linked to the landed aristocracy is heraldry, which provided, in the coat of arms with its quarterings and marks of cadence, an exact register of the continuance, amalgamation and division of family lines. But genealogies and coats of arms could be forged, and a verdict of the too long inexpert heralds on one of their visitations or in the Court of Chivalry might indirectly establish one's claim to the material possessions of a line, along with its insignia. A second phenomenon, caused by the practice of magnates to re-enfeoff their lands to themselves and their wives jointly (an early device for avoiding the feudal obligations of relief, wardship and escheat), was a race of formidable dowagers, disposing of vast properties. One such was the authoress, Lady Russell (1528–1609), whose letters to her powerful kinsman, Lord Burghley, demanding justice for herself and her daughter and containing wonderfully confident verdicts on the complex subject of contingent remainders, fill many pages of the Hatfield MSS. One of her last actions was to write to Garter King of Arms to ask about her funeral – 'what number of mourners were due to her calling . . . the manner of the hearse, of the heralds and church'.[7]

Law-suits about land were the country gentleman's main preoccupation. At any time the average landlord would be carrying on two or three campaigns, each lasting several years, to extend his sway by a combination of law-suits and violent invasion of the disputed land. At the stage of violence criminal law came in as a counter in the private struggle, the J.P. using his duties in case of riot to condemn his rival's aggression and justify his own. An example will show how this was done. In the Autumn of 1589, the earl of Lincoln decided that he had a claim to the Oxfordshire manor of Weston-on-the-Green, then occupied by James Croft as the tenant of Lord Norris of Rycote, and tried to make good his claim by holding a manor-court at Weston. He arrived at Weston House while Croft was away visiting; gained admittance, 'to preserve her majesty's peace' according to his followers, 'riotously' according to his opponents; and, fearing a counter-attack, called upon the constable of Weston to stay in the house overnight. Croft returned, and it so happened that he was a J.P. and had a special claim on the support of the lord-lieutenant of the county, none other than Lord Norris. At the door of his house he cried out in a loud voice, 'constable of Weston-on-the-Green . . . here is a justice of the peace and of the quorum . . . come forth of the house and see her majesty's peace kept'. But from inside came the reply: 'there is here in the house a justice of the peace and quorum, and he [the constable] shall not come forth'. There was deadlock for several days, each side exhorting the other 'to keep her highness's peace', till the Earl had to go away on business and further J.P.s, sent by Norris, decided the issue.[8]

It has been suggested that one of the reasons why the aristocracy became less troublesome at the end of the sixteenth century was the complication of litigation, absorbing all their energies. Violence turned into litigiousness. At the same time, the appearance of a 'rise of the gentry', which has generated so much heat amongst present-day historians, may have been produced by better methods of endowing younger sons, with a consequent enlargement of the gentry class.[9]

In seventeenth-century France, an absolute monarchy was doing something to protect the poor against the landlords. In England, the conciliar courts which attempted to follow suit went down in 1642 before the gentry, along with a would-be absolute monarchy. To a few radicals the landowning class and its law were at last revealed as the true oppressors. An effective revolution, they believed, would have to destroy the Common Law. The myth of a 'Norman Yoke', which in 1066 had descended cataclysmically on the primitive democracy of the Anglo-Saxons and had still to be shaken off, became the answer to Coke's 'Whig interpretation of history', depicting an uninterrupted growth of English freedoms under the rule of law. 'The tedious, unknown, and impossible-to-be-understood Common Law practice in Westminster Hall came in by the will of a tyrant, namely William the Conqueror', wrote John Lilburne in 1646. The source of law, Parliament, was tainted too, for, as Tom Paine said in the 1770s, it was a boon which had been granted by 'crowned ruffians', the successors of the 'French bastard' with his 'armed banditti'. After 1642 radical critics of the Common Law were never to be lacking, and the *Leveller* tradition eventually merged with the Marxist view of law as the tool of the dominant class.[10]

THE LAW AND COMMUNITY

Another form of inequality was expressed in law – the natural inequality of persons of different age and sex. In law, the child and the wife, like the tenant-at-will, were regarded as entirely in the power of someone else – the father or guardian, the husband or the landlord, who must sue on their behalf. They were thus particularly vulnerable and in company with lunatics were extended the protection of Chancery. For the wife, the *feme covert*, her subordination was somewhat compensated by the reduction of her liability for crimes committed under her husband's control. Domestic servants have until very recently stood in the relation of children to their masters, and the same action of trespass on the case (*per quod servitium amisit*) lay for the enticing away of a servant and of a child. This was not so much the law of a few horizontal classes as of many vertical, that is hierarchical, communities in which inequality of status was reconciled by family relationships or land tenure.

Though, as Maitland maintained, a corporation is a moral reality before it is a legal fiction, all groups which are more than mere aggregates must have corporate funds, legal status (as though they were individual persons), and their own rules. The legal advantages of incorporation consisted in the power to undertake contracts and acquire property as a community, symbolized by possession of a common seal. In the sixteenth century many a borough got a charter from the Crown, making it 'a body corporate and politic by the name of the mayor, bailiffs and burgesses', in order to buy up the lands of a dissolved monastery or chantry lying within it. But the original growth of borough corporations was natural and independent of royal grant. Many towns had seals by 1300. London, though not itself formally incorporated till 1608, was invoking the idea of corporate responsibility by 1130, when it obtained the right to distrain any merchant from another town for the debts of his fellow-merchants to Londoners.[11]

The state did and does keep a close control on such versatile bodies as corporations. One of them may last for generations, since it can replace its deceased members, and by a statute of 1391 secular corporations were therefore subjected along with ecclesiastical ones to the necessity of obtaining licences to acquire land in mortmain. The greater communities were marked out by the possession of all the apparatus of law. Long before it was officially incorporated, London legislated in the highest style, claiming on one occasion that the acts of its common council were 'of no less strength than acts of the high court of parliament'. It had its own bar, and its courts punished citizens for pleading in the king's courts.

But the Crown instructed the J.P.s to make a careful scrutiny of the bye-laws of the London guilds and companies and other corporations. For this reason, the Inns of Court and other organizations vested their funds in the alternative device of the trust, which opened the way for a quite un-designed liberty of association.[12]

The lawyers formed a number of important communities within London society. There was the law term, the London 'season', focused on the colourful life of the palace of West-minster, and there were the Inns of Court, nation-wide com-munities of lawyers and country gentlemen, whose loyalty to their 'old colleges' was lifelong. The very fabric of the inns grew by the efforts of members who tacked rickety ex-tensions on to their chambers, frequently enraging neigh-bours in the process, and certainly there were no societies in London to rival them for turbulent life. Shallow, the Glou-cestershire justice in Shakespeare's *Henry IV*, part II, recalls sentimentally 'the mad days that I have spent' at Clement's Inn, with 'little John Doit of Staffordshire, and black George Bare, and Francis Pickbone, and Will Squele a Cotsald man – you had not four such swinge-bucklers in all the Inns-of-court again'. The inns were known for high living and high spirits. Their Christmas revels were famous: Shallow recalled when he was 'Sir Dagonet in Arthur's Show', and it was at Gray's Inn at Christmas 1594 that *The Comedy of Errors* was first performed. The inns had still other attractions. It was said that one Ulveston got himself made steward of the Middle Temple in 1451, and one Isley, steward of the Inner Temple, 'for excuse for dwelling this time from their wives'.[13]

Though the old nobility did not usually attend the inns, those who rose into the nobility through successful politics almost always had done so: of these were Thomas Cromwell, earl of Essex; William Cecil, Lord Burghley; Thomas Went-worth, earl of Strafford; and Edward Hyde, earl of Claren-don. At all stages of their progress such men could make use of the contacts made at the Inns of Court, much as a modern politician might use his youthful contacts at Balliol. The J.P.s who had been to the inns carried into the counties the social and political fashions of London: 'and now is this vice's dagger became a squire', marvelled Falstaff at the sight of Shallow. The more elusive, yet probably more important, influence was the reciprocal one: how far did the students at the inns reflect the loyalties of their localities, which remained the basis of English political life? The inns only intensified the local divisions, in so far as the great families of each county sent their sons into the chambers of some local man who had made good, just as the lesser gentry apprenticed their sons to London tradesmen. But, at the inns also, bonds might be created between different parts of the country, for they were, like parliament, thriving marriage markets.

Within London there were communities created by the law in stranger ways. There were those exotic growths, the criminal societies in the sanctuaries and the debtors' society in the Fleet. Reading 'The Oeconomy of the Fleete or an apologetical answer of Alexander Harris (late Warden there) unto xix articles set forth against him by the prisoners' (c. 1620), one begins to think that more happened inside the prison's walls than outside: 'To the Fleet they will bring their wives, children, and servants to cohabit, women are brought to bed there . . . and no other breeding have some than there; . . . they exempt themselves from house rent, parish duties, and all taxations . . . ; they endeavour to have a chamber in the Fleet, with gardens, yards, places of pleasure, at the third or fourth part that it would cost abroad, so that by excess of families there are two or three menial servants to one prisoner . . . it is better than a hospital, for to an hospital none shall be admitted that hath livelihood abroad. . . . In the Fleet all this may be done, and from the Fleet many will not go though they be cleared or you would force them, because they can . . . follow and solicit law-suits . . . and with a little Fleet reading become counsellors, attorneys, doctors, chirurgeons, scribes, cooks, and all manner of handicrafts to that precinct, where sometimes are plotted robberies abroad, cutting of purses in town . . . and no hue and cry . . . can follow, for the Fleet is a privileged place . . .' The Fleet was 'a law unto itself'.[14]

Only as the Common Law overcame custom did the greatest community of all, the nation, which learnt much from London, become a loyalty stronger than the local community, a man's *patria* or 'country', to whose verdict he had been accustomed to appeal from a criminal accusation. The peripatetic eyres and the swarms of attorneys brought the English counties closer to one another: nothing travelled so much as the law. It must be admitted that the enormous business of litigation was a more important unifying factor than the success of the law in 'healing and settling' disputes. The legal process of distraint was the 'beginning of all wars', according to Simon de Montfort. Litigants were to some eyes 'idle hotheads, busy bodies and troublesome men in the Commonwealth', who would have been better ending matters at home by the mediation of their neighbours than waiting at Westminster 'and gaping upon their rolls and process in the law'.

But the law did make possible the growth of communal responsibility on a national scale. The upkeep of medieval roads, drains and bridges was enforced by the presentment and trial of those who neglected their duties. The welfare of the poor and the sick was, however, left to the church. The puritan radicals of the reformed church took up these responsibilities with an enthusiasm born of the conviction that grace and election were already theirs, but tempered by the same secularism that had filled laymen's pockets with the wealth of the monasteries into a canny emphasis on visible works. If there was a 'puritan ethic' which contributed to the rise of capitalism, it was a sincere religious hatred of the indiscriminate almsgiving, encouraging indigence, which the reformers attributed to the monasteries, and of the endowment of chantries for the benefit of souls in purgatory. The purposes of puritan charity were not entirely new, but the puritan merchants were the first to glimpse the idea of capital investment in the sense of permanent endowments producing material results, and the trust was the legal institution which made their schemes capable of realization. The most typical item in a puritan's will was therefore a bequest of 'stock for the setting of the poor to work'. Trusts might also be set up to provide alms-houses, hospitals, loans as working-capital for young men and marriage subsidies for young women, roads and bridges, schools, workhouses (private charity here far outstripped official measures) and even public libraries.[15]

Of course, benefactions to education and lectureships advanced Puritanism as a movement. By 1629, however, when Thomas Sutton gave the greatest sum of all to found the Blue-Coat school in the London charterhouse, one may feel that charity had become a form of social exhibitionism; and in Jonson's *The Alchemist* it is Sir Epicure Mammon who promises to employ his wealth

all in pious *uses*/Founding of colleges and grammar schools,/ Marrying young virgins, building hospitals,/And now and then a church.

Only a very small part of the sums thus invested has ever been lost, and inflation has now increased their value to several millions of pounds. This durability has been partly the result of the consistent attitude of the law: the list of charitable purposes given in a statute of 1601 protecting charitable trusts was reaffirmed by a legal committee in 1952. Partly it was due to the corporate sense and civic pride of the towns and particularly of London, where the livery companies, whose members the benefactors so often were, became the greatest trustees of all. Conversely, trusts cultivated corporateness and civic pride not in the towns only but in that newer community, the nation, for both London merchants and wealthy country yeomen began to feel responsibility for counties other than their own, where the people were less godly (as in papist Lancashire) or the poor were poorer. If England was ceasing to be medieval by 1642, law played its part in the change, along with religion and trade and government.

THE LAW, THE KING AND THE STATE

The law never played so large a part in the history of English society as in the early years of the seventeenth century, for the political issue then was the rights of the king as against the rights of his subjects. Since the thirteenth century and the first political theory, the king in England had been regarded as 'under God and the law'. Richard Hooker was using the language of Bracton when he wrote, in the sixteenth century, 'so is the power of the king over all and in all limited that unto all his proceedings the law itself is a rule. The axioms of our regal government are these: "*Lex facit regem*" [the law makes the king].' As it was put in the seventeenth century: 'the King's prerogative stretcheth not to the doing of any wrong: for it growth wholly from the reason of the Common Law and is as it were a finger of the hand. . .' The bad king could be deposed because by the very fact of doing wrong he ceased to be king: this line of reasoning led to the crucial distinction between the king for the time being and the Crown as an institution. No new theory was needed to send Charles I the way of Edward II and Richard II.[16]

There was, then, some rudimentary public or constitutional law. But the king's position was much more fully worked out in terms of private law. Bracton thought of the nation in terms of a common element in civil litigation – the joint and inseparable interests of a number of parties to the same suit. Similarly, in the Middle Ages, the king's prerogative meant no more than the special property rights of the crown as supreme feudal overlord, though Edward I's broadening of proceedings on writs of *Quo Warranto* from feudal rights to the usurpation of franchises (all the profitable rights of local government which the king considered his alone to grant) perhaps made the king's prerogative look more like a constitutional power. Since kingship was a complex of property rights it could be entailed and Parliament could regulate the descent of it, as the property of attainted men was taken and restored by act. '. . . The said imperial crown,' ran a statute of 1534, '[shall descend] from son and heir male to son and heir male. . . . And for default of such sons . . . to the eldest issue female, which is the Lady Elizabeth [Mary, Catherine's daughter, being passed over].'[17]

In another sense, however, the king was the source of law.

The courts were his creation. Appropriately, some of the earliest portraits of kings were miniatures within the illuminated capital letters at the beginning of plea-rolls. The basis of every complaint was a breach of the king's peace or protection, and so until very recently the Crown – the departments of government – could not be sued in tort, since this appeared to be suing the king for an offence against himself (as early as 1270, on the other hand, property could be recovered from the Crown by a *petition of right*). As the enforcer of law, the king might strike harder in certain cases – and he had the right also to hold back the blow, to show mercy, to pardon. This power was sometimes resented but could not be effectively challenged, for it was his own right which the king was waiving.[18]

By the early seventeenth century there were thus two known types of prerogative: the king's feudal property rights and his executive rights in matters of war and peace and justice. The Stuarts precipitated a crisis by extending their executive powers too blatantly to dispensation from statute-law: the law and not just the execution of it was identified with the king's will. The Stuarts' extension of their prerogative was aided by the growth of the distinct theory of the divine right of kings, a theory fostered by the circumstances of the Reformation, when many churchmen reconciled themselves to government coercion by the belief that 'we may not in any wise resist . . . the anointed of the Lord'. The civilian, Dr Cowell, deduced absolute prerogative from absolute obedience: 'the King of England is an absolute King,' he wrote in 1607, and he 'is above the law by his absolute power.' Yet oppose prerogative in action, Parliament did.[19]

A connected question was whether the king's powers in time of war and emergency permitted extra-parliamentary taxation of his subjects' property. In *Bate's Case* (1606), the Exchequer (the court for matters of prerogative in the sense of the king's property rights) decided that the king could legitimately impose export and import duties without consulting Parliament. *Hampden's Case* (1637) decided that the king could levy ship-money by writ 'when the good and safety of the kingdom in general is concerned'. For the king these were pyrrhic victories. If the law was against what they conceived to be their fundamental rights, the parliamentarians would be tempted to change it. They began with the (national) *Petition of Right* of 1628, which invoked Magna Carta and other medieval provisions against extra-parliamentary taxation, and asserted that imprisonment at the king's command (discussed inconclusively in the *Five Knights' Case* of the previous year) was not proof against a writ of Habeas Corpus.[20]

The establishment of 'royal supremacy' over the church had been the symbolic affirmation of the king's supremacy in the whole nation; and it was also the subjection of the church's law of sin to the Common Law of peace. A rival legal system was destroyed, and in High Commission the king himself acquired some of the resources of a totalitarian state for prying into a person's conscience and morals. The idea of the two political entities, Church and State, arose from medieval quarrels between bishops and kings, often over matters of jurisdiction. One of the causes of the overthrow of the Roman church in the sixteenth century was the layman's hatred of the petty tyranny of the ecclesiastical courts – tyranny which produced in 1515 the scandal of the death of Richard Hunne in the Bishop of London's prison. The Reformation in England turned upon Parliament's *Supplication against the Ordinaries* or ecclesiastical judges (1532), and the *Act in Restraint of Appeals* to Rome (1533), the latter a declaration that 'this realm of England is an empire . . . a body politic, compact of . . . spirituality and temporality', all owing 'humble obedience' to 'one supreme head and king'. The study of Canon Law was banned at the universities and Roman civil law, the weapon of despotic princes, encouraged in its place. With jurisdiction over blasphemy, heresy and other sins, the Reformation was believed to have restored to the king the 'absolute empire and monarchy' which were rightfully his and anciently had been. But this theory, expressed in *Cawdrey's Case* (1591), and the practice of the

Court of High Commission, were more limbs for the leviathan at which Parliament took fright.[21]

THE COURTS AND THE CONSTITUTION

The medieval constitution might be described as a network of courts. Everyone had to attend some court regularly. There were special eyres for offences against the king's forest rights; a section of the Exchequer court dealt with Jewish cases; and the Cornish tin-miners had their court of the Stannaries. 'Jurisdiction was the first reason for making distinctions' between types of cases; and everyone knew the meaning of 'I will make a Star Chamber matter of it'. In medieval England political power was dispersed, and the arrangement of local courts and itinerant commissions conformed to its distribution. England was in effect a conglomeration of 'countries', held together by its legal system.[22]

There were ruinous conflicts between the courts, for jurisdiction meant profit (in the early seventeenth century, fees paid to Chancery, King's Bench and Common Pleas amounted to over £100,000 per annum, as against about £20,000 to the government). Thus accustomed to a militant independence, the Common Law courts were not inclined to serve the purposes of the Stuarts, who tried to get from them opinions favourable to the prerogative. Richard II had put a series of questions to the judges about his rights, and the Stuarts made such a practice of it that Pym had to complain of 'the extra-judicial declarations of judges, without hearing of counsel or argument'. In *Peacham's Case* (1615), Coke resisted the king's scheme to take the opinions of the judges separately and individually, and in the *Case of Commendams* (1616), which caused his downfall, stood out against the king in collective debate. In the *Case of Proclamations* (1610), the judges, taught by the king the political value of their opinions, had gone on to the offensive, and claimed that the royal prerogative did not extend to the creation of new offences by proclamation. In the reports of a body of judgments largely hostile to the king a written constitution of a sort was making its appearance.[23]

The opposition to the king was focused in the High Court of Parliament. The uniqueness of the English Parliament lay in its combination of the functions of a supreme court and a representative political assembly; and this is why it throve while the separate *Parlements* and Estates-General in France faltered. The petition was the link between the two roles, and, on petition, Parliament possessed entire jurisdiction – civil and criminal, original and appellate, the last including the hearing of errors in the Irish courts. This extraordinary jurisdiction came to be exercised predominantly by the Lords, and in 1400 the lower House petitioned to be relieved from legal business. The Lords already comprised a distinct court, for the very notion of peerage was derived from the privilege of a magnate accused of a criminal offence to be tried by his equals, who were conveniently assembled in the House of Lords and presided over for this purpose by the Lord High Steward of England. The actual jurisdiction of Parliament was reduced by the development of the other courts to the hearing in the Lords of infrequent petitions against errors in King's Bench. As a Common Law court, Parliament did not until the seventeenth century consider itself competent to hear appeals from equity.

In the sixteenth century, the House of Commons began to claim that it was a court by itself, in order to gain for its members the normal privileges of officers and suitors in one of the king's courts. *Strode's Case* (1513) established that an M.P. could not be sued for what he said in the House. Until 1543, a Member arrested by the order of another court could be freed by a writ of privilege sued out of Chancery by the Speaker, but in *Ferrers's Case* of that year the Commons began to act on their own warrant. By this means M.P.s and their servants escaped their creditors, though the House might itself send a defaulting member to the Tower. The next and much harder step for the Commons was to establish freedom of speech and freedom from arrest against the king as well as against other courts. As a court, the Commons also claimed to adjudicate disputed parliamentary elections, though previously these had always been decided in Chancery, which issued the writs of election and received the returns. In *Goodwin's Case* (1604), King James was constrained to recognize the Commons as 'a Court of Record and a judge of returns'.[24]

The seventeenth-century Parliament – Lords and Commons together – fought the king by reasserting its fourteenth-century position as a supreme court. But in 300 years its composition had changed, and after the accession of James I the council which had been its root lost all influence within it. 'The king in his council in parliament' no longer existed; the government and the highest court of the realm had parted company; and a great confrontation between them was possible, perhaps inevitable. The main judicial form of Parliament's attack was the condemnation of the king's ministers by impeachment and attainder. Impeachment was a way of arraigning political figures before the House of Lords, worked out by the magnates and the king against each other in the political crises of Richard II's reign. The Commons had then been employed as the accusors, and in James I's reign they revived the device, unused since 1459, on their own initiative. In March 1621, the Commons attended at the bar of the House of Lords to demand judgment against Sir Giles Mompesson, a monopolist, who was promptly sentenced to life imprisonment. That same year, the Lords were brought to condemn their own 'Speaker', Lord Chancellor Bacon.[25]

To dispose of the earl of Strafford in 1641, the Commons did not plead – they condemned the earl themselves by introducing a bill, to state that his offences 'hath been sufficiently proved' and to enact that he 'be adjudged and attainted of high treason, and shall suffer . . . pains of death . . .' This was murder by act of Parliament, planned to deprive the victim of any defence: 'it must be done before he answer.' Justice and politics had contaminated each other. Yet the solemn process of impeachment still had something to give the constitution. Well into the eighteenth century it was the only reminder to ministers that they were responsible to Commons and people as well as to the king, and it found a permanent place in the constitution of the United States.[26]

LAW, HISTORY AND THE ENGLISH REVOLUTION

All societies appear to have speculated and made myths about the origins of their laws. To invaders like the Normans, emphasis on the continuity of English law was a way of asserting their legitimate succession to English government. In China the same advantage was secured for usurpers by the practice of writing an official history of the displaced dynasty; but in the West mature historiography was a by-product of the political use made of law in the sixteenth century. Men turned to history to justify their view of the constitution, because antiquity was the only undisputed attribute of the fundamental law they all invoked. But English lawyers pushed the argument beyond history: the Common Law had always been as it was. The idea of the antiquity and uniqueness of the English political tradition ('the Whig view of history') followed from this myth of the immemoriality and uniqueness of English law.[27]

Those who opposed an immemorial customary law to royal prerogative obviously could not admit historical legislators. Anyone who put forward a historical account of the growth of English law was immediately suspected of royalism. Sir Henry Spelman (? 1564–1641) was the first to show that all the Common Law's main features could be explained by the historical fact of feudalism. Sir James Harrington (1611–77) could then go on to formulate, in *The Commonwealth of Oceana* (1656), the general theory of the connexion between land tenure and constitutional changes which lies behind the 'rise-of-the-gentry' theory of the English revolution. Spelman, though he may not have known it, provided the historical account of English legal development which the parliamentary lawyers feared. It was easy to show that feudalism came with the Normans: the Conquest was reinstated as the great historical divide: no longer could the immemoriality of

English law, of England's Parliament and liberties, go undisputed. These historical matters were the meat of seventeenth-century political controversy, with better results,
perhaps, for history than for politics.

The pure concept of fundamental law was a political
weapon as two-edged as history. When he said in *Bonham's
Case* that a 'repugnant' act of parliament would be 'controlled' by the courts, Coke was not proposing 'judicial review'
of legislation, such as was later written into the constitution
of the United States. He knew that the judges could not
declare statutes unconstitutional and therefore void; but he
did believe that there were some fundamental principles
behind English law which it was inadvisable for Parliament
to alter, and he was advocating the strictest interpretation of
statutes which appeared to alter them. At their simplest these
principles were the rights of the king and his subjects, often
summed up in the words of Seneca: 'To kings belong power. .
to citizens property.' People were beginning to see that these
rights together made up a 'constitution' – even James I
recognized it. The problem was the demarcation of these
rights, made urgent by the vastly increased responsibilities
of kingship, and of the value of the property on which the king
might call in an emergency. Divergent interpretations of
fundamental law appeared: the king, seeing his prerogative
as the main part of it, used it to justify the impeachment of
five rebellious M.P.s; while, in the Grand Remonstrance of
December 1641, the Commons denounced the king for 'a
malignant and pernicious design of subverting the fundamental laws and principles of government'. Against the
king's cry of necessity, Parliament in the end came to state
fundamental law in a new way – as the good of the people.
'*Salus populi suprema lex*' justified Parliament in acting without
the king.[28]

It has been argued that Parliament was guilty of an error
of tactics in using the weapon of fundamental law (which
admitted too much royal prerogative), rather than Fortescue's intrinsically more modern idea that England was a
'mixed monarchy', where the check on the king was the

political necessity of gaining his subjects' cooperation in his projects. But, in fact, Fortescue's idea was another common formulation of fundamental law, meaning once again that both king and subject had rights. The imprecision, or rather comprehensiveness, of the fundamental law concept is one of its most interesting facets. For it shows that law was the universal political framework: law, not economic interests, still – but for not much longer – shaped men's political thinking.[29]

In the Wars of the Roses the administration of the law in the counties had become the plaything of politics. In the early seventeenth century, politics were near to becoming the playthings of the lawyers and their doctrines; of the Common Law courts; and of the great corporations, like London and the merchant companies, which the law had helped to create. If there had ever been any danger from the civilians, by 1600 the Common Lawyers were triumphant. 'The medieval books poured from the press, new books were written, the decisions of the courts were more diligently reported. . . . We were having a little Renaissance of our own: or a Gothic revival if you please . . .' The ebullient Common Lawyers were natural leaders of a Parliament falling out with the Crown, and their energies were concentrated on the abolition of the 'prerogative courts', Star Chamber and High Commission. Of the courts tainted with Romanism, Requests had been on trial for its life since late in Elizabeth's reign, and in 1599 had been declared by Common Pleas 'no court that had power of judicature'. In the short Parliament of 1640, Edward Hyde made a reputation for himself by launching an attack on the 'upstart court' of Chivalry, in which (so he said) a respectable citizen might be condemned for bidding an insolent waterman 'be gone with his goose' when his badge was really a swan. Under the attentions of a parliamentary committee, the Court of Chivalry ceased to function in 1641, when Requests also came to a silent end.[30]

Star Chamber, High Commission, the Councils in the Marches and the North, and the Palatine Courts of Lancaster and Chester were, on the other hand, abolished with great ceremony on the 5 July 1641, as operating against the ordinary process of law and 'by experience . . . found to be an intolerable burden to the subject, and the means to introduce an arbitrary power and government'. After that consummation, many of the lawyers, Hyde the most notable among them, moved to a position of neutrality or joined the king to oppose Parliament's more outrageous claims. It was not just that the lawyers were born trimmers. Law had a distinctive part to fill in defining and restricting the king's power: in the nature of things it could not work a revolution, which is the transformation of law.[31]

PART THREE

CHAPTER II

THE AGE OF IMPROVISATION, 1642–1789

THE INTERREGNUM: A LOST OPPORTUNITY

IN 1641, Parliament destroyed a sizeable part of the legal system and put nothing in its place: consequently the reform which the lawyers feared became more necessary still. Moreover, the Common Law was as unpopular with the lower classes feeling their way towards political power as the conciliar courts had been unpopular with the Common Lawyers. After 1641, the lawyers were no longer the political leaders, and soon their allies, the Commons, reduced to a bigoted Rump, lost their power to the army. Parliament could not be used to try the king, who was an essential part of the process of impeachment; so a special High Court of Justice was constituted of 150 persons, and the king was condemned to death in 1649 'as a tyrant, traitor, murderer and public enemy to the good people of this nation'. The people had become the final court of appeal, and it was logical two months later to abolish the House of Lords, found 'by too long experience' to be 'useless and dangerous to the people of England'.[1]

The people, represented by the radical elements in the army, turned against Parliament; against the 'hotchpotch of linsey-wolsey laws, so numerous, as not be be learned or comprehended, some so differing as that they contradict and give the lie to one another, so irrational and absurd . . .'; and against the 'Grand Cheat and Abominable Idol Called the Course of ye Courts'. The army was demanding that fundamental law be written down as a constitution which would thenceforth be unchangeable by Parliament. Others wanted 'one plain, complete and methodical treatise or abridgement of the whole common and statute law', to which all judges would have to subscribe 'for settled law', so that 'every man may know his duty, and his danger'.[2]

Though an enthusiastic committee of amateurs found the latter task too much for them, changes were made in the law. The Court of Wards, wardship and the other incidents of feudal tenure, and tenure by knight-service itself, were abolished by an ordinance of 1646. A form of civil marriage before a J.P. was instituted. Fees for certain legal documents were done away with, and in court the pleading of the general issue was encouraged. But many fundamental reforms besides codification were frustrated. It was generally but vainly hoped that Chancery, 'a Mystery of wickedness', would go the way of Star Chamber. Twenty-three thousand cases were believed to be pending before it: yet some which had been there for 30 years and had involved 500 (contradictory) orders would be quickly enough settled 'by a reference to some gentlemen in the country' when clients' purses began to empty. The criminal law was not reformed, though Cromwell denounced the 'wicked abominable laws' which pardoned murderers and hanged men for stealing a shilling. No answer was made to the demand for the replacement of the central courts by omnicompetent county-courts, 'that the people might have right at their own doors', and for registries of deeds in every county. Proposals which got further before defeat would have created courts of law and equity at York, abolished entail, and suppressed fraudulent conveyancing, sale of offices and duels.[3]

A less worthy scheme to restrict equity of redemption, probably in the interest of speculators in land confiscated from the royalists, also came to nothing. Generally, however, it was the retrograde and repressive measures which succeeded. Treason was redefined very widely. Incest and adultery were declared capital felonies. Anglican-inspired laws concerning church attendance were repealed, but penalties were imposed for 'dancing, profanely singing, drinking or tipling' on a Sunday, and for swearing at any time.

The destructive zeal of the Long Parliament and the failures of the Interregnum together condemned English law to years of incompleteness and improvisation, until the job of comprehensive reform was taken up again in the nineteenth century. What the Protectorate did achieve by way of legislation was erased from legal memory at the Restoration (the House of Lords therefore returned to life), but the maiming of 1641 had been properly done by king and parliament, and was not healed. (Only the inessential church-courts, and for the brief period from 1687 to 1700 the Court of Chivalry, were revived.) Perhaps the worst result of the interregnum was the justification it gave for complacency amongst the lawyers. Sir Matthew Hale, chief justice of Common Pleas and 'the last of the great record searching judges', carried into the Restoration a picture of an age-old law which had overcome a temporary adversity. The law 'knew itself to be the perfection of wisdom, and any proposal for drastic legislation would have worn the garb discredited by the tyranny of the Puritan Caesar'.[4]

THE JUSTICES AND POLICING IN A CHANGING SOCIETY

Together, lawyers and aristocracy weathered the storm of the interregnum. The ancient aristocratic government of the country had seemed to be in jeopardy, when Parliament's system of county committees and Cromwell's major-generals ousted the justices of the peace. Political confiscation caused landed families to rise and fall more quickly than before. But the changes proved to be superficial as well as temporary. At the Restoration, the gentry entered an age of prosperity in which the J.P.s could afford to treat popular disorder with comparative leniency. And the constant supervision of the Tudor and early Stuart privy council was one of the things not restored. The Glorious Revolution of 1689 concentrated power in the hands of an oligarchy of Whig nobles and virtually ended interference with the local justices, even by the judges. The basis of local authority was wealth. An act of 1732 disqualified from the office of justice attorneys, solicitors and anyone not possessing an estate worth £100 a year. If he had the money, 'any booby' might be invested 'with the ensigns of magistracy'.[5]

In fact, the few working justices amongst the 250 or so on each county's commission usually acted responsibly, administering the law informally and humanely in their own homes or in village inns. A single justice could fine a drunkard on the spot, give a gambler a month's hard labour and order a parish to relieve a pauper. At petty-sessions within each division were appointed the surveyors of highways and that 'most arbitrary sovereign on earth', the overseer of the poor, and the rate for maintaining the highways was fixed. Divisional Brewster Sessions granted alehouse licences. At quarter-sessions, the justices administered the laws for the upkeep of bridges, gaols and houses of correction, and fixed county rates for these purposes. They heard petitions of disabled soldiers for pensions, issued writs to the sheriff for the distraint of accused persons, and proclaimed new regulations. They fixed wages and prices. Most important of all, they tried indictments for individual offences, and the presentments made by the Grand Jury, by juries of the hundreds and by constables, of neglect of communal obligations. One of these might be: 'We present the highway leading from X to Y to be out of repair (and that the same ought to be repaired by the inhabitants of X).'[6]

As justices, the gentry could afford to see the decay of the ancient private jurisdictions: the courts-leet were dying, except where they provided the government for manors which had burgeoned into industrial towns like Manchester without acquiring borough status. The Tudors had put the parish in the place of the manor as the basic unit of local government, but the parish constables, surveyors of highways and fieldmen, compelled to serve without pay, were treated by the justices much as the village reeve had been by the feudal lord. Supervising these organs of local government, the justice himself escaped supervision. The judges who came from Westminster on commissions of assize, oyer and terminer and gaol delivery were preoccupied with trying the more serious crimes with which the justices of the peace did not presume to deal. (The London Assizes or Old Bailey Sessions, taking their material from the Newgate prison, did far more of the major criminal business than any other court.) Though they might be of great political importance, as in the case of Judge Jeffrey's notorious Western Assize of 1685, the assizes were not any longer an essential part of government. The only effective restraint on the J.P. was a *mandamus* to appear in King's Bench to answer an information that he had exceeded his powers.[7]

Social changes made the traditional justice more and more inadequate. Government by judicial forms – presentments, forfeitures, sentences – could not cope with problems like urban sanitation, even when the justices multiplied their special sessions; so there grew up a maze of independent 'ad hoc' bodies (such as the 1,100 turnpike trusts). Two new factors, party and class, undermined the old ways of government. The lord-lieutenant, who nominated the J.P.s and chose his deputy-lieutenants from amongst them, was at the centre of the party struggle and sometimes fell with the government. And this was the man who commanded the militia and should have acted against the mobs called out by both sides at election time. Economic causes underlay the politics or old-fashioned religious prejudice which brought the mobs into the streets; these were the coming industrialism and the growth of population. In 1780 (nine years before the French Revolution), London was set blazing by gin-sodden mobs urged on by Lord George Gordon against the Roman Catholic Irish inhabitants. Society was used to violence – it could be learnt very well at the public schools – but the Gordon mob has been analysed and its motives shown to contain a novel element of class hatred: the house and precious library of Lord Chief Justice Mansfield went up in the flames, along with other property not belonging to the Irish.[8]

Crime, organized as never before, also contained an element of class warfare. Highwaymen, outrageous murders and robberies were commonplace. A thief made off with the

chancellor's mace in 1677, and would have got the Great
Seal had it not been under the chancellor's pillow. London
and Westminster, said Henry Fielding, were like 'a vast
wood or forest, in which a thief may harbour with as great
security as wild beasts do in the deserts of Africa and Arabia'.
The thronging populace of the prisons and the sanctuaries
(like 'the Mint' in Southwark, which lasted till 1723), the
robbers, murderers, receivers and informers, gaolers and
executioners, Robin of Bagshot and Slippery Sam, comprised a true under*world* with its own law and morality. Like
the Robin Hoods of the medieval forest, the criminals of the
new urban wastes were setting up in derisive opposition to
polite society – the rogues in authority.[9]

The justices of the peace were used to a rural society made
up of many vertical communities, in which they paternally
chastised their own and their neighbours' tenantry. Oppres-
sive legislation in their own interests, like the Game Laws
which Sir Roger de Coverley was so good at expounding, had
begun to divide the gentry even from the agrarian proletariat.
In the cities the justices were soon standing helpless, over
against an anonymous and degraded mass. Horizontal and
nationwide class divisions had by 1700 made the *posse comitatus* unusable as a police force, since it included the very
classes which were prone to riot. Increasingly the army or the
militia had to be called in, but they came when the mobs
were out of hand and the damage was done: it took five days
of Gordon riots and the prospect of an attack on the Bank of
England to turn out the London Military Association. The
constables in the towns were as degraded as the populace,
which they treated with great brutality.[10]

The town justices were corrupted, too. In Middlesex a
responsible squirearchy no longer existed, and the chancellor was compelled to fill the bench with tradesmen who
'were generally the scum of the earth' – the notorious
'basket' or 'trading justices'. In the country there were
several justices equal to the times. In the cities a lone example
was set by Henry Fielding (1707–54), the novelist, sitting at
Bow Street as the self-styled 'principal Westminster magi-

strate', and his brother and successor, Sir John Fielding, 'the Blind Beak'. Unpaid, like other magistrates, they spurned the bribes which gave 'the trading justices' their name and made efforts to reform the young offenders and prostitutes who came before them. They turned the eight Westminster parish constables into the effective police force later known as the Bow Street Runners, whose aid was sought far and wide, simply by encouraging a disillusioned public to come in with exact descriptions of those who robbed them and setting up a primitive criminal record office.[11]

Meanwhile, the generality of magistrates continued, in desperation as much as inhumanity, to hunt 'the undeserving poor' from parish to parish. Parliament lamely backed them up by passing the Riot Act of 1715, which made it a felony for members of 'tumults and riotous assemblies' not to disperse within an hour of being charged to do so by a justice; and by protecting magistrates and constables in 1751 from being sued for their official activities. The industrial revolution did not get into its stride till after 1760, but the justices' incapacity to meet its problems on their own was already evident, and the growing reliance on military forces was ominous.[12]

CRIMINAL LIABILITY, PROCEDURE AND PUNISHMENT

Parliament's main remedy for crime was the lengthening by statute of the list of capital felonies – the only field in which statute did contribute much to law in the eighteenth century. An act of 1576 (18 Eliz. c. 7) had provided that persons claiming benefit of clergy should not be handed over to the church courts but discharged or sentenced to a year's imprisonment. When colonies appeared, clergyable larceny was punished by seven years' transportation. Benefit of clergy was extended to all classes of society so that the old line between clergyable and non-clergyable offences could operate as a distinction between capital and non-capital offences (since all felonies were normally capital), and mitigate the harshness of the law. Beginning in the late seventeenth century, however, Parliament made many forms of larceny from dwelling-houses, which did not amount to burglary, into non-clergyable felonies and therefore punishable by death once more. In 1722, following an outbreak of deer-stealing and hooliganism in Hampshire, came the 'Waltham Black Act', which imposed the death penalty merely for being armed and disguised ('with faces blacked') on high roads, open heaths, or in forests where there were game; for wounding cattle; for cutting down garden trees; and for setting fire to crops. The reigns of the last two Stuart kings and the first three Georges added about 190 capital offences to the 50 or so existing in 1660. Since they prescribed death for many forms of assistance in crime, the eighteenth-century penal statutes also developed the liability of accessories.[13]

In *Curl's Case* (1727), the attorney-general successfully argued that obscene libel was a Common Law misdemeanour and not just a matter for the church courts; and in 1750 a warrant was issued on the request of the bishop of London against the publisher of *The Memoirs of Fanny Hill*. Amongst crimes against the state, *seditious libel* was most prominent. Up to 1641 the printing of libels had been kept down by proclamations enforced in Star Chamber. After that, there were acts which imposed restrictions through a system of licensing, but Parliament refused to renew them in 1694. Thereafter the ordinary courts had to deal with politically dangerous libels. They had to condemn publication on other grounds than that it was unauthorized – and juries had to find whether there had been seditious libel at all. In the *Seven Bishops' Case* (1688) the question was in effect whether it was seditious libel to 'come to the king's face, and tell him . . . that he has acted illegally'; for it was alleged against the bishops that their petition to the king against the Declaration of Indulgence was a libel 'published in Middlesex'. It was this political and legal question (rather than a question of fact) which the jury decided when they found the bishops not guilty.[14]

The judges' coercion of juries to return the verdicts they wanted was curtailed by the judgment of Common Pleas in

Bushell's Case (1670) that a juryman could not be punished for finding 'against the manifest evidence': the duties of a witness to tell the truth, of the jury to infer the truth from evidence, and of the judge to direct the jury on points of law, were – in theory – clearly distinguished. Libel showed the weaknesses of the distinction in practice, for here it is particularly obvious that a verdict depends not so much on facts (that these words were published by *X*) as on 'facts-in-law' (that they do constitute what law calls libel). The judges could, of course, direct the jury on the law of the matter, but juries could disown law which was politically obnoxious to them by returning special verdicts. In the re-trial of the *Dean of St Asaph's Case* (1784), Mansfield asserted that to find a special verdict of publication only was to imply that the offending books were not malicious: that question was a matter of law for the judge to decide, and, if he found malice, the jury must find the accused guilty. At last, in 1792, 'An act to remove doubts respecting the functions of juries in cases of libels' gave the jury complete freedom to decide guilt or innocence, which meant that reasonable political dissent would no longer be condemned.[15]

Criminal procedure is best described by an example. John Smith was assaulted by William Higgins, and complained to a local justice, who perhaps took his deposition but certainly required his recognizance and the recognizances of two sureties and any witnesses to appear at the next quarter-sessions; and the clerk of the peace, perhaps on the basis of Smith's deposition, drew up an indictment endorsed by Smith's witnesses, who might be examined by the Grand Jury before it approved or dismissed the charge. If Higgins acknowledged his guilt at the sessions, he was immediately sentenced: if he 'put himself on his country', the case would be adjourned for a petty jury's verdict. When the case was a serious one, the justice took the recognizances for appearance at assizes and might order the accused to gaol. The essentials of a good warrant of arrest were discussed in *Wilkes* v. *Lord Halifax* (1763): it was declared that a magistrate (in this case, a secretary of state) could not commit 'upon discretion . . .

without any evidence or information', but that the grounds of the charge need not be set out in the warrant. The courts were less happy about search-warrants not specifying any offence. Chief Justice Pratt said in Common Pleas that if the secretary of state had power to break into people's houses and seize their papers, 'and he can delegate this power, it certainly may effect the person and property of every man in this kingdom, and is totally subversive of the liberty of the subject'. Wilkes got £1,000 damages against the secretary of state on this issue.[16]

The conduct of the trial was one aspect of the criminal law which was improved in this period, the reputation of such judges as Jeffreys and Scroggs notwithstanding. The King's Bench resolved in the case of *Rex* v. *Vane and Lambert* (regicides) (1662) that the indictment must be read to the prisoner in English if he understood no Latin, 'for he must answer to the substance and not the form of the case'. The Habeas Corpus Amendment Act of 1679 (31 Charles 2, c. 2) required a gaoler to bring a prisoner to court within three days of the service of a writ of Habeas Corpus (within twenty days if the gaol and the court were more than a hundred miles apart), and provided that any of the judges could issue such a writ in vacation time.[17]

The Trial of Treason Act (1696) was a turning-point in the just regulation of criminal trials. The man accused of treason was to be given a copy of the indictment at least five days before arraignment; he was to have free access to counsel (whom the court would assign at the prisoner's request); and processes were allowed him to summon witnesses on his behalf, who would be sworn. He was not, however, to know the names of witnesses against him; ordinary felons were not allowed counsel till 1837; and there were still few rules on the admissibility of evidence. The verbatim report of the trial of John Donellan for murder, before Mr Justice Buller at Warwick assizes in 1781, shows well-developed methods of cross-examination, with objections to leading questions; but also a willingness to allow expert witnesses (physicians – it was a case of poisoning) to give decisive opinions on the whole question of guilt. The judge's summing-up of the merely circumstantial evidence was weighted against the prisoner. Before the trial, the accused submitted a written defence which was read in court, for he still could not give evidence on oath – a grave disadvantage for a poor and ignorant man, unable to afford an elaborate defence.[18]

On capital charges, juries were generally slow to convict, and bribes increased their inclination to reduce (say) murder to manslaughter. When the verdict of the jury could not be commanded by the judge, the only safeguard against mistaken verdicts was the greater use of re-trials (which had always been possible in extreme cases like the drunkenness of the jury). Thus, the *Dean of St Asaph's Case* went to King's Bench for re-trial on a motion of the Dean's counsel, who alleged that the assize judge had misdirected the jury on the issue of law. But motion for a re-trial (like the use of counsel) was not available to felons: it was permitted only in cases of misdemeanour.

At the Wiltshire Lent Assizes of 1736, before two barons of the Exchequer, eight persons were indicted of felonies. Of three accused of grand larceny (the stealing of one pair of horse traces, six pecks of wheat . . .), two were guilty, one 'confessing'. A woman accused of murder was convicted of manslaughter only; and three men accused of burglary or housebreaking were convicted only of non-capital larceny. A man was convicted of being at large after a sentence of transportation. One indictment was rejected by the grand jury; a man was discharged 'for want of prosecution'; and another, accused of the misdemeanour of laying traps for game, was acquitted.[19]

Punishments ranged from standing in the pillory (which turned out to be a popular triumph for Wilkes's printer), burning in the hand for manslaughter and whipping for petty larceny, to the burning of quite young girls for the high treason of coining (though they were usually strangled before the flames reached them), and the ancient horrors of the execution of male traitors. A number of eighteenth-century theorists believed hanging not punishment enough for ordinary felonies and proposed breaking on the wheel. Their views prevailed, in so far as an act of 1752 (25 Geo. 2, c. 37) was passed 'that some further Terror and peculiar Mark of Infamy be added to the Punishment of Death' for murder: the convicted murderer was to be kept on bread and water in a special cell, and after execution his body was to hang in chains before the public gaze and then go to the surgeons for dissection.[20]

Dr Johnson was one who saw that capital punishment satisfied a sinister human craving for power over others' lives, but did not really deter. Undiscriminating severity simply made criminals more cunning and more desperate, and confused small crimes with great ones. Men were loth to prosecute for 'mere violations of property' and eager to see a criminal pardoned. The truth is that in the period 1805–10, one in five of reported crimes were not prosecuted; and that in the year April 1793 to March 1794, one half of the 1,060 persons committed for trial at the Old Bailey were acquitted (mostly of minor but capital offences). To avoid imposing the death penalty, the courts interpreted the statutes restrictively, exploited technical errors in indictments, and actually requested prosecutors to reduce their valuations of stolen property to less than 1s.[21]

The king granted free pardon, or pardons conditional on service in the armed forces or settlement in the colonies. An act of 1717 (4 Geo. 1, c. 11) allowed the judges to pass sentence of transportation in certain cases. Judges would also grant reprieves (respites of execution) while they recommended the king to show mercy on such grounds as the offender's youth, previous good character, that it was his first offence, or that he had been driven to it by necessity, and the recommendation was almost invariably accepted. At the Old Bailey Sessions of 1761–5, 225 persons were thus reprieved and sentenced to fourteen years transportation each. In Elizabeth's reign, perhaps 140 persons a year had been executed in London and Middlesex alone, and in the period 1749–99 the average was still above 30, the total (for that half-century) amounting to 1,696 of 3,680 capitally convicted (chiefly for crimes against property). But there was in fact a great falling-off in executions during the eighteenth century, although the number of capital crimes was multiplied: 51 of the 90 capitally convicted in London and Middlesex were executed in 1756–8, 23 out of 244 in 1802–4. The system was not as inhuman as it appeared at first sight, but it was unpredictable and arbitrary, discriminated with difficulty between hardened criminals and first offenders, and put a tremendous responsibility on the judges.[22]

Transportation was perhaps for a time the saving of the criminal law, for imprisonment was not in the eighteenth century a reasonable alternative to capital punishment. With the beginnings of a more humane outlook came the dilemma of the modern penal reformer: how to combine appropriate retribution and deterrence with moral rehabilitation in prisons where a man sentenced to a year's imprisonment for a minor offence mingled with felons awaiting trial and execution. In the 1770s and 80s, John Howard was travelling throughout Britain and Europe to produce a more exact account of *The State of the Prisons*. In Newgate (just rebuilt after destruction, along with the Fleet, in the Gordon Riots) Howard found 225 men and 66 women: about 100 were awaiting transportation, 21 execution and 89 the payment of their fines. 'In three or four rooms there were near one hundred and fifty women crowded together, many young creatures with the old and hardened . . . on the felons' side a person stood with cans of beer.' The even more populous Fleet was much as it had been two centuries before, while in hulks on the Thames and around the south-east coast were housed criminals sentenced to hard labour – 'too severe for the far greater number', and not proportioned 'to the several offences'.[23]

LORD CHANCELLOR NOTTINGHAM AND EQUITY

During this period, precedent replaced conscience as the guiding principle of equity. Lord Nottingham, chancellor from 1675 to 1682 and 'the father of modern equity', gave reasons for his decisions with a new scrupulousness, and declared that, 'if conscience be not dispensed by the rules of science, it were better for the subject there were no Chancery at all than that men's estates should depend upon the pleasure of a court which took upon itself to be purely arbitrary'. Yet, Nottingham always tried to see cases with the layman's standards of fairness and reasonableness: like Coke in the Common Law, he rather created precedents than followed them. Lord Hardwicke, chancellor from 1737 to 1756, was the real systematizer of equity, feeling himself 'under an indispensable obligation' to follow his predecessors' decisions. As the principles and business of equity developed, so the scandal of its interminable procedure grew worse. Its delays were due partly to inadequate staff, the amateur element running through English justice: 'The truth is a Court such as that is, with officers and fees proper for a little business such as the judiciary part anciently was, coming to possess almost all the justice of the nation, must needs appear troubled.'[24]

The landed aristocracy – the Whig nobility of the Glorious Revolution of 1689 – were more powerful and more exclusive in the eighteenth century than ever before. The growth of the land law of Chancery helps to explain why. In 1660, the land on which a family's power rested could already be tied up by means of the strict settlement. Still, many families were tottering as a result of civil war confiscations, and the notorious dissipation of some of the eighteenth-century aristocracy would have been expected to increase indebtedness. So, indeed, it did – yet the number of private acts to break settlements, sell up and pay off the debts steadily declined. From the interregnum almost to the twentieth century it was extremely difficult for the rich merchant to find land to buy. This was because the mortgages which were an essential concomitant of the strict settlement had become easier and longer. The settlement was usually renewed when the eldest son came of age or married, and it would include provision for the portions of the children yet unborn and for the bride's jointure, which (added to those already in being for the bridegroom's mother, brothers and sisters) would be raised

from 'trust estates' set aside from the main property. The
strain on the family resources, if many children came or
fortunes declined, was bearable only because other parts of
the estate could now be mortgaged at reasonable interest
without fear of losing them altogether.[25]

By 1800 the Equitable and Sun Fire Offices (insurance
companies) had £776,000 invested in mortgages, and a
wealthy country yeoman might have as much as £800 out at
interest. Indebtedness was a normal and unalarming part of
eighteenth-century land management. If, however, it became chronic and retrenchment was inevitable, the trustees
who were intrinsic to the strict settlement would be called in,
or new ones appointed, to pack the spendthrift heir off
abroad or to Bath and inaugurate a period of economy. The
trust was in addition adapted to the needs of the eighteenth-
century dissenting groups, who were not likely to gain recognition as corporations. Eventually, the Methodists had a
standard form according to which the trustees of a chapel
were to apply their funds 'for promoting the preaching of
the Gospel among the said people called Methodists in the
circuit in which the said chapel shall for the time being be
situated. . . .'[26]

Chancery made the trust more versatile by increasingly
protecting the beneficiary's interest. The final transmutation
of feudal tenure into socage-tenure at the Restoration (12
Charles 2, c. 24), and the commutation of the king's feudal
dues to a tax on brewing, removed most of the objections to
uses which had inspired the statute of 1536, though trusts had
still to be squared with that statute's provisions. According
to old ideas, a trust conferred on the beneficiary – and on the
beneficiary alone – a purely moral claim against the persons
of the trustees, not a piece of property which could be recovered or was assignable. Lord Nottingham, however,
modelled the trust on property rights at Common Law. One
practical result was that claims against the beneficiary could
be satisfied from the lands which others held in trust for him
but were now regarded in a certain sense as his own. Sometimes it was necessary to decide that there was an implied

trust: that an heir held the land in trust which was devised by his father to be sold to provide for other children; or that *B* held in trust for *C* when he bought land from *A* with *C*'s money. But Nottingham was unwilling to presume trusts unnecessarily, lest 'a way is opened to the Lord Chancellor to construe or presume any man in England out of his estate'.[27]

Trustees and executors were not forced to undertake the responsibility and were allowed expenses when they did accept it, but they were made to act unpaid, and the chancellor, while not penalizing their honest mistakes, insisted on standards of care and skill which were too high for a century when the investments open to trust funds were often risky.

The right of the mortgagor to redeem the mortage after the term when he should have repaid his debt was established in the first quarter of the seventeenth century; and in 1629 appeared the correlative right in the creditor and mortgagee to foreclose upon the defaulting debtor (that is, to obtain a Chancery decree giving him full ownership of the land). In Chancery's hands the right to redeem ('equity of redemption') became, like the right of the *cestui que trust*, a peculiar form of property, an 'equitable estate' in the mortgaged land; an estate which, according to Lord Hardwicke, 'will descend, may be granted, devised, entailed, and . . . barred by a common recovery'. Chancery saw the mortgage as above all a security, and so the creditor was not allowed to treat it as his own land for the time being, and any agreement restricting ('clogging') the right of redemption was simply disregarded. This attitude suited the dynastic schemes of the eighteenth-century gentry only too well. They enthusiastically piled mortgage after mortgage on the same properties and left Chancery to sort out the conflicting rights of the various 'incumbrancers'.[28]

The Statute of Frauds of 1677 was a courageous attempt – but one that proved as unlucky as the Statute of Uses – to stop fraudulent conveyancing and render harmless the courts' inexperience in handling parole evidence of transactions, by requiring that wills should always be written, signed and witnessed, and that there should be deeds for the

creation and assignment of all trusts. The statute was followed by attempts to establish an English land register equal
to the Scottish Register of Saisines, and a few local registries
were created. Victims of fraud could in principle find relief
in equity, provided that their own unbusinesslike behaviour
had not been a contributory factor. The trouble was that
frauds, if not dammed at the source, got beyond easy regulation. If Chancery once laid down rules about them, said
Nottingham, it 'would be perpetually eluded by new schemes
which the fertility of men's invention would contrive'.[29] It
was Chancery's business also to relieve 'against penalties and
forfeitures and unconscionable insistence on legal rights'.
Given the dangers of the sixteenth-century trade in credit, it
had been reasonable to write into a loan the condition that
an extra penalty would be payable if repayment was late, or
that the security would be forfeited. In the eighteenth century
it was quite possible that such harsh agreements would be
made by unscrupulous men in the hope that the debtor
would default, and from that time the law has set its face
firmly against penal clauses in contracts.

With the help of the Statute of Distribution of 1670 (22 &
23 Charles 2, c. 10), framed to give one third of an intestate
man's personal property to his widow or 'next-of-kin' and
two thirds to his children, Chancery administered the jurisdiction over wills and intestacy which had once belonged to
the church, and attempted to do justice within the family.
It could give to a married woman, by means of a separate
trust for her benefit, an independence of her husband which
was abhorrent to the Common Law; and to a son relief
against his father's wasting of the family estates. In his most
famous decision, the judgment – reversed by his successor
and restored by the House of Lords – in *The Duke of Norfolk's
Case* (1681), Lord Nottingham invented the modern rule
against perpetuities – that is, settlements endeavouring to tie
up property for all time. He recognized that behind complicated rules against contingent remainders lay the principle
that land should not be taken out of the market for long
periods, and he held that any settlement was bad where the

remainder would not 'vest' – the fee simple be once more in possession – within a certain and reasonably short time. He did much to make English law serve society, and was prepared to model equitable principles on the Common Law where this was sensible, just as afterwards Mansfield introduced equity into the Common Law. But the *separate* existence of equity after 1641, when its procedural usefulness was finished, was a disaster not redeemed till the end of the nineteenth century.[30]

Freed from contact with the plain man in the jury-box, the Chancellors were tempted to forget how plain and rough good law should be, and to screw up the legal standard of reasonable conduct to a height hardly attainable except by those whose purses could command the constant advice of a family solicitor. A court which started with the idea of doing summary justice for the poor became a court which did a highly refined, but tardy justice, suitable only to the rich.[31]

LORD MANSFIELD AND THE COMMON LAW

According to Dr Johnson, 'Much may be made of a Scotchman, if he be *caught* young'. The Doctor was writing of William Murray, Lord Mansfield, Chief Justice of King's Bench from 1756 to 1788, born the younger son of a Scottish peer but educated at Westminster and Oxford. Like Lord Nottingham, Mansfield conformed his judgments to common sense and justice, as well as to strict law, in which he refused to believe that principles of equity had no place. Thus, in construing deeds, mortgages and wills he broke through the professional mystification of conveyancers' forms, to decide from independent evidence of the grantors' intentions: 'the lawful intention, when clearly explained, is to control the legal sense of a term of art unwarily used by the testator'.[32]

The assimilation of law to equity scandalized Mansfield's colleagues; and 'Junius' belaboured him for corrupting the Common Law with 'your unsettled notions of equity and substantial justice. . . . The Roman code, the law of nations and the opinion of foreign civilians, are your perpetual theme. . . . By such treacherous arts the whole simplicity and free spirit of our Saxon laws were first corrupted.' Sir William Holdsworth judged, more soberly, that the breadth of Mansfield's learning 'prevented him from attaining that accurate knowledge of the development of Common Law rules which could only come to an English lawyer who had devoted the largest part of his time to the study of its complex technicalities'. Mansfield's justification is perhaps in his own criticism of *Shelley's Case* and of the contingent remainder rules it enshrined: the sequel to the Statute of Uses had shown, he said, that 'if courts of law will adhere to the mere letter of the law, the great men who preside in Chancery will ever devise new ways to creep out of the lines of law and temper it with equity'; and this indeed would 'render the lines of property very dubious and uncertain, by a difference in judgments in law and equity'.[33]

The benefits of Mansfield's procedural reforms were less controversial. He greatly reduced the volume of litigation by the encouragement of settlements out of court; he ended the haranguing of juries and bullying of witnesses by counsel; and he originated the form and decencies of the modern trial. Both the calculated delay of litigation (to increase the profits) and the unseemly competition for the ear of the bench he prevented by the institution of a calendar of the cases to be heard and by giving counsel, whatever their seniority, an equal chance to put the motions by which a case was kept on the move.[34]

Parties had been encouraged to plead on more general points by legislation of the Interregnum, and by an act of 1705 (4 & 5 Anne, c. 3) which permitted multiple defences at the discretion of the court. Some trading companies set up by Act of Parliament were empowered to plead the general issue at all times, putting in special matter as evidence. Mansfield accepted that special pleading had an object – the production, with precision and brevity, of the decisive issue. Short shrift was given to pleading which produced the opposite result. In *Yates* v. *Carlisle*, the Chief Justice called for a report on the responsibility for the enormous pleadings: 'there were twenty-seven several pleas of Justification' by the defendants, which, with the Declaration, 'Replications, Traverses, Novel Assignments and other engines of Pleading, amounted at length to a Paper Book of near 2,000 sheets', and the counsel who drew the Declaration which started it all was made to pay the whole £1,000 costs in the case.[35]

Rather than embark on this sort of thing, counsel often preferred to arrange a special verdict (acceptable to the judges in civil matters), leaving the court to give judgment on the issue of law; or to present the agreed facts straight away ('a special case') and see the judge direct the jury's verdict according to his legal opinion. Or the general issue would be pleaded – but if this was to become a general practice, the courts had to grow more expert in the handling of evidence. Before the eighteenth century, the law took very little account of anything but written evidence – deeds and the like. As solicitor-general, Mansfield had helped to get the evidence of non-Christians admitted in the courts. As Chief Justice, he worked on the principle that the credibility of a witness was more important than his formal competence in law. And credibility, he knew, defied general rules, requiring to be tested by different methods in different cases. Orders for the re-trial of civil cases after clearly unjust general verdicts had been known since the mid seventeenth century. Mansfield introduced the appeal in the more modern sense of a reconsideration of the legal basis of a judgment, when he allowed plaintiffs non-suited before a judge sitting alone to take the issue before the whole court of King's Bench.[36]

Contract showed Mansfield at his most original. Though assumpsit had in fact unified the whole field, there was still no theory of contract. Mansfield began to provide it when he concentrated on aspects common to all agreements, and chiefly (as in his handling of deeds) on the intention of the parties. He was even loth to disallow a contract on the grounds that its objects were illegal or 'against public policy'. Though disputes about wagers were a nuisance to the courts in the eighteenth century, it was too late to expel them, and Mansfield even found himself upholding an action of assumpsit upon a wager that a certain 'decree of the Court of Chan-

cery would be reversed on appeal to the House of Lords'
(remarking by the way that the wager was quite fair, since
the law was so uncertain). The problem of agreements made
without a plausible consideration, he tackled, first by asserting that no consideration was needed in a written contract,
and then by the doctrine that in any agreement 'the ties of
conscience upon an upright mind are a sufficient consideration'. The duty to keep one's promises was set up as the
essence of the contractual obligation.[37]

A contractual duty was presumed by the courts in situations
where *A* had paid *B* a sum of money by mistake or had been
induced to do so by fraud or duress. Though simple equity
demanded the return of the money – these were in fact, cases
of 'unjustifiable enrichment' (cf. p. 238 above) – the only
remedy at Common Law was an assumpsit, and the liability
to repay was called *quasi-contract*. Mansfield's emphasis on
the moral obligation in all transactions was well-fitted to
extend this branch of the law to many forms of extortion and
unfairness which only Chancery could have dealt with
before. Thus, in *Smith* v. *Bromley* (1760), a woman was allowed to recover the money she paid to her bankrupt
brother's creditor in the belief that it would secure her
brother's discharge.[38] 'The enthusiasm of litigants for a
remedy so strangely akin to common sense,' writes Mr Fifoot,
'threatened the ascendancy of the older writs.' The forms of
action were in solution (they began to disappear within fifty
years of Mansfield's death), and valuable things were certainly threatened with them – the boundaries of jurisdictions
for instance, and the protection to the defendants of narrow
lines of attack, known in advance. Yet the advantages of this
widely-drawn action 'for money had and received' were
obvious to Mansfield's most cautious colleagues. This was
the way the law was going.[39]

LAWYERS AND EIGHTEENTH-CENTURY SOCIETY

Year books and other old law books were being printed at a
great rate around 1700, but contemporary reporting (still in

law-French) languished in the shadow of Coke. The modern standards of law reporting were set by Sir James Burrow, master of the crown office in reports stretching from 1756 to 1772 which first discriminated between facts, arguments and decisions. Abridgements culminated in that of Charles Viner (1678–1756), whose other great work was the endowment of the Vinerian chair at Oxford.[40]

The most successful of the handbooks was *Justices of the Peace* by Richard Burn, a Westmorland vicar and J.P. But textbooks of a more modern type were appearing, setting out the principles of areas of substantive law, rather than procedural rules. Sheppard's *Touchstone of Common Assurances* (1641) on conveyancing had been a forerunner, but the first really scientific study of the land-law was Charles Fearne's polemical *Essay on Contingent Remainders*, an attack on Lord Mansfield's relaxation of the ancient rules. A judge in India, Sir William Jones, wrote an *Essay on the Law of Bailments* (1781) which combined history, analysis and a comparative approach. Jones, who was an F.R.S., President of the Asiatic Society, and an expert in Sanskrit and the Hindu laws, shows the direction in which eighteenth-century jurisprudence was advancing. Englishmen were looking to other legal traditions, first to Scotland, bound to England since 1707 by Parliament as well as Crown, where Lord Kames (1696–1782) was attempting to illuminate law by history; and then to the France of the Enlightenment, where Robert Joseph Pothier (1699–1772) wrote on the general theory of contract, and Montesquieu's *Spirit of the Laws* (1748) engendered the idea that the virtue of the English constitution was a system of checks and balances between executive, legislature and judiciary – a 'separation of powers'.[41]

The thing which Montesquieu sought to explain was the happy outcome of English history in the Glorious Revolution, and William Blackstone's *Commentaries on the Laws of England* (1765) were at least partly intended to justify and preserve the social order which the revolution had established. Indiscriminate as was its praise of the existing state of things – particularly in the field of real property – that 'artistic picture of the laws of England' provided the most intelligent and readable account that had ever been made of a whole legal system; and, re-edited time and time again, it for long determined the layman's picture of the law, especially in America. Blackstone showed law to have been a major factor in England's historical blessedness; but a reverence like Coke's for history was no longer a considerable influence on the law. In a century which was rationalist and anthropological in its interests, there was more willingness (Junius notwithstanding) to borrow from Roman and foreign law, and Mansfield was not alone in being glad that the change to English in the records had drawn a veil over the 'Gothick ignorance' of the Common Law's own past.[42]

Eighteenth-century litigants struggled through crowds of lawyers who lived by watching each other at their clients' expense. The judges had attempted to control the attorneys by requiring five years' apprenticeship before admission to the roll, and even residence at an Inn of Court or Chancery, where documents could be served on them. The Inns retained their revulsion for attorneys, and a different solution was tried in an act of 1729, inspired by the petition of the justices of the West Riding against the plague of unqualified men. This act (2 Geo. 2, c. 23) prescribed an oath to be taken by the attorney on admission and forbade him to have more than two articled apprentices at a time or to allow anyone else to act in his name in the courts; and it provided the basis for the work of the Society of Gentlemen Practisers which had come into existence by 1739. The Society aimed 'to detect and discountenance . . . unfair practice'; had dishonest attorneys removed from the rolls; acted as a pressure-group to get legal reforms through Parliament; and of course gradually established the attorneys' own monopoly against the barristers, who were prosecuted for taking on clients without the intervention of an attorney. Divided yet more absolutely from the barristers and the inns, the attorneys absorbed the similarly excluded solicitors into their organization. Solicitors had been able to work in the Court of Chancery because attorneys were a product of Common Law procedure. The act of 1729 confirmed the position of the solicitor in Chancery, and sworn solicitors were permitted in 1750 to practise as attorneys also. Since Chancery suits were lucrative and the atmosphere of the court dignified, 'solicitor' outdid 'attorney' in social prestige and the attorneys began to assume the more reputable title.[43]

The Commissioners of Customs and Excise employed solicitors soon after the Restoration, and from 1669 there were Treasury solicitors 'to solicit and take care of the prosecution of all debts to the King'; they also took charge of the prosecutions in Jeffreys's Bloody Assize. Some of the early Treasury solicitors were rogues employed in dubious political business; but a government legal office grew up around them, and by 1800, when the single Treasury Solicitor (at the head of the department) received a salary of £2,000 a year, the barristers had elbowed their way into it.[44]

In the country, attorneys acted as trustees for county families, arranged their mortgages and organized their parliamentary election campaigns, costing £10,000 and upwards; and they founded the country banks which set commerce moving in the outlying areas. They were no less essential to the public enterprises – the turnpike trusts and Navigation Companies, the General Infirmaries, Carnation Shows and charity schools. They were solicitors and secretaries to these, and to the older-established authorities; for the principal firm of solicitors in the county town would provide the Deputy Clerk of the Peace, and the attorney's premises in the market town was replacing the justice's mansion as the office for petty-sessional business. In these ways, solicitors contributed especially to the development of the industrial cities. Birmingham and Manchester, with forty each, had more attorneys in 1790 than any other provincial town except the great ports of Bristol and Liverpool. In 1770, Bristol founded its own law society on the model of the London Society of Gentlemen Practisers, and it was followed in 1786 by Yorkshire, in 1800 by Sunderland, by Manchester in 1809, and Birmingham, Hull and Kent in 1818.[45]

The law societies were like medieval craft guilds in their

charitable objects, their oversight of a professional training which was based on apprenticeship, and their preservation of the law as a technical mystery which would impress clients and open their pockets. Gentlemen from all over England sent their sons to be articled to London attorneys, just as they had once sent them to the Inns of Court. Idealists began to argue that a man with so many responsibilities as an attorney must be given a 'liberal education' – like gentlemen at the Inns of Court in the old days. Several judges, including Lord Chancellors Somers, Macclesfield and Hardwicke, received their early training in attorneys' offices like Charles Salkeld's in Great Brook Street. For the Inns of Court and Chancery were more decayed even than the eighteenth-century universities. New chambers were still being built, but Clement's Inn was accommodating local brewers, periwig-makers and comedians from Drury Lane, and demanding dues from members gone abroad and unheard of 'for above fifteen years past'. The inns were used as clubs by the gentlemen of all sorts – politicians, and literary men like Aubrey and Evelyn – who continued to join them. Serious law-students, such as Mansfield, made private arrangements for instruction with special pleaders and conveyancers.[46]

The flow of men from the inns to the attorneys' offices seemed to many to threaten the status of the law as a gentleman's profession. The real gentry were neglecting the inns for the universities and leaving 'the interpretation and enforcement of the laws (which include the entire disposal of our properties, liberties and lives)' to 'obscure and illiterate men'. These words were written by Dr William Blackstone, fellow of All Souls and recorder of Wallingford, who concluded that the universities were the places where future judges and administrators must thenceforth be taught. In lectures on the laws of England which he gave on Mansfield's urging at Oxford in 1753, and as the first Vinerian Professor of the Laws of England there from 1759, Blackstone was providing general principles for gentlemen-beginners – law for barristers, not solicitors. He wished such instruction to become the normal entry to the legal career, and his object was advanced by the announcement of the Inns of Court in 1762 that graduates of Oxford and Cambridge might be called to the bar after three years at the inns instead of five.[47]

By 1800 the attorneys had become respectable. In Common Pleas the 1,000 ill-qualified attorneys of 1728–9 had been greatly reduced, and new admissions dropped from 140 in 1740 to 58 in 1790. An attorney as well as a barrister could amass a fortune sufficient to start his family on the road to nobility: Viscount Melbourne, prime minister from 1834 to 1837, was descended from Peniston Lamb, a Nottingham attorney who made £100,000 in the early eighteenth century.[48]

Law-suits were so expensive that it was not worth a man's while to sue for a £30 debt. Yet a good attorney was probably making his £2,000 a year profit more legitimately in 1800 than earlier. Attorneys were more respectable basically because they were more useful: in litigation it was quite as important to have a good attorney as a good barrister. And, however much the fastidious Blackstone might deplore it, a growing class of professional agents was the unavoidable concomitant of Whig oligarchy. Not only as estate-agents but as election-managers and political go-betweens the attorneys were essential to the aristocracy whose kaleidoscopic groupings formed the eighteenth-century administrations. Thomas Nuthall, in addition to being receiver-general for hackney coaches, a treasury solicitor and solicitor to the East India Company, was attorney to William Pitt, Earl of Chatham, who used him in 1766 as intermediary in attempts to form a government. The attorneys helped to make the image of the nineteenth-century middle class – the sober and trustworthy professional people; or, to Shelley in 1820, the exploiting class of 'attornies and excisemen and directors and government pensioners, usurers, stockjobbers, country bankers . . .' The solicitors were home.[49]

Great advocacy without profound legal knowledge brought fame and the lord chancellorship to Thomas Erskine (1750–1823) after false starts as a midshipman and an officer in the Royal Scots. He was said to have made £150,000 at the bar and was the first to receive a fee of 300 guineas for one case. After the Restoration, as never before, legal ability on its own could lead to the highest places in the land as well as to a fortune. The gentry were not, as formally, looking to the law as a general training for administration, and there were fewer legally trained J.P.s, Furthermore, the lawyers who still made up thirteen per cent of the House of Commons were not a particularly impressive group: they were there for the most part because that was the way to the best legal offices under the Crown, for even the lord chancellorship was confined to professionals after the dismissal of Shaftesbury in 1672. But a few rare personalities were able, by sheer ability, to rise from law to the centre of government. Only his determination in standing up to Pitt brought Mansfield the Leadership of the House of Commons, and in 1756 the duke of Newcastle fought desperately against Mansfield's defection to the position of chief justice and the House of Lords. He could have become prime minister after Newcastle. As it was, he held the chancellorship of the exchequer in the 'caretaker government' of 1757; and, more remarkably, after arranging the coalition of Newcastle and Pitt, he stayed in the cabinet till 1765, having on one occasion to declare illegal in King's Bench the general warrant issued by his cabinet colleague.[50]

The nobles, though more exclusive than ever before, were forced to recognize the great lawyers as their equals, because Parliament was the High Court of Parliament and politics were conducted in legalistic terms. And the development of advocacy – of the art of stating a case you may not believe in, which Johnson defended in a memorable conversation with Boswell – affected the House of Commons as much as the courts. In both, the eloquence of an Erskine too easily sank to mere abuse, but sheer professionalism in debating eventually carried one man, Spencer Perceval (1762–1812), up through the legal political offices to the premiership.

EIGHTEENTH-CENTURY LAW-MAKING

The real legislators of eighteenth-century England were the

local gentry. Their announcements, as J.P.s in quarter-sessions, that they would punish certain conduct, amounted to legislative prohibition of that conduct; and they did not, like a modern county council making bye-laws, have to get their general orders confirmed by the Home Secretary. When parliamentary backing was desired for local regulations, this was obtained not by a general statute but by thousands of separate local acts (. . . *An Act for erecting a Workhouse in the City and County of Norwich . . . An Act for Repairing part of the road from London to Cambridge* . . .), contrived by the gentry of the neighbourhoods concerned, and discussed in Parliament by their representatives. 'In this "age of reason", as we are wont to think it,' Maitland wrote, 'the British parliament seems rarely to rise to the dignity of a general proposition.' Law-making was still far from being regarded as the main function of Parliament; and Locke advocated a separation of powers just because the executive power had to operate constantly, while legislation was an intermittent and extraordinary activity.[51]

The definition of Parliament's legislative sovereignty was an eventful process. It began in the days between the opening of the civil war and Cromwell's dictatorship, when Parliament was left alone to rule. The Anglican Parliaments following the Restoration produced a stream of acts to disable Roman Catholics and dissenters from public office and hinder their worship, and it was then that the king, relying on the aid of Catholic France, asserted as part of his prerogative the right to dispense with the operation of statutes in particular cases, and even to suspend them altogether. In the case of *Godden* v. *Hales* (1686), King's Bench actually declared that the right to dispense with the penal laws for the benefit of Hales, a Roman Catholic army officer, was part 'of the sovereign power and prerogative of the kings of England', since 'the laws of England are the king's laws'. The logical consequences of that decision were the fall of James II and the proclamation in the Bill of Rights (1 Will. & Mar. Sess. 2, c. 2) of the illegality of the 'pretended power' to suspend or dispense with Parliament's laws.[52]

At first Parliament did not understand where its sovereignty lay – namely, in legislation through statute. It was too inclined to see itself as a supreme court which could try and condemn individuals by mere resolution and without due process, especially in cases of Parliamentary privilege and elections. In the *Case of the Aylesbury Men* (1704) the right of the Commons to imprison some electors who had sued the constables of Aylesbury at Common Law for refusing their votes was courageously denied by Chief Justice Holt: the Aylesbury men were perfectly entitled to sue for their rights in an ordinary court, for there was no 'law of Parliament' apart from the Common Law, and that, Holt said, could only be altered through Act of Parliament, by Queen, Lords and Commons together. Consistently with that view, the mere resolution of the Commons that general warrants were illegal was declared by Mansfield to have no force in law.[53]

Though impatient of the law's irrationalities, neither Nottingham nor Mansfield looked to statute for improvement. Despair of making sense from the (in any case technically secret) debates in the Commons may have caused the courts to adopt the strange rule that statutes were to be interpreted literally and without recourse to external evidence of their intention. The general rules of the Common Law were built up in the courts, and one obstinate litigant like John Wilkes made a profounder difference than many statutes. Some judges sanctimoniously weighed the precedents in a case and thought that enough. Yet, the best lawyers could not help wondering how far the cult of precedent was consonant with reason, at a time when 'arguing from authorities be exploded from every other branch of learning'. Mansfield would surrender to a long line of settled cases, and he appreciated the practical advantages of even an irrational certainty in curbing the litigious zeal of corporations. But he had only contempt for the uncritical assembling of corrupt reports, and his instinct was to emphasize basic principles. 'The law of England,' he said, 'would be a strange science indeed, if it were decided upon precedents only. Precedents only serve to illustrate principles . . .'[54]

293

His jurisprudence had the pragmatic spirit of the time. To do justice between men it was necessary to see things as they really were, and he would not enforce rules established in the different social context of an earlier age. As Mr Fifoot says, 'It is impossible not to remark, alike in his choice of interests and in his approach to problems, the symptoms of a changing order. He was the first judge to speak the language of the living law.' But the shape of the law was the product of history. Most of the conciliar courts had gone, but they had left behind the use of interrogatories, depositions, affidavits. After 1641, the Common Law courts added to their own jurisdiction over slander Star Chamber's jurisdiction in those more serious cases of defamation (known as libel) in which criminal malice was imputed to the defamer and truth was not admitted as a defence. In the civil courts 'libel' was thenceforth reserved as the term for the more obviously deliberate and malicious *written* defamation; and thus appeared the modern distinction between the torts of slander and libel, sealed in the case of *King* v. *Lake* (1668) by the decision that in libel special damage need not be proved.[55]

LAW IN THE HISTORY OF
EIGHTEENTH-CENTURY ENGLAND

Of the great constitutional issues, some were new, like the freedom of the press and the independence of the criminal jury (raised by the seditious libel cases), some old, like the process of impeachment (eventually killed by the unpopular prosecution of Warren Hastings) which Sir Robert Walpole lived in fear of: but law was at the heart of most of them. Sir John Holt stood up for the Englishman's rights of liberty and property, resigning the recordership of London rather than condemn a soldier to death for desertion in time of peace, and, as lord chief justice, preventing Queen Anne's Parliament from interfering with the right to vote. Judicial courage was justified in the provision of the Act of Settlement of 1701 (12 and 13 William 3, c. 2) that judges should have fixed salaries and be removable only 'upon the Address of both Houses of

Parliament'. The royal prerogative to impress men for the navy received judicial confirmation; but in the remarkable *Sommersett's Case* (1772) Mansfield held that slavery, which was odious, had no standing in England, so that a writ of Habeas Corpus was good to release a negro slave from a ship on the Thames.[56]

Between the sovereign king-in-parliament and the free individual, the associations of citizens which were essential to a free society were precariously placed. Thomas Hobbes and the French revolutionaries alike condemned corporations as flaws in the structure of the all-powerful state. Charles II had some theoretical backing, therefore, when by process of Quo Warranto he attacked the corporation of London for exceeding its powers and secured the forfeiture of many borough charters in order to grant new ones giving him control over town politics. In some cases, of course, King's Bench's power to interfere in the affairs of corporations by writ of Mandamus amounted to a beneficial 'administrative law': it was used in 1724 to protect Richard Bentley, Master of Trinity College, Cambridge, whose deprivation by the university was held to be 'contrary to natural justice' and to 'the rules for the removing of members of corporations, which cannot be done, without summoning the party, and giving him an opportunity of being heard'.[57]

Transferred to the problem of the American colonies, the law's attitude to associations and the general habit of seeing politics in legal terms contributed to a disaster. 'In one county of Massachusetts the revolution was started with the grand jury indicting the British Parliament as a public nuisance.' Mansfield and Lord Chancellor Thurlow were amongst the hottest against colonial rights, and Edmund Burke had to tell the British Parliament that this was a matter of politics and statesmanship, not law: 'I do not know the method of drawing up an indictment against an whole people.'[58]

Men still talked of their constitutional rights as 'fundamental law', though their ideas of its contents differed widely. Within that way of thinking, the concept of a 'fundamental contract' became predominant, so that James II in 1689 was accused simultaneously of 'having violated the fundamental laws' and 'having endeavoured to subvert the constitution of the kingdom, by breaking the original contract between king and people'. It is not clear how far Locke and the other political philosophers believed in the 'original contract' as an historical fact, dimly perceived in the dark ages: most probably the Whig aristocracy who so often handled contracts saw the very ancient idea of the constitutional contract as just a useful political assumption – they implied a contractual relationship between king and people as contemporary judges would imply one between (say) an innkeeper and his guests. In the Bill of Rights of 1689 the terms of the constitutional contract began to be written down, and the constitution ceased to be entirely 'living custom'.[59]

Equally often, the philosophers, seeking to destroy divine right and reconcile individual rights and sovereign authority, spoke of a *social contract* between the people in a state of nature to submit themselves to a sovereign as the head of a corporation, or to *entrust* him with power. Political trusteeship is, again, a concept found in every age: but the emphasis on trusts and moral obligation in Nottingham's jurisprudence must surely have contributed to its prominence around 1700. The sovereign which emerged from the Glorious Revolution was Parliament, conceived still as a supreme court. The theoretical importance of Parliament's judicial functions led to the conflicts between the Commons and the Lords over their respective roles, and to a dangerous arrogance in the Commons which caused Defoe and others to remind them of their trusteeship and of the fundamental law which bound even them. In the Aylesbury election case of 1704 the Lords joined with Lord Chief Justice Holt to tell the Commons that the vote was the absolute right of a freeholder, and that 'the security of our English constitution' was that 'neither House of Parliament has a power separately to dispose of the liberty or property of the people'.[60]

Law could be seen to be changing all the time, and the

immemorial antiquity of English law was no longer a plausible political argument. 'Junius' appealed to Magna Carta against the innovations of the lawyer, Mansfield, but politicians generally were arguing from abstract legal concepts – contract and trust – rather than from the history of the law. Burke, framing the philosophy of conservatism, appealed once more to the past, but to the virtues of England's political tradition, not the sacred antiquity of her laws; while, in the hands of the utilitarians, Helvetius and Bentham, law-making came to seem an exercise neither in moral philosophy nor in history, but in psychology, a problem of how to give the greatest happiness to the greatest number.

The main impression left by eighteenth-century law is, however, one of practical, unexciting worth, the reflected worth of the gentry who arranged the affairs of England in their county meetings, often assembled at the Assizes. Gone were the heroic attitudes of the law in the seventeenth century, when in a fit of 'legal antinomianism' Milton could argue that it was 'legal' to kill the king. The purpose of English law was not even to put down violence, but – as all the world knew – to defend the Englishman's property. Amongst that property, according to Blackstone, personal possessions, once regarded contemptuously by the law, had begun to achieve an importance equal to land and office, by reason of 'the introduction and extension of trade and commerce, which are entirely occupied in this species of property and have greatly augmented its quantity . . .'[61]

CHAPTER 12

EMPIRE AND COMMERCE: THE EXPANSION OF THE COMMON LAW

ENGLISH LAW IN THE COLONIES

ENGLISH law was colonizing early. The Normans and their feudal tenures established themselves in southern Scotland in the first half of the twelfth century, followed by English writs and English forms of action. Until the Reception of the sixteenth century, Scotland's law, though an autonomous system, was a rather less elaborate version of England's. By the Act of Union of 1706, the Scottish courts were preserved intact; but Scots law became alterable for the future by the United Kingdom Parliament, and cases of 1708 and 1710 established the right of appeal to the House of Lords. Scotland's relationship with England was one of at least theoretical equality. To Ireland, on the other hand, the English went to exploit and dominate. Since it was the land which was exploited – in 1800, some £1,500,000 was going from Ireland in rents to absentee landlords – English tenures and the Common Law were the agents of domination. In 1277 a group of churchmen tried to purchase the Common Law for Ireland: they offered Edward I 7,000 marks in order 'to be able to sell their land more easily than Irish law allowed' and 'to hold their lands in fee and inheritance, with resulting security of tenure'.[1]

Unfortunately, the relationship of the United Kingdom and its early colonies was constructed on the Irish rather than the Scottish model. The 'first British Empire' was regarded as belonging to the king by right of conquest, and the king shared out the new lands as William I had shared out England. The East India Company was granted Bombay in 1669, 'to be holden of us, our heirs and successors as of the manor of East Greenwich in the county of Kent, in free and common socage and not in capite nor by knights service, yielding and paying therefor to us, our heirs and successors at the Custom House, London, the rent . . . of £10 . . . yearly for ever'.[2]

Blackstone held that to an uninhabited country Englishmen carried with them as their birthright as much of English law as was 'applicable to their situation and the condition of an infant colony'. India, however, was far from uninhabited or lacking its own systems of law and custom, and the British were there for trade rather than land. The Mayors' Courts set up from 1726 onwards in the trading towns were empowered by the Company's charters to decide cases between British subjects only, 'according to the laws and customs of merchants . . . and by such ways and means as the judges should think best'. In fact, the Mayors' Courts, because of their efficiency in execution, attracted much litigation between Indians, and soon the British were taking over the jobs of the professional arbitrators outside the towns, supplementing native law by English law where necessary. English procedures were introduced, and English-style negotiable instruments; Indians came to exploit and delight in litigation much like English gentlemen; and native lawyers and jurists appeared to handle the new Anglo-Indian law.[3]

The first settlers in Australia were convicts. At the end of the transportation routes from England was a colonial existence so vicious that in New South Wales 'the number of convictions for highway robbery' exceeded 'convictions for all offences in England'. The first parts of English law to reach Australia were therefore the military and criminal laws, and particularly the regulation by the magistrates of labour and wages. The Criminal Law and Practice Act in Victoria (1864) assumed all the English definitions of crimes and even retained English laws about deer-stalking. In India some of English criminal law was clearly inapplicable – the punishment of bigamy for instance – but, equally, English courts could not tolerate customs like *suttee*, or order penalties like stoning for sexual immorality. Nor would they be influenced by considerations of caste or status. It was this implacability, and the speediness of execution, which scandalized India when Nandakumar was condemned for forgery in 1775. The extent to which English criminal statutes were taken to apply in India is uncertain, but in 1828 Sir Robert Peel's reforms were extended to India by a specific act (9 Geo. 4, c. 74) which did not forget to abolish benefit of clergy. Sir James Stephen spoke of Anglo-Indian criminal law, which he helped to codify between 1860 and 1882, as constituting 'one of the most important bodies of law in the world', allowing 'a handful of unsympathetic foreigners . . . to rule justly and firmly about 200,000,000 persons of many races, languages and creeds'. Canadian criminal law is based on a code which Stephen prepared for England but was never adopted here. In the same way as India, almost every colony came to have its codified version of English criminal law.[4]

The councils of the early colonial trading companies, and the proprietors of the palatine-colonies, created by royal grant to such as Walter Raleigh or William Penn of powers 'like the Bishop of Durham's in his bishopric', received authority to 'make . . . laws . . . forms and ceremonies of government and magistracy'. This usually meant that the governor and his officials acted like the justices of the peace and commissioners of oyer and terminer and gaol delivery which they had known – and perhaps been – in England. As for civil jurisdiction, the Company's Mayors' Courts in India were supplemented by Supreme Courts set up by the British Government at Calcutta, Madras and Bombay between 1774 and 1823, the year in which Australia also was given a Supreme Court. The English judges and attorneys of the Indian Supreme Courts naturally applied the English procedures and precedents they were familiar with at home; and Israel is today a 'Common Law country' for the same reasons: during the Mandate, British judges, sitting in the courts of

Palestine to apply Ottoman law, followed English precedents wherever that law was defective.[5]

The regulations made by corporations, as the trading companies were, came under the scrutiny of the Privy Council; and it was held that the king could legislate for the colonies by orders-in-council since they belonged to him by right of conquest. As soon as the king granted a colony the right to have its own assembly, the supreme law-making authority passed to the British Parliament, which alone, by its Act, might supplement and overrule the colony's legislation: that was Lord Mansfield's decision in 1774 in the case of *Campbell* v. *Hall* which followed Coke's judgment in the *Case of the Postnati* (1608). The relationship of the new colonies to Parliament was following ominously closely to that of Ireland, for which Poynings' Law, a late-fifteenth-century act of the Irish Parliament itself, had accepted the authority of all English statutes then in force. The American War of Independence was fought on this issue of the legislative authority which the British Parliament so obstinately guarded.[6]

But the unity of English and colonial law was judicial rather than legislative. To integrate the variety of sources of law which the Anglo-Indian judges had to apply – English Common Law, statutes and charters; native laws, usages and scriptures – High Courts of Appeal were established in India in the 1860s. What England gave India and the other colonies was not so much a body of law as the English way of making law and binding it together in a hierarchy of courts. In the federal Dominions of Australia and Canada – almost the whole of whose substantive law was inevitably taken from England – High Courts were established which would integrate the judgments of the courts in the separate states and reduce the number of appeals going to the Privy Council in London. The Privy Council was the Imperial court of appeal. The Council and its offshoots, the Courts of Admiralty and Chivalry, had long been the proper bodies to hear the complaints of the king's subjects dwelling in the Channel Islands (for example) or the Isle of Man, beyond the reach of the Common Law. The fertility of the procedure by petition to the king was demonstrated once again, and the Judicial Committee of the Privy Council came to do for the Empire 'somewhat the same service as the Curia Regis formerly did for England'. In 1667 we hear of a committee of the council, for trade and foreign plantations and to hear appeals from Jersey and Guernsey. By 1700 there was a regular colonial appeals committee, consisting of 'the chief legal authorities, the Bishop of London, one or other of the two Secretaries of State', and other interested councillors, working with the assistance of the attorney-general. Like the House of Lords, this committee was largely a court of amateurs in the eighteenth century, and made some bad decisions: but in the nineteenth century its hearings became public, its decisions began to be reported in 1829, and its membership was made more expert.[7]

THE COMMON LAW IN THE UNITED STATES

In the construction of their New England, the settlers who went out to Massachusetts Bay in 1630 used many of the elements of the society they had left behind. The agrarian communities of Salem and Boston, amongst their open fields, followed the traditional ways of English local government; and the Company appointed J.P.s and later established 'quarter-courts' in the principal settlements. John Winthrop, the governor, had been lord of the manor of Groton in Suffolk and a justice of the peace there, and Richard Bellingham, another leading settler, had been recorder of Boston, Lincolnshire. Massachusetts took its peculiar character from the English puritan's idea of justice and the godly magistrate. The colonists followed English statutes concerning the powers of the justices and English rules about dower. They had no alternative to borrowing from English laws and textbooks, but they selected carefully, their purpose to build an ideal community always in mind; and this law, which was theirs, not the king of England's, they codified in 1648 in the form of an abridgement, under the name of *The Laws and Liberties of Massachusetts*. The process was the same in the other American colonies, though the selections were different. South of Massachusetts, courts-baron and courts-leet flourished; and in Virginia a squirearchy ruled as completely as in an English shire. The reception of Blackstone's *Commentaries* in the eighteenth century – 2,500 copies were sold in America before Independence – helped to prevent too much divergence between the colonies, as did the attendance of Americans at the Inns of Court. Private law in America remained English in its principles, but had simpler and fewer procedures: 'actions on the case' covered almost every sort of injury.[8]

England's abuse of her judicial supremacy was one of the subsidiary grievances leading to independence, and Massachusetts tried from the first to intercept appeals to the Privy Council. The culminating judicial outrage was the strengthening of the vice-admiralty courts in the American harbours at the end of the Seven Years War in 1763, in order to draw a revenue from customs (and customs prosecutions) which would pay the cost of colonial defence, and to enforce the hated Stamp Act.[9]

The issues which separated the United States from Britain were mostly legal issues which had already been fought out in England. Jefferson appealed beyond feudalism to the rights of the Anglo-Saxon freeholder, and a later Baltimore school of historians, under the influence of Edward Freeman, was to see American communal institututions as a revival of the ancient Teutonic *mark*. The colonists took their stand on fundamental law against royal prerogative, and in Massachusetts they had the idea of writing it down, even before the English law reformers of the Interregnum did. The American Declaration of Rights of 1774 and the Declaration of Independence itself are in the fundamental law tradition. When they spoke of the Common Law as the American's birthright, and when the Constitution of the United States was proclaimed the supreme 'law of the land', the language was the language of Magna Carta, transmitted by Coke. In two other ways, England's domestic battles were being fought over again. The admiralty courts were 'prerogative courts', hated ostensibly because they operated without a jury. The final issue was that of legislative sovereignty, which the English Parliament had earlier won against the king. The colonists were not to be satisfied by the assertion that, as tenants of the manor of East Greenwich, they were represented in Parliament by the M.P.s for Kent.[10]

In the century after independence, the state legislatures enacted much new law – on the basis, however, of the Common Law, which the state constitutions said was to continue in force. The changes sometimes ran parallel to English changes. The Kentucky penal code of 1798, thirty years before Peel, abolished the death penalty for all but first degree murder. America influenced as well as felt the influence of the nineteenth-century English law reformers; both English and American commercial law was codified late in the century; and English decisions developing the law of tort were followed beyond the Atlantic. The crudities of the American courts under pioneering conditions were merely superficial. Already in 1777 Yale was planning a chair of English law modelled on Blackstone's at Oxford. The Harvard Law School was opened in 1817, and from its first Dane Professor Joseph Story, came a stream of valuable textbooks.[11]

From Virginia, the county system, with its J.P.s, moved westward as the unit of frontier settlement. Here American law faced up to an issue which English lawyers can even now barely imagine: whether, in a democracy, judges should not be elected too. Alexander Hamilton's discussion in no. 78 of *The Federalist Papers* and the debates of the nineteenth-century state constitutional conventions contain some of the best statements anywhere of the place of the judiciary in society.

COLONIZATION, TRADE, MARITIME LAW AND INTERNATIONAL LAW

Colonization was a private enterprise and largely a commercial one, though 'commerce' here must be interpreted widely: the profit which was the object of the joint-stock companies and the lords proprietors came from a mixture of trade, the rents of the settlers and the crops of the plantations. The rustic character of Massachusetts, where corn and beavers served as currency, obscures the crucial step which had been taken to economic freedom and growth, when the feudal bonds of Europe were left behind for the New World of unlimited land on easy terms.[12]

Not the wide lands, but the oceans between, fostered the earliest commercial institutions. Trading over great distances was expensive and required cooperation in a partnership or company. A usual arrangement amongst the medieval Italian merchants was the *commenda*, between an investing partner who stayed on land and a travelling partner who endured the perils of the sea. In the eighteenth century, the role of the travelling agent was still one through which an adventurous young man could become a partner in a reputable London West India merchant house, though sometimes he remained a factor, a mere employee. Many of the plantations were started by merchants and pioneers in partnership; in other cases the planter sold his crops through a factor in England. A more properly maritime institution, developed by the East India Company, was the *ship's husband*, who managed the affairs of a number of vessels for his less expert partners (he had often been a ship's master himself). Still, the merchants could not always find the right ships, so *ships' brokers*, centred on the London coffee-houses – and particularly, after 1774, Lloyd's coffee-house in the Royal Exchange – specialized in bringing husbands and merchants together. Lloyd's extended its activities and built up a world-wide business in marine insurance.

Vessels were usually chartered by a special form of contract, the *charter party*, in which the master covenanted with the merchant to begin his voyage on the first favourable wind after a specified date and the merchant agreed to pay so much a ton freight when the goods were discharged: clauses could be written in to exempt the master from liability for accident or stipulate the proportions in which prizes taken by the ship were to be distributed. A second essential document was the *bill of lading*, evolved by the middle of the sixteenth century, in which the master acknowledged the taking on board of the specified goods and promised to deliver them to the consignee.[13]

Medieval governments had become involved in the affairs of their merchant fleets, which, besides providing a large part of the national revenues, were points of contact between different countries and could spark off wars. Edward I appointed men to 'keep the sea' for the benefit of the merchants, and soon each maritime state was claiming the dominion of the large areas of ocean which it tried to police against pirates. International law began with the demarcation of these areas and a general acceptance of rules about the right of neutrals and belligerents in a maritime war (e.g. the right of belligerent ships to search all vessels for contraband goods). Private maritime wars were legalized by *letters of marque*, allowing a merchant whose ship had been plundered to become a *privateer* and take revenge and compensation from other ships of the offender's nation. Privateering, though not abolished till the Declaration of Paris in 1856, became confined to time of war, when the merchant ships of the belligerent nations brought in huge numbers of 'prizes'.[14]

The Middle Ages knew many customs and several local codes to deal with disputes arising from maritime practices. The most widely observed set of customs, those enforced in the merchants' court of the little island of Oleron in Guienne, already contained the basic principles of modern maritime law. Collisions at sea were investigated carefully, and the loss was either born entirely by the responsible ship, or divided equally if both ships were to blame: these principles were introduced into the Common Law as late as 1945. A vessel could be arrested for the debts of anyone aboard her and sold by the order of the maritime court, for a master would often pledge his ship so as to be able to buy supplies in a foreign harbour: such a loan (called a *contract of bottomry*) was repayable only if the ship arrived home safely, and high interest was therefore charged. The owner of a ship was fully liable for the debts and torts of the master and crew, and enjoyed any rights they contracted.[15]

Maritime law was drawn, through the Court of Admiralty, into English commercial law, partly because much of even the domestic trade of England went by sea before the days of canals and surfaced roads. In 1775 there were some 1,800 vessels in the coastal coal trade, and Shropshire pig iron went to Chester down the Severn and through the Irish Sea. Some maritime rules profoundly modified the Common Law. Thus, in *Boson* v. *Sandford* (1691), Holt derived the modern principle of the employer's liability for the torts of his employee from the peculiar responsibility of the owner for his crew. It was in the eighteenth century that the merchants became predominant and English law ceased to be supremely a law of land. Until the seventeenth century there was no true 'law-merchant' to be received – just a mass of local maritime customs, which were only then welded under civilian influence into public international law (its growth marked by the disputes of Selden and Grotius about the dominion of the seas) and *private international law*, dealing with private disputes between the subjects of different nations. Private international law is sometimes discussed under the title, *conflict of laws*, because it is concerned to decide which national body of law should apply to the case at issue. In more than one case we find Mansfield employed in this task. We must now see how commercial law got into the English courts.[16]

THE ORIGINS OF ENGLISH COMMERCIAL LAW

In medieval England, the customs of merchants, including all sorts of contracts which the Common Law ignored, were enforced by special local courts. The courts and legal peculiarities of the boroughs, and the merchant guilds which were often the earliest town governments, owed their existence primarily to trade. At one extreme, the hustings court of London was begun to settle disputes with Danes coming to the city in the peaceful way of commerce; at the other, every market and fair in the country had its court of *piepowder*, so named from the dusty feet (*pieds poudrés*) of the wandering pedlars whose bargains it enforced. In England, the local mercantile courts did not, however, benefit like their continental equivalents from the seventeenth-century consolidation of the law-merchant. They were in fact in decline before the Court of Admiralty, with its special knowledge of maritime and foreign laws.[17]

The court which was sitting by 1357 under the Lord High Admiral of England, the lineal successor of the keepers of the sea, was a manifestation of the Council's concern with foreign affairs and trading problems, and the Judicial Committee of the Privy Council still hears appeals from the Admiralty Division of the High Court in prize cases (prizes had to be confirmed to their captors in a court). Despite the envious attacks of the Common Law courts, the sixteenth-century Court of Admiralty dealt according to maritime and civil law with a tremendous body of litigation. Some of the cases were veritable sagas. In 1602 half-freight was awarded to the crew of *The Primrose*, which had brought its cargo back to London after being attacked by the Portuguese: surprised and imprisoned below hatches as the merchants' factors dallied on shore at Lagos, the crew had blown up the decks, blasted their captors into the sea, and nursed their vessel home. To handle the disputes which arose from the thronging life of the coastal waters and the sea-shore – the 'Mariners, Fishermen, Fowlers, Shipwrights, Sandwalkers, Cadgers and Wreckburners' – vice-admiralty courts were set up in the harbours of provincial England, and, later, of the American colonies. In the seventeenth century, the court at York, where the archbishop was titular vice-admiral, heard cases concerning wreck, flotsam, royal fish and the activities of enemy privateers on the coastal trade routes. Prize cases and wage disputes between masters and crew took up most of the time of the American courts; and the prizes from the great wars of the eighteenth century allowed the High Court of Admiralty in London to enjoy 'a short St Martin's summer' under Sir William Scott (Lord Stowell), appropriately the son of a Newcastle coal-shipper.[18]

But the Admiralty Court suffered the same hostility as the other conciliar courts, and in the eighteenth century the

Common Law courts were making inroads into the jurisdiction which they had struggled for generations to keep beyond the tide-line. They had begun by pretending in particular cases that incidents abroad had happened 'in the parish of St Mary-le-Bow in the ward of Cheap'. At the end of the seventeenth century, statutes came to the aid of fiction, when, for the convenience of trade, arbitration awards between merchants were made enforceable by any of the king's courts (9 and 10 Will. 3, c. 15). The piepowder courts themselves had always been reckoned as the king's, and their judgments had gone under writs of error to be reviewed at Westminster. The Law Merchant was thus affected by decisions in Westminster Hall, and by the eighteenth century merchants were recognizing virtues in the Common Law: 'Where cases are so faithfully and equitably reported as in England, a man of sense, though not bred to the law . . . may himself form a good judgment in most cases whether he is in the wrong or the right in going to law.' The Common Lawyers therefore began more confidently to claim that 'the Law Merchant is part of the laws of this Realm'; and the incorporation of it into the Common Law was taking place well before Mansfield, who has often been given credit for the task. Sometimes the merchants had cause to complain that their affairs were not understood in Westminster Hall. In *Ekins* v. *Maclish* (1753), however, Lord Hardwicke showed sympathy for their feelings and accepted their interpretation: 'the credit of the funds depends on the facility of transacting them,' he said, and mercantile usage was therefore to be preferred to 'nice and critical construction'.[19]

In its own way the Common Law of buying and selling was as developed as the law-merchant's, and as essential to the growth of trade. The right to hold a weekly market or annual fair, which the king had granted and controlled since Anglo-Saxon times, was protected by the Assize of Nuisance. In the eighteenth century new markets were still being created, like the White Cloth Hall at Leeds; and Abraham Darby of Coalbrookdale disposed of his pots and kettles at the annual fairs of Chester, Wrexham and Stourbridge. The great mass of sales were on credit and poorly recorded, but the Common Law provided safeguards in the form of assumpsit, and Chancery did so by its power to compel discovery of written evidence or objects, and to give remedy against fraudulent or unfair dealing. Customs cases were heard in the Court of the Exchequer, which further supervised the remarkable statutory process of Account against a dishonest bailiff or commercial agent: the plaintiff in such a case appointed auditors who might commit the accountant to prison until the debt was cleared.[20]

The Common Law was inclined to see commercial life as made up of masters and servants, of classes of person, each with its place and function in the social order, rather than in terms of individual enterprise and contracts. From the beginning of the action on the case, the 'common callings' – innkeepers and carriers for instance – incurred special liabilities at Common Law; but, in *Coggs* v. *Bernard* (1705), Holt introduced to the Common Law the maritime exceptions to carrier's liability, 'act of God and the King's enemies'. Conversely, the carrier's absolute liability for the theft of goods in his care was extended from the Common Law to maritime law as this was captured from Admiralty. Since larceny was a violation of possession, which the carrier was presumed to have (and since a man cannot steal from himself), the carrier's own misappropriation of the goods in his charge was punished as the new felony of *breaking bulk*, invented in 1473 to punish a carrier who opened a bale and sold the contents. Similarly, in the eighteenth century, the various new industries got their own laws of 'quasi-theft' to proscribe the *purloining* by factory workers of articles in their charge; and an act of 1799 (39 Geo. 3, c. 85) began to classify as *embezzlement* the misapplication of effects received in the course of their work by clerks, brokers, bankers and the like.

TRADING ASSOCIATIONS, MONOPOLIES AND JOINT-STOCK COMPANIES

Produce reached eighteenth-century London along a chain of intermediate dealers. Corn was passed from farmer to

factor to miller to mealman to baker; coal reached the consumer by way of 'Tyneside fitters, shipmasters, London
crimps, wholesale dealers, and hawkers'. Between principal
and factor or agent the Common Law was slow to learn from
mercantile custom how to apportion responsibility. The
reason was probably the confusion of the principal–agent
relationship with that of master and servant, in which the
master bore 'vicarious liability' for only those actions of his
servant which he had expressly authorized. Chancery began
to see that this analogy was too restricting for commerce, and
instead to compare principal and agent with *cestui que trust*
and trustee; while Holt began to import the relevant maritime law piecemeal into the English courts.[21]

Most of the great firms have started from the enterprise of
one individual. Then, as the business became too much for
one man, even with a team of agents, he began to take in
partners (perhaps from amongst his apprentices), each of
whom was legally an agent of the firm and of the other partners. Incorporation was often desirable, so that (like the
Newfoundland Co.) the partners and their successors might
'by the name aforesaid . . . plead and be impleaded before
any of [the king's] Judges or Justices in any of [his] Courts
and in any actions or suits whatsoever . . .'[22]

We saw that incorporation, granted by royal charter,
began with the medieval towns and their merchant guilds.
Though membership was by birth or apprenticeship, the
craft guilds or livery companies which arose in London
around 1300 – the butchers, bakers and candlestick-makers –
represented a further step towards the modern company:
accounts were kept and profits sometimes shared between
members, and the idea of the private trading corporation
began to separate from the idea of the public body with its
area of jurisdiction. For very good reasons the separation
remained incomplete in the overseas trading companies
which began to be incorporated at the end of the fourteenth
century. The king scrutinized the bye-laws of these 'regulated companies' very carefully, for they were outlying parts
of his government, elements in his foreign policy. The public

aspect became exclusive in those colonial companies, like the Massachusetts Bay Company, which grew into independent nations. Other colonial companies kept their headquarters in London, where they could protect their chartered monopolies in the courts against the independent merchants who were always trying to break in, and exert pressure on Parliament for favourable legislation like the Navigation Acts.[23]

The monopolistic practices which had begun in the medieval guilds and were continued in the trading companies were recognized as being to the national harm. The London companies in particular were attacked by Parliament for 'selling of dear stuff, exceeding price reasonable' and 'by reason of their corporations' making ordinances 'in common hurt of the king's liege people'.[24] Unfortunately, the king had learnt in the thirteenth century how advantageous it was for him to channel the wool trade through staple ports and a single Company of the Staple, which he might constantly milk by way of taxes. So the Crown was willing to institute a new type of monopoly in the mid sixteenth century – the exclusive right under letters-patent to exploit new manufacturing processes. What seems to be the first patent of invention was granted in 1552 to Henry Smyth, a London merchant, who proposed to introduce the making of Normandy glass, on the consideration of its 'great commodity to our realm' and the condition that Smyth taught the art to others. In the last years of Elizabeth's reign, Parliament launched a tremendous attack on these contracts between Queen and subject 'in restraint of trade'. But the Statute of Monopolies of 1624 (21 Jac. 1, c. 3 – an act which further outlawed patents for more than fourteen years) did not succeed in its attempt to destroy the jurisdiction of the Privy Council over monopolies and patents, though some notable test-cases like *Darcy* v. *Allen* (see p. 223 above) did find their way into the Common Law courts. For another century the Council decided on the novelty of the products or processes in question, hearing the *caveats* of opposers and perhaps requiring the lodging of a specimen or model with the attorney-general. In the 1690s,

Chancery began to put its powers of injunction at the disposal of the patentee whose monopoly had been infringed.[25]

After the Statute of Monopolies, an inventor could hope to keep ahead of his rivals only through the resources of a corporation; the 'projector' became a company promoter. Incorporation as a way of assembling capital rather than to regulate trade began, like so much else, in the merchant fleets. A merchant would buy shares in several vessels – an eighth here, a sixteenth there – and reap proportionate amounts of their profits. In Elizabeth's reign, the African Company raised a separate joint-stock for each voyage of the fleet, and divided the profits on its return, every venture thus taking the form of a large partnership, sometimes including the Queen herself. The East India Co. began to use the same stock for a number of voyages, threw that of 1617 open to a public subscription (drawing in one and a half million pounds), and in 1657 set up a permanent capital fund: the 'New General Stock'.[26]

Industry quickly caught the idea. Large partnerships like the Mineral and Battery Works got incorporation from Elizabeth so that capital subscription could be better organized, shares easily transferred between investors (as *choses in action* they were not transferable between ordinary individuals), and the members' liability for the company's debts limited. The last was the crucial matter. The company had now begun to separate from the firm, to become a mere investing device. The investor did not share in the running of the firm but in the administration of its stock or capital, and his votes in company meetings were soon proportional to the size of his share. Investment would have been discouraged if shareholders had been liable for all the debts incurred through the inefficient management of the firm or other people's unbusinesslike dealings with it. Fortunately, the members of a sixteenth-century corporation were already regarded in law as to a certain extent distinct from the corporation itself and not liable for its debts.[27]

The rush for incorporation as joint-stock companies slackened in the mid seventeenth century, only to be revived by another kind of enterprise – the lending of money at interest to the state. In 1694, the government incorporated a group of its creditors as the Bank of England. The interest on loans to the government seemed an inexhaustible source of income, on the basis of which the Company of 1694 could trade as a bank, and the South Sea Company, which outbid the Bank in 1719 with an offer of £7½ million for the privilege of taking over the whole £31 million of the National Debt, could work its monopoly of the South American trade. In the 1690s appeared for the first time the novel and disturbing phenomenon of stock exchange speculation. Groups of businessmen bought up the charters of dying companies, considered themselves incorporate, and indulged in any venture which offered itself. Companies for developing perpetual motion were projected, and the value of shares followed South Sea stock up to fantastic heights. Then, in September 1720, when the government prosecuted four of the bubble companies for trespassing on the South Sea Company's preserve, the whole edifice came tumbling down again to ruin.[28]

In the crisis, Parliament passed 'the Bubble Act' (6 Geo. 1, c. 18), which, instead of imposing stricter rules for the conduct of corporations, made the privilege of incorporation almost unattainable and imposed the severest penalties for acting as a company without it. But it was not at all clear what was meant by 'acting as a company'. In fact, the development of the small partnerships which led the way in the industrial revolution was stimulated by the Bubble Act as the alternative to incorporation. Mansfield, in a number of cases, worked out the obligations of partners to each other and third parties. Chancery meanwhile, with its extraordinary facility for opening up a new line of growth when statute had blocked an old one, treated the unincorporate business association as a trust. The company-by-trust was formed by a deed of settlement between the shareholders and the trustees which was the forerunner of the articles of association required by nineteenth-century company legislation – and into the deed could be written a limitation of the shareholders' liability more complete than the corporation had ever known. The way was then open for Lord Hardwicke to model the director's responsibilities on the trustee's.[29]

The Bubble Act had fortunately not stunted the growth of private enterprise, but nor had it solved the public problems: stock speculation may have been checked, but as a debtor the business association had been shattered into a number of elusive individuals. And in any case, Parliament had to pass a host of private acts to incorporate new joint-stock 'public utility companies', such as built the canals for which £13 million was subscribed between 1758 and 1802. When the king's authority was overthrown in America, companies there claimed incorporation as a right (businesses in the United States are therefore generally 'inc.' rather than 'co.' or 'ltd'), and the success of the American corporations prepared the way for the repeal of the Bubble Act in England in 1825.[30]

The progress of the Industrial Revolution was marked by peaks in the issuing of patents of invention and in litigation about them: in 1825, the number of inventions patented (their object mainly economy of labour) reached 250. Mansfield was successful in the case of Dr James's fever powder (1752) in persuading the Council to surrender its important jurisdiction over patents to the Common Law courts.[31]

THE FACILITATION OF CREDIT

Legal processes for recovering debt were as vital to commerce as protection of seisin was to agriculture, for without them no business would have been transacted on credit. The creditor trusted in the courts as much as in the debtor. The medieval wine trade passed through the hands of a succession of middlemen, each of whom sold on credit to the next. In the wool trade, not the payment, but the production of the goods was deferred, some Cistercian monasteries mortgaging their crops years in advance. By the eighteenth century, indebtedness had become a normal part of estate management as well; and huge quantities of credit were required to power colonial trade, and for the establishment and competitive operation of retail shops.[32]

Because foreign merchants could not stay to see the Common Law actions pursue their ponderous course, Edward I, in the Statutes of Acton Burnell and Merchants (1283 and 1285), provided a swifter process for the recovery of debts made 'of record' in rolls to be kept in the great fairs and by the mayors of certain ports. To foster new commerce – and because a merchant might have no land from which the debt could be raised – the law returned to the old expedient of retaliation against the defaulter's person: he was to be imprisoned, and his possessions subjected to compulsory sale. When the debt was recorded, the lending merchant was given a bond (sealed with a special seal) called a *statute merchant* or (after 1353) a *statute staple*, which continued in constant use till the staple ports themselves declined in the sixteenth century.[33]

Accessibility as well as speed was required in the machinery for debt enforcement. Between 1660 and 1846 something like 400 district 'courts of request' or 'courts of conscience' were created by local acts of Parliament to hear pleas of debt (and eventually of assumpsit), as a rule involving no sum greater than five pounds. Proceeding according to a robust common sense, these benches of town councillors and small traders could explore the facts of cases more widely than the courts of Common Law, and order the debts to be paid into court by instalments. In the new industrial cities they did an immense business amongst the growing ranks of shopkeepers and manufacturers and their working-class customers and employees, and 'prevented thousands from starving'; for the network of credit stretched in all directions, the manufacturer being as often as not in arrears with the worker's pay.[34]

A bankruptcy does not arise from a single debt, which a man whose credit is sound can always pay off by borrowing elsewhere: it is the breakdown of a man's credit, the failure of an essential piece of his trading equipment, due to his inexpertness as often as to his dishonesty and sometimes to circumstances beyond his control. Even in the sixteenth century the splendours and miseries of the Fleet were scarcely an enlightened cure for indebtedness. Moreover, the law's yardsticks were clumsy ones for detecting real insolvency amongst the merchant's complicated affairs – there was a statutory list of 'acts of bankruptcy', such as fleeing the country and taking sanctuary. An important act of 1571 (13 Eliz. 1, c. 7) gave the chancellor power to appoint commissioners who would deal with the bankrupt and share his assets in due proportion between the creditors. The chancellor appointed the commissions as an official, and it was only in 1676 that, in the person of Lord Nottingham, he began to hear appeals from them as a judge. After that, the tyranny and profiteering of the commissions required his continual vigilance; and the receivers of the bankrupt's assets, appointed by the creditors under an act of 1706 (6 Anne, c. 22), were, as trustees, further subjects for Chancery supervision. Bankruptcy became one of the most valuable parts of Chancery's jurisdiction.[35]

Fraudulent disposal of his goods by a bankrupt was created a non-clergyable felony by statutes of 1705–6 (4 and 5 Anne, c. 17; 6 Anne, c. 22): but at the same time provision was made (perhaps only as an emergency measure in the midst of a ruinous war) for the discharge from prison of a cooperative bankrupt, who could also be allowed five per cent of his assets when they were sufficient to give his creditors eight shillings in the pound. These acts remained the basis of bankruptcy law till the nineteenth century. The most important development of that law took place in King's Bench, to which issues arising from bankruptcies might be referred by the chancellor or come in the shape of Common Law actions by the receivers to obtain the bankrupt's dispersed assets. Thus, in *Alderson* v. *Temple* (1768) and *Rust* v. *Cooper* (1777), Mansfield was able to resolve much law about the man who paid one of his creditors when on the verge of bankruptcy into the simple idea of *fraudulent preference*, which made all such transactions void. The background to this legal development was a rise in the number of bankruptcies listed in *The London Gazette* from an average of about 200 a year in the

1740s to about 700 a year in the 1790s. The significance of these figures becomes clearer when it is remarked that the application of bankruptcy law was expressly confined to traders (as it is to this day in many countries) – because, said Blackstone, the laws of England were 'cautious of encouraging prodigality and extravagance by indulgence to debtors'.[36]

NEGOTIABLE INSTRUMENTS

When merchants assigned debts owed to them from one to another, credit became a sort of money. True *assignment* must pass the right to sue for the debt (the *chose in action*) to the assignee, and against this the Common Law always set its face, through fear of encouraging litigiousness and perhaps even maintenance. These objections were overcome amongst the medieval Jewish money-lenders by the practice of giving to the assignee full powers to sue in the assignor's name : and of extracting from the debtor a *writing obligatory* binding him to pay the creditor 'or his attorney'; while the Tudors found that loans were easier to come by if they made the exchequer tallies and bills which recorded royal debts transferable to the creditors' 'heirs and assigns'. Beginning in the seventeenth century, Chancery would in certain circumstances relieve an assignee who had not been given powers of attorney, as though the assignor (the original creditor) held the debt in trust for him. Because the virtual abolition of imprisonment for debt in 1870 made the temper of one creditor no more dangerous than another's, the Judicature Act of 1873 (36 and 37 Vict. c. 66) was able to compel debtors to accept obligations to any assignees.[37]

Informal bonds were passed freely from merchant to merchant in late-medieval England, but they had no legal status. On the other hand, the *bills of exchange* probably introduced to England by Italian merchants in the fourteenth century were recognized at least in the mercantile and admiralty courts. A bill of exchange was a formal letter authorizing the drawer's creditor abroad to get his money from one of the drawer's debtors in the same country : it was a 'traveller's

cheque' as much as a way of paying debts. It was payable, as
far as the courts were concerned, to the creditor 'or his assigns', but apparently not – in medieval England – 'to
bearer'. Assignment by simply writing the name of another
payee on the back of the bill was sufficient, however, to
create a thriving discount market, in which an assignee could
have his bill cashed by a third party before it fell due; and,
proclaiming that 'merchants can no more be without exchanges ... than ships at sea without water', Sir Thomas
Gresham built the first Royal Exchange as a centre for the
business in 1566. Even the Common Law courts learnt how
to enforce a bill of exchange, at first by assumpsit, and then,
after *Woodward* v. *Rowe* (1666), when the court stated bluntly
that 'the law of merchants is the law of the land', by 'an
action on the case upon the custom of merchants'.[38]

The seventeenth century saw the development of the old
'writings obligatory' into 'promissory notes', the ancestors
of modern banknotes. A banker is a man who borrows from
some people in order to lend – at interest – to others: and the
scriveners were engaged in this business on a large scale at
the beginning of the seventeenth century. The goldsmiths,
with whom merchants began to deposit their surplus cash for
security during the Civil War, were however the first to
issue promissory notes – of any denomination – in exchange
for deposits, which they then lent to Cromwell. They also
invented the *cheque*, which is a bill of exchange drawn on a
banker. Since the time of the great medieval Italian banks,
the lending side of banking had been directed towards the
state, and as early as 1571 there was a proposal for a bank to
take over the national debt. The suspicion of the Crown as a
debtor which frustrated such schemes appeared justified by
the famous 'Stop of the Exchequer' in 1672, when the in-
ability of the Crown to pay its debts on time placed the goldsmiths and their depositors in difficulties. The judges in
Exchequer Chamber, led by Holt, helped to save the situation in *The Bankers' Case* (1696–1700), which established
that a creditor of the king could claim his money by petition
of right. The Bank of England had been set up two years

before that case began, to lend £1,200,000 to the government. On the interest of this loan, the Bank seemed to think itself entitled to lend to private persons without limit by means of promissory notes, and the issuing of notes, soon of fixed denominations, became much more important for it than deposit business. An act of 1708 (7 Anne, c. 7) gave it a virtual monopoly of note-issuing and forced private banks to rely on cheques, which had the advantage, anyway, that clients could make them payable to the exact sums required.[39]

By 1700 the pressure was therefore irresistible that the promissory note should be not just assignable, but *negotiable* like a coin; and negotiability, which depends on whether the law will allow an action for value to the bearer of a note without asking how he has come by it, was duly conferred by the Promissory Notes Act of 1704 (3 and 4 Anne, c. 9). Mansfield's achievement in this matter, as in others, was the brilliant definition of what had already emerged. Deciding, in *Miller* v. *Race* (1758), for a plaintiff who had been refused payment by the Bank of England on a note which had been stolen at an earlier stage of its history, Mansfield declared that the fallacy of the defendant's argument had been to compare 'bank notes to what they do not resemble . . . viz. to goods, or to securities, or documents for debts', when they were in fact treated 'as money, as cash . . . by the general consent of mankind'.[40]

Through the defects of the Mint and an unreasonably high gold-to-silver exchange ratio, the supply of money in England in the eighteenth century 'was far from adequate to the needs of an expanding economy'. Hence the importance of the development of negotiable paper (we have not mentioned the more curious varieties, such as lottery tickets) and the springing up of private banks. In remote areas such as the Highlands of Scotland, where money was almost non-existent, a vigorous trade was carried on through bills of exchange before banks and promissory notes began to appear in the latter half of the century. Paper money brought its own abuses. The act of 1708 had not prevented employers from paying their workers in promissory notes of their own manu-

facture, sometimes for as little as 6d. and negotiable only at
a discount: it was against this abuse that an act was passed in
1775 prohibiting the negotiation of notes at less than £1.[41]

INSURANCE

Insurance is a contract by which the insurer (or 'underwriter'), in consideration of a premium, promises to indemnify the insured (or 'policy-holder') against a specific loss.
The high interest charged on the medieval sea-loan or contract of bottomry was very like an insurance premium, since
the lender lost his money if the ship foundered, and the terms
'premium' and 'policy' appeared in that connexion. But,
in the late fourteenth century, maritime insurance became
modelled on the contract of sale, and the property insured
was regarded as sold to the insurer on the condition that if it
arrived safely it would be re-conveyed to the insured. The
analogy gives us important principles: that the insured must
have some interest in the goods in the first place – the insurance must not be a mere wager on the safe passage of anyone's
vessel – and that payment for total loss entitles the insurer
to any of the property which can be recovered.[42]

The earliest policy sued upon in an English court was an
Italian one: the year was 1548, and the court, predictably,
the Court of Admiralty. Policies were not sealed and so could
not be enforced at Common Law, and, although in 1601 the
government gave statutory approval to the Chancellor's
practice of appointing commissions to deal with insurance
disputes (43 Eliz. c. 12), insurance law remained in a poor
way throughout the seventeenth century, when London was
becoming the world headquarters of the business. The eighteenth century was the century of Lloyd's. Amongst the
insurance brokers who resorted to the coffee-house in Lom-
bard Street from c. 1720, and the merchants who did the
actual underwriting as just one of their varied activities,
flourished the careful judgement of risks and premiums, of
the danger of hurricanes in the West Indies and ice in the
Baltic, which has always been the insurer's particular skill.

All this reflected the spread of England's maritime power. For most of the century the broker, providing credit facilities for both insurer and insured and some guarantee of the other party's reliability, exercised a sort of tyranny; but he failed to adapt himself to the mounting complexity of the trade and dropped behind his cousin, the bill-broker, in the climb to opulence. In marine insurance he was bypassed by that uniquely English phenomenon, the underwriter (by then a specialist), who operated not in a joint-stock company but as an individual from his box in Lloyd's.[43]

The eighteenth century was the one in which the Common Law moved into the commercial field, and since a large risk would be underwritten by several insurers the courts had to permit the 'consolidation' of actions: by this method, one of a number of identical actions, as by a policy-holder against several underwriters, was taken as deciding the whole group. Mansfield was the first judge to understand to the full that an insurance was a contract, and he particularly emphasized the need for good faith in marine insurance, which was open to monstrous frauds on the part of the shipowners. In *Carter* v. *Boehm* (1766), between an underwriter and the governor of a Sumatran trading station who insured his charge against capture and then capitulated to the French, he laid down the obligation of a policy-seeker to disclose all his circumstances.[44]

Gerard Malynes (*d.* 1641), the pioneer English authority on mercantile law, said that 'men cannot invent or imagine anything but the value of it may be assured'. Yet there was for long no true *life assurance*, as distinct from insurance against death from a particular misfortune – pregnancy or plague – within a limited period of time. Insuring life did not become commercially feasible until the end of the eighteenth century, when the growth of actuarial science made it possible to estimate the expectation of life, and there was a large middle-class clientele of clergymen, lawyers and millowners, living in a reasonably settled political climate. An act of 1774 assisted, by forbidding wagering policies on lives in which the policy-holders had no legitimate interest (14 Geo. 3, c. 48) – though it did not prevent bets of this sort on Napoleon's fortunes.[45]

The first successful fire insurance scheme was inspired by the Great Fire of London and made an acceptable risk by the higher building standards of the new city. The Sun Insurance Office, now the oldest surviving insurance company in the world, was founded in 1708. The fire insurance companies provided the earliest fire-fighting services and sent out inspectors of the insured properties to impose safety standards. (In the nineteenth century, life assurance similarly stimulated medical services.) The progress of the industrial revolution can be followed in the diversification of fire insurance risks towards 1800. Around that year only the big London breweries led the richest nobility in the size of their policies (the Duke of Bedford had Woburn Abbey insured for £80,000), but factories made up an increasing percentage of the whole £80 million insured with the Sun. The large section of the business involved in the insuring of London's docks and warehouses is a measure of the extent to which the industrial revolution was built on a commercial revolution. The Gordon rioters of 1780 burnt down Thomas Langdale's Holborn distillery, insured with the Sun. In the leading case of *Langdale* v. *Mason and others*, the courts upheld the clauses in all fire insurances exempting companies from liability for damage by 'Invasion, Foreign Enemy, Civil Commotion, or any military or usurped power'. It was in the deeds of settlement of insurance companies (which were particularly likely to suffer disastrous calls on their funds) that the liability of shareholders was first limited.[46]

LAW AND THE INDUSTRIAL REVOLUTION

The pressure of commercial cases upon the Common Law courts grew steadily throughout the eighteenth century, because judges like Mansfield understood that law's business was to assist every legitimate social activity. The law possessed ancient devices adaptable to its new task – the chancellor's power to arrange arbitration; that wonderful vehicle of cooperative enterprise, the trust; and the jury, which, composed of merchants, would find the appropriate commercial usages as easily as the facts of a case. There was no necessary conflict between law and commerce; but there were some troublesome differences of temperament. Merchants relied too much on custom and were apt to be slovenly in the drawing up of agreements: lawyers were too rigid in their demand for certainty of usage and in their assertion of privity of contract (the doctrine that none but the original contractors or the original creditor could sue for the benefit of a transaction). Mansfield's achievement was to sink these differences in a few general principles. He trained up a veritable corps of merchant-jurymen, but he did not abdicate to them. It was the commercial judge's task to transform a particular verdict as to mercantile custom into 'the general policy of law', effective in future cases. Soon contracts were being made 'in the sense of the judicial determinations', and after one of Mansfield's decisions the underwriters altered their insurance policies. Textbooks of commercial law had by the end of the eighteenth century separated from the encyclopedias of trading practice and the laws of the sea.[47]

By following the needs of commerce, law helped to prepare the way for industry. Patents granting monopolies of trade led to patents of invention, the earliest of which coincided exactly with the onset of large-scale mining projects in the mid sixteenth century. (Inventions always happen: it is the exploitation of them which counts.) By 1700, England, which in the sixteenth century was only catching up with Germany in technological development, had seen its capital city surpass Antwerp as a centre of exchange, and the way opened to the world's first industrial revolution. Probably all that remained to be done was to divert mercantile investment from land to the factories. Law to some extent determined the form which money took, but how did it affect the flow of money? Partly in a sense hostile to industrial growth, for the mortgage market channelled most capital into land, and the strict settlement hindered even the development of scientific farming by severely limiting the landlord's powers of disposition. Conversely, a law dominated by land was suffused by Blackstone's prejudice against the trader, and

reluctant to accept the local courts of requests which subjected 'persons of quality' to 'a company of shopkeepers'.[48]

Yet commerce, capitalism and industry of necessity grew
up in a society of landlords and peasants. The industrial
revolution happened in the first country where the rural
community had become stratified into absentee landowners,
'a class of agricultural entrepreneurs, the farmers, and a
large agrarian proletariat'. Enclosures forced the peasantry
into the towns; and, as the land was tied up in the senior line,
the younger sons of the squire were forced into commerce, to
make that fertile union of the governing and the mercantile
classes represented by the modern board of directors. The
industrial power of a pioneer magnate of industry like Sir
Ambrose Crowley was based and modelled on the social
dominance of the feudal magnate, and the English nobility
was getting richer in the eighteenth century because it was
exploiting the industrial potentialities of its estates: there
was a 'landlord phase' of the industrial revolution. The law
of land had its part in fostering trade. The judges frowned on
contracts in restraint of trade as they frowned on perpetuities.
The trustees of landed estates were encouraged by the chancellor to invest in joint-stock companies. By its very concentration on land, the Common Law left the merchants
with no secure mode of inheriting wealth and compelled
new enterprise in each generation. In a negative way,
even the eighteenth-century strict settlement assisted trade
by keeping land out of the market and driving merchant
capital back into the funds – incidentally dividing the
'landed interest' from the 'moneyed interest' for the first
time.[49]

For legal history, one of the major events of the eighteenth
century is the subsequent abdication of the law of the land
before this moneyed interest. Until then, everyone had believed in the careful regulation of trade as of the rest of life in
the close-knit community of the land. The J.P. had administered a whole collection of medieval assizes concerning
weights and measures and the price of bread and ale; and
the Navigation Acts showed the same instinct to control

transferred to the high seas. Adam Smith looked across an ideological gulf at a medieval world which feared *engrossing* and *regrating* (the wholesale buying up of produce to retail it at an unreasonable profit) as much as it feared witchcraft; a world in which 'the law of the market' was the obligation to buy 'in market overt', and not to *forestall* the vendor before he got there. The statutes against these practices were repealed in 1772 (12 Geo. 3, c. 71), though they remained misdemeanours at Common Law till 1844. By setting permitted rates of interest the law had been accommodating itself to the fact of usury ever since 1545. There was perhaps more reason than Adam Smith realized in the medieval attitude, for an economy unregulated by the law was one controlled by monopolists. There was a principle of English law that a man should be able to exercise his trade in freedom, so that contracts 'in restraint of trade' were invalid and combinations for that purpose criminal conspiracies. But these rules did not apply to the king. He lived by his prerogative of *purveyance*, which was forestalling elevated to a system, and he could authorize others to exercise monopolies. Adam Smith's doctrine of free trade and the principle of '*laissez-faire*' destroyed the old controls and monopolies but only encouraged the modern type of cartel, the spontaneous combination of producers to keep up prices.[50]

The 'laws of the market-place' prevailed, and their beauty was their exclusion of any positive regulation: the great firm escaped legal control as effectively as the feudal magnate long ago. From that time onwards economics rather than law was to be the chief language of politics. The industrial revolution brought about by individual enterprise replaced the 'social contract' as the great social myth, and it was a myth that enshrined in the nation's consciousness not only the economic leap forward but an accompanying disruption of society. The size of the industrial firm and the strangeness of factory work to the proletariat which flocked in from the countryside demanded a discipline which often degenerated into a tyranny of masters over men. The organization of the Crowley works in the early eighteenth century seems an absurdly

Gothic construction: in fact, it represents the moment of transition from medieval communalism to modern management, from the domestic to the factory system, from the paternalism of the squire–J.P. to rabid exploitation. The Crowley's iron-works in County Durham, their collieries to provide fuel, their farms to raise draught-horses, and their coastal vessels to ship the nails south, were ruled through the eighteenth century from the Crowley residence at Greenwich by means of a council, a court of arbitrators and a network of committees; the entire society being regulated by a continually amended code of laws ('the ancient constitution'), which included a process of outlawry and relied on an elaborate system of informers.[51]

The Crowley kingdom obtained its own laws as the laws of England gave up trying to control industrial relationships. The pre-industrial master enjoyed tremendous power over his apprentices, but within a code which assured reciprocal rights to the employee: in the eighteenth century, the law withdrew its protection from the worker. The J.P.s ceased to exercise the discretionary power to fix wage-rates given them in 1563 by the Statute of Artificers as soon as the vigilance of the privy council was relaxed, and Henry Fielding believed that, because the J.P.s would not ensure them a proper wage, men of independent mind took to crime. Generally, the workers followed an alternative course: they formed trade unions to take the law's place in enforcing reasonable wage-rates. The law which, by its omissions, made the unions necessary, outlawed them as conspiracies in restraint of trade. True, the combinations of masters were also indictable conspiracies at law, and Adam Smith knew that masters everywhere were 'in a constant and uniform combination' to keep down wages. But the desperate and sometimes violent combinations of the workers which the masters' actions provoked were the ones which attracted attention and gave an excuse for repressive statutes.[52]

Parliament looked kindly upon the friendly societies, the mutual insurance clubs of the workers, which were more truly descended from the medieval guilds than the trade unions, founded specifically to fight the employers for better wages. An act of 1793 (33 Geo. 3, c. 54) gave extensive privileges to friendly societies: they could sue in any court of law through their treasurers or trustees; disputes between members would be settled by the justices of the peace, to whom the societies' rules had to be submitted for approval in quarter-sessions; and Chancery was required to hear suits against the societies' officers free of all fees. Trade unions, on the other hand, were the target of a pair of general combination acts, rushed through Parliament in 1799–1800 when it seemed as though the French Revolution might be repeated in England. These acts declared any organization by the workers to increase their wages or reduce hours of work a criminal offence punishable by imprisonment; and there was to be no appeal from quarter-sessions against conviction (39 Geo. 3, c. 81; 39 and 40 Geo. 3, c. 106).[53]

It is true that these acts merely reinforced the Common Law's proscription of combinations as conspiracies. Their novelty was the surrender of the offending workmen into the power of the millowner–J.P., which hastened the stratification of industrial society into opposing classes. In the guild the absorption of the leading workmen into the ranks of the masters prevented workers' organizations, and the Crowley ironworks preserved the 'vertical community' of the feudal estate in an industrial setting. In the nineteenth century, however, the Crowley works became a centre of Chartism. 'The powers and duties of the medieval guild' were broken up, and the fragments left were 'the friendly society and the trade union, the capitalist syndicate and the employers' association . . .' For this result the law bore much responsibility, and becoming more exclusively the law of the upper classes it deserved to lose the workers' respect. By the tragic withdrawal with which we must end this chapter on the advance of the law into trade a great number of problems were stored up for the future, problems still not entirely solved. Sir William Holdsworth believed that it was the late-eighteenth century refusal of Parliament, on the basis of *laissez-faire* doctrines, 'to set up any legal machinery for the equitable adjustment of industrial disputes', which made it 'possible in 1906 to pass a statute which perpetrated the enormous injustice of freeing trade unions of masters and men from liability for tort. . .'[54]

CHAPTER 13

LAW REFORM
IN THE NINETEENTH CENTURY:
THE LEGAL SYSTEM

STAGNANT LAW IN A CHANGING SOCIETY

THE myth of the Industrial Revolution covers a variety of
social changes. The population of England and Wales rose
from eight million in 1780 to thirteen million in 1831 and
eighteen million in 1851, and at the same time it became a
predominantly urban population, fed by an agricultural
'industry' which was transformed by the inpouring of
capital. Great shifts of industry and population were made
possible by the criss-cross of railways engraved on the
countryside by the 'railway mania' of the 1840s – this but
one example of the chaotic vitality of Victorian England,
which for the sake of worker, shareholder, landowner, traveller and consumer, badly wanted discipline. By the mid-
nineteenth century, the law was struggling to catch up with
a rate of change which was accelerating, for population rose
by a further twenty-five per cent between 1851 and 1871, and
the national income grew from £523 million to £916 million
a year.[1]

Fifty years earlier, the law needed persuading that there
was any race to enter. Government at that moment was
carried on with a cheerful amateurishness which would be
unimaginable by mid century: as well as running the Court
of Chancery, the Lord Chancellor was required to handle
the mad king (who called him 'Baggs', after the pouch he
carried the Great Seal in) and the unspeakable Prince of
Wales. That particular chancellor was just the wrong man

330

for the times. Stowell's brother, Lord Eldon, chancellor from 1801 to 1806 and from 1807 to 1827 knew far too much law to reach moderately expeditious judgments, though as a young man he had found the initiative to elope to Scotland with the daughter of a Newcastle banker. 'He hugs indecision to his breast, and takes home a modest doubt or a nice point to solace himself with it in protracted, luxurious dalliance.' The plight of the litigant in Chancery was well described in *Bleak House*, for Charles Dickens had himself brought copyright suits in the court. What was Richard of Anstey's case in Henry II's reign to that Monument of Chancery Practice, *Jarndyce* v. *Jarndyce*? 'Equity sends questions to Law, Law sends questions back to Equity; Law finds it can't do this, Equity finds it can't do that; neither can so much as say it can't do anything, without this solicitor instructing and this counsel appearing. . . . Innumerable children have been born into the cause; innumerable young people have married into it; innumerable old people have died out of it. Scores of persons have deliriously found themselves made parties in Jarndyce and Jarndyce, without knowing how or why . . .' The whole thing represented 'waste, want and beggared misery', for men were literally ruined by suits in Chancery, and a defeated party, unable to pay, might find himself in the Fleet for life.[2]

Not only did Eldon do nothing to reform the scandal of his court, but he 'believed in everything which it is impossible to believe in – the danger of Parliamentary Reform, the danger of Catholic Emancipation . . . , the danger of abolishing capital punishment for trivial thefts, the danger of making landowners pay their debts, the danger of making anything more, the danger of making anything less'. He stood for all the repressive measures provoked by the French Revolution, so that it is tempting to attribute the legal stagnation of the period to the control by such a man of a court so important to commercial growth – and even to see the reforming zeal of Whigs like Brougham as mere hatred of an uncompromising Tory. Increasing trade, it might be argued, had itself contributed to the legal crisis, for the most unjust

331

and inefficient part of Chancery jurisdiction was probably that exercised in London by the fourteen lists of bankruptcy commissioners: a skilful commissioner, it was said, could manage (or put off) thirty cases in a morning and net £300 a year in fees. But the complaints against the law in the early nineteenth century were the same as those voiced under the Protectorate and they embraced every part of the law. It was the Protectorate's unfinished business which had to be resumed.[3]

The stream of law-reform tracts so strong in the 1650s flowed swiftly again from about 1750, schemes for the registration of land transactions still to the fore. The calm of the early eighteenth century was due partly to the optimism inspired by the Glorious Revolution; but the conviction that law and constitution were perfect declined into the Blackstonian complacency which aroused Bentham's anger. After Mansfield's departure, King's Bench sank back into lethargy, and, on the accession of Queen Victoria, 300 cases, mostly of two years standing, awaited decision. Jurisdiction and procedure were supported by fictions and pretence which were thickest in the law of bail: Mr Pickwick, brought to the judges' chambers at Serjeants' Inn for committal to the Fleet, passed a screen of shabby little men who lived by going bail for anyone at half-a-crown a time. Nonsuiting was still the penalty for making the wrong selection from the seventy varieties of action – choosing Trespass instead of Case, for instance, when the damage was indirect and due to negligence. Pleading had long since ceased to convey any true information, though the rules against 'duplicity' might require a party to admit all but one of his opponent's falsehoods. Yet it was actually in the first half of the nineteenth century that the labyrinths of pleading were traced with the most loving care by Serjeant Stephen in his *Principles of Pleading* (1824) and by Baron Parke on the bench of the Exchequer. The greatest absurdity of all was the rule that no interested persons, including the parties in the action, might give evidence. 'The merchant whose name was forged to a bill of exchange had to sit by, silent and unheard, while his acquaintances were called to offer conjectures and beliefs as to the authenticity of the disputed signature.'[4]

Private law and criminal law shared a malaise which affected the whole of the state and is perhaps better known in its public aspects: the inadequacy and corruption of town government, the alternate harshness and waste of the poor law, the sinecures weighing down the government no less than the courts, the narrowness of parliamentary 'representation'. During the Napoleonic wars, the results of this incongruity between social conditions and legal institutions were aggravated by the use of the law to repress social radicalism.[5]

BENTHAM AND BROUGHAM

To some extent, the malaise was a temporary loss of confidence before a social revolution which in the end generated the intellectual energy to modernize the law. There is much still to be explained about the transformation of thought and sensibility in the later eighteenth century. It was not just a revulsion against industrial squalor, for some of its earliest targets were the independent scandals of slavery, the boy chimney-sweeps and the brutality meted out to women and servants within the confines of the home (in 1834 there were still three times as many female domestic servants as there were workers in the cotton mills). A characteristic product of the new humanitarianism was the Apprentice and Servant Act of 1851 (14 and 15 Vict. c. 11), occasioned by a lawyer's vicious treatment of his pauper servant-girl, such treatment as could be punished, after the Act, by three years' hard labour. What needs to be explained, therefore, is the appearance of the 'Victorian' virtues and vices – a sensitive humanity (in some directions), moral indignation, moral theorizing, respectability, cant, the sudden revulsion against the traditional corruption and sinecurism of government.[6]

Reform began with Parliament and the administration as early as the 1780s. It was then a Whig movement, bent on eliminating the jobbery through which the king was alleged to exert an excessive political influence. The attack was quickly extended to the anomalies of parliamentary representation and to the law courts, and achieved a popular form in John Wade's *Black Book* (1820), which purported to give facts and figures about the all-pervading corruption and sinecurism. The Whigs had reaped a whirlwind, and they were soon arguing that reform was necessary to appease the masses. Burke spoke of the courts as Macaulay was to speak of the unreformed Parliament in 1832: 'People crushed by law have no hopes but from power. If laws are their enemies, they will be enemies to laws; and . . . will always be dangerous, more or less.'[7]

Political reform and increasing democracy demanded social reform and created a Parliament able to accomplish it. Jeremy Bentham was a theorist crying in the wilderness because the great parliamentary Reform Bill was passed only in the year of his death (1832). As a law student he had heard Mansfield in King's Bench with admiration and Blackstone's lectures at Oxford with scorn. In his *Fragment on Government* (1776) he attacked Blackstone's *Commentaries*, with their encomium on the Gothic structure of the British constitution, and, forsaking his profession, devoted himself to that study of the underlying principles of law which issued, in the stirring year of 1789, in *The Principles of Morals and Legislation*. The purpose of government, he asserted, was to secure the greatest happiness of the greatest number; institutions were to be judged by their fruits; and they must be continually reformed by radical legislation. He was perhaps unconsciously imitating the despised Blackstone in 'examining how far each part' of English law was 'connected with the rest', but he took the further and 'mighty step of trying the whole province of our jurisprudence by the test of expediency'. Bentham was a figure of the Enlightenment, convinced of the perfectability of man through his own common sense, and thus one of a group of European reformers – Montesquieu, Voltaire and Beccaria were others – concerned with the punishment and reform of criminals. His influence was 'purely intellectual', and his schemes were highly unpracti-

cal: he proposed to put culprits into what he called a Panopticon, 'a sort of circular prison, with open cells like a glass
bee-hive', where the prisoners would set each other an example of industry. But as a critic of the working of the law
he was penetrating and fantastically comprehensive. He
offered codes – which he thought should replace judicial law-
making – to half the nations of the world, and his name was
famous as far as 'the plains of Chili and the mines of Mexico'.
The Americans actually built a Panopticon.[8]

Simply because his works were so many and such enormous collations of facts, there were few of the reforms which
were carried out after his death that Bentham did not hint
at. Brougham and Edwin Chadwick were just two of his
disciples, but their empirical, piecemeal, parliamentary legislation was closer to judicial law-making (which, though
Bentham despised it, was to share the burden of reform) than
it was to his encyclopedic rationalism. Bentham was, in fact,
bitterly disappointed by Brougham's great six-hour Commons speech of 1828, sustained by the constant sucking of
oranges, which kept Members from their dinners and in-
augurated the period of general law reform. Henry Brougham was a Romantic rather than an Enlightenment man,
who fought (with speeches that ran away with him through
an excess of indignation and contempt) in a crusade against
cruelty and injustice which was as old as Hogarth – certainly
older than Benthamism. And, though by Bentham's standards the speech of 1828 may have been woefully unsystematic, concrete results soon followed the noble peroration
which urged the king to make his boast that 'he had found
law dear and left it cheap, found it a sealed book – left it a
living letter; found it a patrimony of the rich – left it the
inheritance of the poor; found it the two-edged sword of
craft and oppression – left it the staff of honesty and the shield
of innocence'. The Tory government promptly appointed
two Royal Commissions of eminent lawyers, one to inquire
into the practice and procedure of the Common Law courts,
the other into the law of real property; and Brougham himself, whom Eldon lived to see on the woolsack in the Whig

335

government of 1830, was responsible for implementing several of their recommendations.[9]

The group of reformers round Bentham included only one real jurist, John Austin, whose identification of law with command and admiration for the Prussian monarchy reflected the utilitarians' faith in legislation. The problems of colonial justice also encouraged authoritarianism in the reformers. In 1825, a young clerk at India House, John Stuart Mill, was busy arranging Bentham's manuscript on the law of evidence, and Benthamism had a large part in transforming the Indian administration Bill Hickey knew into the *élite* of public servants whose descendants have since contributed many of Britain's intellectual leaders. From India, where the feasibility of major alterations to the law had been demonstrated, Benthamism returned to England with redoubled force in such persons as James Fitzjames Stephen, an Austinian by conviction and, after three crowded years (1869–72) as legal member of the Governor-General's council, an experienced and insatiable codifier. In 1877 he was officially instructed to draft a Criminal Code (Indictable Offences) Bill.[10]

The bill never passed, and the scheme foundered on the opposition of the Lord Chief Justice. Once again codification proved not to be the way of the reformers, whose families, like Stephen's own, had worked professionally for generations within the empirical tradition of English law. The law reformed itself in its own way. A Tory lord chancellor, Lyndhurst, took up the suggestions of Brougham's speech, and many of the reforming ideas of the beginning of the century were orthodoxy for the great judges, Bramwell, Blackburn and Willes, who led the Bench between 1852 and 1875. Judicial legislation and parliamentary legislation worked together. Decisions of the much-maligned Chancery eroded prejudices against a married woman's separate property, so that a series of Married Women's Property Acts, beginning in 1870, could fairly quickly confer a separate estate and contractual capacity on every wife. Concerning the sale of goods, statutes no more than consolidated judge-made law. Judicial legislation was safe but generally slow, and needed the complement of statutes, which sometimes, however, simply created new problems by ignoring general principles and logical consistency, or, like the act of 1853 against wife-beating (16 and 17 Vict. c. 30), by providing crude punitive remedies for deep-seated social ills.[11]

Statute was the good blunt instrument which the hands of the law reformers itched to bring down on the crust of procedural fictions. Bentham did not have to teach them the use of the statute: the modern period of legislative activity is only the last of four, the others occurring under Edward I, under the Tudors, and during the Commonwealth, and Brougham looked back to them in his great speech. But the effect of nineteenth-century parliamentary reform was to compel the parties to have competitive legislative programmes on every subject, so that there could never be another period of legislative quiescence. The early reformers had, however, to work out the technique for promoting legislation. This was to raise support in Parliament, move for a select committee of one of the Houses (which might lead, if the lord chancellor was agreeable, to that oldest of judicial forms, a Royal Commission of inquiry), supply the committee with expert witnesses and draft bills, and finally carry through legislation on the wave of popular feeling created by a best-selling (and sometimes illustrated) *Report*.[12]

Peel wrote in 1820 of 'that great compound of folly, weakness, prejudice, wrong feeling, right feeling, obstinacy and newspaper paragraphs, which is called public opinion'. The reformers worked on it through journals like the *Edinburgh Review* or James Stephen's *Saturday Review*, and through national associations not all as eccentric as Brougham's Society for the Diffusion of Useful Knowledge, which in 1862 took over the House of Lords for its congress. In Parliament, where all the elements in reform came together – public opinion, the government, the chancellor, judges and law officers – the individual reformers enjoyed the initiative because there was not the modern separation between Government Bills and Private Members' Bills or even Private Bills. The individual Member with a scheme of reform engineered the favourable report of a committee as did the ordinary citizen seeking a private act. Between 1800 and 1831 alone over sixty commissions of inquiry were appointed into various aspects of the administration, and the technique of unremitting pressure can be seen in the history of the improvement of the statutory forms themselves. In 1796, Charles Abbott persuaded the House of Commons to appoint a committee of inquiry into the publication of statutes and another in 1800 into the state of the public records, the second leading to the Record Commission and the publication of an authoritative edition of the statutes. Brougham set up a Royal Commission on the revision of the statute-book in 1833; in 1836 there was another select committee on publication.[13]

As in the time of the Commonwealth, there were ambitious schemes for digests of the whole law. At least the piecemeal consolidation of statute-law got under way in 1825, when 12 acts (6 Geo. 4, cc. 105–16) repealed and replaced 442 earlier ones on customs revenue. In 1854, Lord Chancellor Cranworth appointed a Statute Law Commission which was intended to produce a Code Victoria, but it was allowed to expire by Lord Chancellor Campbell after a few years of expensive work, only six of its ninety-three bills to consolidate criminal law being passed in 1861 (24 and 25 Vict. cc. 94–100). That same year saw, however, the first of the continuing series of Statute Law Revision Acts to erase obsolete statutes, and in 1868 the task of revision little by little passed under the chancellor's Statute Law Committee, which also continues. Better drafting of new statutes was the subject of 'Brougham's Act' of 1850 and a committee of 1875. An early example of the simpler, clearer style which emerged was the Merchant Shipping Act of 1854, drawn by Mr Henry Thring, one of the succession of barristers known as 'parliamentary counsel' who had been employed by the Home Office on drafting since the late eighteenth century. Thring managed to turn his occasional employment into the permanent office of First Parliamentary Counsel to the Treasury, who took immediate responsibility, under the Statute Law Committee, for the condition of the Statute Book.[14]

In the heroic age before 1869, the reformer had to draft his own bills and campaign for them in parliament. He was fortunate if the Lords – in which law reform bills are often introduced on account of the House's legal expertise – was not in a mood for rejecting the bills of 'the dilettanti ... *one* after *another*'. But, in the long run, the very success of the reformers in cleaning up the statute book and impressing the government with the need for legislation of all sorts took the initiative from the private member. The Reform Act of 1832 was the first of a great series of Public General Acts put through by the government of the day; and at the other extreme private bill procedure became quite distinct from national legislation. Law reform in particular suffered because the procedure of statute law revision seemed able to operate automatically, needing little of Parliament's precious debating time.[15]

THE REFORM OF THE CIVIL COURTS

At the beginning of the nineteenth century the chief hazard facing the litigant was a bewildering multiplicity of expensive and largely medieval courts. It was fatal for the plaintiff to make a wrong choice between them, but the defendant could play off Equity against the Common Law courts indefinitely. So in 1810 there began a series of inquiries into the superfluity and sale of offices in the courts which gradually extended its scope to the condition of the whole judicial system.[16]

Equity procedure had the merits that there was but one form of action, that formal mistakes were not irretrievable, and that a dubious decision could be remedied by a straightforward reconsideration; Common Law procedure, the merits that it aimed by fixed and easy routes at substantial justice, not (through the consideration of every aspect of a

339

case) at comprehensive justice, an ideal quite out of proportion to Chancery's resources. The obvious solution, then already adopted in America, and in England accepted by parallel commissions of 1851 on Chancery and the Common Law courts, was to combine the best features of the two. The Chancery Procedure Act of 1852 and the Common Law Procedure Act of 1854 abolished the Masters in Chancery and the chancellor's dilatory practice of referring questions to the masters or the Common Law judges: Chancery was empowered to hear oral evidence and use a jury, the Common Law courts to grant injunctions and admit other equitable procedures.[17]

The separate strands of jurisdiction were first gathered together at the top – at the level of appeals. The review of decisions followed different lines in law and in equity and was very slow, but appeals were common because they involved stays of execution. There was a separate appeal court for almost every court of first instance. In 1830, however, the jurisdiction of King's Bench over errors in Common Pleas was abolished, and the separate courts of Exchequer Chamber hearing errors and considering difficult cases in the Common Law courts were amalgamated: thenceforward the trial judges of the other two superior courts would determine errors in any one of them (11 Geo. 4 and 1 Will. 4, c. 70). In his great speech, Brougham particularly condemned the Privy Council, the court of appeal for a whole empire yet an amateur body which disposed of the property of the king's subjects with the utmost frivolity. Five years later Brougham secured an act (3 and 4 Will. 4, c. 41) creating the lord chancellor, the chief justices and other legal officers a permanent and professional 'Judicial Committee of the Privy Council' to hear appeals from the Empire, including maritime cases which had previously gone to the High Court of Admiralty. The Judicial Committee also swallowed up the jurisdiction over appeals from the other civilian courts such as the Court of Chivalry and from the ecclesiastical courts, which Chancery had exercised through courts of delegates. (The Judicial Committee was thus able in 1860 to 'dismiss hell with costs' by upholding the appeal of the authors of the famous *Essays and Reviews* against conviction in the Court of Arches for denial of the doctrine of eternal punishment.) By the mid-nineteenth century there were basically two final courts of appeal: the House of Lords for the Common Law and Equity, and the Judicial Committee of the Privy Council for the church and the colonies.[18]

The 1860 report of the Commissioners on the Supreme Courts of Law recounted with some complacency the course of reform to that date, and had only a 'few suggestions' for improvement. The more remarkable was the abandonment within a decade of the method of piecemeal readjustment for the most thoroughgoing revolution in English legal history. Much of the old mischief remained, concluded the First Report of the Judicature Commission in 1868, and the only solution was 'the consolidation of all the Superior Courts of Law and Equity, together with the Courts of Probate, Divorce and Admiralty, into one Court'. The Judicature Act of 1873 (36 and 37 Vict. c. 66), drafted and nursed through Parliament by Lord Selborne, Gladstone's lord chancellor, accordingly erected one Supreme Court of Judicature divided into a High Court of Justice and a Court of Appeal. All the existing judges were created 'Justices of the Supreme Court', whose ranks would be filled for the future from the barristers of ten years' standing. The High Court's jurisdiction could in most cases be exercised by a single judge, though a 'divisional court' of at least two judges was required to sit for the hearing of appeals from inferior courts, and the High Court was split for convenience of business into divisions corresponding to the abolished courts (but any judge might sit in any division, as required). The Common Pleas and Exchequer Divisions were merged in the Queen's Bench Division by an order-in-council of 1880, and the chief justice of Queen's Bench became the Lord Chief Justice of England: the other two divisions were Chancery; and Probate, Divorce and Admiralty.[19]

Not without some confusion or in such a way that the two streams lost their substantive identities, the fusion of the common law and equitable processes was gradually achieved. The Judicature Act's express adoption into the Common Law of assignment of debt and the protection of mortgagors in possession was more effective here than its general precept that, in case of conflict between Common Law and Equity, the latter should prevail in all divisions of the new court.[20]

The Judicature Act created a single civil Court of Appeal, comprised of the lord chancellor, the lord chief justice, the president of the probate, divorce and admiralty division, any previous lord chancellor invited to act, and up to five specially appointed lords justices of appeal. Any three judges of the court had jurisdiction, and they were to follow Chancery's practice to simply reconsider the issues rather than the old Common Law procedure in error, which could only put the parties back to the beginning of the case. The Act would have abolished further appeal to the House of Lords, but the clauses to do this were removed before they could take effect, and so the Appellate Jurisdiction Act of 1876 was passed to reform the Lords as an appeal court. In the debate on the Judicature Act the attorney-general described the Lords – in their judicial capacity – as an 'utterly irresponsible' and 'perfectly indefensible' institution. The Lords had, however, become accustomed to ask and to accept the advice of the judges in their midst, and the lay peers did not vote on appeals after 1844, when they withdrew from the House during the hearing of *The Queen* v. *O'Connell and Others*. After 1876, appeals brought by petition for review 'before Her Majesty the Queen in her Court of Parliament' were to be heard only in the presence of three of the law lords, and the numbers of these were to be reinforced by two Lords of Appeal in Ordinary (life-barons), chosen from judges of two and barristers of fifteen years' standing, who would also be appointed to the Judicial Committee of the Privy Council as vacancies occurred. In this way provision was made for the uniting of the personnel of the two supreme appeal courts of the Empire.[21]

In 1846, an act of Brougham's 'nationalized' the local

courts of requests, which before that time had stood rather apart from the English judicial system, by making them formally branches of the ancient shire-courts, moribund but still possessing exclusive power to proclaim outlawry. Following an earlier experiment in Middlesex, the act provided for the appointment of experienced barristers as paid judges, each to go on circuit through a number of counties and at various places within them to hold ' county-courts ' and determine small claims. The result was something like the American county-court, where the J.P.s had been compelled to deal with common pleas and chancery business as well as crimes, since the earliest settlements. For routine business the English county-courts have since become by the steady accretion of statutory powers the most important courts in the land.[22]

In the 1870s was completed the purging of that clerical organization of the courts, based on fee and sinecure, which had been the original target of the reformers and their major obstacle. In 1810 the Commissioners upon Saleable Offices in the Courts of Law reported that more than half the work was performed by deputies, who in King's Bench were paid only £1,356 13s. 0d. of the £15,022 19s. 3d. their masters received in fees. The number of offices in a particular court bore little relation to the extent of its business – at the judicial level, Chancery was ludicrously understaffed, and, because of the prolixity of procedure, such as taking bail, the Common Law judges were overburdened with work in chambers. Procedural reform and the pooling of resources in the Supreme Court automatically cured some of these defects, and the idea of office as property was just then being destroyed by the new civil service. Many of the legal sinecures were abolished, and the remaining offices were formed by an act of 1879 (42 and 43 Vict. c. 78) into the Central Office of the Supreme Court. After 700 years of service, the plea-rolls gave way in November 1875 to brief judgment papers.[23]

A more fundamental break with the past took place in 1884, when the Courts, which had already moved out of Westminster Hall to adjacent premises completed in 1828, left Westminster altogether for Street's new buildings in the Strand. Justice moved away from Parliament into the lawyers' quarter, where the inns, the judges' chambers and the court offices had long been gathered, and greater efficiency resulted. Out of term, the lord chancellor had previously kept his court where Dickens found it, in Lincoln's Inn Hall, as a sort of tenant-at-will of the Benchers, and the judges of Common Pleas, whose business also overflowed the term, had used the Guildhall. The Royal Courts of Justice sealed the fusion of the courts and by providing office accommodation also curtailed the squalor of chamber business – the fights to get into the judge's rooms, and the administering of oaths through windows to deponents in the courtyard.[24]

THE CRIMINAL COURTS

Industrial misery and disorders, not fees and delay, were the conditions demanding reform on the criminal side. Disorder was urban and mostly directed against the Poor Laws. During the Chartist disturbances of the 1830s and the 1840s, the magistrates, particularly the bourgeois element, taking less joy than the old landed aristocracy in fighting their own battles, were very quick to call in the military, which the railways allowed to be transferred quickly to the trouble-spots. Both justices and workers, in the new society of horizontal classes, were looking to the government in London. Fortunately, the Home Secretary gave up trying to rouse the magistrates to their policing responsibilities, yet recognized along with the intelligent and humane military commander of the Northern District, Sir Charles Napier, the dangers of using the army. Instead, by lending out the Metropolitan 'Peelers' in local emergencies and through permissive legislation, he spread the idea of a regular police drawn from the lower classes themselves, using local knowledge in preference to force, and responsible for its general efficiency to him.[25]

Administration from Whitehall, though introduced in the guise of a mere 'superintending' of local administration which was compatible with local discretion, attacked the ancient aristocratic system of government at its roots. Tory gentry and urban radicals combined to resist (unsuccessfully) the trend from legislation merely permitting the creation of county police forces out of the rates, by way of the increasing employment of inspectors, to the 'despicable despotism' of the 1856 County and Borough Police Act which made the raising of county police obligatory and provided Treasury grants in aid. The widening floods of social legislation did not go to the J.P.s for enforcement; but nor were the localities entirely deprived of responsibility. The middle course was to provide summary processes to be executed by new local authorities supervised by government ministers or boards. Watch committees set up within the elected borough councils by the Municipal Corporations Act (5 and 6 Will. 4, c. 76) appointed police constables and reported upon them quarterly to the Home Secretary. The county was retained as a unit of government, but the justices in quarter sessions, a sort of 'rural House of Lords', were compelled – four years after the parliamentary Reform Act of 1884 – to surrender their remaining administrative powers to democratically elected county councils. By 1888, however, the J.P.s were no longer predominately gentry; not 'social leaders', but 'public persons'; of that middle class of business men which also supplied the county and borough councillors. The landed interest had been pushed into second place by free trade and agricultural depression.[26]

The emancipation of the boroughs from the gentry was symbolized in 1846 by Manchester town council's purchase of the court-leet from Sir Oswald Mosley at the price of £200,000. In some towns – but it is perhaps remarkable how few – the justices were actually thrown into the shade by new stipendiary magistrates. The reason – as for the appointment of salaried *resident magistrates* in Ireland and the colonies – was the lack of residents in the cities, beside the parish clergy, who would make responsible unpaid justices. In 1792, seven 'public offices' (later called 'police offices') were set up in 'the parts of Middlesex and Surrey contiguous to the City of London', every one of them having a staff of three justices, each justice receiving a salary of £400. All fees were to be paid to a receiver accountable to the treasury, so that the trading justices would be put out of business. A Thames Police Office at Wapping, added in 1800, was the headquarters of the river police built up by Patrick Colquhoun, and this and the other police forces assembled on the Bow Street model around the stipendiary magistrates led in 1829 to the Metropolitan Police. The Municipal Corporations Act required each borough having quarter-sessions to appoint a coroner, who should make returns of inquests to the Home Secretary, and permitted it to petition the Crown for the appointment of a paid judge, called the Recorder: other boroughs might ask for Police Magistrates to replace petty sessions.[27]

Though it had been objected in 1792 that the stipendiary magistrates should not be barristers, because they were 'utterly destitute of common sense', five years at the bar was the qualification set in 1835. The duties of the local justices were being reduced to the purely judicial. With the increase in the number of capital offences which the J.P.s left to the assizes, these judical functions threatened to melt away also; and, at the same time that Peel abolished many capital felonies, quarter-sessions were excluded from jurisdiction over crimes punishable with penal servitude for life. Yet in 1857 petty sessions were still handling twenty times as many criminal cases as all other courts. The complications of industrial society, particularly the increase of road traffic, multiplied the number of actual cases with which the justices had to deal, and the county's quarter-sessions soon needed a panel of experienced chairmen.[28]

As their administrative duties fell away, quarter-sessions were left under the exclusive control of the High Court, the judges of which, by the act of 1873, took over the duties of the justices of assize, and with them the commissions of *nisi prius*, gaol delivery and oyer and terminer. For London and Middlesex an assize court (again formally part of the High Court) was to be held throughout the year at the Central Criminal Court, established in 1834 at the Old Bailey (4 and 5 Will. 4, c. 36); this had already taken over Admiralty's jurisdiction concerning crimes on the high seas and abroad, and it began to have referred to it cases which could not be tried at provincial assizes because of local prejudice.[29]

Till the beginning of the twentieth century there was strictly speaking no appeal in criminal cases. Writs of error, brought by leave of the attorney-general, concerned technicalities only and were rare. A new trial would sometimes be granted after conviction for misdemeanour, on a motion that the jury had found 'against the weight of the evidence', but even this process seems to have been applied only to trial at *nisi prius*. The idea of the sanctity of jury trial delayed the setting-up of a court of criminal appeal able to review the whole conduct of the proceedings and quash a conviction. Judges had become accustomed, however, to discuss difficult criminal cases informally at Serjeants' Inn, just as they had discussed civil cases in Exchequer Chamber, and in 1848 the practice led to the creation of the Court of Crown Cases Reserved, comprised after the Judicature Act of 1873 of the Chief Justice of England and any four judges of the High Court. After conviction, a judge, recorder or chairman of quarter-sessions could submit to the court a question of law, and the court could alter the judgment and sentence. The verdict on the facts could not be set aside, and the criminal had no right of appeal.[30]

THE RENAISSANCE OF JURISPRUDENCE

In 1846, a Select Committee of the House of Commons reported on legal education and found that the education of solicitors by apprenticeship still gave too little of that grounding in principles which was proper to gentlemen of a liberal profession. Yet, the present Law Society had been founded in 1825, took over the remnants of the Society of Gentlemen Practisers, in a few years possessed a reasonable library at its buildings in Chancery Lane, and instituted in 1836 an examination for articled clerks. Intending solicitors came to their legal training from the narrow education of the grammar schools, intending barristers from the expansive idleness of the unreformed universities. In 1850, the creation at Oxford of a new combined School of Jurisprudence and Modern History, and in the following year the replacement of the farcical disputations by a serious examination for the degree of Bachelor of Civil Law, meant that the conscientious student did learn something useful in his future career; but it was agreed that the universities should not go beyond teaching lawyers general principles and a liberal culture. At Oxford, Roundell Palmer, the future Lord Selborne, won the Newdigate prize for poetry and the Ireland Greek scholarship; and James Stephen left Cambridge with little but some Union successes behind him, undecided whether his career should be in church, law or medicine.[31]

The 1852 Universities Commission could think of no better reason for beginning a barrister's education at a university than that the young would thus be spared the 'temptations and distractions of London life'. In fact, the mid-nineteenth century Inn of Court, which did nothing but call a man to the bar and provide him with a club, seems to have borrowed its plumbing and arrangements, its swells and sets, from the Oxford colleges to which the inmates looked back with nostalgia. The inns, however, were near the law-courts, and only there, decided the committee of 1846, could the practice of law be taught, if students were to be rescued from the legal jungle of the conveyancers' and special pleaders' chambers. Sir Richard Bethell (Lord Chancellor Westbury in 1861) inspired the creation of a Council for Legal Education, which was comprised of representatives from the inns and appointed five readers within them, Sir Henry Maine being the most distinguished. In 1872 an examination was made compulsory for admission to the bar, despite protests that it would deter country gentlemen who wished 'merely to acquire such status and so much professional knowledge as would be useful to them as Magistrates, Politicians, Legislators and Statesmen'. The bar was being infected by the same professionalism which had overcome the Indian Civil Service and was attacking the English one.[32] But the Inns presented a stubborn and successful resistance to real reforms such as

Selborne's proposal for a London School of Law, and clung to their medieval privileges with equal tenacity against the Bar Committee (later Bar Council) set up in 1883 to protect the interests of the rank and file of the barristers.

It was at the revived universities that the pace was set in the late-nineteenth-century renaissance of jurisprudence. From 1868 to 1881, the place of the absentee Vinerian Professor at Oxford was filled by Vinerian Readers, the first of whom was Kenelm Digby, author of a classic *History of Real Property*, the third and last Sir William Anson, whose *Law of Contract* entered its twenty-second edition in 1964. A chair of International Law was set up at Oxford in 1859, and a chair of Jurisprudence – to attract Maine – in 1869; and in 1870 James Bryce, the author of a great book on *The Holy Roman Empire* and later another on *The American Commonwealth*, succeeded to the Regius chair. Then there came the illustrious A. V. Dicey to virtually refound the Vinerian chair, in the same year (1882) that his friend, Oliver Wendell Holmes, became a professor at Harvard. From 1874 to his death in 1932, Holmes corresponded with Sir Frederick Pollock (in his last years, with Harold Laski, too); and Pollock (1845–1937), professor of jurisprudence at Oxford in 1883, founder of the *Law Quarterly Review* in 1885 and its editor for thirty-four years, chairman of the Royal Commission on the Public Records in 1910 and Privy Councillor in 1911, was a new type of figure in English law – a jurist whose opinion was constantly sought by government and judges.[33]

Along with every other branch of learning in the mid nineteenth century, jurisprudence felt the winds blowing from Germany, the 'historical spirit' of Ranke and the 'ethical spirit' of the German theologians. The juristic influence of Pothier and the Code Civile was replaced – in America first – by the power of Savigny, who was not only an expert historian of Roman Law, but, in Maitland's words, 'the herald of evolution' who substituted 'organism for mechanism'. This idea of natural growth, strengthened by the publication of Darwin's work in 1859, was applied to legal institutions by Maine in *Ancient Law* (1861). Under its inspiration Holmes and Maitland finally rendered out of date Blackstone's and Austin's over-tidy maps of English law.[34]

But Holme's analysis of *The Common Law* (1881) and Pollock and Maitland's *History of English Law before the time of Edward I* (1895), Digby's *Real Property* and L. O. Pike's editions of the Year Books in the Record Commission's *Rolls Series* also tapped an old vein of native historical scholarship from which had come John Reeve's *History of the English Law* (1783–1814), F. M. Nichols's edition of *Britton* (1865) and Sir Travers Twiss's rather unsatisfactory edition of *Bracton* (1878–83). The native tradition was tied to the medieval records, amongst which a Russian scholar, Paul Vinogradoff, discovered *Bracton's Note Book*, edited by Maitland in 1887. The public records, by which was originally meant legal records, were being housed under the supervision of the Master of the Rolls in the Public Record Office, the shadow of which had begun in 1851 to creep towards the judges' chambers in Serjeants' Inn. Early in the century the Record Commission was busy printing such legal records as Domesday Book (which was cited in Queen's Bench in 1961) and the thirteenth-century Quo Warranto proceedings. Maitland and others founded the Selden Society in 1887 to publish documents and treatises important to legal history. Jurisprudence was influenced by historical research, and reciprocally the university schools of modern history were acquiring a legal, or at least constitutional, bias which is only today being corrected.[35]

The Record Commission's work in publishing *The Statutes of the Realm* to 1713 (1810–28) was, of course, work of the greatest practical importance, which was carried forward in the Stationery Office volumes of the statutes of each year, in the official *Statutes Revised* (begun in 1870, 3rd edition in 1951), in the annual chronological table and index of statutes (also begun in 1870), and in Lord Chancellor Halsbury's *Laws of England*, a great and continuing work of private enterprise. In the reporting of cases, too, legal history and practical law went together. The judges needed the reporters. Pollock was sent to the Year Books by Mr Justice Willes, and learnt that one must go 'back to its medieval origins and development' to understand modern English law. Along the bond of case-law, history led to jurisprudence, and from case-law worked over by historically-minded jurists came the modern law journal, and textbooks to replace the still medieval texts of the beginning of the century. In *The American Law Review* (1866), the *Law Quarterly Review* (1884) and the *Harvard Law Review* (1887), essays on branches of the law were interspersed with notes on contemporary cases.[36]

THE LEGAL PROFESSION

Between 1802 and 1832 the number of certificated solicitors rose from 5,270 to 8,702, an increase proportional to the growth of the national population but larger than the growth of the upper classes who had a use for lawyers. The average solicitor earned no more than £200 or £300 a year, and, since this income was built up from the petty fees set for every step of procedure without consideration of the responsibilities involved or the efficiency displayed, solicitors were naturally opposed to any procedural reform unaccompanied by a new method of taxing costs. A compromise was to leave more discretion to the courts (through their Taxing Masters), whose interest in the matter was that they had early grasped the idea of discouraging frivolous suits by making defeated parties pay some of the victors' expenses, and to which since 1729 clients had possessed the right to submit their attorneys' bills for scrutiny.[37]

The way of the young man setting up as a solicitor was made harder by the loss of debt-collecting business on the inception of the new County Courts, and a new race of accountants were encroaching on other areas of his preserve. The future in London and in the provinces lay with the firms. Some partners in London firms were important figures like Edwin Field, a founder of the Law Amendment Society, who inspired several improvements in company law and was instrumental in the moving of the law-courts. The provincial

conveyancer and family confidant, like Dickens's Mr Tul-
kinghorn, was eclipsed by the solicitor specializing in commercial or criminal cases, and the gap between solicitor and
barrister narrowed. Against the barristers' attempts at a
monopoly, the solicitors succeeded in guarding their right
to be advocates at least in the magistrates' courts and the
county courts, and they even dreamed of a fusion of the two
parts of the legal profession. But it was still true that solicitors
were people who had to work hard for a living, while barristers were often men of independent means.[38]

The bar, as described by Thackeray, was a lottery: 'There
may be a great parliamentary counsel on the ground floor [of
the inn], who drives off to Belgravia at dinner-time. . . . But
a short time since he was hungry and briefless in some garret
of the inn; lived by stealthy literature; hoped, and waited,
and sickened, and no clients came. . . .' James Stephen described in rather less romantic terms the bar on the Midland
Circuit in the 1850s: 'They are a robust, hard-headed, and
rather hard-handed set of men, with an imperious, audacious,
combative turn of mind, sometimes, though rarely, capable
of becoming eloquent', but 'with a most sagacious adaptation to the practical business of life'. As the legal processes
were brought up to date, the special pleaders went out of
business and the conveyancing specialists turned their curious
expertise to the commercial bar. The order of serjeants-at-
law, having lost their monopoly of audience in Common
Pleas in 1846, was dissolved by the Judicature Act of 1873
and their inn was sold up.[39]

The county courts and recorderships had multiplied the
judicial offices open to the barrister, and the introduction of
bar examinations divided these professional judgeships more
sharply from the commission of the peace. The judges of the
Supreme Court could remain a relatively small *élite*, because
at first instance they now heard cases singly and met in
benches only to hear appeals; and also because much process
before and after trial was handled by the still powerful
clerical officials, the Masters of the Queen's Bench and
Chancery Divisions and the Registrars of the Probate,

Divorce and Admiralty Division. Simple professional brilliance was the way to a puisne-judgeship. When Lord Chancellor Campbell appointed him to Queen's Bench in 1859 Blackburn had written a *Treatise on the Contract of Sale* but was not a Q.C.: nor was Willes, appointed to Common Pleas in 1855, who had made his name as counsel for the Treasury and Lloyd's. Accomplishment in jurisprudence alone was not a qualification for the judiciary. Since the legal career had been focused for centuries past on the courts in London and controlled not by the universities but the inns, there could be no English equivalent of Oliver Wendell Holmes, the professor who rose to the Supreme Judicial Court of Massachusetts on the strength of his book on *The Common Law* and went on to be the most celebrated judge in American history.[40]

The offices of chancellor and chief justice were generally the inheritance of the law officers of the Crown. Eldon maintained that it was not profitable to become solicitor-general, because he had to spend too much time learning up 'international law, public law and the laws of revenue and other matters' and received only 3 guineas for acting in a government case as against 10–25 guineas in a private one. But, as chancellor, Eldon was reckoned to enjoy perquisites amounting to £35,000 a year, and his brother, Lord Stowell, died with a quarter of a million in the funds and a rent roll of £8,000. Moreover, the chancellor and the law officers were members of the government, and the chancellor enjoyed patronage as well as power, for he recommended the judges. The Whigs opposed the creation of the London Police Offices in 1792 on the grounds that salaried magistrates would be agents of the government, and Brougham asserted in 1828 that all the judges were chosen on party considerations and therefore biased in political cases. This abuse was gradually remedied, and the place of chief justice was felt to be incompatible with a seat in the cabinet: it became something of a refuge for lawyers who did not really enjoy politics but knew the law offices to be the quickest way to the top. Even the chancellors preserved a certain independence in politics, and perhaps for this reason, perhaps because the legal manner was not any longer the best political equipment, rarely became leading statesmen. Lord Selborne, for instance, felt little obligation to follow Gladstone on the question of church disestablishment, and, conversely, Palmerston sacrificed Lord Westbury without a fight when the chancellor was compromised by his bankrupt son.[41]

Even for a Scotsman at the beginning of the nineteenth century, Westminster Hall was the way to St Stephen's, and men with a legàl education seem to have made up about twenty per cent of the House of Commons in 1830: but it is not clear how many of these practised (Disraeli did not, though he attended Lincoln's Inn for a time). To the Lords, where of all the legal officers who had sat on the woolsacks only the chancellor was left, the number of judges necessary to the House's judicial functions were – with some misgivings – admitted as peers (the chancellor and chief justice had, of course, often been ennobled as a reward). When Parke was given a life peerage in 1856, the lawyers feared that they would never again receive hereditary titles, and the lay peers believed that since the reform of the legal profession no judge could make a fortune equal to the expenses of nobility. But lawyers' families were in fact to provide a staple element of an upper House slowly becoming a more utilitarian and less plutocratic institution. Roundell Palmer, made lord chancellor and baron Selborne in 1872, promoted to be earl Selborne on the opening of the law-courts in 1882, was never a rich man: but his son was a First Lord of the Admiralty and son-in-law to the marquess of Salisbury, his grandson Minister of Economic Warfare from 1942-5.[42]

Socially, barristers still ranked above businessmen and so, unlike the solicitors, they did not in the later nineteenth century lose recruits to business. They were not, however, aristocrats, but rather products of intellectual middle-class families: Lord Chancellor Campbell's father was a Scottish minister, Selborne's an English parson. That remarkable interrelated group of jurists and intellectuals at the end of Victoria's reign – Dicey was second cousin to the Stephens,

Leslie Stephen married firstly Thackeray's daughter and secondly Julia Duckworth, Maitland's aunt, and their children were Virginia Woolf and Vanessa Bell – finished the work of making the law intellectually respectable and were prominent amongst the founders of the British Academy in 1899.

CASE-LAW

The variety of forms in which the law appears is one of the chief characteristics of English law, and a change in the balance between them a very important event in legal history. The change which upset the balance in the nineteenth century was the vast increase in parliamentary legislation. This had two other new aspects besides its bulk which concerned the courts. Firstly, much of it was social legislation, dealing with matters like drainage or the handling of food, on which the judges were inexpert, but law for all that. And, secondly, when it dealt with 'legal' matters, it went into the same detail as if the question had concerned public health. The Tudor statutes spoke in general terms because they were expected to be completed by a mass of case-law. The modern statute provides for many more special cases, and the judges become grammarians who spend their days construing a mass of technical phrases, each petty in itself.[43]

On occasion, statutes meddled quite incompetently with the Common Law, and the judges then had to use a discretion in interpretation which was occasionally turned into an impertinent amendment of social legislation. Lawyers are necessarily concerned with individual rights rather than social policy, and socialism could be combated under the rule of construction that the legislature was to be presumed not to have intended by general words an 'enormous injustice' – say, the taking of a man's property for public use. According to Pollock, 'our modern law of real property is simply founded on judicial evasions of Acts of Parliament'. The narrow interpretation of the statutory rights of trade unions in the late nineteenth century and of welfare legislation affecting private property in the twentieth seems to reflect the social attitudes of those generations of judges. Judicial evasion had the 'back-effect' of compelling Parliament to make its statutes even more particular in their terms and wider in their operation.[44]

But, if the judges have consistently tried to obstruct social legislation, they have not been very successful. It is fairer to attribute most of their writhings to a real disease. A storm-driven ship damaged a pier after the crew had been taken off: in the subsequent case of *The River Wear Commissioners* v. *Adamson* (1877) the separate judges of the Court of Appeal, and then of the House of Lords, found all manner of different reasons to exclude the owners from liability, in the face of a three-year-old statute which said that the 'owner of every vessel . . . shall be answerable . . . for any damage . . . to the harbour, dock or pier'. This case provoked Lord Blackburn to lay down the rule that a statute should be interpreted with the same strictness as a deed; but it is not obvious that public measures ought to be 'bound with the same trammels as private transactions'. One solution which has been repeatedly offered to the problems created by the nineteenth century's use of the same instrument of statute to reform both technical law and social conditions is a classification of acts as (say) 'constitutional', 'social' and 'technical', to which different rules of interpretation would apply. But is this not merely to introduce new terms for misinterpretation?[45]

While statute law revision certainly helped the judges by at least making clear what statutes were in force, improvements in reporting – a cynic might argue – only cramped the judges' style by preventing them from ignoring inconvenient precedents as Lord Mansfield had done. Since any report vouched for by a barrister could be cited, new series of reports multiplied, especially in periodicals such as the *Law Journal*, the *Legal Observer* and the *Law Times*, until, from considerations of the market, it was better to combine. The Law Amendment Society's proposal for an official reporting organization was rejected in favour of W.T.S. Daniel's scheme for a voluntary body set up by the inns and independent of government and judiciary. The Council for Law

Reporting began to issue its *Law Reports* in 1866 and was incorporated in 1870.[46]

So the equipment for using precedents remained curiously unofficial, though the reform of the system of courts allowed the judiciary to set precedents and make law in a more decisive fashion. The House of Lords was the final court of appeal not only for the litigant, but (in a sense) for the judge whose interpretation of a statute or earlier case was disputed. The new courts of appeal were concerned almost exclusively with questions of law, focused attention upon them as never before, and provided a means of settling them conclusively. It was certain by the nineteenth century that inferior courts were bound by the decisions of superior ones. The major uncertainties remaining after 1873 were how far the judges of the Supreme Court had to follow each other's precedents, and how far it was even desirable that the House of Lords should, in consistency, follow its own. Lord Chancellor Campbell told the Lords in 1861, 'that rule of law which your Lordships lay down as the ground of your judgment, sitting judicially, as the last and supreme Court of Appeal for this Empire, must be taken for law till altered by an act of Parliament' – for the Lords subsequently to give a conflicting decision would be to claim the right to legislate alone. But Campbell's view was not at that time generally accepted.[47]

As a way of laying down the law, judicial decisions had many drawbacks. Which rules came up for definition depended on the accidents of litigation. Bentham, the would-be legislator, said that the judges made law as a man trained his dog: 'When your dog does anything you want to break him of, you wait till he does it and then beat him.' And a judge's incautious *obiter dictum* might by simple repetition become binding on future generations. Yet these were defects in the working rather than in the principle of case-law. The fact was, as Dicey stated, that the judges had made nine tenths of the law of contract, almost the whole of the law of torts and – in a mere eighty years – almost all the rules about the conflict of laws (that is, the decision of cases containing a foreign element).[48]

Sometimes the courts made law which was in advance of public morality – their extension of rights to married women is an example – but sometimes, usually in technical matters like procedure, they were behind public opinion. Everything depended on the appointment of independent-minded judges, for, while the numbers of the judges were now sufficient to confine 'judicial valour' within a corporate sense of responsibility, there was no remedy for timid and uncritical acceptance of the decisions of the past. The Victorian judges had the strength of personality to bring the rules up to date, and the academic jurists were there to criticize their decisions and relate them to the Common Law as a whole; for another element in case-law is a body of textbooks which returns the law to the courts as an easily handled body of principles.[49]

CHAPTER 14

LAW REFORM
IN THE NINETEENTH CENTURY:
THE SUBSTANTIVE LAW

CRIMINAL LAW: THE PROTECTION OF THE PERSON

IN 1811, the Home Office began to publish statistics of crime, from which it appears that the annual number of those convicted at assizes rose from 3,163 to 14,947 between 1811 and 1832. Much of the increase can be explained by the growth of urban population, some by better policing. Moreover, it consisted chiefly of petty larcenies: a select committee of 1819 could detect no growth of murder or other crimes of violence and believed that 'many statutes denouncing capital punishment might be safely and wisely repealed'. Beccaria in the eighteenth century had established that the object of punishment was to protect society, and the nineteenth century came to agree with Bentham that the deterrent was best which achieved its purpose with the least human suffering. The criminal law of the nineteenth century was concerned more with the welfare of the individual – whether criminal or victim – than with the defence of property.[1]

The new humanity was middle class. The lower classes continued to enjoy public executions till they were abolished in 1868. Long before that, tradesmen had refused to prosecute for larceny if the offenders' execution was to be laid at their doors, and between 1811 and 1832 hangings stayed down at an average of fifty a year. In 1790 the burning of women for treason was stopped, and in 1817 the public whipping of women; in 1834, the hanging of felons' bodies on the gibbet, and by 1861 almost all corporal punishment. The antique doctrine of the corruption of the felon's blood disappeared, and the consequent forfeiture of his property. Characteristically English, perhaps, but sensible enough, was the linking of the mitigation of punishments to human beings with a campaign against cruelty to animals. Distaste as well as humanitarianism inspired the abolition in 1816 of the pillory, its effectiveness dependent on 'the caprice of the multitude', and of other forms of public disgrace. By mid century there was a reaction against a sentimental humanitarianism which seemed to have gone too far. New threats to public order had arisen – Orangemen's organizations, and 'the Tenets and Proceedings of a Society under the Name of Socialists' into which the Lords wanted an inquiry in 1840. The sponsor of the Garroters Bill of 1863, which would have prescribed flogging for crimes of violence, appealed to a general feeling that 'punishment had become too weak and uncertain to stop crime'. The modern penal controversy had begun.[2]

The most spectacular change in the substance of the criminal law was the reduction of the number of capital offences from some 200 in 1826 to 4 in 1861 (the 4 were treason, murder and offences against the Dockyards Protection Act and the Piracy Act). The Treason Felony Act of 1848 even reduced the punishment of constructive treasons (e.g. forcible attempts to change government policy, construed as 'levying war against the king in his realm') to life imprisonment.[3]

While capital felonies against property were abolished, new specific offences were defined, mostly for the protection of the person, though further protection to every type of property was given by the Malicious Damage Act of 1861. Before the 1851 Apprentices and Servants Act it was no offence to starve a dependent of mature age. For the ill-treatment of wives, a number of remedies were tried, until F. P. Cobbe's *Wife Torture* suggested the device of legal separation in 1878. Some of the 'protection' now looks like impertinent moral paternalism. In the debate on the Obscene Publications Bill of 1857 Lord Chancellor Campbell too easily persuaded the legislature of its duty to protect people from moral contamination. Should bigamy, defined by the 1861 Offences against the Person Act, be punished criminally at all? The legislature which passed the Metropolitan Police Act of 1839 providing punishment for 'threatening, abusive or insulting words and behaviour . . . whereby a breach of the peace might have been occasioned' had no scruples about restricting people's freedom for what it considered to be the people's own good.[4]

Penal legislation, applied in the past to the regulation of men's economic behaviour, proved to be equally useful in the hundred and one social reforms the Victorians projected. The Poor Law Amendment Act of 1834 made it a misdemeanour to disobey the order of a Poor Law Commissioner; the Food and Drugs Act of 1875 required quarter-sessions to submit to the Home Secretary reports prepared by a public analyst on the condition of food. One stage of every attack on the socially intolerable was the provision of penalties and summary procedures against those responsible for it.[5]

CRIMINAL JURISPRUDENCE:
THE TRIUMPH OF MORALITY

The criminal law was manufactured piecemeal by statutes listing offences with a minute particularity which had long ago obscured any general principles. Textbooks mirrored the statute book in their 'utter incapacity to take general views'. In India, however, lawyers had been compelled to think about the criminal law, which needed clever adaptation to be applicable to local needs, and, returning from India, James Stephen began a renaissance of criminal jurisprudence. Though, as an Austinian, he believed that all law was command and therefore in a sense criminal law, Stephen emphasized malice, wickedness or *mens rea* as the mark of crime properly so-called, and distinguished statutes imposing true criminal liability from those creating administrative offences. The judges followed Stephen's conclusion that negligence, which underlay so much of tort, could not be a basis for criminal liability: only in the case of manslaughter would they admit that 'gross and culpable negligence' (the language is that of Willes in *Regina* v. *Spencer*, 1867) might 'amount to a culpable wrong and show an evil mind' – in plain words, be criminal.[6]

Emphasis on *mens rea* went along with Stephen's acceptance of the Hobbesian view of law as a science, the necessarily rather brutal science of a society which, without discipline, would sink into anarchy: a rational and resolute criminal law could deter positive wickedness, but not (Stephen thought) lack of care. Partly, however, the emphasis just reflected the moral earnestness of the times. Justice, says Mr Fifoot, with a suggestion of approval, 'reflected faithfully the contemporary egoism that sought neither the fraternal discipline of the police state nor the *diablerie* of the psychiatrist', but rather a conformity to the accepted moral standards. Such attitudes were in fact too simple to be the basis of an adequate criminal jurisprudence. Holmes may have gone to the other extreme in asserting that wickedness and disgust had nothing to do with the criminal law, which existed to reconcile the fact of 'self-preference' with the need to live in a community, but his theory at least admitted – as the English judges were reluctant to do – the increasingly important crimes of 'strict liability', the statutory offences (e.g. by traders against clean food acts) for which *mens rea* was not required.[7]

The prevailing concept of crime was too simple not only in what it excluded, but in the great variety of conduct it lumped together. The judges were rather too willing to condemn an action because the agent appeared to them a cad. More serious, their concept of *mens rea* condemned the judges to a great deal of heart-searching when confronted with prisoners who had acted from psychological abnormality, which was of many types. The famous M'Naghten Rules, composed by the judges in 1843 after the controversial acquittal of one M'Naghten, the sufferer from a persecution mania who had killed Sir Robert Peel's secretary in mistake for the Prime Minister himself, allowed the acquittal of the man who could not understand the moral significance of his deed but not the man who acted under irresistible impulse. The prisoner shown to have been ignorant of the moral significance of his acts was freed from blame, though Queen Victoria, who had her own ideas on moral questions, got the appropriate verdict changed from 'not guilty because insane' to 'guilty but insane' (the earlier verdict has in 1964 been reinstated, though in a slightly different form of words).[8]

Legal concepts, to be useful, should be somewhere between the over-general, which make none of the necessary working distinctions, and the too-particular, which cannot be extended to new situations. The story of the concept of *possession* shows the late-nineteenth-century jurists trying to find a universal meaning, within which the judges then had to make absurd distinctions in order to solve individual cases. There was no reason why possession should have meant the same in criminal as in civil law. The jurists decided, however, that possession was always and essentially a mental quality – it was a matter of knowing that one had something in one's possession. In crime, meanwhile, larceny was the violation of possession. Then, did a shepherd who in ignorance drove away a neighbour's lamb with his own flock on a misty morning, and when he discovered the extra lamb sold it with the rest, commit larceny? And, if so, when? In that case, *Regina v. Riley* (1853), the Court of Crown Cases Reserved decided that the accused 'took' the lamb unwittingly ('taking' was the term in civil law for obtaining a thing tortiously, without the owner's consent), and that, when he knew he had the lamb, he automatically converted the tort into the crime of larceny.

What then of the man who was given a sovereign in mistake for a shilling, and kept it? In this case, *Regina v. Ashwell* (1885), the same court was prepared to say that the 'taking' also was postponed till the moment that the prisoner knew that the coin in his pocket was different from the one his benefactor had intended to give him. Only two of the judges protested against the apparent feeling that, since the accused had been dishonest, the bench had somehow or other to find a crime which fitted him.[9]

CRIMINAL PROCEDURE AND PUNISHMENT

Appeals of felony were hastily abolished after an attempt to resuscitate the procedure in *Ashford* v. *Thornton* (1819); and the Wiltshire grand jury appears to have stopped making presentments in assizes about 1850. There remained prosecution by the information of the private citizen, and in more serious cases the indictment, gradually shedding its clogging formalities, such as the requirement (which might not be satisfied in the case of a pickpocket on public transport) of the name of the county in which the offence had been committed. Indictment, of course, began with the complaint of a private citizen or policeman, but in the nineteenth century the Crown took a firmer control over it, exercised after 1879 through a new law officer, the Director of Public Prosecutions, who could stop any criminal proceeding. In matters of national importance, such as the Chartist riots, the strategy of prosecutions was decided by the attorney-general.[10]

The advent of an efficient police force changed the whole nature of prosecution without changing its forms. In England the police constable prosecutes an offence triable summarily just as a private citizen would: the case is (P.C.) *Smith* v. *Jones*, not *Regina* v. *Jones*, for the case is not handed over for prosecution to a Procurator Fiscal (as in Scotland) or a District Attorney (as in the United States). The police are left with a largely beneficial discretion as to which of the many petty offences coming to their notice should be taken further. Inevitably, however, prosecution was made more 'official' by a police supervised however loosely by the Home Secretary and relying on better detective methods to catch criminals instead of the old system of rewards to informers.[11]

The law as to the summary jurisdiction of magistrates was codified by the Summary Jurisdiction Act of 1848. The use of the criminal law to enforce social legislation has vastly extended this summary jurisdiction, and many indictable offences have been made triable summarily at the wish of the accused. The existence of police detectives meant that the preliminary examination by magistrates of men accused of serious crimes could cease to be inquisitorial and become judicial hearings, at which the prisoners were given all the facilities to clear themselves which they would have in a higher court – though they might prefer to reserve their defence. The magistrates' control of preliminary hearings was a protection for the accused when the magistrates were no longer interested in detecting and proving crimes.[12]

The process continued of conceding the accused a more equal position in the criminal trial. In a number of offences triable summarily the accused was allowed to opt for trial by jury in quarter-sessions; and because of local prejudice against William Palmer, the Staffordshire poisoner, in 1856, an Act of Parliament was passed to authorize his trial at the Old Bailey. In 1836, against the opposition of most of the judges, who regarded themselves as the prisoner's advocates, the Prisoners' Counsel Act was passed to give to the man accused of felony the same right as one accused of treason or misdemeanour to address the jury through counsel, and to all prisoners the right to have copies of the depositions against them. In Palmer's trial no reference was made to the other crimes of which he was suspected, lest the jury be prejudiced on the charge against him. It was necessary to prove the charge beyond reasonable doubt, and in 1859 the convicted poisoner, Thomas Smethurst, was granted a free pardon because medical experts persuaded the Home Secretary that such doubt existed. In a criminal, as in a civil case, the judge exercised a vigilant control over procedure. He was entitled to exclude unfair and irrelevant evidence, even to direct the jurymen that there was no real evidence for the prisoner to answer and they must acquit him, or that the evidence would not permit a verdict of insanity. This is but one more illustration of the complexity of the relationship between judge and jury, reflecting the intricate mingling of law and fact.[13]

The greater effectiveness of the police in catching criminals was no deterrent without appropriate punishment, but the humanitarianism which abolished the more savage penalties and – in conjunction with colonial feeling – soon ended transportation as well, created a problem for the judge as he came to sentence. The Penal Servitude Acts of 1853 and 1857 replaced transportation by equivalent terms of penal servitude at home. The magnitude of the problem which then confronted the prisons can be deduced from the fact that between 1811 and 1832 sentences of imprisonment for more than one year had risen from 145 to 233, of transportation for periods between seven years and life from 563 to 3,915. The commissions sat again; new prisons were built (Dartmoor, Brixton, Pentonville, Wandsworth and Holloway were all working as convict prisons by 1852, though the Fleet was mercifully pulled down, now that debtors were rarely incarcerated); inspectors were appointed by the Home Secretary to begin the work of centralization; and acts of Parliament like the Prisons Act of 1865 aimed at uniformity in the provisions for the prisoners' physical and mental health.[14]

The weaknesses of imprisonment as a deterrent were discovered almost as soon as it became a general form of punishment – the problems of penal reform were catching up on each other. Brougham observed that 'people do not come out of gaols as they went in'; no, indeed – boys committed in their hundreds for poaching came out as trained criminals. Commissions therefore considered the expediency of trying juveniles summarily, placing them in separate prisons, and creating for them reformatory and industrial schools. Lunatic offenders were syphoned off by the Broadmoor asylum, opened in 1877. The proper regimen to prevent the mutual corruption of the ordinary prisoners was the subject of a long controversy between the advocates of the 'separate system' – incarceration in individual cells – and the 'silent system' – communal work at the treadmill or oakum-picking under a strict rule of silence. Despite all this, a large number of habitual criminals were still produced by the prisons, to be helped a little by the voluntary Discharged Prisoners' Aid Societies, and hounded back behind bars by an unsympathetic public. Some positively medieval clauses of the Habitual Criminals Act (32 and 33 Vict. c. 99) for a time allowed the police to arrest any discharged prisoner on mere suspicion, and placed upon the accused the onus of proving that he had been living honestly.[15]

The judges were untrained in penal theory and resisted the suggestion that there should be policy and uniformity in their sentencing. A more flexible system of penalties was, however, gradually provided by statutes like the ones of 1861 and 1879 which authorized the judges to punish certain felonies by fines only, and magistrates to fine a person convicted summarily up to £25. Under the Forfeiture Act of 1870 a man convicted of felony could be ordered to pay a maximum of £100 compensation to anyone whose property had suffered by his offences. Acts of 1877 and 1879 allowed magistrates to suspend the sentences upon first offenders under probation, and the Police Courts Mission instituted in 1876 by the Church of England Temperance Society was the beginning of a system of probation officers. Yet Hazlitt's criticism of the criminal law remained true: it was made by the rich and respectable for 'the refuse of the community' which they did not understand. There was no data to proceed upon – 'the *criminal mind* of the country is a book sealed'.[16]

MODERN CIVIL PROCEDURE

Finding their fellow barrister, James Boswell – the biographer of Johnson – lying dead drunk in a Lancaster street during assizes, the future Lord Eldon and his friends invented and sent to him a new writ: *Quare adhesit pavimento*. By then, however, the forms of action were in decline. The practice of dispensing with the original writ and starting with the order for arrest had spread out from the process by bill of Middlesex; and a few general causes of action – Mansfield's action 'for money had and received', and 'trespass on the case upon promises' – were beginning to oust the others, particularly in America. Further, the amalgamation of jurisdictions in the nineteenth century implied the amalgamation of procedures, for a main purpose of each of the old forms was to bring the matter to the appropriate court. The merging of the courts also forced upon the Common Law the example of equity's single original process of subpoena.[17]

The Uniformity of Process Act of 1832 recognized the growing uniformity of original process by instituting a single form of writ for the personal actions (primarily actions of trespass or case), and the Real Property Limitation Act of the following year swept away almost all the land actions except ejectment, which was already enjoying a practical monopoly. The Common Law Procedure Act of 1852 provided that it 'should not be necessary to mention any form or cause of action in any writ of summons'. These earlier measures only postponed the unavoidable choice of action to the stage of pleading: but the rules made by the High Court under the 1873 Judicature Act abolished the need of choice altogether, or rather left it to the judges, for they required that a pleading should 'contain and contain only, a statement in a summary form of the material facts on which the party pleading relies'. A modern writ therefore commands the defendant to enter an appearance within eight days in the appropriate division of the High Court and indicates by an endorsement the general nature of the action: 'The plaintiff's claim is for damages for breach of contract'.[18]

A variety of procedures of course remained. Some cases would entail trial by jury, some not. But thenceforth the course of proceedings was not determined by the original writ but worked out in exchanges between the solicitors and at pre-trial hearings before masters of the court. In the seventeenth and eighteenth centuries it had been found that interlocutory proceedings – such as an application for the amending of the plea-roll – could be more cheaply and efficiently dealt with by a single judge in his chambers than by the full court. An attorney could handle this 'summons and order' procedure, while counsel was necessary for 'motion and rule' before the whole bench. By 1860, the judges in chambers had been given statutory powers to order the discovery of documents and interrogation, and even to give judgment on default. The Judges' Chambers (Despatch of Business) Act of 1867 transferred almost all of these powers to the five *masters* of each of the Common Law courts.[19]

The old actions took with them many of the fictions of pleading designed to squeeze new grievances within an existing form. Yet the notorious Hilary Rules of 1834, drawn up by the judges under the influence of Serjeant Stephen, who believed special pleading to be a science of extraordinary rigour, actually insisted on it in preference to the general issue (that is, the defendant's reply: 'I admit nothing and want to see what you can make of it'). This remarkable step backward was not redeemed until the Judicature Act; but the exclusion of the evidence of interested parties was ended between 1846 and 1869, first of all in the county courts. In the mass of actions in the county courts – as in criminal cases before magistrates – juries were dispensed with unless the parties insisted. The Court of Appeal – never using a jury – would admit new evidence in civil cases as well as reconsidering the issue of law, and could change the judgment as it liked.[20]

Costs, apportioned by the judge but calculated by the 'taxing masters', regulated the stream of litigation, discouraging the merely vexatious. When counsel could no longer spin out a clear case by procedural tricks, all the costs could be fairly awarded against the defeated party whose obstinacy had dragged out the case, and the plaintiff with a genuine grievance not made to lose by his suit.

TOWARDS A LAW OF TORT

The scrapping of so much rusty machinery did not alter the principles of English law, which (to change the metaphor) had grown upon the framework of the forms of action but were now coherent enough to stand alone. The plaintiff need no longer commit himself at the beginning to one procedure and one remedy, but he must prove a body of facts in which the judge can detect one of the old causes of action, and they will be described in the old terms of the art. When the judges assumed the task of finding the cause of action, they naturally looked for still more general principles to go by – they wanted, for example, a single formula for divining liability in tort. Social movements demanded the recognition of new torts. In *Pasley* v. *Freeman* (1789), the modern tort of fraud appears. It is the knowingly false representation of circumstances (in the 1789 case of a third party's credit) upon which the plaintiff acts to his loss. Modern transport and machinery greatly extended the torts of personal injury. Lord Campbell's Fatal Accidents Act of 1846 overrode both the principle that a personal action died with the person wronged and the rule in *Baker* v. *Bolton* (1808) that death was not an injury which could be valued in terms of damage to anyone else: thenceforth a dead man's family could sue for the earnings he would have received in the remainder of his working life.[21]

Could old torts and new be brought under a single principle? Blackstone had distinguished breaches of contract (which were in fact tortious in historical origin) from torts proper. The nineteenth century discovered that in most torts liability could be traced to negligence, which was emphasized by the crop of personal accidents. But *negligence* on its own was far too wide, and the judges therefore limited liability to cases where the defendant could be said to have owed the plaintiff a special duty of care. The problem was merely postponed, for duties of care have proved no easier to generalize about. Thus, Bevan's *Principles of the Law of Negligence* (1889) listed fifty-six separate duties of this sort, and some people argued that the existence of a duty in a particular case was a matter of fact to be decided by a jury. The instance most hotly debated was the liability of an occupier of unsafe premises to a visitor suffering injury. The mangled victims necessary to judicial experiment – as Mr Fifoot puts it – were duly forthcoming, and in *Indermaur* v. *Dames* (1866) and *Gautret* v. *Egerton* (1867) Mr Justice Willes was able to elaborate the test of liability. It was, reasonably enough, the character of the entrant – whether he came on business, or by invitation or as a trespasser.[22]

If negligence was in some ways too wide a concept, there were also undeniable torts it did not include. Conspiracy, maintenance and malicious prosecution could be sued as torts when specific damage to the plaintiffs was demonstrable, although the criterion of their existence was the 'criminal' one of malice. Neglect of a statutory duty (e.g. to fence dangerous machinery) also hovered between crime and tort: a worker injured thereby could obtain damages – unless, as in ordinary negligence, his own carelessness had contributed to the accident – although the duty imposed was a public one.[23]

Holmes, following the general shift of emphasis from the practical criterion of loss to the moral one of blame, hit on the concept of *fault* as one which would embrace both negligent and malicious torts. But there was a precedent for liability without any personal fault, in the *vicarious liability* of the master for the torts of his servant. Furthermore, the possibility of insurance against all manner of eventualities made the judges willing to recognize some accidents for which it was fair to hold a man responsible though he had not been in any way to blame. In the leading case of *Rylands* v. *Fletcher* (1868), consequent on the unpredictable flooding of Fletcher's mines by a reservoir which Rylands had built upon his own land, the House of Lords affirmed that 'The person who for his own purposes brings on his land and collects and keeps there anything likely to do mischief if it escapes [explosives are a good example] must keep it in at his peril, and if he does not do so is . . . answerable for all the damage. . .'[24]

MARRIAGE AND DIVORCE

The act of 1836 which for the first time allowed marriage elsewhere than in the parish church – either at a registry office or in a nonconformist chapel in the presence of a registrar – was carried through on a rising tide of resentment against Anglican privileges. Marriage was beginning to be looked upon as a sort of contract, which like other contracts was dissoluble. For more than two centuries, proper divorce (allowing re-marriage) had been available to those persons only who could afford to call upon the legislative supremacy of Parliament. The divorces of the great, ten per cent of whose marriages, it has been calculated, came to a bad end, were familiar scandals by 1700. Before divorce by private act of Parliament, separation from bed and board by an ecclesiastical court was necessary and was granted on proof of adultery or, after 1801, the husband's outrageous cruelty. The wronged husband or wife might also sue the 'paramour' for his tort, which was rather strangely termed 'criminal conversation' (Lord Melbourne, while prime minister, was the defendant in a case of this type).

None of these procedures were open to the poor, as Mr Justice Maule pointed out when sentencing a man to one day's imprisonment for bigamy in 1845. He told the prisoner that he had 'acted under a very serious misapprehension' about his proper course when his wife left him for an adulterer: the ecclesiastical courts, the action for criminal conversation and the private bill had all been at his disposal. 'It is quite true,' Maule continued with irony, 'that these proceedings would have cost you many hundreds of pounds, whereas you probably have not as many pence. But the law knows no distinction between rich and poor.' Twelve years later, the Divorce Act merged the three processes in the jurisdiction of a new Court of Probate and Divorce (from 1873 a division of the High Court), so that judicial separation, an absolute divorce and compensation for the injured party could be gained by one and the same action. Divorce has since been brought into the reach of all classes by the development of legal aid.

The Divorce Act took the last important jurisdiction from the established church. Yet the secular courts could not translate marriage entirely into the equations of civil liability, and divorce drew them deeper into questions of morals and humanity. The Matrimonial Causes Act of 1878 began to impose upon the magistrates what is now one of their heaviest burdens, the prevention of domestic suffering by separation and maintenance orders.[25]

TOWARDS A LAW OF PROPERTY

The land law from which English law had originally sprung was sinking into second place in the nineteenth century, but it was as remarkably tenacious as the aristocracy which relied upon it. In 1830, it was still being argued that the great landed families should be preserved by making entail compulsory upon the peerage, and in 1848 perhaps two thirds of the land was tied up under marriage settlements. Bills to make the real property of intestates equally divisible amongst their dependants, like personal property, were condemned as 'tending to republicanism'. Mobs of retainers still fought each other for estates and livings, and the legal adventures from 1871 to 1874 of the claimant to the Tichborne baronetcy enthralled people of every class. The aristocracy was persuaded of the indispensability of the old land law by the conveyancers, the only people who understood it enough to reform it but whose interests were that it should not be reformed.[26]

The judges for their part were still haunted by a superstitious fear of perpetuities, which had become fused with an equally 'superstitious fear of the power of compound interest' exemplified in the episode of Peter Thellusson's will. Thellusson, a West Indian merchant who died in 1797, left an estate worth some £600,000 to accumulate interest in the hands of trustees during the lives of his sons and grandsons living at his death, and then to be shared between the eldest male descendants of his three sons. He hoped (and his hope was fulfilled) that the money would in due time carry one of his descendants to the House of Lords. Under Lord Nottingham's perpetuity rule the estate Thellusson created would vest before the reasonable time-limit, which was defined as the lifetime of the longest-lived heir in being when the interest was created plus a further twenty-one years. What people were now worried about, however, was not the inalienability of land but the accumulation of capital, which in the Thellusson case was estimated as possibly £100 million (sums like that were not then so commonplace in business as they are now). An Accumulations Act was therefore passed in 1800 (and re-enacted as part of the 1925 Law of Property Act), limiting accumulation at interest to a normal period of twenty-one years. The methods of the antiquated land law were expected to curb the terrors of modern finance.[27]

At length the aristocracy and their land law had to give ground to the bourgeoise. Primogeniture and entail were abolished in most American states at the time of the

Revolution. The demands of the Manchester School for the abolition of primogeniture and for free trade in land in England were taken up by the Chamberlainite radicals in the 1880s, and again by the Liberals between 1909 and 1914. Maitland launched a glorious onslaught in 1879 on primogeniture and the rule that a man's most distant paternal relative would succeed to his land (but not his goods) before his nearest maternal one – even his mother herself: '. . . why should women be postponed? It must be out of respect for some one's memory. But whose? Is it Ethelbert or Cnut, is it Salagast, Bodogast and Widogast, or Choke, Croke and Coke, is it Howel Dda or Dynwal Moel Mud? The Conservative Party is a historical party, let it explain to the uninitiated the exact form which its ancestor-worship takes.' But agitation achieved less than agricultural depression, which produced the revolutionary Settled Land Act of 1882. This gave the tenant for life freedom to dispose of the land (the other beneficiaries of the entail were left only with certain rights in a fund); and mustard kings and brewers moved in on the estates of indebted peers like the duke of Newcastle and the earl of Carlisle. Land, however, had lost its fascination for everyone. Landlords who wanted to sell up and transfer their assets to stocks and shares found buyers surprisingly scarce.[28]

The orthodox solution to the jungle of conveyancing – the one recommended again by the Real Property Commission in 1829 – was a land register, but no one was prepared to compel registration. The land actions except for ejectment, however, and the conjuring trick of the common recovery, had gone in 1833, and at last 'on the 24th day of October, 1852', that faithful pair, John Doe and Richard Roe, 'died of broken hearts', forsaken by their friends, the Common Law Commissioners. The land law lost its fascination, and real property some of its peculiarity. Realty was made liable, like personalty, for the deceased owner's debts; and by the Land Transfer Act of 1897 it devolved along with the personal property upon his executor or (in case of intestacy) administrator, often the true next-of-kin, though the heir, if he was a different person, retained an equitable interest in it. With the ending of the Church's separate jurisdiction over wills (cf. p. 161 above), the law concerning real property and the law concerning personal property had begun to grow together into a single law of property.[29]

At this point, the virtue of the old real property law became once more apparent. Behind its excessively luxuriant undergrowth was the clear logic of equitable interests and legal estates; the first (which goes back to the use, protected by Chancery) allowing a complex pattern of endowment, the second (the even older Common Law forms) regulating the necessarily more concentrated power to manage and dispose of the property. The equitable interest has in modern times become simply a right to the income from a capital fund, the nature of which may be continually changing; for the trustees who have the legal estate may sell the land and reinvest the proceeds in other property or in securities. The ancient abstractions have thus enabled the land law to adapt itself to a world in which 'real property' takes the form of stocks and shares.[29a]

THE EMANCIPATION OF THE COMPANY

Despite the efforts of Chancery, the unincorporated business association worked under great difficulties. In a firm like this there might be 2,000 'partners' who, by the Common Law of partnership, had to sue and be sued individually for the firm's debts and could not call to account those of their number who were the actual managers. A commercial boom in 1825 finally compelled the repeal of the unintelligible but intimidating Bubble Act; and a fading of that suspicion of big business evident in the affair of Peter Thellusson's will made Parliament more liberal with incorporation, less inclined to use it as a means of strictly controlling economic development: thus, in 1826 and 1833, the Bank of England's privileges in joint-stock banking were abolished. Company law became the subject of frequent commissions of inquiry and vigorous parliamentary debate. The report of Bellenden Ker on the law of partnership (1837) revealed the disabilities of the unincorporated trading association and proposed the recognition as legal corporations of all companies which published their objects and constitution in an official register.[30]

Eventually Ker's answer proved to be the right one, but the Common Law was reluctant to break away from its concepts of partnership, and the government from its reliance on the charter of incorporation. The immediate reform in 1837 was the authorization of the Board of Trade to incorporate the equitable companies, those trading associations with deeds of settlement and limited liability which Chancery had fostered. It was left to six great acts, passed in 1844–5 at the height of the railway mania, to introduce the joint-stock company incorporated by simple registration (all new trading associations with transferable shares and more than twenty-five members were obliged to register), lay down a common-form deed of settlement, and state the procedure for winding up a bankrupt company. Another restriction on companies was removed in 1856, when they were given a general licence to hold lands in mortmain.

As yet only the shareholders in public utility and railway companies generally enjoyed limited liability, but the winding-up procedure at least permitted the shareholder to stay technically solvent while the company went bankrupt. In the early 1850s, when trade was picking up again after a depression, the campaign for general limited liability won the day. The government spokesman for the 1856 Joint Stock Companies Bill, Robert Lowe, argued that fraud was not to be presumed the normal occupation of traders. Nor was it the function of the government to tell men how to run their businesses. The principle of freedom of contract, Lowe said, entailed limited liability, which safeguarded not the fraudulent promoter but the ordinary shareholder – it was the company with unlimited liability which was short of capital and liable to bankruptcy. The bill was passed, and as consolidated in the giant Companies Act of 1862 is the basis of modern company law. The deed of settlement was abandoned and a company was formed thenceforth by the deposit of a Memorandum of Association, stating its purpose, with the registrar of joint-stock companies. The constitution of the company is embodied in articles of association. The company itself must keep a register which is conclusive evidence as to the ownership of shares, and it must file a yearly balance-sheet with the registrar.[31]

The Larceny Act of 1861 protects the prospective investor from the fraudulent promoter by making the publication of an intentionally misleading prospectus a criminal offence; and the case of *Erlanger* v. *New Sombrero Phosphate Co.* (1878) gave the shareholders a remedy against the promoter who used their capital to make a secret profit. The rule in *Foss* v. *Harbottle* (1843) laid down the principle that the courts would not normally interfere in the internal management of a company at the instance of a minority of shareholders, but the act of 1856 provided for the protection of minority interests within the shareholding body by means of a Board of Trade inquiry. Purporting to rescue the shareholders from their own speculative frenzy, the judges decided in *Coleman* v. *Eastern Counties Railway Company* (1846) and *Riche* v. *Ashbury Railway Carriage Company* (1874) that dealings which were beyond the company's express purpose – for example, plans by the railway to run a passenger ship between Harwich and the continent – were *ultra vires* and void. Between 1856 and 1868, 7,056 companies were formed with a capital of £893 million. Company cases poured into the courts, and the fact that in the same dealings the director of a company was regarded by Chancery as a trustee and by the Common Law as an agent for his company was one of the reasons for the fusion of the courts in the 1870s.[32]

Nineteenth-century statutes thus extended freedom of commercial association, but they also interfered with freedom of contract to protect the citizen as consumer. The consolidating act of 1893, on which the modern law concerning the sale of goods is based, even shows a modification of the old rule *caveat emptor*: the seller remains liable for defects in goods 'bought by description' (that is, by asking for a standard item by its usual name), and also if the goods do not fit the purpose for which they were sold. (Unfortunately, these warranties may be excluded by 'contracts' between vendors and purchasers, printed inconspicuously on labels.) In the case of food, where the danger to the consumer was great, criminal sanctions were applied by legislation stretching from the Adulteration of Food Act, 1860, to the Sale of Food and Drugs Act, 1899. The Infants Relief Act of 1874 protected the young against the blandishments of salesmen by confirming and extending the Common Law rules which made a contract with an infant unenforceable. The Factors Act of 1889 modified *nemo dat quod non habet* ('a man cannot give what he has not got'), one of the prime examples of the power of simple maxims in English law. Thenceforth an honest purchaser from a salesman who misappropriated a manufacturer's goods for his own profit was not liable to forfeit his purchases. But it is an injustice (admittedly one very difficult to avoid) that this clause applies only where the salesman has obtained the goods with the manufacturer's consent, not – for example – where they are stolen. The nineteenth century remained reluctant to foster commercial transactions to the detriment of property rights.[33]

THE RIGHTS OF THE WORKER

Since the emancipated company was at an unfair advantage in its dealings with the individual, its freedom of contract with consumer and worker had to be restricted. Tory philanthropy, conveniently discovering that Liberal *laissez-faire* delivered the working population into the hands of the manufacturers, embarked on a programme of inquiry and legislation about industrial conditions and the legal relationship of employers and workmen. In 1875, Disraeli's government passed the Employers and Workmen Act, which removed the workman's breach of his contract of service from the list of criminal offences and the threat of imprisonment from the strike-breaking employer's armoury. (Though a wilful breach of contract of service likely to interrupt water supplies and other essential public services was preserved as a crime by the 1875 Conspiracy and Protection of Property Act.)[34]

Compensation for workmen injured in their employment was the result of changes in the law of vicarious liability. It was of course more profitable to sue the employer rather than the employee for an injury caused by the latter in the course of his work, and the judges had accepted that the employer was liable in strict trespass if he had directly ordered the act which injured, and liable in trespass on the case if it was performed on his standing authority. The abolition of the forms of action and the rise of the company, which necessarily acted through officials with a large discretion, concentrated attention on the limits of this delegated authority. It was easier, as it turned out, to say when a company official had perpetrated a tort while acting *ultra vires*, than when a factory-worker or a van-driver injured a stranger in the course of his employment. Was the bus company liable, for instance, when two off-duty drivers took their buses out for a race and injured a bystander? What particularly worried the trade unions was the situation where the injured man and the tortfeasor were fellow-workers. In the *laissez-faire* 1830s the courts said flatly that an employer could never be vicariously liable for the damage which his employee inflicted by negligence on a fellow-workman, who accepted the risks along with the profits of his employment; and so manufacturers were virtually relieved of responsibility for accidents in the factories.[35]

In the more socialistic atmosphere at the end of the century, the pendulum swung the other way. By a long process, lasting from 1880 to 1947, this doctrine of 'common employment' was discarded, and the employer made as vicariously liable to his employee as to a stranger, and directly liable for accidents caused by neglecting his common-law duty of care, or his statutory duties, in the provision of working conditions; while the Workmen's Compensation Act of 1897 introduced the new principle that the employer must pay compensation to a workman for any injury incident to his work – that is, insure his workers against accidents. In law, a master and servant were still jointly liable for the servant's torts and the master could indemnify himself against the servant for a share of the damages he had to pay. The recent case of *Lister* v. *Romford Ice Cold Storage Co.* (1957) has even attributed to the employee a contractual liability to indemnify the employer or his insurance company for all the expense his negligence causes in damages. But at least in the case of factory accidents the balance of risk was transferred in the nineteenth century to the employer. [36]

This result was partly due to the pressure of the trade unions, at last admitted to legal equality with the other quasi-corporate organizations into which society was being marshalled in Victorian Britain. Friendly societies, savings banks and building societies had continued to enjoy the encouragement of the state and were accorded some of the advantages without the form of incorporation. The equitable company and the trade union the state was forced to recognize as corporate organizations existing in fact, to which formal incorporation was therefore irrelevant and privileges more appropriate to their needs could be granted piecemeal. There is no doubt that combinations of workers existed despite the law, at the beginning of the nineteenth century, for much of the employers' *truck* system – such as the compulsion of the workers to spend their wages in the company's stores at company prices – seems to have been designed to circumvent wage agreements negotiated with workers' representatives. In 1824, the government realized that the ban on combinations merely encouraged secret conspiracies, and that freedom of contract should logically be extended to a body of workers as to a firm. It therefore agreed (in the year before the Bubble Act against companies was repealed) to an act which cancelled the combination laws and exempted combinations to raise wages from the Common Law of conspiracy. But another act of 1825 restored the law of conspiracy and imposed penalties for the use of violence by combinations to interfere with the freedom of contract of individual worker and employer.[37]

Only with the ending of the political riots of the 1830s and 1840s, during which the government had invoked the sedition laws against the pathetic association of the Tolpuddle men, and the concentration of the workers on social rather than political action, did the authorities begin to see positive merits in the unions. Gladstone's Trade Union Act of 1871 declared that unions were not to be held unlawful simply because they operated 'in restraint of trade'. But it was Disraeli's government in 1875 which gave the unions freedom of action by abolishing the statutory offences with which they could be charged. Violence was left to the Common Law and criminal conspiracy confined to the concerting of actions criminal in themselves. (In the *Gas Stokers' Case* of 1872 some London gasworkers had been given a year's hard labour for conspiring to break contracts – i.e. going on strike.)

LAW AND THE MODERN CORPORATIVE STATE

The law was more just by the end of the nineteenth century, because it dealt more efficiently with a greater range of social interests. Everyone was equal before a law which at least spared no one. Compulsory vaccination, control of the sale of arsenic, regulation of female labour – in all directions the freedom of individuals was restricted for their own good, and everyone, high and low, was 'protected' by some law which allowed no 'contracting out'. In the matters of divorce and married women's property, the wife was put on a more equal footing with the husband and the lower classes with the rich.[38]

The law adapted itself to industrial society. All the way up the profession lawyers were specializing, and in 1895 a 'commercial list' of cases, heard by specialist judges using special techniques, was instituted in the Queen's Bench Division. The courts were already submitting to the drudgery of traffic cases, for by 1870 steam wagons capable of 20 m.p.h. were causing havoc on the roads. The lawyers no longer sneered at the shopkeepers' 'little affairs' but talked of reforming company law so as to allow 'workmen to enter upon the formation of companies for themselves'. They must be given credit for turning away from land law when it had become barely relevant to modern society, thus helping to ensure that British industry did not, like its German equivalent, retain the imprint of an aristocratic class structure. After jettisoning medieval protectionism in the name of freedom of trade, the law quickly and still more remarkably grasped the need to reimpose a different sort of protection for the individual shareholder, consumer and worker. It was as consumer and worker that the ordinary person achieved a meaningful equality in the courts, and from a law which talked of strict liability for tort and the duty to insure grew the protection of the citizen in the welfare state.[39]

English law was also widening its horizons in a straightforward sense – it was looking to see, for instance, how foreign systems handled the relations of master and servant. And the same forces which had transformed the law at home – humanitarianism and trade – stimulated the growth of international law. Products of humanitarianism were the multilateral treaty of 1841, which placed the slave trade on a level with piracy, and the 1864 Geneva Convention on the Amelioration of the Condition of the Wounded of Armies in the Field; products of trade, the International Telegraphic Union of 1865, the Universal Postal Union of 1874, and the Copyright Union of 1886. The Conference of Paris, which in 1856 issued the famous declaration on the rules of maritime warfare, marks the beginning of an international constitution and conscious international legislation. Then, by submitting to arbitration at Geneva the American claims for the damage caused by the *Alabama*, a warship built at Liverpool for the confederate side in the American Civil War, Britain and the United States opened the way in 1871 for an international court.

Britain led in the promotion of the first international public legislation against the slave trade and piracy. Yet it was perhaps in the field of international law that the slackening of enterprise and initiative in English jurisprudence first showed itself after the mid-Victorian achievements. In the *Franconia* case of 1876 the English judges declined to deal with a crime by a foreign ship in English waters as international law demanded, on the grounds that at Common

Law the jurisdiction was unclear. The lapse into insularity is partly to be explained by the decline in the teaching of the traditional language of international relations, Roman Law, since the time when Mansfield had asserted that 'the law of nations in its full extent is part of the law of England'. Bishops with a knowledge of Roman–Canon Law had helped to negotiate treaties up to that of Utrecht in 1713, but Doctors' Commons was dissolved in 1857 because the domestic ecclesiastical courts had lost all importance, and the handling of international cases became the function of the attorney-general and solicitor-general (Roundell Palmer acted for Britain in the *Alabama* Case). It was doubly difficult to maintain an international law bar in England after the decline of prize cases, which had made Stowell one of the greatest of international lawyers.[40]

The most formidable new challenge to English law was, however, the growth not of international government but of national administration. The industrial revolution stimulated organization throughout society, in the form of companies, friendly societies, trade unions and professional associations, and these were the units with which the government had to deal. Inevitably there was a demand that the state should take over completely those monopolistic but essential corporations, like the railways, which it had done so much to create. The Post Office became the first (and is still the greatest) of the nationalized industries, and in many places slaughter-houses, markets, tramways and water-works were municipalized. The government itself took on the forms of industrial organization, working through such public corporations (half government department, half business company) as the Mersey Docks and Harbour Board, set up in 1857. If further proof were needed of the importance of corporations within the modern state, which is itself the greatest 'public service corporation' of all, it would be found in the obsession of Maitland and his fellow jurists with the theory of corporations, and in such movements as guild socialism.[41]

Communities are often intolerant of individual freedom,

and when communal organizations are invested with the authority of the state, the law must be tough which will prevent oppression. Not that the mid-Victorian state was voracious for power – in fact, it was a general belief in free competition and self-help, combined with government parsimony, that caused unavoidable tasks of administration to be left to a host of separate authorities, enjoying those wide powers of executive discretion and subordinate legislation which are the main concern of *administrative law*. Executive discretion often assumed a judicial character – the authority sat in judgment and imposed a penalty on the uncooperative citizen. Of course, this was how England had been governed for centuries by 'the amphibious old justice of the peace who did administrative work under judicial forms'.[42]

Subordinate legislation – the scrutiny of which is the other main concern of administrative law – is even less separable than judicial discretion is from the business of administration. The making of bye-laws was always a privilege of corporations, but the scope of subordinate legislation was enormously increased in the nineteenth century by the new practice of including in the statutes setting up special authorites grants of the power to make detailed regulations. To the proclamations which the Privy Council issued independently of Parliament were added a vast number of orders – e.g. on the lighting and ventilation of cow-sheds – which were issued by the Privy Council (really quite ignorant of their subject-matter) on behalf of government departments and under the authority of Acts of Parliament. The departments, which already enjoyed the right to scrutinize private acts affecting their concerns, began to issue orders themselves, once the Poor Law Commissioners had been empowered by the statute of 1834 to make rules for 'the management of the poor'. By statutes like the Public Health Acts of 1875–1939, local authorities were permitted to enact bye-laws on everything from burials to public libraries (summary conviction of their infringement carrying a £5 fine). The systematic publication of *Statutory Rules and Orders*, by then twice as bulky as the statutes themselves, dates from 1890.[43]

Three years earlier, Maitland pointed out the magnitude of the change which was occurring. 'The traditional lawyer's view of the constitution [Parliament as sole legislature and king as the executive, advised by ministers responsible to Parliament] has become untrue to fact and to law. . . . To a very large extent indeed England is now ruled by means of statutory powers which are not in any sense . . . the powers of the King. . . . Year by year the subordinate Government of England is becoming more and more important. . . . We are becoming a much governed nation, governed by all manner of councils and boards and officers, central and local, high and low, exercising the powers which have been committed to them by modern statutes.'[44]

ADMINISTRATIVE LAW

Administrative law is based on the principle that the exercise of administrative power is subject like every other action to measures of fairness and natural justice kept by the courts. Just when the control of the administration was becoming an acute problem, Dicey confused the issue by attacking the special courts which existed in France to adjudicate public actions and suggesting that *droit administratif* somehow put officials outside the rule of law. His complacent denial that any such thing as administrative law existed in England obscured the need for it – indeed that it was even then being rapidly developed in the ordinary courts. Dicey himself pointed out the remedy of the private citizen against tyrannical officials – an ordinary action for tort in the Common Law courts – without recognizing it as a distinctively English form of administrative law, which is a matter not of courts but of principles.[45]

The rise of powerful departments of government caused changes in the law concerning actions against Crown servants. Here again, it was more profitable to sue the employer than the employee, but since the Crown could do no wrong it could not be vicariously liable in tort, as an ex-speaker of the House of Commons discovered in 1842 when he claimed

damages for the burning down of his house (along with the
House of Commons itself) through the negligence of some
workmen in the Crown's employ. (The good principle that a
Crown servant who acts wrongfully cannot plead a defence
of 'superior orders' follows from the idea that the Crown is
also incapable of ordering a wrong.) However the case of
Mersey Docks and Harbour Board Trustees v. *Gibbs* (1866)
decided that public corporations erected by statute were
separate from the Crown and incurred the liabilities of
ordinary employers.[46]

The modelling of government on the corporation suggested
the ways in which law might curb the arbitrary use of administrative powers. Just as a company and its servants will be
called to account if they act outside the sphere demarcated in
the Memorandum of Association, so will a public authority
if it goes beyond its statutory powers. The courts have defined
certain special ways in which an authority may act *ultra vires*,
such as by delegating its discretion still further, exercising it
under an outside influence, or making contracts which restrict it for the future. The authority must act not only within
its powers, but (secondly) with good motives, reasonably,
and in good faith, 'according to law and not humour'; but,
naturally, the courts must stop short of censoring government policy, and have nothing to do with honest mistakes
(the necessary distinctions are fine ones). Thirdly, in certain
situations, where it seems to act in a judicial way, an authority must obey the rules of natural justice and not take
action without giving a hearing to someone who may suffer
thereby; and in *Cooper* v. *Wandsworth Board of Works* (1863)
a builder recovered damages against the local authoriy
which had demolished without notice a house he was admittedly building against regulations.[47]

Amongst the remedies which the High Court gives against
administrative abuses are the prerogative writs of certiorari,
prohibition and mandamus which King's Bench had used
for centuries to curb those all-powerful local authorities, the
J.P.s. And there was, after all, a similarity between the review
of the legality of a hearing in a local court and of the exercise

of its discretion by a local authority. The 1834 act, which in its second section permitted the Poor Law Commissioners to hold inquiries and examine witnesses on oath, expressly enacted in its 105th section that the commissioners' rulings should be 'removable by Writ of Certiorari into . . . His Majesty's Court of King's Bench at Westminster'. Thus certiorari may sometimes lead to the quashing of an administrative decision. Mandamus – the injunction of public law – will order a wide range of positive action by authorities; for instance, will command a returning office to hold an election properly, a taxation officer to reimburse a taxpayer, a railway company to fulfil its statutory duties, a court to hear a particular case. There may be a question as to whether the complainant is properly concerned in the matter, but there is often a particular victim – Mr Smith – whose standing is clear, and the case will then be cited as (e.g.) *Regina* v. *The . . . Rent Tribunal ex parte Smith*.[48]

It was but a step from reviewing administrative actions to scrutinizing the regulations made by public authorities, for no doctrine of parliamentary sovereignty prevented the judicial review of delegated legislation. Here the principle that no one might be condemned unheard reappeared as the precept that where possible interested parties should be consulted before a regulation was made. Such consultation is not a Common Law right, however, and the courts have relied rather on a strict interpretation of the statutes conferring rule-making powers, and on the various measures of *ultra vires*. Parliament will be presumed not to have authorized the making of rules infringing a citizen's fundamental rights or partial to a particular class; nor to have delegated the imposing of taxes, which under the Bill of Rights is Parliament's exclusive function.[49]

The older types of constitutional question still arose from time to time, especially during the revolutionary scare at the beginning of the period, when the protection of Habeas Corpus was suspended by statute and Erskine made his name defending political prisoners. Later, the law about public meetings was defined in some notable cases. Acts of 1868 and

1883 gave the ordinary courts jurisdiction over electoral corruption (the general election of 1880 was the most expensive in English history) and power to certify the Speaker that an election was void. Parliamentary privilege took a new turn. The House of Commons changed its view that to publish its proceedings was a breach of privilege to one that it had a constitutional duty to publish, and that the publisher could not be arraigned in an ordinary court for a libel contained in parliamentary papers. In the cases of *Stockdale* v. *Hansard* (1839) and *Wason* v. *Walter* (1868), King's Bench showed its usual jealousy for private rights, denying in the first that the Commons could by mere resolution authorize what was intrinsically unlawful, but confirming in the second that when fairly reporting parliamentary debates newspapers enjoyed a privilege which safeguarded them from libel suits.[50]

In other areas, the law was less relevant to politics than in the past. For example, the conventions of ministerial responsibility had dispensed with judicial impeachment. But to the ordinary citizen ministerial responsibility gives less satisfaction than the right to challenge 'the powers-that-be' in the ordinary courts, a right which the judges went some way to establishing in the middle years of the nineteenth century. The adumbration at that time of an 'administrative law' to control the exercise of government perhaps stands on a level in British history with the definition of the legal basis of government – 'constitutional law' – by Coke and his friends some three centuries earlier. For administrative law is now the more controversial half of public law and the real battlefield between governors and governed, though it has not fulfilled its nineteenth-century promise.[51]

EPILOGUE: REFORM CONTINUED?

IT is not the historian's business to criticize the present state of the law. But he may ask how its recent development measures up to its earlier history, and he will probably conclude that a falling-off from the nineteenth-century impetus of reform is one of the causes of present dissatisfaction.

A CONSERVATIVE PROFESSION

The nine law lords, the eleven judges of the Appeal Court (who are also privy councillors), the sixty or so High Court judges and the eighty or so county-court judges – these figures have steadily increased – are chosen from a mere 1,900 practising barristers, who are not selected with the same care as administrative civil servants and are no longer the unchallenged *élite* of the professions. Admission to the bar is still controlled by the Inns of Court, although there has been a democratically elected Bar Council since 1883. It is often said that the benchers of the inns are obscurantists who use their power irresponsibly, refuse to cooperate with the bar council, and provide a narrow technical training which has no regard for the social implications of the law. Until recently, the inns showed themselves particularly ill-equipped to handle the overseas students, including many Africans and such future statesmen as Mr Nehru, who by 1960 made up two thirds of all those called to the English bar. English law students preferred 'crammers' to the efforts of the Council for Legal Education.

The work of the barristers is governed by archaic rules and conventions. One barrister may not form a business partnership with another, though several will work from the same chambers and have the same 'barrister's clerk' to organize their time. The bar has in effect two divisions. To the juniors – those who are not Q.C.s – is reserved the work of drafting pleadings, so that the man who 'takes silk' must start all over again, with as much chance of failing as he ever had. The division between juniors and Q.C.s is another of those distinctions (like that between barrister and solicitor) which creates stubbornly defended privileges and interests, and forces the litigant to buy what seems to him a series of redundant services. Why was it necessary to engage a junior along with a Q.C. and pay him exactly two thirds of what the Q.C. received? The answer is, because the barrister lives by honoraria and to get the best income must take as many briefs as he can: but because of the lack of a fixed programme in English courts, two of his cases might come on simultaneously in different courts, and then one litigant would find that only a junior was in court to act for him. Since the junior could not be a business partner of the Q.C., he must be paid separately.[1]

The main vested interest of the 20,000 solicitors is in conveyancing charges, described by their own journal in 1962 as 'probably one of the largest single price-fixing agreements in the country', which made them persistent opponents of land registration. The solicitors have since 1950 been eligible for appointment as stipendiary magistrates, but they remain excluded from the judiciary, although their legal education is now considerably more thorough than the barristers'. Since 1 January 1963 an aspiring solicitor must serve two years unbroken apprenticeship at the very minimum, if he does not have university degree. In fact, the Law Society puts a higher premium on a law degree than does the bar, and since 1922 the proportion of graduates among the solicitors has risen from seventeen per cent to sixty per cent. The argument is therefore heard that the solicitors, combining the liberal education of the universities with a professional training that makes them both technically competent and adaptable, drawn from a wider social and political background and organized for business in efficient partnerships, are at least as qualified as barristers to be judges of the High Court.[2]

The continued division of the legal profession can be justified by reference to the special functions of each branch. Particularly outside London, the solicitor has a lot of important work – the drafting and executing of wills, for example – unconnected with litigation. The prospective litigant engages, in the solicitor, a strategist who knows how to choose between barristers as between court tacticians. The barrister is in touch with the state of judicial opinion, but in the interests of an impartial trial he sees nothing of his witnesses until he calls them into court – it is the solicitor who seeks them out and arranges for their appearance. If the judge is likewise regarded as a specialist in court proceedings, his choice from the barristers alone is reasonable.[3] It seems, however, that the divided structure of the profession has too often worked against a rational structure for the law it administers, and the arguments for at least partial fusion seem strong. A common education of the two parts of the profession is particularly urgent now that many students return to countries where the profession is 'fused'.

The cost of legal services is still popularly regarded as scandalous, though the vacancies for solicitors and the decline in the numbers of all lawyers in the past sixty years from 1/1,400 to 1/1,200 of the population suggest that the legal profession is now not as sensationally well paid as it used to be. The median income of the barristers in 1955 was £1,620 – less than the solicitors' or the doctors' – though thirty or so earned more than £10,000 a year and ten might have been getting more than £20,000. The charge for counsel's opinion varied from five to a hundred guineas, according to the problem and the status of the barrister, and brief fees were of course higher, but the really big fees came from company litigants well able to pay them. Barristers were ostensibly not doing well by comparison with businessmen, and considerable numbers of them were tempted from law into business (in which they may not operate while at the bar). But as a result of a determined campaign by the Bar Council for higher fees, accompanied by an up-turn in the volume of litigation and an extension of legal aid, incomes have greatly improved since 1955 and it appears that the profession has easily kept up with the cost of living. The number of new recruits has begun to rise again.

Public dissatisfaction with legal costs is probably due to a feeling that the machinery of the law has not been brought up to modern standards of efficiency and economy, and to the knowledge that a good proportion of lawyers' fees come out of the public purse in the form of legal aid. As a result of the Evershed Committee on supreme court practice and procedure (1947–53), something was done to simplify the interlocutory proceedings of the High Court towards the level of the county-courts. But an action would come on in the county-court within about two months of commencement; in the High Court, perhaps not within a year. When a case went to the Lords on appeal, the costs might run into five or six figures.

It could be said that in the last fifty years English lawyers, in marked contrast to their American counterparts, have lost their position as 'the priesthood of industry' and the leading profession to the accountants, though the fact has been obscured by the lawyers' pomp and tradition. The lawyers' social exclusiveness sometimes looks like a social isolation which shows itself in a natural conservatism, and in the remoteness from modern life which allowed the prosecuting counsel in the *Lady Chatterley's Lover* trial to ask the jury whether it was a book they would wish their servants to read. In the early years of this century, English judges spurned 'public policy' as a reason for widening the interpretation of legal rules and showed a class bias in cases involving trade unions. After 1945, on the other hand, they seemed on occasion to abdicate from their function of criticizing administrative actions through anxiety not to appear hostile to the Labour government. There is no suggestion, however, that judgments have been significantly biased by the judges political opinions.[4] The danger has been rather a complacency and lack of imagination in judges who are too often described as the infallible guardians of English liberties and morals, are supposed to possess an unrivalled insight into human nature, and are surrounded, throughout overlong careers, with pomp and circumstance. Nothing seemed to shake the judges in their almost solitary faith in corporal punishment, and some of them were outraged that legal aid should be regarded as the right of poor persons, rather than as charity.

In politics, barristers are still the largest professional group and most of them are Conservatives: there were sixty-six barristers and eleven solicitors on the government benches in the 1959–64 parliament, twenty-seven barristers and nine solicitors were in the opposition, and the speaker was a former solicitor-general as well as being the son-in-law of a previous speaker. Lawyers seem to move naturally to the political right, for Dicey was the greatest opponent outside Parliament of Irish Home rule, and Halsbury, at the age of eighty-seven, led the party in the Lords which resisted the 1911 Parliament Bill 'to the last ditch'. Yet Halsbury, who had won the position of solicitor-general in Disraeli's government by saving Conservative seats in trials of election petitions, is the only lord chancellor who may have appointed the odd judge on grounds of political loyalty.[5]

Lloyd George is the only solicitor to have become Prime Minister, and Asquith was the last barrister to do so. Asquith had not been a law officer. As politics have become more professional, a political career has been less easy to combine with a legal one, so that the lord chancellor, who is a member of the cabinet, has been more frequently chosen from success-ful politicians who happen to have the necessary legal quali-fications, whether or not they have held the law offices. But, because it carries a peerage, the lord chancellorship has also meant, under modern parliamentary democracy, an end to the highest political ambitions, and the office of Home Secre-tary has therefore become a better stepping-stone for the lawyer–politician. This was Asquith's first government office, and it was Sir David Maxwell Fyfe's when he appar-ently gave up a chance of being Prime Minister by accepting the lord chancellorship in 1954. Sir Thomas Inskip may have given up a similar opportunity in the same way in 1939, but he was a somewhat unwilling politician who had been made Minister of Defence in 1936 to keep out Churchill, and in 1940 he was the first ex-lord chancellor to be appointed lord chief justice. Since the war the chancellor has had less time for his judicial work in the Lords as a court of appeal. His importance is now as an administrator of the legislative and judicial machinery. And Lord Dilhorne's activities on Mr Macmillan's resignation suggest that he is still, as in Eldon's day, the natural political go-between.[6]

THE MACHINERY OF LAW-REFORM

Of the mass of twentieth-century legislation, very little beside the Property Acts of 1925 has changed 'lawyers' law', and ancient statutes have had to be ingeniously construed to cover modern inventions such as broadcasting and modern offences like the opening of car doors to the injury of passers-by. Even the piecemeal codifying of the law has languished since the Bills of Exchange Act of 1882 and the Sale of Goods Act of 1893; though there has been a continuous succession of the consolidating acts, which do not re-state the law in a more logical fashion but only bring together miscellaneous enactments on the same subjects.[7]

In the nineteenth century, law reform was an integral part of social reform through legislation (cf. p. 361 above). By 1900, however, social reform had passed from the stage of adjusting general principles to that of detailed regulation, and there was little time left in Parliament for statutes on 'lawyers' law'. Now that there seems to be again a wide demand for law reform, the machinery for carrying it through is the first target for criticism. An attempt at reform still usually begins with investigation of the particular problem by a commission, often chaired by a judge and composed (as in the case of the 1943-5 Cohen Committee on Commercial Law and Practice) of lawyers, academic lawyers and laymen experienced in the field of society or industry which the problem concerns. There has also been since 1952 the lord chancellor's Law Reform Committee, a reincarnation of the Law

Revision Committee of 1934–9. When it comes to implementing the recommendations of committees, however, the lord chancellor has too often been refused adequate parliamentary time by his government colleagues. There has been no possibility of steady, planned reform, and even piecemeal improvement has been left to struggle through or go under as a private member's bill.[8]

Thus, of the ten reports of the Law Reform Committee in its first decade, one was implemented by a government bill (as the 1957 Occupiers' Liability Act) and five by the initiative of private members. Other government departments than the lord chancellor's have been better able to put through legislation, and have kept up to date the less purely 'lawyers' law' (an example is the Board of Trade's company legislation); and in 1959 the Home Secretary appointed his own Criminal Law Revision Committee, which quickly produced the Indecency with Children Act (1960) and the Suicide Act (1961). Law reformers have therefore argued that the post-war strengthening of the Lord Chancellor's Office should be continued till it becomes the Ministry of Justice so often proposed in the last hundred years; and that this should coordinate the legislation of other government departments, continually review the law itself, and promote an annual Law Reform Act. There is a crying need for more codification, for there are now something like 50 volumes of statute-law, 100 of delegated legislation and over 300,000 reported judgments, and all three sources must be consulted in almost every case. Delegated legislation, the vehicle of the welfare state as the Public General Act was of nineteenth-century liberalism, has particular problems.[9]

There are many pressure groups seeking to persuade Parliament to alter the law in their interests, but public opinion as a whole has been apathetic or reactionary in its attitude towards law reform. The Conservative government's Homicide Act of 1957 and steps towards a milder penal law appear to have been contrary to the strong feelings of the majority of Conservative supporters. As in the nineteenth century, penal reform has been the work of a group of non-party humanitarian enthusiasts, not of the political public nor of the lawyers as a body, though lawyers naturally predominate in the unofficial organizations like 'Justice' which lobby the Law Reform Committee. Why law reform should not be as much a party issue as (say) economic policy – no less technical and no more important to the individual citizen – or whether it would then do better, are questions not to be answered here.[10]

Of course, the assumptions of the ordinary 'reasonable' man are accorded great respect in the operation of English law and so affect its content, usually in a conservative direction. The ideas of the ordinary man (for instance, that obscenity corrupts) are often prejudices unjustified or disproved by science. The presence of the jury has acted as a brake on the assimilation of modern scientific knowledge, for the judges have doubted its capacity to appreciate technical issues, and for this reason even as recently as 1888 the law would not allow damages for injury allegedly caused by nervous shock. True, there are now many successful actions for injury alleged to have affected the plaintiff's personality, and recent advances in gynaecology have led to the rejection of precedent decisions which turned on the legitimacy of children and the possible limits of the period of gestation. But judges and juries appear to share a reluctance to recognize the findings of psychology and a tendency to retreat from exact distinctions into a cloud of moral reprobation.[11]

The dislike of experts now apparently takes in the academic lawyers, who nevertheless comprise a fifth (amounting to three members) of the Law Reform Committee. The normal reply to the reformers' idea of five permanent law commissioners under a Minister of Justice has been that successful barristers would not leave their work for such positions, and the job would have to be done by academics without experience of the law's practical defects. Furthermore, to have legislation planned by experts, who represent no one, is said to be less democratic than ordeal by private member's bill. In opposition, radical reformism became centred in the universities, where men like Dr Glanville

Williams have deplored the state of official jurisprudence and called for the appointment of judges from the law schools, as in the United States. Certainly there have been no English jurists equal in influence to Dicey or Pollock at the beginning of the century, or to Mr Justice Cardozo or Roscoe Pound in America. A committee on legal education in 1934 recommended greater coordination between universities and professional bodies and facilities for legal research, as a result of which an Institute of Advanced Legal Studies was created in the University of London in 1948.[12]

THE ATTITUDE OF THE COURTS

The usefulness of the system of courts as a law-adapting mechanism has been diminished by a still more exact regard for precedent. *Young* v. *the Bristol Aeroplane Co.* (1944) settled the fact that the Court of Appeal was normally bound by its past decisions and those of the earlier court of Exchequer Chamber, and ever since *London Street Tramways* v. *London County Council* (1895) the Lords have renounced the power to depart from one of their own precedents, even when they think their earlier decision was probably wrong. But the sheer bulk of important decisions in the Common Law world threatens to cause a breakdown of *stare decisis* (as it may already have done in the United States). Vital precedents are overlooked by counsel, and a whole line of authorities begins to grow in the wrong direction. Perhaps only the computer can save the situation.[13]

More and more cases rest on the interpretation of legislation, which becomes increasingly intricate. Yet the classifying of statutes and the provision of different rules of interpretation, even a separate body of interpreters, for 'technical' statutes like The Rent Restriction, Restrictive Practices or Taxation Acts seems a dangerous solution for the judges' difficulties: this is the legislation which affects the average citizen most and needs to be applied according to the strictest standards of the Common Law. The difficulties are accompanied by greater power and responsibility, if the courts choose to use it, for the rules of statutory interpretation are less precise than those of *stare decisis*. In *Roberts* v. *Hopwood* (1925) the Lords seem to have used this power to whittle away 'social legislation', when they construed a statute enabling local authorities to fix their employees' wages 'as they think fit' to mean 'as they think reasonably fit', and found the minimum of £4 a week set by one borough council extravagant and dictated by 'eccentric principles of socialist philanthropy'. But since that time the judges have often shown appreciation for the social purposes of statutes, and have also been less inclined to construe taxation acts in favour of the individual. In *Latilla* v. *Inland Revenue* (1943) the lord chancellor went so far as to deprecate the tendency to regard tax evasion 'as a commendable exercise in ingenuity or as a discharge of the duties of good citizenship'.[14]

The complaint against the courts is now rather that they pay too much attention to the letter of a statute, and attempt to impose a rigidity of statutory interpretation on a rigidity of *stare decisis*, which is intolerable in combination. Taxation cases have reached a level of intricacy where no ethical consideration is any longer relevant. They are battles of ingenuity in the construction of statutes which seem to be decided on the spin of a coin. For, despite the *Index of Statutory Definitions*, no word has a constant significance. Because the meaning of a term varies according to context – the particular statute and the circumstances of the case in hand – hundreds of actions arose from the single phrase in the 1906 Workmen's Compensation Act, 'an accident arising out of and in the course of his employment', and many have turned on whether linoleum is furniture within the meaning of the Rent Restriction Acts.

Words mean nothing by themselves, and it is difficult to see how they can be given a meaning without reference to the Parliament or department which framed them. The difficulties of discovering the legislator's intention might be overcome by allowing the courts to consult the White Papers and other explanatory memoranda which already accompany bills in Parliament. Though the meaning of such expressions as 'reputed thief' and 'idle or disorderly person' could not have been known without breaches of the rule against parliamentary history, the doctrine still seems to be that it is 'a naked usurpation of the legislative function' for the courts to attempt to fulfil the legislator's purpose.[15]

The Common Law would not exist if in past centuries judges had not been prepared to condemn certain conduct as plainly unjust. In *Reynolds* v. *General and Finance Facilities Ltd* (1963), one judge did indeed say that the behaviour of the defendant (a hire-purchase company) had been 'most harsh and unconscionable and revolting to one's sense of fair dealing' – but this was not the *ratio decidendi* and since Mansfield could never have been such where there was a clear precedent. But the moral feelings of judges still have a place: not the bludgeon of moral indignation, but the subtle and more difficult instrument of moral restraint, which tries to balance competing interests fairly. It is indeed desirable that there should always be an element of indeterminacy and free choice in judicial decisions, for otherwise law and the society which depends upon it would be closed systems, incapable of adapting themselves to changed circumstances. There is virtue in the fact that principles evolved in cases about stage-coaches can be applied to motor-cars.[16]

In 1950, the Court of Criminal Appeal made a choice which fundamentally altered the law, when in *Rex* v. *Taylor* it refused to be bound by one of its own previous decisions in a case involving the liberty of the subject. But by their more rigid adherence to precedent, the courts as a whole seem to have deliberately restricted their own freedom of choice at a time when social change has diminished faster and faster the convenience of deciding as in the past. No statute has imposed the strictness of the modern rule: the judges have imposed it on themselves. True, they have shown more willingness in recent years to recognize that two precedents set by the same court are not infrequently contradictory, leaving a choice of principles still to be made; and that decisions are sometimes reached *per incuriam* – that is, in ignorance of the relevant statutes and precedents – and cannot bind. And, of course, the judgments of a higher court may expressly or by implication overrule the decisions of an inferior one.[17]

These qualifications of the rule may in fact destroy any value it possesses. 'An absolute rule concerning precedent,' to quote Dr Goodhart, 'has at least the virtue of certainty. A semi-absolute precedent has no more virtue than a semi-fresh egg.' For this reason there is danger, too, in the suggestion that the House of Lords should reassume or have restored by statute the power to overrule its own previous decisions. But absolute certainty is incompatible with any legal growth. Why should the Lords (as a court) not fashion the better law which the legislature will not provide? Only in the twentieth century have the judges disowned the role of law-makers. In the nineteenth century, as we saw on pp. 336, 358, they reformed many parts of the law by their judgments, and Parliament tidied up the loose ends: now, they disclaim any power to remedy gross anomalies and appeal vainly for a statute to do the whole job.[18]

PROPERTY AND FAMILY LAW

The one substantial piece of law reform this century has been the series of Property Acts of 1922–5. These abolished copy-hold-tenure and its irksome formalities, so erasing the last vestiges of the manor-courts. Conveyancing was immensely simplified by the repeal of the Statute of Uses and by the reduction of legal estates in land to two, the 'fee simple absolute and in possession' and the 'term of years absolute' (i.e. leasehold). Such changes in substantive law were possible because registration of interests in land was no longer regarded as the complete panacea: indeed, it was realized that there could not be a successful scheme of registration while those interests remained so multifarious. The 1925 legislation provided for the eventual registering of all titles (only a third are registered yet), and for the recording of special charges like restrictive covenants, mortgages and town-planning regulations.[19]

The substance of the property acts was the relegation to equity of future estates, and indeed of all estates but the fee-simple in possession and leasehold. This means that the trustee, the tenant-farmer and the builder alone have the management of land, and can see that the property retains its original form. Any equitable interest, on the other hand, may be 'overreached'; that is, transferred from one form of capital to another as the trustees, having the legal estate, may decide. The farmer needs land as such: the equitable interest is merely a right to income. Securities, not land, are now the substance of the normal family settlement. Property-owners so much adopted the methods of commerce that in 1930 a statute was necessary to check families from turning themselves into limited companies to avoid taxation. The wider application of the trust and the unification of the rules of succession have gone far towards completing the assimilation of the law of land to the law of personal property which began in the nineteenth century (p. 375 above).[20]

The transformation of the land-law followed the greatest transfer of land in English history. Death duties and the slaughter of heirs in the Great War produced in 1919 an avalanche of sales by the peerage, which had already been invaded by bankers, brewers and newspaper proprietors with virtually no land to their names. The opposition to the Parliament Bill of 1911 was the last ditch of the old nobility, and their enemy, Asquith, was the first non-landed Prime Minister apart from the peculiar case of Disraeli. It was not merely that the property passed to new men: the old pattern of land-ownership was broken up as the sitting tenants – the farmers – very often acquired the freehold. Weighed down by mortgages, the farmers then found themselves under pressure from one side by companies eager to develop the land as industrial or housing estates and from the other by a government shown the importance of agricultural planning by the war and more than ever conscious that land meant power to be controlled. Many of the legal complications surviving from the hey-day of private property in land – easements of light, for instance, and theoretical ownership of the air-space above one's land and 'a cone-shaped segment' below it 'with its point at the earth's centre' – seem to many people to be inappropriate in this present age of planned development. The same is true of the restrictive covenants under which land has sometimes been sold, preventing the purchaser and his successors from building more than one house per half-acre, or their wives from hanging out their washing on Sundays.[21]

The hardship caused by the reversion to the landowner at the end of a long lease of the homes built upon the property has found no remedy acceptable to all the interests concerned; but the Labour government which came to power in October 1964 quickly promoted a Leasehold Enfranchisement Act, to give the leaseholder the right to purchase the freehold when a lease of more than twenty-one years expires. Since 1915 there has been a series of acts to control the rents of houses and particularly of the furnished accommodation for which the Rents Tribunal was set up in 1946, and to prevent the ending of tenancies without good reason. The courts now spend much time on cases arising from this 'landlord and tenant' legislation.

The methods of real property law could perhaps contribute now to solving the problems which arise in the transference of goods. Here, as in land transactions, it is the separation of ownership and possession which causes difficulties: equal justice cannot be done both to the true owner of the goods and to the *bona fide* purchaser from a thief or someone who merely had possession of the goods. Registration of title to valuable articles (particularly those which are the subject of hire-purchase) might prevent such conflicts of interest from occurring at all. But it seems more likely that the key to the intricacies of property in goods will be found in commercial law. In the United States, title to goods often passes in the form of a document – a development of the old bill of lading – which is recognized by the courts and may be negotiable.[22]

The predominance of concern for individual welfare over strict considerations of property is further apparent in family law, where the continued political and social emancipation of women has assisted the general trend. The principle of distinguishing the husband's and the wife's estates which underlies the Married Women's Property Acts was recognized in *Allen* v. *Allen* (1961) to be not entirely adequate to a joint venture like marriage: in that case a wife claimed in equity a half-share of a bungalow the purchase of which, though in the husband's sole name, had been made possible by the use of her earnings for all the household expenses. The Inheritance (Family Provision) Act of 1938 went beyond the old Statutes of Distribution (which applied only in cases of intestacy) to allow a widow and her children to appeal against a will which neglected to provide for them. A great deal of the Chancery Division's most important work is now in the area of family law. The processes of legitimation and adoption are there controlled under the terms of a series of twentieth-century Legitimacy Acts and Adoption Acts (most adoption orders are in fact made in the County or Magistrates' Courts); guardianship of a child of separated parents is awarded to husband or wife; and infants are made wards of court to prevent undesirable marriages.[23]

There were royal commissions on divorce law in 1912 and 1956. Yet only in 1937 were the grounds of divorce extended from adultery to cruelty, desertion and insanity, and then it was by the efforts of a private member, Sir Alan Herbert. The Judicial Proceedings Act of 1926 restricts the reporting of details of matrimonial cases in the Press, and the judges (in common with society at large) have shown a more understanding attitude to matrimonial problems, no longer singling out the adulterous wife for especially harsh treatment. But the use, until 1963, of the M'Naghten Rules to excuse insane cruelty and refuse divorce on that ground shows that unfortunate hints of criminality still attach to a divorce suit (there is generally too much talk of the 'innocent' and the 'guilty' party). Legal Aid reached a new level of organization when the Law Society created a salaried staff during the last war to conduct the divorce suits of poor persons in the armed services.[24]

THE PREDOMINANCE OF PERSONAL INJURIES

The great majority of civil actions concern torts, mostly negligence in motor and industrial accidents, and here emphasis has been shifting from penalizing carelessness to compensating for injury. This change has gone in step with the spread of the strict liability which the law first recognized in *Rylands* v. *Fletcher* (p. 371 above): in more and more situations the courts have translated the duty to take care into a duty to ensure that another person does not lose by one's actions, and statutes have sometimes made this a duty to contribute to actual insurance schemes from which injured persons can be compensated. Why should not all suggestion of wrong-doing be dropped from tort? What reason was there, apart from the extra inducement to the employer to observe safety regulations, for the 1948 Law Reform (Personal Injuries) Act to leave an injured employee the possibility of suing in tort as well as claiming from national insurance? Would it not also be beneficial to take 'running-down' cases out of the courts by strengthening the insurance protection for third parties and perhaps enacting a national system of insurance against injury on the roads?[25]

The law of torts moved further from punishment to compensation in 1945, when a statute replaced the Common Law principle that evidence of the plaintiff's partial responsibility for an accident excused the defendant entirely, by the Admiralty rule that it should lead to a fair apportionment of blame and loss. With the Common Law's peculiar obsession with the 'contributory negligence' of the last person who could have avoided the accident (usually the victim) vanished the age-old opposition of negligence to inevitability. Equally important, the power in tort of the doctrine of privity (cf. p. 106 above) was destroyed by the House of Lords in *Donoghue* v. *Stevenson* (1932), where the person taken ill after drinking a bottle of ginger beer and finding a decomposed snail at the bottom gained damages against the manufacturer although there had been no immediate transaction between them. Given that life would be too complicated if a man was legally responsible for all the harmful effects of his actions, the best limitation of his liability would seem to be to those effects which he can reasonably foresee; and this obligation of reasonable foresight was firmly established by *Donoghue* v. *Stevenson*.[26]

Even in tort, where the judges headed by Lord Atkin and Lord Wright did considerably improve the law during this century, there has since been a renewal of conservatism. The particular area from which *Rylands* v. *Fletcher* and modern strict liability arose – a landowner's responsibility for dangerous objects on his property – has proved especially difficult to extend; and, despite the coming of the motor-car and the findings of a committee of 1952–3, a farmer has no more duty to fence in his cattle from the roads than he did when England was a purely agricultural community. But the decisions of the House of Lords, by their very unhelpfulness, have here inspired one piece of reforming legislation – the 1957 Occupiers' Liability Act. In a very different field, the High Court refused in *Candler* v. *Crane, Christmas and Co.* (1951) to impose liability on a negligent firm of accountants for a loss of profits caused by their advice, but this decision was overruled twelve years later by the House of Lords. A Right of Privacy Bill which would have made over-persistent salesmen, reporters and the like, guilty of a new tort was destroyed in 1961 by government opposition.[27]

Strict liability had also, and less beneficially, crept into libel. It had ceased to be necessary to prove intention to injure, or even negligence, in a libel, and the authors of novels were liable to heavy damages just because they had hit upon the names of living persons for their less reputable characters. The 1952 Defamation Act made broadcast defamation a libel, but did permit one who published a defamatory statement 'innocently' (i.e. without malice or negligence) to make an offer of reasonable amends which would be a good defence if the victim persisted in legal proceedings. It also continued the process of giving 'qualified privilege' to newspapers which fairly and accurately report parliamentary debates and court cases. Papers can advance the common-sense argument that much of what they say is not to be taken as fact but as 'fair comment on matters of public interest'. A simpler improvement would surely be to remove the distinction between libel and slander caused by the accidents of seventeenth-century history (cf. p. 294 above), and to require proof of special damage in libel also. This is in fact already done, to the extent that the jury may award a mere halfpenny, as it did in *Dering* v. *Uris and Others* (1964), when the libel turns out to have been substantially true: 'no injury is done to the plaintiff by his reputation's being reduced to its true level'.[28]

Because the defence that the libel is true is virtually equivalent to a charge against the plaintiff, the continued use of a jury is appropriate here, but it has steadily declined almost everywhere else in civil proceedings. After 1933 (which therefore marked the end of a 'golden age of advocacy' aimed at swaying the juryman) a jury could be claimed by the parties only in cases of libel and slander, fraud, breach of promise of marriage, false imprisonment, malicious prosecution and seduction; and during the last war the civil jury was temporarily abolished altogether.[29]

The judge is much better able to weigh complicated evidence, and there seems no reason for the retention of the highly complicated rules of evidence (e.g. excluding most but not all hearsay) which once ensured against a jury's stupidity. Because of the minute examination in court of every bit of evidence – much of it as technical as pleading and procedure used to be – the length of the civil trial has multiplied by four or five times since 1875. This has counterbalanced the simplification last century of pleading (which takes place before trial) and the erection of each of the Queen's Bench Masters into a distinct tribunal for interlocutory matters. At the pre-trial 'summons for directions' the Master, from whom appeal lies to a judge in chambers, arranges the date of the trial, the amending of pleadings, and the taking of affidavits from witnesses who cannot attend in court; he may authorize a compromise between the parties, enter judgment for default, and order execution against a judgment debtor. It is mainly due to his work that only 1,350 of the 50,000 cases begun each year in the Queen's Bench come to trial.[30]

None of this has much reduced the expense of litigation, which is particularly important because the defeated party will probably be made to pay the winner's 'taxed costs' (those approved by the Taxing Master), as well as his own. This is a way of discouraging irresponsible litigation: in *Dering* v. *Uris and Others*, the plaintiff was landed with £20,000 costs because he went on with the case after the defendants had offered him £2 by way of compromise – just nine hundred and sixty times what the jury eventually decided was his due. The costs of many poor plaintiffs who could not otherwise have sued at all are paid by the state under the Legal Aid and Advice Act of 1949; and very recently an obvious injustice has been righted by allowing the defendant who succeeds against a legally aided plaintiff to get his costs also from the fund. Before 1926, most poor litigants had to go to voluntary 'Poor Man's Lawyer' organizations for help, but in that year the government placed the responsibility on the Law Society, because a solicitor is what a poor litigant wants first of all. The state has spent £20 million on legal aid since 1950; 450,000 legal aid certificates have been issued; and eighty-eight per cent of legally aided actions have succeeded.[31]

The basis of the law of tort has always been a legal conundrum. Is there now, at last, a chance of merging its various compartments on the single principle of strict liability for harm done to others? Of course, this would mean that insurance companies would virtually replace the courts (even now, most personal injury claims are settled by negotiation between them). And there would still remain the question: what is harm in the complicated world of today? How plausible is a claim for shock which is alleged to have altered an artist's personality? How are 'gold-digging' plaintiffs to be excluded, especially from libel actions? How much can a man (or even an insurance company) reasonably be made to pay for a pure accident? In cases of defamation and personal injury, juries (which may be used at the judges' discretion) are apt to award inflated damages, and in a number of recent instances the Court of Appeal has declared that a case of very serious injury is not one for a jury, which often has no idea of the right way to go about assessing damages. Though the figures set by the judges alone may be consistently too low and show a disregard of actuarial science, this does seem to be the place for the judge's particular expertise, to balance one interest against another, and to resist the temptation of the juristic 'short cut', the undiscriminating general principle.[32]

INDUSTRY: THE TREND TO CORPORATENESS CONTINUED

The courts have come to realize in the last eighty years that those old Common Law preoccupations, conspiracy and individual freedom, are not the answer to commercial disputes. In *The Nordenfelt Case* (1894), the House of Lords acknowledged that agreements to restrict competition between manufacturers might be reasonable and in the public interest. *Crofter Harris Tweed Company* v. *Veitch* (1942) finally established that group pressure was a legitimate weapon of modern economic life; and in that instance the opposition was not between management and union, but between certain employers and workers in conjunction and the non-union mills which threatened all their livelihoods. The greatest change has been the law's extension to the trade unions (until a few months ago) of the policy of 'collectivist *laissez-faire*', which in the nineteenth century already exempted the 'conspiracies' of the employers from interference. The Trade Union Act of 1871 had, by expressly legitimizing combinations in restraint of trade, begun the legislative policy of making unions immune from judge-made doctrines (which have rarely favoured the unions), but at the price of denying them any help from the judges in their internal affairs: it merely allowed a union to register with the Registrar of Friendly Societies if it chose. [33]

The judges found, however, that the attribution of corporateness to a registered union was a way of keeping it within what they considered proper bounds. The discrepancy between the judicial attitude to employer and to worker was made clear by the *Mogul Case* (1892), in which an organized boycott of a rival trader was decided not to be tortious, and the celebrated *Taff Vale Case* (1901), in which Lord Halsbury declared the Amalgamated Society of Railway Servants vicariously liable in tort for the action of its officials when they induced workmen to break their contracts of employment. The *Taff Vale* decision meant in law that the union was recognized as a quasi-corporation, like the companies it fought; but by the same token that its only economic weapon and reason for existence, strike action, was paralysed by the fear that its funds would dissolve in damages. The Liberal Government in 1906 neutralized the *Taff Vale* decision by the Trade Disputes Act. This supplemented the Conspiracy and Protection of Property Act by a clause which exempted from civil as well as criminal liability any conspiracy to commit an act in itself lawful and (by express words) any inducement to break a contract of service, if these things were done 'in contemplation or furtherance of a trade dispute'; it declared peaceful picketing lawful; and, most drastically, it exempted unions from all liability for the torts of their agents.[34]

The act did not, it must be noted, abolish the breach of his contract of employment by an individual workman as a civil wrong. In 1956, officials of the Association of Engineering and Shipbuilding Draughtsmen persuaded B.O.A.C. to dismiss a non-union man, Mr D. E. Rookes, by threat of an immediate strike. Rookes sued the officials, won his case in the High Court, saw the decision reversed in the Court of Appeal, and finally, on 12 January 1964, reaffirmed in the House of Lords (*Rookes* v. *Barnard and Others*). The Trade Disputes Act had exempted trade-union officials from liability for conspiracy to do what was lawful for an individual, and as separate individuals from liability for *inducing* strikes in breach of contract. But the House of Lords decided in *Rookes* v. *Barnard,* with evident satisfaction, that to *threaten* a strike was to conspire actually to break contracts (i.e. to do what is unlawful in itself) and not just to 'induce a breach', and that here it was the tort of intimidation, for which in all previous cases violence had been necessary. In the case of *J. T. Stratford and Son Ltd* v. *Lindley and Another* (1964), a judge of the Court of Appeal said that *Rookes* v. *Barnard* might cause 'industrial chaos' if the scope of the decision was not limited. It must be understood that the legal issue in *Rookes* v. *Barnard* was not the closed shop, which the courts accepted as legitimate back in 1924. Nor was it anything to do with the fact that the contracts of employment included an undertaking not to strike without negotiating first: it is equally a breach of contract to strike without giving due notice as if one is terminating one's employment. The issue was whether the union officials had committed a tort unprotected by the Trade Disputes Act; and the Lords were able to conclude that they had, only by equating a threat to break a contract with (as Mr George Woodcock put it) a threat to 'bash a man's face to pulp'.

The result of the unsympathetic handling of trade unions is a general feeling that law is no longer of much service to industry and sometimes obstructs its working. The Common Law courts are said – and not only by the unions – to be uncomprehending about the purpose of trade unionism, and to have no place in the collective bargaining of employers and unions. In 1913 the Industrial Council of the Board of Trade recommended that industrial agreements, which were easiest to arrive at where there was the greatest organization of management and men, should be enforced by special conciliation boards and joint councils of the two sides. Despite continuous efforts to provide legal sanctions for collective agreements, there have in fact been no lasting changes in labour law since the 1906 act. Even the Industrial Court set up in recent years only decides whether the terms of a collective agreement are reasonable. The courts recognize only the individual contracts of employment, which mean nothing to the average worker. A collective bargain has no legal status, except insofar as its terms are written into the individual contracts, and appears to be unenforceable except by further 'industrial action'.[35]

The registered company has been such a success that it has ousted the trust even as the basis of charitable organizations. The separation of the company from the firm was advanced by the case of *Salomon* v. *Salomon and Co. Ltd* (1897) and completed by the Limited Partnerships Act of 1907: the case decided that Mr Salomon, who had turned his shoe factory into a family company, was entitled, when the company was wound up, to have its debts to himself, secured by debentures, paid before the unsecured debts of outside creditors; and the act allowed unincorporated firms to include 'limited partners' who did nothing but provide capital and whose liability was proportional to their contribution to the funds. The Companies Act of 1907 created the *private company*, which cannot invite public subscription and is restricted to fifty members, but actually needs only two members (as against seven for a public company) and can conduct its affairs with far greater privacy.[36]

The old remedy of franker disclosure suggested by the regular series of Company Law Amendment Committees – the most recent was the Jenkins Committee appointed in 1959 – has not ended the peculiar abuses which the private company makes possible. One enterprise can form a large number of private companies and borrow money through them which it transfers to one or two going concerns, the others then being liquidated with little fear that the creditors will throw good money after bad by instituting proceedings. To avoid estate duty the private company can sometimes be utilized, rather as the trust was in past centuries. It is the public company, however, which is used in 'take-over bids'. These involve the purchase of the shares of the companies to be taken over, and may cause an inflation of share prices, the closing down of old firms, and the sacking of employees: all this without the shareholders knowing the true position of the concern they surrender. Since part of the trouble is the vagueness of the director's responsibility at law and the shareholder's lack of interest in the running of the firm, there are suggestions that it is time to reverse the historical development – for the shareholder and the firm to be brought closer together again, the limitation of liability not so freely conceded, and the separate existence of the private company ended.[37]

The recent history of restrictive practices demonstrates the courts' acceptance of the facts of modern commercial life and recognition of the internal contradictions of the concept of 'freedom' in trade. There is no simple answer to the great industrial trust, any more than there is to the trade union: the encouragement of corporate discipline must here go along with the prevention of corporate excesses. The judges have to escape from their own illusion that they are concerned only with rights and freedoms, to take sides in economic matters and decide what is reasonable in terms of the general welfare. In *Thorne* v. *the Motor Trade Association* (1937) the House of Lords found it perfectly legitimate for an association of wholesalers and retailers to black-list price-cutters and refuse to supply them. But a Ministry of Reconstruction Report after the First World War had recommended the creation of a special tribunal on combinations of manufacturers, which were increasing alarmingly at that time, and after the Second World War the Monopolies and Restrictive Practices (Inquiry and Control) Act (1948) set up a Monopolies Commission to which the Board of Trade could submit restrictive practices for consideration of their effects. A Restrictive Practices Court of judges and lay members was set up in 1956 to decide on the lawfulness of any restrictive arrangements brought to the Registrar of Restrictive Trading Agreements for registration. It was a unique experiment which must be presumed to have failed: only a tiny number of new agreements have been looked at by the Court. In March 1965, the Labour Government introduced a bill to restrict mergers creating undesirable monopolies, especially in the newspaper world.[38]

The acceptance of corporate organization in labour, manufacturing and distribution left the consumer as the underprivileged party in commerce; and that he too has begun to organize is shown by the Consumers' Association (publishers of *Which?*) and the belated controversies over trading stamps (the subject of a committee before the First World War) and resale price maintenance (reported on by another in 1948–9). The consumer's interest is focused on the law of the contract of sale, and, though in some respects the harshness of that law's first principle – *caveat emptor* – has been mitigated, in others the snares which face the consumer seem to have multiplied. The chief of these are the 'standard form contracts' printed on laundry and railway tickets, insurance policies, hire-purchase agreements and 'guarantees' (the latter restricting the normal liability of the manufacturers as often as safeguarding the purchaser). The consumer is frequently bound by unfavourable conditions in 'contracts' which he had no part in framing and no encouragement to read. On the other hand the potential purchaser has no way of enforcing a seven-day option given by a dealer, because there is no consideration for such a promise to keep an offer open.

The courts have shown themselves conscious that the Common Law freedom to draft a contract as one pleases has now removed real freedom from many fields of commerce. But, since the problem is that contract becomes more and more 'institutionalized', that it ceases to be 'the instrument by which millions of individual parties bargain with each other' and is rather the quasi-legislative form in which large organizations impose their economic policies, it seems that the answer must again be found in Parliament.[39]

Since the foundation of the Commercial Court in 1895 – which was apparently due to a spectacular demonstration of ineptitude in a charter-party case by Mr Justice Lawrance – the judges seem to have lost their ability to foster commercial institutions. The work of the Commercial Court itself has declined from 107 cases tried in 1907 to 16 in 1957, because businessmen have lost interest in the law and prefer their own arbitrating tribunals. Official committees propose new bodies to solve commercial problems, as the Molony Committee proposed the recently instituted Consumer Council; and official tribunals like the Industrial Court and the Restrictive Practices Court rely more on the device of registration (which may, however, owe something to developments in the law of conveyancing) than they do on the ordinary judicial forms.[40]

A BACKWARD CRIMINAL LAW?

When we look at crime, which changes with society no less than the subject-matter of civil actions, we may feel that English law trails behind as much as it did in Hazlitt's day in the understanding of the criminal mind (cf. p. 367 above). Since the work of Cesare Lombroso in the second half of the nineteenth century, criminology has indeed developed quickly in Europe and America. We know more about delinquent subcultures, and about the dangerous fascination of the criminal which was already evident in eighteenth-century London. Many books have been written on the replacement of poverty as a chief cause of crime by adolescence in the midst of affluence and broadcast sensationalism. There have been many statutory reforms in the administration of English criminal justice. But the provision in 1964 of a special court to deal with the backlog of minor traffic offences is hardly an answer to 6,000 road deaths a year. The substance, the lawyer's part, of the criminal law has not kept up with modern problems. The number of indictable offences recorded each year stands above the million mark – and perhaps only fifteen per cent of actual crimes are detected. There are something like four and a half million men and one million women in Britain who have been convicted of indictable offences, and 400,000 of them have had at least eleven convictions. Improvements in detecting and recording make a comparison with the nineteenth century impossible, but it can be said that serious crimes have been increasing recently by around ten per cent a year, against a population increase of less than one per cent, and violence by youths aged fourteen to sixteen increased by an average of twenty-one per cent.[41]

The definition of crime still seems bedevilled by the moralistic theorizing of the Victorians (cf. p. 362 above). Against the restatement by the Wolfenden report of John Stuart Mill's principle that immoral conduct should be punished only when it injures other people, Lord Justice Devlin argued in a now celebrated lecture that 'the suppression of vice is as much the law's business as the suppression of subversive activities'. What is injurious is in fact a matter of judgment. Though it would be futile as well as tyrannical to regard all sins as crimes, outrageous affronts to generally held moral feelings might very properly be included in the criminal category. Large concepts are not very helpful in the debatable ground between crime and simple immorality: the law must work as an empirical social science and take careful note of the actual effects on society of men's actions. There was nothing wrong in principle in the publication of a list of prostitutes' addresses being held to be criminal under the headings of 'a conspiracy to corrupt public morals' and 'an act tending to the public mischief', as it was in *Shaw* v. *D.P.P.* (1961). What is important is how the judges use the wide discretion to create new offences given them by a concept like public mischief. It does seem that justice would be better served if the criminal courts were sometimes less moralistic and more technical in attitude (and, conversely, the civil courts larger in outlook, and willing to construe almost all kinds of harm as tort). Crimes would then be just those particularly serious and wicked injuries for the deterrence of which the state brings its resources into play; which may again – if present schemes for compensating the victims of crimes of violence are a success – carry private compensation as in the dawn of English law.[42]

There is plenty of disagreement as to which forms of gross immorality are in fact injurious to the public and should be punished at the cost of individual freedom and happiness. Is incest, which was made a criminal offence by statute as late as 1908? Should not the desirability of abortion be assessed in particular medical decisions, rather than comprehensively denied by the law? The recognition that attempted suicide at least was a matter for treatment, not punishment, was marked by the Suicide Act of 1961, which abolished the offence, but English law has been very reluctant to adapt itself to the Freudian revolution. Parliament not long ago refused to advance the bottom limit for criminal responsibility beyond the age of ten, and occasionally the courts appear to take pride in their ignorance of the findings of psychology. This may be the result of a temporary moralistic bias in the criminal law, or of an obscure feeling that psychology challenges the very idea of moral responsibility on which the law rests. The Homicide Act of 1957 did, however, compromise with psychology in a way which a select committee had said in 1931 was futile: instead of abolishing capital punishment altogether, it distinguished three degrees of responsibility for intentional killing and retained the death penalty only for the highest. The lowest is manslaughter, which the jury must find if the defence proves diminished responsibility, a concept (borrowed from Scottish law) covering the emotional disturbance which insanity under the M'Naghten Rules excluded (cf. p. 362 above). The task of the defence is not easy in such a case, but in the first twenty-seven months of the act's operation, diminished responsibility was argued in seventy-three instances and in fifty-three of them verdicts of manslaughter were returned.[43]

The inadequacy in the twentieth century of intentional wickedness as a measure of crime is obvious, too, from the fact that it would exclude all punishment of the stupid carelessness which kills fifty on the road for every single murder. In a complicated modern society people must sometimes be penalized for breaking regulations when even carelessness is hardly discernible – 'strict responsibility' has developed for the same reasons as 'strict liability'. Emphasis in both civil and criminal law has necessarily shifted from individual motivation to the effect of certain actions on delicate social mechanisms; from the *mens rea* to the *actus reus*.[44]

Good criminal law continues to depend very much on fair and rigorous procedure, and it is here that the present situation is least satisfactory. At the preliminary stage of police investigation, the tension between the need to check crime and the demands of justice to the suspected persons is particularly great. It may seem unreasonable to restrict the police in their detective work, but what a suspect says to them in a moment of stress may prejudice his entire trial; and, unfortunately, it is the innocent citizen who is most vulnerable and the hardened criminal who knows his rights – that he is not obliged to go to a police station unless he is actually arrested, nor to answer questions. In 1912 and 1918, the judges laid down rules for the questioning of suspects by the police, the disregarding of which might lead to a conviction being quashed. 'The Judges' Rules' were amended in January 1964 to require the cautioning of a man (that he need not answer) as soon as he is suspected and not just when he is charged. This concentration on what a suspect blurts out injudiciously, perhaps, but quite voluntarily, is a survival from the days before 1898 when it was thought in some way to be a protection to the accused that he was debarred from giving evidence at any stage. It would surely be more realistic to stop the eliciting of information by keeping people for long hours at police stations.[45]

Appointment to the benches of magistrates before which so much of criminal proceedings takes place has yet to be extricated from local politics. J.P.s are chosen by advisory committees for counties and boroughs nominated by the lord chancellor, the composition of which is secret and therefore beyond public criticism. In 1948 a royal commission did report that lay justices were chosen too much on a political basis, and that younger people, the lower income groups, and teachers and other suitable persons were thereby under-represented, even when the choice showed no political bias. But the government retained the automatic appointment of prominent councillors as a concession to 'local government sentiment'. The preliminary hearing of serious charges before magistrates is an example of the way in which criminal procedure has slipped out of gear, and protections for the accused become disadvantages (cf. p. 365 above). The publicity given at that stage in the press may very well prejudice the jury in the higher court, and steps are being taken to restrict it. As a way of detecting possible murderers and committing them for trial, an inquest in a coroner's court seems (considering the resources of the modern police) inefficient and unnecessary as well as unfair: should the coroner be abolished after 900 years of service?[46]

TRIAL AND PUNISHMENT

Fairness of trial depends on whether the judge, with the help of a rigorous procedure, can succeed in holding the balance between two deliberately biased arguments. The Criminal Evidence Act of 1898, following the admission of interested parties as witnesses in civil trials (cf. pp. 332, 369 above), permitted accused persons to go into the witness-box. As a result, that most effective device of English criminal law, cross-examination, has conclusively exposed a number of criminals, and innocent men have had a greater opportunity to clear themselves under the sympathetic questioning of the counsel assured to them by the legal aid acts of 1903 and 1949. The order of speeches by counsel in criminal trials, which gave the prosecution the immense advantage of the last word to the jury (before the judge's summing-up), has just now been revised. These are matters for statutory improvement, but almost everything still depends on the judge's success in keeping prejudicial influences from the jury. Hearsay evidence and reference to the accused's previous convictions must be suppressed, since the jury may be swayed by it without being able to assess its worth.[47]

The jury is the problem. No one has been allowed to study the jurymen making up their minds, but it seems inevitable that they decide from general impressions rather than any just assessment of evidence, and certain that their decisions are sometimes capricious and even frivolous. Unfortunately, juries are exposed to insidious influences not so well allowed for as (say) mention of the accused's previous character. If a man is indicted of a large number of sensational charges, the jury is liable to think he must be guilty of something. Even where the old rule that a man is to be presumed innocent till proved guilty has not been abrogated by statutes placing on the defence the burden of proving innocence, it may be subtly undermined by the terms used to refer to the man in the dock – not 'Mr Smith', but 'Smith' or 'the accused'. An unguarded expression of disgust by the judge, or the type of witticism for which Mr Justice Darling was notorious, influence juries to an extent of which judges seem unaware. The moralistic streak which has been prominent in the English judicial attitude since Victoria's reign does not favour cool judgment on the jury's part, and it is difficult not to feel that Dr Stephen Ward was convicted of being an immoral man, rather than of any specific crime.[48]

The root of the trouble is not the moral arrogance of High Court judges, but that in present conditions the responsibility for determining guilt falls between judge and jury: the judge, deciding by himself, would make an effort to discount those prejudices which he conveys to the jury without knowing it and which the jury relies upon as guidance to a verdict. Not since the controversial trial of Dr Jameson of 'Jameson's Raid' in 1896 has a criminal judge asked the jury to find special verdicts on a number of questions of fact, and then directed it to give the general verdict which followed in law. The necessity of exact guidance to the jury is nevertheless recognized by the judge's summing-up, which since the early nineteenth century has covered the evidential as well as the legal issues. Powerful arguments are therefore being advanced for the abolition of the criminal jury and the placing of the responsibility for determining guilt on a bench of judges, or a judge and a few assessors. As it is, offences triable summarily already outnumber indictable offences by six to one, and eighty-four per cent of indictable offences are also tried summarily; such small desire does the accused offender show for trial by his peers, when he has the choice. The only occasions when juries now regularly refuse to convict – and then not very admirably – is in cases of bad driving: was the jury ever the palladium of English liberties except possibly in the sedition trials of the eighteenth century?

There is no reason why the bench of judges should not preserve, just as well as the jury, the orality and publicity of the English trial (which is in any case being whittled down by the use of confessions); and anyone reading the account of the E.T.U. trial, in which, as a civil case, there was no jury, must be impressed with the fairness and skill with which a judge can handle complicated facts.[49]

The tragic but by no means isolated case of Adolf Beck, who had a double who was addicted to crime, at last in 1907 provoked the establishment of a court of Criminal Appeal which could quash a conviction or alter a sentence as it thought fit. In the first nine months of the court's operation there were twenty-nine appeals, in no less than eighteen of which the conviction was quashed: what numberless injustices took place before it was created? Yet, out of undue reverence for the verdict of the jury, the court is even now generally inhibited from reconsidering questions of fact or hearing fresh evidence, so that miscarriages of justice of the Beck type have recurred. Nor, before the Criminal Appeal Act of 1964, could the court order a re-trial, and for this reason a guilty man whose trial was technically faulty might escape scot-free; while its much-used power to increase sentences may deter the appeals of the genuinely innocent. Hitherto, the Home Secretary has acted as a sort of 'long-stop', reluctantly ordering special inquiries in apparent cases of injustice (e.g. conviction on allegedly false evidence) where the Court of Criminal Appeal will do nothing.[50]

Unlike their continental equivalents, English judges are not trained in penal methods. The glaring inconsistency of sentences for similar crimes by different judges led to the institution in 1964 of courses on sentencing for magistrates and of conferences for other judges. There remains the much more fundamental disagreement about what punishment is for. Lady Wootton believes that the Homicide Act of 1957 was vitiated by the wish, 'now increasingly manifest in our penal practice, to ride two horses simultaneously in opposite directions' – the old horse of retribution and the new one of rehabilitation. Penal reformers perhaps underestimate the necessity even today of the criminal law's original function – official retribution as the only alternative to the anarchy of private revenge. On the inefficiency of harsh punishments as deterrents to potential criminals they seem, however, to have had the better of the argument: fines turn out to be the best. The 1931 Select Committee on Capital Punishment recognized that the abolition of the death penalty for crimes against property had not led to an increase in such crimes, and that there was no reason to think that hanging deterred murders either. The crime of attempted suicide was abolished when it was accepted that suicide is the result of psychological disturbances impervious to rational deterrence. Yet the majority of murders are also the products of emotional stress within the family: one half of all murderers kill near relatives and a third immediately commit suicide.[51]

Forty-five per cent of murderers sentenced to death were being reprieved, before the Homicide Act of 1957 replaced the death penalty by life imprisonment for all but capital murder, namely the murder of a policeman, murder using firearms and murder in the course of robbery. But the dreadful irrevocability of the death penalty drove some reformers to take up the position that no sort of murderer was responsible for his crime; which easily becomes the dogma that responsibility is an outdated concept in every part of the criminal law. They can point to the large number of recidivists, the people of generally low intelligence who, despite the penalties, go on committing crimes throughout their lives; and to the body of evidence, resting on Henry Maudsley's *Responsibility in Mental Disease* (1874) and Charles Goring's official study *The English Convict* (1913), that delinquency is at least partly determined by a man's environment and constitution. On the other hand, many psychiatrists will admit that 'psychopaths' are not sick in the same sense that mental patients are sick, that eighty per cent of criminals are 'normal', and that the idea of responsibility before the law therefore remains indispensable. It is fascinating to observe, moreover, that one modern treatment of the offender, group psychotherapy, makes him responsible to a sort of folk-moot of his own kind.

We are certainly still a long way from a dispassionate treatment of criminals: little use is made of the Mental Health Act (1959) which allows a judge to send a violent criminal to hospital instead of prison. Nevertheless, there has been for some years a Home Office Advisory Council on the Treatment of Offenders; since the Children Act of 1908 juvenile delinquents have had special attention in Juvenile Courts; and under the Probation of Offenders Act of 1907 one in every five persons accused of indictable offences is released on probation, whereas 150 years ago every second offence was punishable by death. In 1964 there was appointed a Royal Commission on the Penal System, under the chairmanship of Lord Amory, to make the first comprehensive study of the treatment of offenders since 1895.[52]

By the Homicide Act of 1957, executions for murder were reduced to an average of four a year, but few were satisfied with the compromise the Act represented, or were not soon convinced that a just demarcation between capital and non-capital murders was impossible to arrive at. In December 1964, Mr Sydney Silverman introduced a bill to abolish the death penalty for murder, and the bill became law in November 1965.

THE CONDITION OF PUBLIC LAW

The courts may disallow only those administrative actions which go beyond the authority delegated by Parliament: they cannot criticize the powers which Parliament chooses to confer, and in time of war or serious strikes these may be very wide (the Defence of the Realm Act of 1914 even gave the king in council wide powers to impose trial by court-martial upon civilians). Yet the rule of law survived two world wars, and the old practice of embodying emergency legislation in a special class of temporary acts ensured that the defence regulations eventually lapsed – although it has taken twenty-five years for some of the 1939 ones to do so.[53]

Administrative law has not kept up with the permanent growth of government, nor coped with the 'administrative feudalism' of the great public corporations like B.O.A.C. set up since 1945. The courts have been hard put to it to counter the statutory conferment upon Ministers of 'subjective powers' – authority to act 'if they are satisfied' that certain situations exist – which effectively removes from the courts the right to judge the reasonableness of the actions. Though in *Liversidge* v. *Anderson* (1942), Lord Atkin made a famous protest against those judges who in cases 'involving the liberty of the subject show themselves more executive minded than the executive', the House of Lords decided that Defence Regulation 18b, allowing the secretary of state to detain anyone he had 'reasonable cause to believe . . . to be of hostile origin or associations', placed the Minister's subjective judgment beyond criticism. In 1961 there were at least two thousand independent administrative tribunals – Rent Tribunals, National Insurance Appeal Tribunals and so on – operating under a chaos of improvised procedures. The use of public inquiries before clearance and planning orders are made – inquiries in which the Minister, or rather his inspector, acts as judge between local authorities and objectors – is another essentially beneficial development of administrative method which has brought its own problems: firmness of administrative policy has to be reconciled with requirements of fairness in what has become a 'quasi-judicial' proceeding.[54]

As late as 1929, Lord Chief Justice Hewart exhibited, in his book, *The New Despotism*, a hatred of the very idea of administrative law. But its necessity has since been recognized everywhere, and the Crichel Down affair of 1954, which could be settled only by the political decision to order a special inquiry and the resignation of a blameless Minister of Agriculture, suggested that there was indeed too little of it. The problem in that case was the inscrutability of the king's administration, which statutes and courts together have done something to reduce. The use of *relator* actions, brought against public bodies by the attorney-general on the relation or information of private citizens, has provided a new line of attack. The departments of central government which, as part of the Crown, could not be sued in tort (cf. p. 355 above), yet accepted responsibility for defending actions against their officials and would nominate defendants when there was doubt about which official to sue. A private individual cannot be allowed to halt the processes of government by suing out an injunction against a crown servant (such as a minister). The *declaratory judgment* which states the law on a matter but is followed by no order for execution, is, however, respected by the government whenever it is applied to administrative issues, and this nineteenth-century device threatens to replace the more narrowly judicial prerogative writs like *certiorari* as the great administrative remedy.

The courts disliked the makeshift of the nominated defendant procedure. The Crown Proceedings Act (1947) therefore enacted that the Crown should have the same liability in tort as 'if it were a private person of full age and capacity', and departments as if they were ordinary employers. The new standard procedure against the department or attorney-general was also extended to matters of property and contract once dealt with by the petition of right, which was thus abandoned.[55]

The dispute is no longer about the necessity of administrative law, but about the place of the ordinary courts in enforcing it. The Common Law courts, which first asserted the standards of administrative action (cf. p. 386 above), seem to have lost their creativeness here. They have limited themselves to criticizing those bodies which, 'having the duty to act judicially, act in excess of their legal authority'; and, in application, their idea that only some administrative acts are thus 'quasi-judicial' has confused rather than controlled the processes of government. It is vital that the rule of law should pervade administrative operations, but it seems that the special administrative courts (the judicial element built into the civil service which Dicey feared) can now assert it better, by more expertly and realistically distinguishing policy from prejudice. The Franks Committee which followed the Crichel Down affair sensibly welcomed the administrative tribunal, as no previous committee had, and pointed out the impossibility of classifying procedures 'as purely administrative or purely judicial'. It could then go on to recommend improvements in the constitution of tribunals and inquiries which make them more just to individuals (to the official defendants who are 'tried by tribunal' as well as to the complainants), and hand over in 1958 to a permanent Council on Tribunals.[56]

In the important case of *Ridge* v. *Baldwin* (1963), a suit by the ex-chief constable of Brighton against the watch committee which had dismissed him with loss of pension rights, the House of Lord seems to have held that the principles of natural justice, including the principle 'hear the other side', which the watch committee had neglected, were still binding in some cases of dismissal by a local authority. (Though, 'Master and Servant' law allows no restriction of an ordinary employer's right to dismiss.) Administrative law is after all very much concerned with the individual's rights against the organization, an issue which goes far outside public administration (cf. pp. 243–4, 295 above). Professional disciplinary bodies like the General Medical Council are subjected from time to time to the power of certiorari, and 'there is a belated recognition that ... not only the Houses of Parliament and the Ministry of Labour, but also the General Council of the Trade Union Congress, the British Employers' Confederation, Imperial Chemical Industries Ltd, the Prudential Assurance Company, and The Transport and General Workers Union are part of the British Constitution'. None the less, the major defect of English public law is the absence of any general law of associations which would recognize an 'inherent right' of a member of an association to legal protection in respect of his status as a member.[57]

Moreover, there are now many issues between the state and private interests to which the traditional concepts of administrative law are irrelevant. For instance, no adequate law has been evolved on public contracts. The Ferranti case, where the firm could only be invited to make a voluntary repayment of excess profits from a government contract; the Burmah Oil case, in which the courts awarded compensation to a company for the destruction of its installations on government orders during the war, only to have the decision nullified by act of Parliament; and *Pfizer Corporation* v. *the Ministry of Health* (1965), which decided that patent rights may be infringed 'for the services of the Crown': all these show in their different ways the lack of fair criteria for settling disputes between the government and the firms with which it deals. Administrative law needs firm concepts of public utility and its limits, as well as ideas of natural justice, which relate to the procedure rather than the substance of administrative decisions.

THE LAW AND POLITICS

The power of the trade union over the livelihood of individual workers has achieved notoriety because of its political bearing and the stringency of the discipline which was once necessary if the trade unions were to be effective. The unions might now be wise to relax that discipline a little, but the ordinary courts gave up the right to interfere when they first refused to recognize the existence of associations of workers, and then – with admirable consistency – to intervene in the internal arrangements of unions more than with those of a company, the Stock Exchange or the Carlton Club. Since *Bonsor* v. *Musicians Union* (1956), unions have been open to damages for wrongful expulsion; and the Common Law action for conspiracy was sufficient to overthrow the rigged E.T.U. election; but any further protection for the rank and file of trade unionists will probably have to come from the Registrar of Friendly Societies and a special body of labour law. In February 1965, Lord Donovan was appointed to head a royal commission to inquire into 'relations between management and employees and the role of trade unions and employers' associations in promoting the interests of their members and in accelerating the social and economic advance of the

426

nation with particular reference to the law affecting the activities of these bodies. . . . '58

Law and politics are entangled at many points, of which the status of trade unions is a good example because of the separation of employers and workers along party lines. Another example is the application of commissions headed by judges, and special tribunals under the 1921 Tribunals of Inquiry Act, to major political issues – a budget leak, ministerial corruption, the government of Nyasaland. The use of these legal procedures as an apparent escape route for hard-pressed administrations is in itself a political question, and it is sometimes argued that standards of government should properly be safeguarded by permanent committees of the House of Commons, or by an *ombudsman* on the lines of the Paliamentary Commissioner appointed in New Zealand in 1962. The attorney-general, a member of the government, is responsible for much of the conduct of special inquiries, and, while it is long since charges of political pressure on the judges were justified, it was not very long ago – in 1924 – that a Labour government was overthrown by allegations that it ordered its attorney-general, Sir Patrick Hastings, to withdraw a prosecution against the *Workers Weekly* for incitement to mutiny. The reconciliation of freedom of speech with the restraint of libel is still a political problem of some magnitude. It is arguable that fear of libel actions makes the British press less free than others and, in situations like the Profumo affair, more cautious than the public interest allows. Perhaps newspapers should be given special licence to libel public institutions and officials, as trade unions have special licence to commit torts, since it is their function to do these things.[59]

As for the constitution of the British Commonwealth, the judicial supremacy of the mother country has not been allowed to become such a disruptive issue as her legislative supremacy in the eighteenth century. The Statute of Westminster (1931) made it possible for colonies which had become independent to abolish appeal to the Judicial Committee. Canada, India, Pakistan, Ghana, Cyprus, Nigeria and Tanganyika have taken advantage of that provision;

Australia, New Zealand, Ceylon, Trinidad and Jamaica have not. The Common Law remains the ordinary law of many parts of the world. The 'uniformity and certainty' of legal rules which the Privy Council proclaimed as its object in 1765 was to an extraordinary extent attained by the authority throughout the colonies of the Council's own decisions and the mutual respect accorded by the courts beneath its umbrella to the judgments of each other. The influence of English decisions has therefore not ended where appeals have been cut off – the courts of India still refer to them often. The newly-independent colonies' objection to retaining appeals is the historical identity of the Judicial Committee with English government. A Commonwealth appeal court clearly separate from the Privy Council, its authority purely judicial in form as well as fact, might commend itself to everyone.[60]

In the development of the still wider field of international law Britain's recent part has been unenthusiastic and disappointing (cf. p. 382 above). International law has changed from being a code for the conduct of war and commerce to being one for the prevention of war, just as English law developed from the regulation to the prevention of private feuds. International litigation has grown enormously, and also the international legislation binding upon Britain, which is now far more bulky than domestic statute-law; and at the same time the emphasis has moved from technical agreements to fundamental concepts of crime against peace and humanity. In 1950, some of the member-states of the Council of Europe drew up a European Convention on Human Rights, and in 1958 established a European Court of Human Rights, which may, for instance, decide that a trial in a national court was unfair because there was not procedural equality between the accused and the public prosecutor. The United Kingdom has not yet accepted the Court's jurisdiction. The teaching of international law in Britain is still inadequate, and diplomats required to work with subtle legal distinctions, such as between the *de facto* and *de jure* recognition of East Germany, are perilously ill-equipped.

Yet, international law can help not only in the strengthening of peace but in the protection and therefore encouragement of world trade, and it was good to see the Foreign Secretary in the Labour Government of 1964 appoint an advisory committee of international lawyers to study methods of conciliation.[61]

LAW AND CONTEMPORARY HISTORY

It is merely odd that trial by peers was abolished only in 1948, that the last vestiges of the medieval ceremony of appointing an attorney disappeared only in 1956; and that the Court of Chivalry was actually revived a second time in 1954 to hear the petition of Manchester Corporation against the Manchester Palace of Varieties, which was displaying the city's coat of arms on its façade. Less harmless amongst the historical curiosities of which English law is full are the procedural differences between trials for felony and for misdemeanour, classifications which no longer correspond to the relative seriousness of offences and are due to be abolished on the recommendation of the Criminal Law Revision Committee; and the grip that the Anglo-Saxon pattern of local jurisdiction still has on police organization, preventing the modern detective from being as mobile as the crook (the recent creation of nine regional crime squads is doing something to mitigate the ill-effects of county boundaries). On the other hand, medieval statutes against livery remain useful against militant political groups, and statutes against embracery, to punish the improper influencing of juries; and the procedural devices of estoppel and perhaps non-suit still have a useful part to play in civil actions.[62]

The ending of the dominance of land over law and society, which happened only yesterday in terms of historical perspective, was something of a 'great divide' in the development of English law. Yet the continuities are obvious, and pay a certain tribute to the law's worth and adaptability. Adaptability became real creativeness in the matter of industrial injuries, for it was the judges who developed employer's liability and laid the foundation of the social insurance which Dicey found shocking.[63] The past exerts its hold on English law through the uniquely English principle of the binding precedent. True, this encourages the attitude that to do anything new is to 'set a dangerous precedent'. True, a civil law code, expressed in reasonably general terms and interpreted by a body of jurisprudence sensitive to changes in society, may reconcile certainty and adaptability without the technical obscurantism which goes with *stare decisis*. It is just another historical fact that English law has never been codified, so that the certainty of the binding precedent was the necessary substitute for the certainty of a code. But the law, and the administration which is bound up with it, do seem to have been marking time for too long. The deadening effect which precedent may have is seen in the recent tendency of the judges, when 'construing an act which changes the law', to 'minimize or neutralize its operation by introducing notions . . . inspired by the old law'.[64]

In particular, the structure of the legal system has not kept up with the advance of democracy – the Common Law is still too much the law of the upper and middle classes. The development of legal aid has moved very little faster than the rise in legal costs, and there is still no adequate system of free legal advice, to be available apart from litigation. The old prejudice against encouraging litigiousness in the lower classes is not quite dead, or the fear that subsidizing their divorce actions (the main inspiration of legal aid) will cause them to take marriage lightly. The structure of the courts points to the same conclusions. The great majority of criminal cases take place 'at the bottom', in the local magistrates' courts; and the decentralization of criminal justice was carried further by the establishment of permanent Crown Courts ('Old Baileys') at Manchester and Liverpool in 1956, and in 1962 by the authorizing of quarter-sessions to sit continuously and the insistence that they must have legally qualified chairmen. On the other hand, it is only with great reluctance that *civil* remedies have been put within easier reach of everyone by extending the jurisdiction of the county courts. No wonder the ordinary man still thinks of the law as entirely a matter of crime and punishment.

But legal history is a record of alternating decline and revival; periodic bursts of criticism and reform are part of it, and we are now into what may prove one of the more notable of these. A number of mishandled cases in the past few years have made people less complacent about the judiciary (there is less inclination to leave the law to the judges); and at the same time some have detected a new stirring of 'judicial valour' and responsibility. Bodies of Law Commissioners, charged with the promotion of law reform, have begun work in both England and Scotland. After a slump in the mid-fifties the number of High Court cases has steadily risen. Moreover, it is unfair to look only at the old courts and the Common Law in its narrow sense, for 'what matters is the law of England', and the administrative tribunals and machinery of industrial conciliation (for instance) are also derived from the empirical tradition of English law, which has been spontaneously generating new courts throughout the centuries. Law goes wider still, permeating the country's life and institutions. Burke said that the law was nowhere so general a study as it was in the American colonies which were about to create the United States. This study made 'men acute, inquisitive, dexterous, prompt in attack, ready in defence, full of resources. . . . They augur misgovernment at a distance, and snuff the approach of tyranny in every tainted breeze.' Though it can hardly match Burke's description, a new interest in the law does seem to be in the air, and should be welcomed.[65]

ABBREVIATIONS

ENGLISH HISTORICAL DOCUMENTS *E.H.D.*

TRANSACTIONS OF THE ROYAL HISTORICAL SOCIETY *T.R.H.S.*

THE ENGLISH HISTORICAL REVIEW *E.H.R.*

CAMBRIDGE LAW JOURNAL *C.L.J.*

BULLETIN OF THE INSTITUTE OF HISTORICAL RESEARCH *B.I.H.R.*

LAW QUARTERLY REVIEW *L.Q.R.*

BREVIATE OF PARLIAMENTARY PAPERS *B.P.P.*

BIBLIOGRAPHY AND REFERENCES

THE following works have been used extensively, and specific references are not normally given to them:

PLUCKNETT, T. F. T., *A Concise History of the Common Law* (5th ed., 1956).

HOLDSWORTH, W. S., *A History of English Law* [to 1875] (16 vols., 1903–, of which XVI is still to be published).

SIMPSON, A. W. B., *An Introduction to the History of the Land Law* (1961).

STEPHEN, J. F., *A History of the Criminal Law of England* (3 vols., 1883).

And, for the early chapters:

POLLOCK, F. and MAITLAND, F. W., *The History of English Law before the time of Edward I* (2nd ed., 1898).

Generally useful are also:

GIUSEPPI, M. S., *Guide to the Contents of the Public Record Office* (2 vols., revised 1963).

KIRALFY, A. K. R., and JONES, G. H., *Guide to the Publications of the Selden Society* (1960).

INTRODUCTION: LAW AND HISTORY

1. W. S. Holdsworth, *Essays in Law and History* (ed. Goodhart and Hanbury), pp. 21–3; F. W. Maitland, *Historical Essays* (ed. Helen Cam), pp. xi–xii.
2. J. G. A. Pocock, *The Ancient Constitution and the Feudal Law;* Maitland, *Collected Papers* (ed. H. A. L. Fisher), I, 490–1.
3. Holdsworth, *Essays*, pp. 25–9; *Diary and Correspondence of John Evelyn* (ed. W. Bray), p. 730.

I. OLD ENGLISH LAW

1. These and subsequent laws are quoted from *E.H.D.*, I (ed. Dorothy Whitelock).

2. The reflections on the feud are from M. Gluckman, *Custom and Conflict in Africa;* cf. J. M. Wallace-Hadrill, 'The Bloodfeud of the Franks' in *The Bulletin of the John Rylands Library* (1959).

3. *Njal's Saga* is translated in the Penguin Classics series; see Bede, *A History of the English Church and People* (Penguin Classics), p. 238, for the settlement of a feud between two English kings.

4. See Sir Henry Maine, *Ancient Law* (Everyman), p. 99, for the suggestion that the peace has patriarchal origins.

5. T. H. Aston, 'The Origins of the Manor in England', *T.R.H.S.* (1958); Joan Thirsk, 'The Common Fields', *Past and Present* (1964).

6. Helen Cam, 'The Evolution of the Medieval English Franchise', *Speculum* (1957).

7. *E.H.D.*, I, 556.

8. On Wulfstan and the laws, see Whitelock in *E.H.R.* (1948).

9. For examples of Anglo-Saxon land-books and wills, and their interrelationship, see *E.H.D.*, I, 472, 482-4, 549; for the latest discussion of them, E. John, *Land Tenure in Early England.*

10. Naomi Hurnard argues for the English origins of the jury in *E.H.R.* (1941).

11. V. H. Galbraith in *Proceedings of the British Academy* (1935); many examples in *E.H.D.*; T. A. M. Bishop and P. Chaplais, *Facsimiles of English Royal Writs presented to V. H. Galbraith.*

12. Florence Harmer, *Anglo-Saxon Writs*; G. Barraclough in *History* (1954).

2. THE COMMON LAW TAKES SHAPE

1. This chapter as a whole relies on H. G. Richardson and G. O. Sayles, *The Governance of Medieval England*; for the continuing argument about the origins of feudalism in England, see J. O. Prestwich in *Past and Present* (1963).

2. For the details of feudalism, see F. M. Stenton, *The First Century of English Feudalism*, and S. Painter, *Studies in the History of the Feudal Barony.*

3. J. Hurstfield, *The Queen's Wards.*

4. V. H. Galbraith in *E.H.R.* (1929); S. E. Thorne in the *C.L.J.* (1959); R. H. C. Davis in *History* (1964).

5. R. W. Southern in *Proceedings of the British Academy* (1962); J. C. Holt, *The Northerners*, p. 18.

6. *E.H.D.*, II (ed. D. C. Douglas and G. W. Greenaway), p. 433.

7. *E.H.D.*, II, 604.

8. *E.H.D.*, II, 486–583.
9. Richardson and Sayles, *Governance*.
10. V. H. Galbraith, *The Making of Domesday Book*; R. C. van Caenegem, *Royal Writs in England from the Conquest to Glanvill* (Selden Society, vol. 77), pp. 59 and 69 ff.
11. E. Miller in *E.H.R.* (1947).
12. Naomi Hurnard in *E.H.R.* (1941).
13. For the Assizes, see *E.H.D.*, II, 407–13, and Richardson and Sayles, *Governance*, appx iv.
14. See R. H. Evans, *Government*, plate 15, for a picture of a judicial combat in 1249.
15. The work of R. C. van Caenegem is the basis of what follows (see note 10).
16. F. W. Maitland, *The Forms of Action at Common Law*.
17. R. F. Hunnisett, *The Medieval Coroner*.
18. See Evans, *Government*, plate 16, for an eleventh-century picture of a king dispensing justice; the origins of the central courts are explored in detail by G. O. Sayles in *Select Cases in the Court of King's Bench* (Selden Society, vols. 55, 57, 58, 74, 76).
19. For the development of the Palace of Westminster, see now the official history of *The King's Works*, ed. R. A. Brown, H. M. Colvin and A. J. Taylor.
20. Doris Stenton in *Proceedings of the British Academy* (1958).
21. On the meaning of 'record' see S. E. Thorne in *Toronto Law Journal* (1937–8); the earliest plea-rolls were edited by Maitland for the Pipe Roll Society in 1891.
22. V. H. Galbraith, *Studies in the Public Records*.
23. Galbraith, *The Making of Domesday Book*.
24. S. J. Bailey in *C.L.J.* (1961).
25. The concepts of law and custom in Magna Carta are explored by Holt, *The Northerners;* see also, now, Professor Holt's book devoted to Magna Carta.
26. J. E. A. Jolliffe, *Angevin Kingship*. A certain violence of language became conventional in the king's writs: see Holt, *King John* (Historical Association Pamphlet).
27. Richardson and Sayles, *Governance*, p. 369.

3. ALL SORTS OF JUSTICES: THE CRIMINAL LAW TO 1642

1. A number of eyre-rolls have been edited by Doris Stenton for the Selden Society. See also C. A. F. Meekings, *Wiltshire Record*

Society (1961), for the most detailed account of the criminal side of the eyre. Much of this chapter is based on the writer's own unpublished work on the Shropshire eyre-roll of 1256.

2. Richardson and Sayles, *Select Cases of Procedure without Writ* (Selden Society, vol. 60), p. cxxxiii.

3. *ibid*; and W. C. Bolland, *Select Bills in Eyre* (Selden Society, vol. 30).

4. See Helen Cam, *Studies in the Hundred Rolls*, for a list of the eyres.

5. Indeed, it looks as though the commission of oyer and terminer was developed in the thirteenth century to deal with the spate of trespasses: see the various forms of the commission in the *Registrum Brevium* (1531).

6. A. Harding in *T.R.H.S.* (1960).

7. On the provost-marshal, see L. Boynton in *E.H.R.* (1962).

8. See Bertha Putnam, *Proceedings before the Justices of the Peace in the Fourteenth and Fifteenth Centuries*, and the bibliography there of Professor Putnam's other works.

9. E. L. G. Stones, *T.R.H.S.* (1957).

10. Cf. Helen Cam in *E.H.R.* (1924).

11. Sir Thomas Smith, *De Republica Anglorum*.

12. On the lists of J.P.s, see T. G. Barnes and A. Hassell Smith in the *B.I.H.R.* (1959).

13. T. G. Barnes, *The Clerk of the Peace in Caroline Somerset*; Gladys S. Thomson, *Lords Lieutenants in the Sixteenth Century*.

14. J. Hurstfield in the *Victoria County History of Wiltshire*, V (a mine of information on the history of local government); T. G. Barnes, *Somerset 1625–1640*; L. Hotson, *Shakespeare* v. *Shallow*, p. 175.

15. H. C. Johnson, *Minutes of Proceedings in Session, 1563, 1574, 1592* (Wiltshire Archaeological Society).

16. See, for example, A. K. R. Kiralfy, *A Source Book of English Law*, p. 321.

17. An up-to-date account of Star Chamber will be found in G. R. Elton, *The Tudor Constitution, Documents and Commentary*.

18. See L. Hotson, *Shakespeare* v. *Shallow*, p. 160, for an example of an information, and G. R. Elton in the *Cambridge Historical Journal* (1954) for informing as a business.

19. Sayles, *King's Bench*, IV, lxvii.

20. T. F. T. Plucknett, *T.R.H.S.* (1942); M. H. Keen, *T.R.H.S.* (1962).

21. For the medieval statutes on treason, see S. B. Chrimes and A. L. Brown, *Select Documents of English Constitutional History, 1307–1485*.

22. Evans, *Government*, plate 50.
23. P. Winfield in the *L.Q.R.* (1919).
24. Sayles, *King's Bench*, III, liv–lxxi; on maintenance, see A. L. Goodhart in *The Law in Action* (ed. R. E. Megarry), Vol. II.
25. This attitude was expressed in a famous case of 1605, *Rex* v. *Pickering*: see Kiralfy, *Source Book*, p. 321.
26. See Elton, *Tudor Constitution*, p. 175.
27. C. H. S. Fifoot, *English Law and Its Background*, p. 96.
28. For what follows, see Professor Plucknett's commentary in Putnam, *Proceedings before the Justices of the Peace*.
29. Evans, *Government*, plates 48 and 162; T. F. T. Plucknett, *Edward I and the Criminal Law*, p. 90; R. B. Pugh in *T.R.H.S.* (1955).
30. John Stow, *Survey of London*; Sir Thomas Smith, *De Republica Anglorum*; Henry Brinklow, *The Complaynt of Roderyck Mors* (Early English Text Society, 1874), pp. 27–8.
31. *William Lambarde and Local Government* (ed. Conyers Read); Evans, *Government*, plates 26–7.

4. PRIVATE LAW TO 1642

1. See W. Stubbs, *Select Charters*, for the text of Mortmain, Quia Emptores, and De Donis; and Plucknett, *The Legislation of Edward I*, for commentary.
2. H. E. Bell, *History of the Court of Wards*; J. Hurstfield in *L.Q.R.* (1949).
3. See F. H. Lawson, *The Rational Strength of English Law*, pp. 82–91.
4. C. Brooke and M. M. Postan, *Carte Nativorum* (Northamptonshire Record Society); E. A. Kosminsky, *Studies in the Agrarian History of England*.
5. M. E. Finch, *The Wealth of Five Northamptonshire Families* (Northamptonshire Record Society).
6. R. S. Hoyt, *The Royal Demesne in English Constitutional History*; on copyhold, C. M. Gray, *Copyhold, Equity and the Common Law*.
7. Richardson and Sayles, *Select Cases of Procedure without Writ*; S. F. C. Milsom in *L.Q.R.* (1958). For examples of the writ of trespass and the other new writs mentioned in this chapter, see Holdsworth, *History of English Law*, III. appx 1. For important cases, see Fifoot, *History and sources of the common law. Tort and contract*.
8. Milsom, *L.Q.R.* (1958).
9. Kiralfy, *Source Book*, pp. 128, 134; cf. Winfield in *L.Q.R.* (1926).

10. Kiralfy, *Source Book*, p. 147, for an example of the excuse of a vendor's deceit by the neglect of the buyer to have the goods weighed.
11. H. Hall, *Select Cases Concerning the Law Merchant*, II (Selden Society, vol. 46), p. xxi.
12. Kiralfy, *Source Book*, p. 197.
13. H. G. Richardson, *The English Jewry under the Angevin Kings*.
14. Finch, *Five Northamptonshire Families*, Isham of Lamport.
15. See Elton, *Tudor Constitution*, for the parliamentary opposition to the statute.
16. Simpson, *Land Law*, pp. 206 ff., for further explanation.
17. Kiralfy, *Source Book*, p. 268.
18. Finch, *Five Northamptonshire Families*.
19. J. P. Dawson, *A History of Lay Judges*, for the activity of the local courts.
20. Simpson, *Land Law*, p. 160; R. L. Henry, *Contracts in the Local Courts of Medieval England*.

5. THE OLD PROCEDURE

1. For all procedure, see Maitland, *Forms of Action*.
2. The bill of Middlesex is discussed by Marjorie Blatcher, in *Elizabethan Government and Society* (ed. S. T. Bindoff, J. Hurstfield and C. H. Williams).
3. On essoins, see Doris M. Stenton, *Pleas Before the King or His Justices*, I (Selden Society, vol. 67).
4. Patricia M. Barnes, 'The Anstey Case', in *A Medieval Miscellany for Doris Mary Stenton* (Pipe Roll Society, 1960).
5. Holdsworth, *History of English Law*, III., appx 7.
6. Kiralfy, *Source Book*, p. 49, for an example. On the general development of pleading, see *Novae Narrationes*, ed. Elsie Shanks and S. F. C. Milsom (Selden Society, Vol. 80), pp. xxv–xxxix.
7. Plucknett, *Concise History*, pp. 122–3.
8. Sir Thomas Smith, *De Republica Anglorum*.
9. Margaret Hastings, *The Court of Common Pleas in Fifteenth-Century England*, is the authority on late-medieval changes in procedure.
10. W. Ullmann in *L.Q.R.* (1946).
11. The thesis is J. P. Dawson's in *A History of Lay Judges*.
12. C. H. Williams, 'A Fifteenth-Century Law-Suit' in *L.Q.R.* (1924).
13. G. J. Turner and T. F. T. Plucknett, *Brevia Placitata* (Selden Society, vol. 66), pp. 20, 26.

14. C. Johnson on thirteenth-century procedure in *E.H.R.* (1947).
15. W. C. Bolland, *Chief Justice William Bereford.*
16. Kiralfy, *Source Book*, pp. 27, 43.
17. Kiralfy, *Source Book*, pp. 150, 187; *Year Book for 33 Edward I* (Rolls Series 1879), p. 64.
18. 2 Brownlow 255 at 264–6; 123 E.R. 928, at 933–4; cf. Coke's own report, 8 Co. Rep. 113b.
19. Plucknett, *Concise History*, p. 132.

6. THE NEW PROCEDURE AND NEW COURTS

1. Hastings, *Common Pleas*, pp. 186–7.
2. Dawson, *Lay Judges*; P. M. Barnes in *A Medieval Miscellany*, p. 6.
3. R. G. Marsden, *Select Pleas in the Court of Admiralty*, I (Selden Society, vol. 6), pp. 149 ff.
4. Kiralfy, *Source Book*, pp. 50–51.
5. Sayles, *Court of King's Bench*, II (Selden Society, vol. 57), pp. ci–cii.
6. Hastings, *Common Pleas*, pp. 31, 37, 40–41.
7. Elton, *Tudor Constitution*, p. 155.
8. Kiralfy, *Source Book*, pp. 272–3.
9. See the Public Record Office *Calendar of Miscellaneous Inquisitions*.
10. H. Coing on the *Denunciatio Evangelica* in *L.Q.R.* (1955); and A. D. Hargreaves on the Latin side of Chancery in *L.Q.R.* (1952).
11. Hargreaves, *L.Q.R.* (1952).
12. Kiralfy, *Source Book*, pp. 260–61.
13. W. P. Baildon, *Select Cases in the Court of Chancery* (1364–1471) (Selden Society, vol. 10), p. 30; Kiralfy, *Source Book*, p. 264.
14. Kiralfy, *Source Book*, p. 260.
15. Kiralfy, *Source Book*, p. 282; W. J. Jones on the Elizabethan Chancery, *American Journal of Legal History* (1961 and 1962).
16. J. Ritchie, *Reports of Cases decided in Chancery by Francis Bacon*, p. 173.
17. I. S. Leadam, *Select Cases before the King's Council in the Star Chamber* (Selden Society, vol. 16), p. xxii.
18. Elton, *Tudor Constitution*, p. 154.
19. J. R. Lander in *E.H.R.* (1958).
20. Elton, *Tudor Constitution*, pp. 87 ff.
21. Elton, *Tudor Constitution*, pp. 104, 107–9, 111.

22. Elton, *Tudor Constitution*, pp. 112, 114.
23. Elton, *Tudor Constitution*, p. 154.
24. Elton, *Tudor Constitution*, pp. 89, 161; S. E. Lehmberg in *Huntington Library Quarterly* (1961).
25. Kiralfy, *Source Book*, pp. 313, 319–20; Elton, *Tudor Constitution*, p. 178.
26. C. Ogilvie, *The King's Government and the Common Law*, p. 101.
27. C. G. Bayne and W. H. Dunham, *Select Cases in the Council of Henry VII* (Selden Society, vol. 75), pp. clxiii–clxiv.
28. Elton, *Tudor Constitution*, pp. 165, 172.
29. Kiralfy, *Source Book*, p. 325.
30. T. G. Barnes in *American Journal of Legal History* (1961 and 1962).
31. Bayne and Dunham, *Select Cases in the Council*, pp. xxiv ff.
32. Elton, *Tudor Constitution*, pp. 188, 191; Kiralfy, *Source Book*, p. 302; I. S. Leadam, *Select Pleas in the Court of Requests* (Selden Society, vol. 12), pp. liv ff.
33. C. A. J. Skeel, *The Council in the Marches of Wales*; P. Williams, *The Council in the Marches of Wales under Elizabeth*; R. R. Reid, *The King's Council in the North*; Evans, *Government*, plates 61–3; Elton, *Tudor Constitution*, p. 210.
34. Kiralfy, *Source Book*, p. 304.
35. R. Somerville on the Court of Duchy Chamber in *T.R.H.S.* (1941).
36. Bayne and Dunham, *Select Cases in the Council*, pp. liv ff.
37. Plucknett in *T.R.H.S.* (1936); Elton in *B.I.H.R.* (1952); Bayne and Dunham, *Select Cases in the Council*, p. lxii; Elton, *Tudor Constitution*, pp. 160, 168, 185.
38. Bayne and Dunham, *Select Cases in the Council*, pp. xxv ff.; Somerville in *E.H.R.* (1939); Elton, *Tudor Constitution*, pp. 128–46.
39. B. L. Woodcock, *Medieval Ecclesiastical Courts in the Diocese of Canterbury*.
40. Woodcock, *Ecclesiastical Courts*; R. A. Marchant, *The Puritans and the Church Courts in the Diocese of York*.
41. Ogilvie, *The King's Government*, p. 100; Elton, *The Tudor Constitution*, pp. 206, 223.
42. G. D. Squibb, *The High Court of Chivalry*.
43. D. Hay in *T.R.H.S.* (1954).
44. Cf. p. 78 above; M. Keen, *T.R.H.S.* (1962).
45. Squibb, *Court of Chivalry*, pp. 59–60, 138–61.
46. Squibb, *Court of Chivalry*, p. 165.

7. THE LEGAL PROFESSION

1. Richardson and Sayles, *The Governance of Medieval England*, pp. 269 ff.; N. Denholm-Young, *Seignorial Administration*; R. Somerville, *History of the Duchy of Lancaster*, Vol. I.
2. Maitland, quoted Plucknett, *Concise History*, p. 220.
3. See Lady Stenton's account in vol. 53 of the Selden Society.
4. Sayles, *King's Bench*, I; for the staff of Common Pleas, see Hastings.
5. Sayles, *King's Bench*, IV, ix ff.
6. M. Birks, *Gentlemen of the Law*.
7. Plucknett, *Concise History*, pp. 217–18.
8. Pollock and Maitland, *History of English Law*, I, 211 ff.
9. Sayles, *King's Bench*, V, xxix ff.
10. *The Canterbury Tales* (ed. N. Coghill, Penguin Books), pp. 33–4.
11. Sir John Fortescue, *De Laudibus Legum Anglie* (ed. S. B. Chrimes).
12. Bolland, *Bereford*; Kiralfy, *Source Book*, pp. 27, 259.
13. *The Paston Letters* (ed. Gairdner), I, 135, 139, 222, 407; II, 423.
14. Ogilvie, *The King's Government*, p. 83.
15. Bishop and Chaplais, *Facsimiles of English Royal Writs*; Chaplais in *A Medieval Miscellany*.
16. On the court officials, see Hastings, *Common Pleas*, and G. E. Aylmer, *The King's Servants*.
17. Sayles, *King's Bench*, V, xxix ff.; Bolland in Selden Society, vol. 45, pp. xliv ff.; J. Ll. J. Edwards, *The Law Officers of the Crown* (which appeared too late to be fully utilized).
18. Kiralfy, *Source Book*, p. 31.
19. Conyers Read, *William Lambarde and Local Government*, p. 69.
20. R. Hilton in *E.H.R.* (1941).
21. T. G. Barnes, *The Clerk of the Peace in Caroline Somerset*.
22. J. E. Neale, *Elizabeth I and her Parliaments*, I, 92.
23. John Stow, *Survey of London*; Fortescue, *De Laudibus*.
24. C. Carr, *Pension Book of Clement's Inn* (Selden Society, vol. 78); R. Roxburgh, *The Origins of Lincoln's Inn*.
25. T. F. Tout in *Collected Papers*, II, on Inns of Chancery.
26. Maitland on the records of Lincoln's Inn, in *Collected Papers*, III.
27. See the invaluable admissions and minute books of the various Inns of Court.
28. Carr, *Clement's Inn*, p. 220; G. J. Turner in Selden Society, vol. 26; S. E. Thorne, *Readings and Moots at the Inns of Court* (Selden Society, vol. 71).

29. Fortescue, *De Laudibus*, pp. 195–6; H. G. Richardson in *L.Q.R.* (1941) and the *Bulletin of the John Rylands Library* (1939).
30. J. H. Hexter in *Journal of Modern History* (1950).
31. W. J. Jones in *American Journal of Legal History* (1961 and 1962).
32. T. G. Barnes in *American Journal of Legal History* (1961 and 1962); Kiralfy, *Source Book*, p. 334; Elton, *Tudor Constitution*, pp. 140, 176; Squibb, *Court of Chivalry*.
33. Marchant, *The Church Courts*, p. 53, for the career of Edward Mottershed; Squibb, *Court of Chivalry*.
34. Elton, *Tudor Constitution*, p. 214; P. M. Barnes in *A Medieval Miscellany*, pp. 7, 16; C. Duggan in *B.I.H.R.* (1962); Dawson, *Lay Judges*.

8. LAWYERS AND LAW BOOKS

1. See generally, T. F. T. Plucknett, *Early English Legal Literature*; P. H. Winfield, *The Chief Sources of English Legal History*.
2. Maitland on the Register of Writs in *Collected Papers*, II; Holdsworth, *History of English Law*, II, appx 5.
3. *E.H.D.*, II, 475; H. A. Hollond on legal authors in *C.L.J.* (1947).
4. Richardson in *L.Q.R.* (1941) and *Bulletin of the John Rylands Library* (1939); Bolland in Selden Society, vol. 27, pp. xliv–xlvii; Maitland on a thirteenth-century conveyancer in *Collected Papers*, II.
5. Kiralfy, *Source Book*, pp. 192 ff.
6. The debate on the Year Books is best followed in the *Guide to the Publications of the Selden Society*, pp. 50, 53, 55, 57, 73, 79, 118; see also Kiralfy, *Source Book*, p. 131; A. W. B. Simpson in *L.Q.R.* (1957); H. G. Richardson's review in *L.Q.R.* (1954).
7. On sixteenth-century legal literature, see B. H. Putnam, *Early Treatises on the Practice of the Justices of the Peace*.
8. Simpson on Keilwey's Reports in *L.Q.R.* (1957).
9. J. W. Wallace, *The Reporters Arranged and Characterized*; Evans, *Government*, plate 68.
10. The most modern edition of Bracton is by G. E. Woodbine; the translation is from Sir Travers Twiss's edition in the Rolls Series (1878–83).
11. Teetor in *American Journal of Legal History* (1963); Maitland, *English Law and the Renaissance*; Evans, *Government*, plate 66.
12. Fortescue, *De Laudibus*, ed. Chrimes.
13. Smith, *De Republica Anglorum*, ed. L. Alston; F. Bacon, *The Advancement of Learning*; *Essay on Revenge*.

14. Selden, *Table Talk, sub* 'Conscience' and 'Equity'.
15. Selden, *Dissertatio ad Fletam*, ed. Ogg; *Table Talk, sub* 'Jurisdiction' and 'Marriage'; Thorne in *Toronto Law Journal* (1937–8).
16. Maitland, *English Law and the Renaissance*; Putnam, *Early Treatises*.
17. J. P. Collas in Selden Society, vol. 70; Richardson's review in *L.Q.R.* (1954).
18. J. E. S. Simon in *L.Q.R.* (1960–62).
19. Hastings, *Common Pleas*, p. 29; W. N. Hargreaves-Mawdsley, *A History of Legal Dress*.
20. W. Ives in *L.Q.R.* (1959); Sayles, *King's Bench*, IV; Squibb, *Court of Chivalry*, p. 176.
21. Sylvia Thrupp, *The Merchant Class of Medieval London*; A. R. Wagner, *English Genealogy*, pp. 164–5; Hastings, *Common Pleas*, cap. 5.
22. Finch, *Five Northamptonshire Families*; A. Simpson, *The Wealth of the Gentry*; will at Somerset House, PCC 90 Capell.
23. Aylmer, *The King's Servants*, pp. 328 ff.; see, for comparison, Simpson, *The Wealth of the Gentry*, on the merchant, Cullum.
24. Aylmer, *The King's Servants*, pp. 223, 231–2, 295 ff.; Hastings, *Common Pleas*, cap. vii.
25. Hastings, *Common Pleas*, pp. 104, 252; Sayles, *King's Bench*, V; Ogilvie, *The King's Government*, p. 85.
26. Aylmer, *The King's Servants*, pp. 179, 210; Sayles, *King's Bench*, I and IV; Hastings, *Common Pleas*, p. 95.
27. Ogilvie, *The King's Government*, p. 84; Hastings, *Common Pleas*, pp. 17–18, 170; Birks, *Gentlemen of the Law*, pp. 115–16; P.R.O., St. Ch. 3/2/7 (I owe this reference to Mr A. Malkiewicz).
28. Ogilvie, *The King's Government*, p. 41; G. R. Owst, *Literature and the Pulpit in Medieval England*, pp. 341–2, 346; L. Hotson, *Shakespeare v. Shallow*; Shakespeare, *The Merchant of Venice*.
29. J. S. Roskell, *The Commons in the Parliament of 1422*; May McKisack, *The Parliamentary Representation of the English Boroughs*; J. E. Neale, *The Elizabethan House of Commons*, p. 304.
30. Neale, *Elizabethan Commons*, pp. 372, 377; *Elizabeth and her Parliaments* (2 vols.).
31. Neale, *Elizabethan Commons*, p. 306; Ogilvie, *The King's Government*, p. 151.
32. Thorne, *Sir Edward Coke* (Selden Society lecture); Fuller, *The Worthies of England*.
33. R. G. Usher in *E.H.R.* (1903).

34. Neale, *Elizabethan Commons*, pp. 354–5, 359, 376, 396, 405;
Elizabeth and her Parliaments, II, 248–50, 313–17, 320.

9. LAW IN THE MAKING

1. See, generally, C. K. Allen, *Law in the Making* (7th ed., 1964);
and, on the relationship between law and society, H. L. A.
Hart, *The Concept of Law*; Maine, *Ancient Law*; and Lucy Mair,
Primitive Government.
2. Plucknett, *The Legislation of Edward I*; Simpson, *Land Law*, pp.
104, 115.
3. Quoted by J. G. A. Pocock, *The Ancient Constitution*.
4. Allen, *Law in the Making*, pp. 134, 144, 154; Kiralfy, *Source
Book*, p. 259; D. A. Binchy on 'The Irish Law Tracts' in *The
Proceedings of the British Academy* (1943).
5. W. Rees, *South Wales and the March*.
6. Simpson, *Land Law*, pp. 42–3.
7. Allen, *Law in the Making*, p. 367.
8. Sayles, *King's Bench*, cviii ff.; Shakespeare, *The Merchant of Venice*.
9. On the forged Year Book, see Vernon Harcourt, *His Grace the
Steward and Trial by Peers*, p. 416; on the general development of
stare decisis, T. E. Lewis in *L.Q.R.* (1930); see also Kiralfy,
Source Book, p. 27; Mary Hemmant, *Select Cases in the Exchequer
Chamber* (Selden Society, vols. 51 and 64).
10. Thorne, *Sir Edward Coke*.
11. D. O. Wagner in the *Economic History Review* (1935–6).
12. Plucknett, *Legislation of Edward I*, cap. I; F. Kern, *Kingship and
Law in the Middle Ages;* Winfield, *Sources of Legal History*, pp.
72–3.
13. B. Wilkinson on the creation of writs in his *Studies in the Constitutional History of the Thirteenth and Fourteenth Centuries*.
14. Richardson and Sayles in *L.Q.R.* (1961).
15. Maitland, *Memoranda de Parliamento* (Rolls Series, 1893); J. G.
Edwards on justice in early parliaments in *B.I.H.R.* (1954);
G. L. Haskins on petitions in *E.H.R.* (1938); Richardson and
Sayles on the early statutes in *L.Q.R.* (1934).
16. Doris Rayner in *E.H.R.* (1941) and A. R. Myers in *E.H.R.*
(1937) on petitions; see Evans, *Government*, plates 98, 153, for the
petition as the modern legislative form.
17. R. W. K. Hinton in *Cambridge Historical Journal* (1957).
18. C. Hughes, *The British Statute Book*, cap. 3; O. C. Williams,
History of Private Bill Procedure.

19. Allen, *Law in the Making*, p. 309; Plucknett, *Statutes and their Interpretation in the Fourteenth Century*.

20. W. Ullmann, *Principles of Government and Politics in the Middle Ages*; Sayles, *King's Bench*, III, xxxix ff.; Helen Cam, 'The Legislators of Medieval England', *Proceedings of the British Academy* (1945).

21. Holdsworth, *Essays in Law and History*, pp. 153–4.

22. Elton, *Tudor Constitution*, pp. 113, 179–84, 209.

23. Steele, *Tudor Proclamations*; Paul L. Hughes and James F. Larkin, *Tudor Royal Proclamations*, I (1964); Hinton in *Cambridge Historical Journal* (1957); Elton, *Tudor Constitution*, pp. 20–23, 26–7, 469; G. Barraclough in *L.Q.R.* (1940).

24. Plucknett, *Statutes and their Interpretation*; Sayles in *E.H.R.* (1937) and *King's Bench*, III; Allen, *Law in the Making*, p. 440.

25. See Plucknett's review of Thorne's edition of the Discourse in *L.Q.R.* (1944); Allen, *Law in the Making*, pp. 491, 495.

26. Allen, *Law in the Making*, pp. 456–7, 496–9; Kiralfy, *Source Book*, p. 30.

27. Barraclough in *L.Q.R.* (1940); Cam, *Proceedings of the British Academy* (1945); Plucknett, *Legislation of Edward I*, pp. 84–6; Bindoff in *Elizabethan Government and Society* (ed. Bindoff, Hurstfield and Williams).

28. Cam, *Proceedings of the British Academy* (1945), pp. 151, 156–7.

29. Allen, *Law in the Making*, pp. 467, 473; Elton in *E.H.R.* (1949 and 1951) and *B.I.H.R.* (1952); *Tudor Constitution*, p. 131; L. Stone in *B.I.H.R.* (1951).

30. Allen, *Law in the Making*, pp. 285 ff.

31. Simpson, *Land Law*, pp. 34, 42–3; Allen, *Law in the Making*, pp. 44, 302–8; S. J. Bailey in *L.Q.R.* (1932).

32. Edmund Dudley, *The Tree of Commonwealth* (ed. D. M. Brodie); W. Ullmann in the *Reports of the 11th Congress of Historical Sciences* (Stockholm, 1960), Vol. III.

33. A. P. d'Entrèves, *Natural Law*; Maitland, *English Law and the Renaissance*, p. 150; J. W. Gough, *Fundamental Law in English History*, pp. 18–20, 24; Allen, *Law in the Making*, p. 447.

34. Thrupp, *The Merchant Class of Medieval London*; Plucknett in *T.R.H.S.* (1936); Gough, *Fundamental Law*, pp. 4, 12.

35. Allen, *Law in the Making*, pp. 387–407; Gough, *Fundamental Law*, pp. 9, 14, 19, 27; Kiralfy, *Source Book*, p. 267; P. Vinogradoff in *L.Q.R.* (1908).

36. P. Vinogradoff, *Roman Law in Medieval Europe*; J. K. B. Nicholas,

Roman Law, pp. 23 ff.; F. Schulz in *The Juridical Review* (1942); Jane Sayers in *B.I.H.R.* (1962).

37. Maitland, *English Law and the Renaissance*, p. 144; H. C. Lea, *The Inquisition* (introduction by W. Ullmann).

38. Allen, *Law in the Making*, pp. 272 ff.

10. LAW IN ENGLISH HISTORY

1. Hastings, *Common Pleas*, p. 82; Aylmer, *The King's Servants*, p. 109.

2. Hastings, *Common Pleas*, p. 94; Sayles, *King's Bench*, II, lxxxiv; Evans, *Government*, plate 58; J. D. M. Derrett on the trial of Sir Thomas More in *E.H.R.* (1964); H. L. Stephen in *T.R.H.S.* (1919) on the trial of Sir Walter Raleigh.

3. Ogilvie, *The King's Government*, p. 86.

4. Edith G. Henderson, *The Foundations of English Administrative Law*; Kiralfy, *Source Book*, p. 38.

5. G. R. Owst, *Literature and the Pulpit in Medieval England*, p. 344; W. J. Jones in the *American Journal of Legal History* (1962); H. Brinklow, *The Complaynt of Roderyck Mors*, (Early English Text Society, 1874).

6. Thrupp, *Merchant Class*, p. 298; Neale, *Elizabeth and her Parliaments*, II, 399; Dawson, *Lay Judges*.

7. R. W. Southern, *St Anselm and his Biographer*, p. 112; *Calendar of the Hatfield MSS* (Historical MSS Commission).

8. N. J. O'Conor, *Godes Peace and the Queenes*; for campaigns of litigation, see also L. Hotson, *Shakespeare v. Shallow*.

9. P. Williams in the *Bulletin of the Board of Celtic Studies* (1954–6), p. 295.

10. C. Hill, 'The Norman Yoke', in *Puritanism and Revolution*.

11. Maitland on corporations in *Collected Papers*, Vol. III; M. Weinbaum, *The Incorporation of Boroughs*.

12. G. A. Williams, *Medieval London*, pp. 78 ff.; Helen Miller in *B.I.H.R.* (1962).

13. Evans, *Government*, plates 19, 22, 29, 46, 119; *Paston Letters* (ed. Gairdner), I, 186.

14. Camden Society (1879).

15. On the burst of charitable enterprises, see the recent works of W. K. Jordan.

16. Elton, *Tudor Constitution*, p. 17; B. Tierney in *Speculum* (1963); J. P. Cooper in *Britain and The Netherlands*, ed. J. S. Bromley and E. H. Kossmann.

17. G. Post in *Traditio* (1945–6); Pollock and Maitland, *History of English Law*, I, 336; Helen Cam in *History* (1926); Elton, *Tudor Constitution*, p. 9.

18. Elton, *Tudor Constitution*, pp. 19–20; Sayles, *King's Bench*, III, xli, xliii–liii; Vinogradoff in *L.Q.R.* (1913).

19. J. R. Tanner, *Constitutional Documents of the Reign of James I*, pp. 6, 13.

20. G. D. G. Hall in *L.Q.R.* (1953); S. R. Gardiner, *Constitutional Documents of the Puritan Revolution*, pp. 57 ff., 66 ff., 105 ff.

21. Tanner, *Documents*, pp. 7–8; Brinklow, *Roderyck Mors*, pp. 29 ff.; A. Ogle, *The Tragedy of the Lollard's Tower*; Elton, *Tudor Constitution*, pp. 226, 324–6, 344–9; in *E.H.R.* (1951); J. P. Cooper in *E.H.R.* (1957).

22. Shakespeare, *The Merry Wives of Windsor*, I, I, i; Elton, *Tudor Constitution*, p. 97.

23. Aylmer, *The King's Servants*, p. 246; Elton, *Tudor Constitution*, p. 188; Kiralfy, *Source Book*, pp. 47, 364; Hastings, *Common Pleas*, p. 162; S. B. Chrimes in *L.Q.R.* (1956); Tanner, *Documents*, pp. 174–5; G. A. Schubert in *Toronto Law Journal* (1951–2).

24. Elton, *Tudor Constitution*, pp. 254 ff.; Tanner, *Documents*, pp. 215, 272 ff., 319; Gough, *Fundamental Law*, pp. 7–8; S. E. Thorne in *Toronto Law Journal* (1937–8).

25. W. Notestein in *Proceedings of the British Academy* (1924); Plucknett, *T.R.H.S.* (1942, 1951–3); Gardiner, *Documents*, pp. 3 ff.

26. Gardiner, *Documents*, pp. 156 ff.; *MSS of the House of Lords*, XI (ed. M. F. Bond for the Historical MSS Commission), p. 238.

27. Maine, *Ancient Law*, p. 68; W. G. Beasley and E. G. Pulleyblank, *Historians of China and Japan*, pp. 46, etc.; Maitland, *English Law and the Renaissance*. Much of the following is based on Pocock, *The Ancient Constitution and the Feudal Law*.

28. Gough, *Fundamental Law*; S. E. Thorne, 'Dr Bonham's Case', *L.Q.R.* (1938).

29. Hinton, *E.H.R.* (1960); Fortescue, *De Laudibus*, cap. xxxvi; C. B. MacPherson, *The Political Theory of Possessive Individualism*.

30. Ogilvie, *The King's Government*, pp. 132, 151–2; Maitland, *English Law and the Renaissance*; Elton, *Tudor Constitution*, p. 189; Kiralfy, *Source Book*, p. 312; Squibb, *Court of Chivalry*, pp. 62–7.

31. Gardiner, *Documents*, pp. 179 ff.; Ogilvie, *The King's Government*, p. 151; Aylmer, *The King's Servants*, pp. 418–19.

II. THE AGE OF IMPROVISATION, 1642–1789

1. Gardiner, *Constitutional Documents*, pp. 357–80, 387.
2. F. A. Inderwick, *The Interregnum*; G. B. Nourse in *L.Q.R.* (1959); Gough, *Fundamental Law*; Ogilvie, *The King's Government*, p. 113.
3. Gardiner, *Constitutional Documents*, p. 290; W. E. Tate, *The Parish Chest*, pp. 46–7.
4. F. W. Maitland, *Historical Essays* (ed. Helen Cam), p. 113.
5. D. H. Pennington and I. A. Roots, *The Committee at Stafford*; Max Beloff, *Public Order and Popular Disturbances, 1660–1714*; Sidney and Beatrice Webb, *The Development of English Local Government* (Oxford, 1963), pp. 3, 6, 54; W. C. Costin and J. Steven Watson, *The Law and Working of the Constitution*, I, 130.
6. G. E. Mingay, *English Landed Society in the Eighteenth Century*. p. 119; Henry Fielding, *Tom Jones*, Book 2, cap. vi; E. Neville Williams, *The Eighteenth-Century Constitution*, pp. 280, 287, 289, 290, 293, 318; William Cowper, *Letters* (Everyman), p. 362; *Wiltshire Quarter-Sessions and Assizes*, 1736 (ed. J. P. M. Fowle), pp. xxxiii–iv, xxxix, 41.
7. Dawson, *History of Lay Judges*; Court Leet Records of the Manor of Manchester, 1552 – 1846 (12 vols., Manchester, 1884 – 90); Tate, *The Parish Chest*; Williams, *The Eighteenth-Century Constitution*, pp. 271, 302; G. W. Keeton on Jeffreys in *Welsh History Review* (1962).
7. Dawson, *History of Lay Judges*; Tate, *The Parish Chest*; Williams, *The Eighteenth-Century Constitution*, pp. 271, 302; G. W. Keeton on Jeffreys in *Welsh History Review* (1962).
8. *Sir Peter Leicester's Charges* (ed. Elizabeth M. Halcrow, Chetham Society, 1953); Webbs, *The Development of English Local Government*, pp. 12, 50, 57; Williams, *The Eighteenth-Century Constitution*, pp. 279–82, 313; *Pepys's Diary*, 24 March 1668; Horace Walpole, *Selected Letters* (Everyman), pp. 368, 502, 515; R. J. Mitchell and M. D. R. Leys, *A History of London Life* (Pelican Books), pp. 243–6; G. Rudé on the Gordon Riots in *T.R.H.S.* (1956).
9. Walpole, *Letters*, pp. 505–6; *Life and Times of Anthony à Wood* (World's Classics), p. 221; Webbs, *The Development of English Local Government*, pp. 83–4; John Gay, *The Beggar's Opera*.
10. Beloff, *Public Order*; Walpole, *Letters*, pp. 496–7.
11. Webbs, *The Development of English Local Government*, p. 55; Min-

gay, *English Landed Society*, p. 118; Mitchell and Leys, *London Life*, pp. 234–8; L. Radzinowicz, *A History of English Criminal Law*, III. 29 ff.; Evans, *Government*, plate 155.

12. Mingay, *English Landed Society*, p. 276; Costin and Watson, I, 123, 133, 135; Evans, *Government*, plate 157.

13. Radzinowicz, *Criminal Law*, I, 4, 41 ff.; J. Heath, *Eighteenth Century Penal Theory*, pp. 18–23; Kiralfy, *Source Book*, pp. 32, 313, 335.

14. David Foxon in *The Book Collector* (Winter, 1963); Costin and Watson, I, 258 ff., 285–6; Williams, *Eighteenth-Century Constitution*, p. 399; A. F. Havighurst in *L.Q.R.* (1953).

15. Costin and Watson, I, 226, 245, 252; Williams, *Eighteenth-Century Constitution*, p. 404; C. H. S. Fifoot, *Lord Mansfield*, pp. 42 ff.; Lord Denning, *From Precedent to Precedent* (Romanes Lecture), pp. 5–8.

16. *Wiltshire Quarter-Sessions*, pp. xxxi, xlvi; Costin and Watson, I, 291 ff.

17. Costin and Watson, I, 46 ff.

18. Costin and Watson, I, 80 ff.; Stephen, *History of the Criminal Law*, III, 371–88.

19. *Wiltshire Quarter-Sessions*, p. 119.

20. Evans, *Government*, plates 168–70; Walpole, *Letters*, p. 501; Radzinowicz, *Criminal Law*, I, 206 ff.

21. Johnson, *The Rambler*, no. 114; Radzinowicz, *Criminal Law*, I, 83 ff.

22. Radzinowicz, *Criminal Law*, I, 107 ff., 140 ff.; Evans, *Government*, plate 172.

23. cf. Wiltshire Quarter-Sessions, p. 119; Fielding, *Amelia*, I, caps. 3–4.

24. C .K .Allen, *Law in the Making*, pp. 380–81; D. E. C. Yale, *Lord Nottingham's Chancery Cases*, I (Selden Society, vol. 73), pp. xii–lxiii; Ogilvie, *The King's Government*, p. 91.

25. C. H. S. Fifoot, *English Law and Its Background*, pp. 123–5; H. J. Habbakuk in *Britain and the Netherlands*, ed. J. S. Bromley and E. H. Kossmann; Mingay, *English Landed Society*, pp. 34 ff., 87.

26. Mingay, *English Landed Society*, pp. 48–9, 67–70; Fifoot, *English Law*, p. 138.

27. Yale, *Lord Nottingham's Chancery Cases*, II (Selden Society, vol. 79), pp. 30–62, 87 ff., 100 ff.

28. Yale, II, 30–62.

29. Yale, II, 8, 65–6; W. E. Tate on the local registries in *B.I.H.R.* (1943–5).

30. Kiralfy, *Source Book*, p. 296; Yale, I, p. lxxxiv.
31. Maitland, *Historical Essays*, p. 116.
32. Fifoot, *Lord Mansfield*, pp. 136, 158–97.
33. Fifoot, *Lord Mansfield*, pp. 183, 188; Holdsworth's opinion is quoted in Plucknett, *Concise History*, p. 250.
34. Fifoot, *Lord Mansfield*, pp. 52–81.
35. Fifoot, *Lord Mansfield*, p. 62.
36. Fifoot, *Lord Mansfield*, p. 53; *Lord Eldon's Anecdote Book* (ed. A. L. J. Lincoln and R. L. McEwen), pp. 159 ff.; M. J. Pritchard in *C.L.J.* (1960).
37. Kiralfy, *Source Book*, pp. 157 ff.; Fifoot, *Lord Mansfield*, p. 23.
38. Fifoot, *Lord Mansfield*, pp. 118–57; Holdsworth, *L.Q.R.* (1939).
39. Fifoot, *Lord Mansfield*, p. 151; *English Law*, p. 102.
40. Holdsworth, *History of English Law*, VI, appx 4; Fifoot, *Lord Mansfield*, p. 14.
41. Fifoot, *Lord Mansfield*, pp. 4, 177; Costin and Watson, I, 378–82.
42. Fifoot, *English Law*, pp. 116–20, 126–30; Maitland, *Historical Essays*, p. 116; Costin and Watson, I, 129.
43. Oliver Goldsmith, *Citizen of the World*, letter xcvii; R. Robson, *The Attorney in Eighteenth-Century England*; Birks, *Gentlemen of the Law*, pp. 118 ff.
44. Birks, *Gentlemen of the Law*, p. 128.
45. Robson, *The Attorney*, pp. 72, 167; R. L. Hine, *Confessions of an Uncommon Attorney*.
46. Carr, *Clements' Inn*, pp. xxx, xxxiv; Fifoot, *Lord Mansfield*, pp. 29–30.
47. Paul Lucas in *E.H.R.* (1962), p. 456; H. G. Hanbury, *The Vinerian Chair and Legal Education*; Robson, *The Attorney*, p. 45.
48. Robson, *The Attorney*, pp. 10, 18–19, 29, 185; Birks, *Gentlemen of the Law*, pp. 135, 142.
49. Robson, *The Attorney*, pp. 80–81, 119–33, 147, 152–4, 162; Birks, *Gentlemen of the Law*, p. 134.
50. Yale, *Lord Nottingham's Chancery Cases*, I, p. xiv; Lucas, *E.H.R.* (1962); L. B. Namier, *The Structure of Politics at the Accession of George III* (2nd ed.), pp. 42–4; Fifoot, *Lord Mansfield*, pp. 36 ff.
51. Webbs, *The Development of English Local Government*, pp. 3–4; Williams, *Eighteenth-Century Constitution*, pp. 314 ff.; Mingay, *English Landed Society*, pp. 180 ff.; J. Simmons, *Transport*, plate 46.
52. Costin and Watson, I, 69, 163–6, 249, 256–8.
53. Gough, *Fundamental Law*, p. 133; Costin and Watson, I, 193 ff., 207, 228, 278 ff.

54. Allen, *Law in the Making*, p. 482; Goldsmith, *Citizen of the World*, letter xcvii; Fifoot, *Lord Mansfield*, pp. 78, 203 ff.
55. Kiralfy, *Source Book*, pp. 154 ff.; H. R. Gray, *The Law of Civil Injuries*, p. 85.
56. Costin and Watson, I, 289, 315; Evans, *Government*, plates 112, 118.
57. Costin and Watson, I, 254, 288.
58. Namier, *Structure of Politics*, p. 43.
59. Gough, *Fundamental Law*, p. 1; *Locke's Political Philosophy*, pp. 29–30; Pocock, *The Ancient Constitution*, p. 229.
60. Costin and Watson, I, 236, 278–81, 313.
61. Williams, *Eighteenth-Century Constitution*, p. 171; Goldsmith, *Citizen of the World*, letter xcvii; Fifoot, *English Law*, p. 129.

12. EMPIRE AND COMMERCE: THE EXPANSION OF THE COMMON LAW

1. G. W. S. Barrow, *B.I.H.R.* (1956); Costin and Watson, I, 102; *Introduction to Scottish Legal History* (Stair Society, vol. 20), pp. 50–51, 55; F. Moran in *L.Q.R.* (1960); Mingay, *English Landed Society*, pp. 43–7; A. Gwynn in *T.R.H.S.* (1960).
2. Maitland, *English Law and the Renaissance*, pp. 93–4; M. Clark, *Sources of Australian History*, p. 113; A. S. Keith, *Speeches and Documents on British Colonial Policy*, I, 7, 61–2, 79; articles by J. Latham and G. V. V. Nicholls in *L.Q.R.* (1960).
3. V. Bose in *L.Q.R.* (1960); J. D. M. Derrett in *Comparative Studies in Society and History* (1961–2).
4. Clark, *Sources of Australian History*, pp. 137–8, 213; Stephen, *History of the Criminal Law*, III, 283–4, 294, 344–5; J. Steven Watson, *The Reign of George III*, p. 312.
5. C. T. Carr, *Select Charters of Trading Companies* (Selden Society, vol. 28), pp. xxvii, 56; Stephen, *Criminal Law*, III, 290, 343; *The Memoirs of Bill Hickey* (for the Supreme Court of Calcutta in the 1770s); N. Bentwich, *L.Q.R.* (1960).
6. F. Moran, *L.Q.R.* (1960), p. 70; Carr, *Charters*, p. lxxxviii; Keith, *Documents*, I, 35 ff.; and, for the rules as to which English statutes automatically applied in the colonies, E. G. Brown in *American Journal of Legal History* (1963).
7. Derrett, in *Comparative Studies in Society and History* (1961–2); J. H. Smith, *Appeals to the Privy Council from the American Plantations*; Holdsworth, *History of English Law*, I, 523.
8. For the following paragraphs, see G. L. Haskins, *Law and*

Authority in Early Massachusetts; R. Pound in *L.Q.R.* (1951); M. DeWolfe Howe in *L.Q.R.* (1960); Julius Goebel in *Publications of Colonial Lords of Manors in America* (Baltimore 1928); A. O. Porter, *County Government in Virginia*; *Johns Hopkins University Studies in Historical and Political Science* (Baltimore 1882—); J. H. Smith, *Colonial Justice in Western Massachusetts*.

9. Keith, *Documents*, p. 70; *Evelyn's Diary*, 3 August 1671; C. Ubbelohde, *The Vice-Admiralty Courts and the American Revolution*.

10. Gough, *Fundamental Law*; Haskins, *Law and Authority*, pp. 36, 191; Namier, *Structure of Politics*, p. 43; on lawyers as leaders of the revolution, see Daniel J. Boorstin, *The Americans, The Colonial Experience* (Pelican edition, 1965), pp. 230–4.

11. Hanbury, *The Vinerian Chair*, pp. 18–19; on the history of American law generally, see E. W. Griswold, *Law and Lawyers in the United States* (1964); J. W. Hurst, *The Growth of American Law, The Law Makers*; and *Readings in American Legal History*, compiled by Mark DeWolfe Howe (Cambridge, Mass., 1952).

12. Adam Smith, *The Wealth of Nations*, Book IV, cap. vii; R. Pares, *Merchants and Planters*, (Economic History Review Supplement, no. 4), pp. 2–4; Haskins, *Law and Authority*, pp. 9–10, 115; E. J. Hobsbawm, *The Age of Revolution*, cap. 8.

13. *The Cambridge Economic History of Europe*, III, 49–54, 58; R. Pares, *Merchants and Planters*, pp. 5, 33, and in *Essays presented to Sir Lewis Namier*; T. S. Willan, *Studies in Elizabethan Foreign Trade*; J. Webb, *Great Tooley of Ipswich*, pp. 38 ff.; Lucy S. Sutherland, *A London Merchant, 1695–1774*, pp. 81–125; T. S. Ashton, *An Economic History of England, the Eighteenth Century*, pp. 131–4; R. G. Marsden, *Select Pleas in the Court of Admiralty*, I (Selden Society, vol. 6), p. xvi; Kiralfy, *Source Book*, pp. 247, 383.

14. J. L. Brierley, *The Law of Nations* (6th ed.), pp. 304 ff.; D. H. N. Johnson, 'The English Tradition in International Law' in *The International and Comparative Law Quarterly* (1962), p. 431; T. W. Fulton, *The Sovereignty of the Sea*; H. A. Smith, *The Law and Custom of the Sea*; D. A. Gardiner in *L.Q.R.* (1932); Pares, *Merchants and Planters*, p. 12.

15. Kiralfy, *Source Book*, pp. 349–50, 355, 374, 384; Marsden, *Court of Admiralty*, II, p. xxxi.

16. Ashton, *The Eighteenth Century*, pp. 71–2; Lucy S. Sutherland in *T.R.H.S.* (1934); J. A. C. Thomas, *Private International Law*; Fifoot, *Mansfield*, pp. 56–7.

17. C. Gross, *Select Cases Concerning the Law Merchant*, I (Selden Society, vol. 23); Kiralfy, *Source Book*, pp. 238, 245, 351.

18. Marsden, *Court of Admiralty*, II, 205–6; J. S. Purvis, *St Anthony's Hall Publications*, no. 22; Webb, *Great Tooley* (for the court at Ipswich).
19. D. E. Kennedy in *Mariner's Mirror* (1962); Sutherland, *T.R.H.S* (1934), pp. 165–6; W. H. D. Winder, *L.Q.R.* (1936); Kiralfy, *Source Book*, pp. 238, 254, 351; *Select Cases Concerning the Law Merchant*, II (devoted to matters coming to the king's court on writs of error); Fifoot, *Mansfield*, p. 23; R. S. T. Chorley in *L.Q.R.* (1932).
20. W. H. Chaloner and A. E. Musson, *Industry and Technology*, plate 191; Ashton, *The Eighteenth Century*, pp. 63, 76; Webb, *Great Tooley*, pp. 30, 108–15; Yale, *Nottingham's Chancery Cases*, I, p. xcv; Elton in *Cambridge Historical Journal* (1954).
21. Ashton, *The Eighteenth Century*, p. 64; Willan, *Elizabethan Foreign Trade*, pp. 1–33, 240–65.
22. A. Simpson, *The Wealth of the Gentry, 1540–1640*, on the firm of Sir Thomas Cullum, draper; Carr, *Charters of Trading Companies*, p. 52.
23. Carr, *Charters*, pp. xi–xii; Pares, *Merchants and Planters*, pp. 27–8.
24. C. A. Cooke, *Corporation, Trust and Company*, pp. 30, 53, 64; Helen Miller, *B.I.H.R.* (1962), p. 133.
25. Chaloner and Musson, *Industry and Technology*, plate 190 (for the late survival of the staple system); E. W. Hulme in *L.Q.R.* (1917); D. S. Davies in *L.Q.R.* (1932); M. B. Donald, *Elizabethan Monopolies*, pp. 19–21, cap. 9 and appx II; Tanner, *Constitutional Documents of James I*, p. 271; Willan, *Elizabethan Foreign Trade*, cap. 2.
26. Cooke, *Corporation, Trust and Company*, pp. 54, 56–8; W. R. Scott, *Constitution of the Joint Stock Companies to 1720*; *Cambridge Economic History*, III, 58; Kiralfy, *Source Book*, p. 363.
27. Donald, *Elizabethan Monopolies*, caps. 5–6; Cooke, *Corporation, Trust and Company*, pp. 56, 59–60, 73; K. G. Davies in *Economic History Review* (1952).
28. L. C. B. Gower in *L.Q.R.* (1952); Cooke, *Corporation, Trust and Company*, p. 81.
29. H. A. Shannon in *Economic History* (1931); A. B. Dubois, *The English Business Company, 1720–1800*; Ashton, *The Industrial Revolution*, p. 96; Cooke, *Corporation, Trust and Company*, pp. 75–6, 85–8; G. W. Keeton, *Social Change in the Law of Trusts*, pp. 61 ff.
30. Ashton, *The Industrial Revolution*, pp. 128–9; *The Eighteenth Century*, pp. 75, 81–5.
31. Ashton in *Essays in Economic History* (ed. E. M. Carus-Wilson),

Vol. III; Fifoot, *Mansfield*, pp. 222–6; D. S. Davies in *L.Q.R.* (1934).

M. M. Postan in *Economic History Review* (1928); Ashton, *The*
32. *Eighteenth Century*, pp. 69–70; Pares, *Merchants and Planters*, pp. 49–50.
33. Plucknett, *Legislation of Edward I*, pp. 136–48; *Select Cases in the Law Merchant*, III (Selden Society, vol. 49), pp. xi ff.; Holdsworth, *History of English Law*, III, appx 5.
34. Winder in *L.Q.R.* (1936); Ashton, *Eighteenth Century*, p. 207.
35. Yale, *Nottingham's Chancery Cases*, I, pp. cxiv–cxx.
36. Fifoot, *Mansfield*, pp. 86, 220; Ashton, *Eighteenth Century*, p. 254.
37. J. M. Holden, *History of Negotiable Instruments in English Law*; S. J. Bailey in *L.Q.R.* (1931–2).
38. Kiralfy, *Source Book*, p. 244; Holden, *Negotiable Instruments*, pp. 25–6, for an example of a bill of exchange.
39. Holden, *Negotiable Instruments*, pp. 327–8 and plates I to V; Costin and Watson, I, 77–9, 271–8; Ashton, *Eighteenth Century*, pp. 178–9.
40. Quoted by Holden, p. 115.
41. Ashton, *Eighteenth Century*, pp. 167–200; D. M. Joslin in *Economic History Review* (1954); A. R. B. Haldane, *The Drove Roads of Scotland*, pp. 48–9; M. W. Flinn, *The Law Book of the Crowley Ironworks* (Surtees Society, 1952), pp. 54–6; P. Mathias, *English Trade Tokens*.
42. H. E. Raynes, *A History of British Insurance*.
43. W. J. Jones in *Business History* (1960); Marsden, *Court of Admiralty*, II, 45; Sutherland, *A London Merchant*, pp. 42–80.
44. Fifoot, *Mansfield*, pp. 88, 94, 116; *Cambridge Economic History*, III, 99–100.
45. Tate, *The Parish Chest*, pp. 119 ff.; C. Gill and A. Briggs, *History of Birmingham*, I, 127; P. G. M. Dickson, *The Sun Insurance Office*, 1710–1960, cap. 6.
46. Dickson, *Sun Insurance Office*; J. Simmons, *Transport*, plate 158; G. Kitson Clark, *The Making of Victorian England*, p. 100.
47. Fifoot, *Mansfield*, pp. 13, 93–4, 102, 104–9, 114–7; Chorley in *L.Q.R.* (1932); Sutherland, *T.R.H.S.* (1934), pp. 161–71.
48. Chaloner and Musson, *Industry and Technology*, pp. 32–3; J. U. Nef in *Economic History Review* (1934); Ashton, *The Industrial Revolution*, pp. 12–13; Mingay, *English Landed Society*, pp. 36 and 87; Winder, *L.Q.R.* (1936).
49. Postan in *Economic History Review* (1928); E. J. Hobsbawm, *The Age of Revolution*, p. 17; W. G. Hoskins, *The Midland Peasant*;

Keeton, *Social Change in the Law of Trusts*, pp. 11 ff.; Sylvia Thrupp, *The Merchant Class of Medieval London*, pp. 312–14; H. J. Habbakuk in *Britain and the Netherlands*, ed. Bromley and Kossmann.

50. *Select Cases in the Law Merchant*, II, pp. xlii ff.; Ashton, *Eighteenth Century*, pp. 136–8, 165–6; *The Industrial Revolution*, pp. 128–32.
51. Flinn, *The Law Book of the Crowley Ironworks*.
52. Webb, *Great Tooley*, p. 17; Ashton, *Eighteenth Century*, pp. 66, 122–4, 218–19, 224, 226–230; Holdsworth, *History of English Law*, XI, 461–71.
53. Costin and Watson, II, 18–20; H. Pelling, *A History of British Trade Unionism* (Pelican Books), pp. 25–8; Ashton, *Eighteenth Century*, p. 231.
54. Chaloner and Musson, *Industry and Technology*, p. 21; Ashton, *Eighteenth Century*, pp. 227–8; Holdsworth, *History of English Law*, XI, 500.

13. LAW REFORM IN THE NINETEENTH CENTURY: THE LEGAL SYSTEM

1. B. R. Mitchell and Phyllis Deane, *Abstract of British Historical Statistics*; W. L. Burn, *The Age of Equipoise*, p. 132.
2. *Lord Eldon's Anecdote Book*; W. Hazlitt, *The Spirit of the Age*; Holdsworth, *History of English Law*, IX, app. 2, XII, app. 2; *Charles Dickens as a Legal Historian*, cap. 3; *E.H.D.* XII (1) (ed. G. M. Young and W. D. Handcock), p. 525.
3. Walter Bagehot, quoted Holdsworth, *History of English Law*, XIII, 606.
4. W. H. & L. F. Maxwell, *A Legal Bibliography of the British Commonwealth*, I, 248–54; A. V. Dicey, *Law and Public Opinion in England in the Nineteenth Century* (2nd ed.), pp. 71, 89, 91–4; Fifoot, *Mansfield*, 231; Holdsworth, *Dickens as a Legal Historian*, pp. 123–6, 134, 139; Holdsworth, *History of English Law*, IX, 424; Fifoot, *English Law and Its Background*, p. 150.
5. Dicey, *Law and Public Opinion*, p. 115.
6. Burn, *Age of Equipoise*, pp. 139, 154–5, 179, 194; Kitson Clark, *The Making of Victorian England*, pp. 37–8.
7. *E.H.D.* XI (ed. A. Aspinall), pp. 299 ff.
8. G. W. Keeton and G. Schwarzenberger, *Jeremy Bentham and the Law: A Symposium*; Mary P. Mack, *Jeremy Bentham*; Dicey, *Law and Public Opinion*, pp. 126 ff.; Heath, *Eighteenth-Century Penal Theory*; Hazlitt, *Spirit of the Age*.

9. Kitson Clark, *The Making of Victorian England*, p. 19; Carr, *A Victorian Law Reformer's Correspondence* (Selden Society Lecture), pp. 10–13; C. New, *A Life of Henry Brougham to 1830*, especially cap. xxi; Dicey, *Law and Public Opinion*, pp. 106 ff.; *Greville's Diary* (Batsford Paperback), pp. 63, 148.

10. Dicey, *Law and Public Opinion*, pp. 163–4; Fifoot, *Judge and Jurist in the Reign of Victoria*, pp. 113–14, 117; Radzinowicz, *Sir James Fitzjames Stephen* (Selden Society Lecture).

11. Dicey, *Law and Public Opinion*, pp. 362, 369, 371–98; Fifoot, *Judge and Jurist*, pp. 15–18; Burn, *Age of Equipoise*, 137–8, 155.

12. Dicey, *Law and Public Opinion*, pp. 18, 85; Kitson Clark, *Making of Victorian England*, p. 100.

13. Dicey, *Law and Public Opinion*, pp. 11–12, 20, 187; Radzinowicz, *Stephen*, p. 9; Carr, *A Law Reformer's Correspondence*, p. 12; P. & G. Ford, *Select List of Parliamentary Papers*, 1833–99.

14. Carr, *Law Reformer's Correspondence*, pp. 8–9, 21; C. Hughes, *The British Statute Book*, pp. 27, 63–4, 111–14.

15. Carr, *Law Reformer's Correspondence*, p. 16; O. C. Williams, *History of Private Bill Procedure*; Hughes, *Statute Book*, p. 29.

16. Evans, *Government*, plates 120–21; P. & G. Ford, *List of Parliamentary Papers*, pp. 104–7; Holdsworth, *Dickens as a Legal Historian*, pp. 144–6.

17. For all the commissions and acts, see *E.H.D.* XII (1).

18. New, *Brougham*, p. 395; Fifoot, *Judge and Jurist*, p. 6.

19. *E.H.D.* XII (1), pp. 531–50.

20. Evans, *Government*, plate 160; Holdsworth in *L.Q.R.* (1935).

21. *E.H.D.* XII (1), pp. 541, 550; Denning, *From Precedent to Precedent*, p. 28; Costin and Watson, II, 278–82.

22. Winder in *L.Q.R.* (1936); *E.H.D.* XII (1), pp. 529–30.

23. Holdsworth, *History of English Law*, I, appx 25, 26, 29, 30; New, *Brougham*, pp. 392–3; *Guide to the Public Record Office*, I, 141–4.

24. Holdsworth, *Dickens as a Legal Historian*, pp. 12–30.

25. F. C. Mather, *Public Order in the Age of the Chartists*; *Victoria County History of Wiltshire*, V, 232; Evans, *Government*, plates 157–8; Costin and Watson, II, 259, 262.

26. Costin and Watson, II, 69–79, 87–8, 171, 174; Burn, *The Age of Equipoise*, pp. 153, 167–76, 189, 222; *VCH Wiltshire*, V, 231, 233, 263; J. M. Lee, *Social Leaders and Public Persons*, pp. 30–31.

27. F. W. Maitland, *Justice and Police*, pp. 99–102; Costin and Watson, II, 86, 89–90.

28. *VCH Wiltshire*, V.

29. Maitland, *Justice and Police*, pp. 163–4; Evans, *Government*, plate 161; Holdsworth, *Dickens as a Legal Historian*, p. 16.

30. Maitland, *Justice and Police*, pp. 171–3.

31. Robson, *The Attorney in the Eighteenth Century*, pp. 33, 66; Birks, *Gentlemen of the Law*, pp. 154–60, 236; Hanbury, *The Vinerian Chair*, pp. 83, 92; Fifoot, *Judge and Jurist*, pp. 23–26.

32. Holdsworth, *Dickens as a Legal Historian*, pp. 36–9; W. M. Thackeray, *Pendennis*, caps. xxviii–ix; Fifoot, *Judge and Jurist*, pp. 21–3; P. Lucas in *E.H.R.* (1962), pp. 480–81.

33. Hanbury, *The Vinerian Chair*, pp. 95–8; M. De Wolfe Howe's biography of Holmes, I, 227, II, 31.

34. Fifoot, *Judge and Jurist*, pp. 5, 7; *Law and History in the Nineteenth Century* (Selden Society Lecture), pp. 4–5, 10–11, 30; Maitland, *Historical Essays*, p. 118.

35. Fifoot, *Judge and Jurist*, p. 10; *Law and History*, pp. 7–8; DeWolfe Howe, *Holmes*, II, 138 ff.; *Guide to the Public Record Office*, I, 1–2; [1961] 1 Q.B. 232.

36. Hughes, *Statute Book*, pp. 84, 113, 161, 163; Fifoot, *Judge and Jurist*, p. 9; *Law and History*, pp. 6, 17; *English Law and Its Background*, pp. 183–6; Dicey, *Law and Public Opinion*, p. 365; Allen, *Law in the Making*, p. 269.

37. Birks, *Gentlemen of the Law*, pp. 174, 208–14, 222–6, 233.

38. Birks, *Gentlemen of the Law*, pp. 23–4, 235, 240, 243–4; Holdsworth, *Dickens as a Legal Historian*, pp. 40, 51–2, 57–8.

39. Thackeray, *Pendennis*; Radzinowicz, *Stephen*, p. 7; Holdsworth, *Dickens as a Legal Historian*, pp. 65, 67, 74.

40. A. S. Diamond in *L.Q.R.* (1960); Fifoot, *Judge and Jurist*, pp. 16–17, 29; *Radzinowicz*, Stephen, p. 36; DeWolfe Howe, *Holmes*, II, 132.

41. *Lord Eldon's Anecdote Book*, p. 116; F. M. L. Thompson, *English Landed Society in the Nineteenth Century*, p. 55; New, *Brougham*, p. 393; Carr, *Law Reformer's Correspondence*, pp. 5, 16; Costin and Watson, II, 160; J. B. Atlay, *The Victorian Chancellors*.

42. P. Lucas in *E.H.R.* (1962), p. 488; Carr, *Clement's Inn*, p. lviii; Burn, *The Age of Equipoise*, p. 9; Thompson, *Landed Society in the Nineteenth Century*, pp. 51–8.

43. Lord Evershed, *The Impact of Statute on the Law of England* (British Academy Lecture), pp. 248, 251, 255; Dicey, *Law and Public Opinion*, p. 487.

44. Fifoot, *English Law*, p. 170; Allen, *Law in the Making*, pp. 456–7; Hughes, *Statute Book*, pp. 56–8, 62, 71.

45. Allen, *Law in the Making*, pp. 503, 512, 528–9; Evershed, *Impact of Statute*, p. 262.
46. Holdsworth, *Essays in Law and History* (ed. Goodhart and Hanbury), pp. 284 ff.
47. Dicey, *Law and Opinion*, pp. 484–6; Holdsworth, *Essays*, p. 148; A. R. N. Cross, *Precedent in English Law*, p. 8.
48. Allen, *Law in the Making*, pp. 263, 313, 321–5, 330; Holdsworth, *Essays*, pp. 160, 163; Dicey, *Law and Public Opinion*, pp. 362–3.
49. Dicey, *Law and Public Opinion*, pp. 365, 368–9; Fifoot, *Judge and Jurist*, pp. 134–5.

14. LAW REFORM IN THE NINETEENTH CENTURY: THE SUBSTANTIVE LAW

1. *E.H.D.* XII, 386, 392; P. J. Fitzgerald, *Criminal Law and Punishment*, pp. 207–8.
2. O. Chadwick, *Victorian Miniature*, pp. 108–17; Kitson Clark, *Making of Victorian England*, p. 60; Hobsbawm, *Age of Revolution*, plate 61; Burn, *Age of Equipoise*, pp. 83, 156, 182–3; *E.H.D.* XI, 388, 399, 400–401; Fitzgerald, *Criminal Law*, p. 228; Holdsworth, *History of English Law*, XIII, 266; P. & G. Ford, *List of Parliamentary Papers*, p. 115.
3. Stephen, *Criminal Law*, I, 472–4; Holdsworth, *History of English Law*, XIII, 286; Costin and Watson, II, 98–9; Fitzgerald, *Criminal Law*, p. 88.
4. Burn, *Age of Equipoise*, pp. 153–6, 161, 224; Fitzgerald, *Criminal Law*, pp. 69, 77.
5. Costin and Watson, II, 69; Dicey, *Law and Public Opinion*, p. 263.
6. Fitzgerald, *Criminal Law*, p. 53; Fifoot, *Judge and Jurist*, pp. 111–17, 128; Radzinowicz, *Stephen*, pp. 16 ff.; Burn, *Age of Equipoise*, p. 181.
7. Fifoot, *Judge and Jurist*, pp. 119, 123, 125, 132–3; DeWolfe Howe, *Holmes*, II, 168–83; Fitzgerald, *Criminal Law*, p. 117.
8. Fifoot, *Judge and Jurist*, p. 133; Fitzgerald, *Criminal Law*, pp. 133–8; Stephen, *Criminal Law*, III, 426–37.
9. Fifoot, *Judge and Jurist*, pp. 99–104.
10. *Wiltshire Quarter-Sessions* (ed. Fowle), p. xxv; Fitzgerald, *Criminal Law*, p. 158; Mather, *Public Order*.
11. Costin and Watson, II, 175 (for the Home Secretary's responsibility); P. & G. Ford, *List of Parliamentary Papers*, p. 107.
12. F. T. Giles, *The Magistrates' Courts* (Pelican Books), pp. 12, 213–17.
13. Giles, *The Magistrates' Courts*, appx; see Stephen, *Criminal Law*,

III, for accounts of the trials of Palmer and Smethurst; Fitzgerald, *Criminal Law*, p. 162.

14. *E.H.D.* XI, 386; *E.H.D.* XII (1), pp. 505, 506, 513; Burn, *Age of Equipoise*, pp. 176–94.

15. Fitzgerald, *Criminal Law*, p. 213; New, *Brougham*, p. 396; Burn, *Age of Equipoise*, pp. 177–81, 185, 191–3; Evans, *Government*, plates 163–5, 171.

16. Fitzgerald, *Criminal Law*, pp. 248, 251, 254; *E.H.D.* XI, p. 387; Hazlitt, *Spirit of the Age*.

17. *Lord Eldon's Anecdote Book*, p. 19; Hastings, *Common Pleas in the Fifteenth Century*, p. 162; Fifoot, *Mansfield*, p. 151; J. H. Smith, *The Pynchon Court Record*.

18. Maitland, *The Forms of Action*, pp. 7–8, 79–81; Fifoot, *English Law*, pp. 69, 161.

19. Maitland, *Forms of Action*, p. 9; Diamond in *L.Q.R.* (1960).

20. Holdsworth in *C.L.J.* (1921–3).

21. Fifoot, *English Law*, p. 162; T. O. Elias, *British Colonial Law*, pp. 32–3; H. R. Gray, *The Law of Civil Injuries*, p. 102; J. Simmons, *Transport*.

22. Fifoot, *Judge and Jurist*, pp. 31 ff.; Gray, *Civil Injuries*, pp. 28, 41; De Wolfe Howe, *Holmes*, II, 86.

23. Gray, *Civil Injuries*, pp. 15, 36, 118, 120.

24. De Wolfe Howe, *Holmes*, II, 188–9; Gray, *Civil Injuries*, pp. 66–70.

25. Dicey, *Law and Public Opinion*, pp. 81, 190–91, 343; *E.H.D.* XII(1), pp. 512–13, 528–9; Kiralfy, *Source Book*, pp. 410–22; Holdsworth, *Dickens as a Legal Historian*, pp. 68–9; Burn, *Age of Equipoise*, p. 156; Margaret Puxon, *The Family and the Law* (Pelican Books), pp. 81 ff.

26. Thompson, *Landed Society in the Nineteenth Century*, pp. 64–9; Chadwick, *Victorian Miniature*; V. H. H. Green, *Oxford Common Room*; Simpson, *Land Law*, pp. 202–3, 252.

27. Keeton, *Social Change in the Law of Trusts*, pp. 39–50.

28. Hobsbawm, *Age of Revolution*, pp. 149–52; Thompson, *Landed Society*, pp. 69, 283–5, 319; Maitland, *Collected Papers*, I, 178.

29. Holdsworth, *History of English Law*, IX, 432; Maitland, *Collected Papers*, I, 171, 182.

29a. F. H. Lawson, *The Rational Strength of English Law*, pp. 75–106; *The Law of Property*.

30. Cooke, *Corporation, Trust and Company*, pp. 95 ff.; Dicey, *Law and Public Opinion*, p. 201; *E.H.D.* XII (1), p. 234.

31. *E.H.D.* XII (1), pp. 261, 278–92.

32. J. A. Hornby, *An Introduction to Company Law*, pp. 46, 64, 145–8; K. W. Wedderburn in *C.L.J.* (1957–8); Fifoot, *Judge and Jurist*, pp. 59–60, 63–4; Keeton, *Social Change in the Law of Trusts*, cap. vi; Cooke, *Corporation, Trust and Company*, p. 175.

33. P. S. Atiyah, *The Sale of Goods*; G. Borrie and A. L. Diamond, *The Consumer, Society and the Law* (Pelican Books), cap. i; Dicey, *Law and Public Opinion*, p. 263; G. H. Treitel and P. S. Atiyah in *L.Q.R.* (1957–8).

34. Dicey, *Law and Public Opinion*, pp. 211–40; P. & G. Ford, *List of Parliamentary Papers*, pp. 17, 64–7, 70–71; Pelling, *Trade Unionism*, pp. 63–4, 75–6; and now, on labour law generally, K. W. Wedderburn, *The Worker and the Law* (Pelican Books, 1965).

35. Fifoot, *Judge and Jurist*, pp. 67–70; Hornby, *Company Law*, pp. 136–8; Gray, *Civil Injuries*, p. 146, Dicey, *Law and Public Opinion*, pp. 280–83.

36. Pelling, *Trade Unionism*, p. 85; G. Gardiner and A. Martin, *Law Reform Now*, p. 221.

37. P. & G. Ford, *List of Parliamentary Papers*, pp. 43–4; Cooke, *Corporation, Trust and Company*, pp. 115–18; G. W. Hilton, *The Truck System*; Dicey, *Law and Public Opinion*, pp. 190–201; Costin and Watson, II, 40.

38. Burn, *Age of Equipoise*, pp. 160, 198–215; Dicey, *Law and Public Opinion*, pp. 261–3, 384; Costin and Watson, II, 192–4.

39. Simmons, *Transport*, p. 60 and plates 25, 150–52, 211; *E.H.D.* XII (1), p. 281.

40. G. Schwarzenberger, *The Frontiers of International Law*, pp. 199, 256; Brierly, *Law of Nations*, pp. 95–6, 98, 102–3, 348; D. H. N. Johnson in *The International and Comparative Law Quarterly* (1962).

41. Cooke, *Corporation, Trust and Company*, p. 179; Dicey, *Law and Public Opinion*, pp. 245, 248, 284–6; H. W. R. Wade, *Administrative Law*, pp. 15, 30–34; L. C. Webb, *Legal Personality and Political Pluralism*.

42. O. MacDonagh in *Victorian Studies* (1958); Burn, *Age of Equipoise*, pp. 135, 147, 151, 212–17; Costin and Watson, II, 174; Wade, *Administrative Law*, pp. 27–30, 100; Dicey, *Law and Public Opinion*, pp. 273–5.

43. Allen, *Law in the Making*, pp. 535–42; Allen, *Law and Orders*; M. A. Sieghart, *Government by Decree*; Wade, *Administrative Law*, pp. 24, 251.

44. Costin and Watson, II, 446–7.

45. Dicey, *The Law of the Constitution*; Wade, *Administrative Law*, pp.

83–6; for Dicey's altered view at the end of his life, see *L.Q.R.* (1915).

46. Wade, *Administrative Law*, pp. 41, 212–13.
47. Wade, *Administrative Law*, pp. 49–54, 130–45.
48. S. A. de Smith, *The Judicial Review of Administrative Acts;* Wade, *Administrative Law*, pp. 97, 100, 119–24; Burn, *Age of Equipoise*, p. 147; Costin and Watson, II, 69–79.
49. Wade, *Administrative Law*, pp. 257–63, 272.
50. Costin and Watson, II, 7, 107, 168, 263–4, 287; Harry Street, *Freedom, the Individual and the Law* (Pelican Books), cap. 2.
51. Wade, *Administrative Law*, pp. 3, 7, 11, 18, 38.

EPILOGUE: REFORM CONTINUED?

1. A. Sampson, *Anatomy of Britain*, cap. 10; B. Chapman, *British Government Observed* (a hostile view, used throughout this chapter); R. E. Megarry, *Lawyer and Litigant in England*, pp. 86–8.
2. Glanville Williams (ed.), *The Reform of the Law*, pp. 31, 210; G. Gardiner and A. Martin, *Law Reform Now* (1963), is the most recent compendium of criticisms of the law, particularly interesting now that one of the authors has become lord chancellor, and the other a law commissioner, and it has been drawn on extensively in this chapter.
3. Megarry, *Lawyer and Litigant* (a detailed account of lawyers' work); Hine, *Confessions of an Uncommon Attorney*; Birks, *Gentlemen of the Law*, pp. 2–3.
4. Sampson, *Anatomy*, p. 466; R. F. V. Heuston, *Lives of the Lord Chancellors, 1885–1940*, pp. 76, 81; Morris Ginsberg (ed.), *Law and Opinion in England in the Twentieth Century*, pp. 120, 241–2; Ludovic Kennedy, *The Trial of Stephen Ward*.
5. D. E. Butler and R. Rose, *The British General Election of 1959*; Heuston, *Lord Chancellors*, pp. 21, 36–66, 69.
6. Heuston, *Lord Chancellors*, pp. xviii–xx, 588, 600; *Political Adventure, The Memoirs of the Earl of Kilmuir*.
7. Allen, *Law in the Making*, pp. 352–3, 476, 480, 499; Fifoot, *English Law*, p. 203.
8. P. & G. Ford, *B.P.P. 1940–54*, pp. 164, 451–501; E. C. S. Wade, 'The Machinery of Law Reform' in *Modern Law Review* (1961); Heuston, *Lord Chancellors*, p. xix.
9. Evershed, *Impact of Statute Law*, p. 253; Fifoot, *English Law*, pp. 189, 191; Hughes, *Statute Book*, pp. 45, 132–4; Allen, *Law in the Making*, pp. 552–3.

10. I. Jennings, *Parliament* (2nd ed. 1957), cap. vii: 'Who Makes the Laws?'; S. E. Finer, *Anonymous Empire* (on pressure groups); Ginsberg, *Law and Opinion*, pp. 55–7, 233, 270, 276–7; Holdsworth, *Essays*, p. 34; Allen, *Law in the Making*, p. 311.

11. Fifoot, *English Law*, p. 251; Allen, *Law in the Making*, p. 300; Kennedy, *Ward Trial*, p. 102.

12. For the old dislike of 'socialist' experts, see Dicey, *Law and Public Opinion*, p. lxxvi.

13. Cross, *Precedent*, pp. 18, 109, 114; Denning, *From Precedent to Precedent*, pp. 22–31; Allen, *Law in the Making*, pp. 312, 315, 367–79.

14. W. Friedmann, *Law and Social Change in Contemporary Britain*, pp. 164, 237–8, 243, 247; Allen, *Law in the Making*, pp. 503, 529.

15. See Lord Evershed's views, reported in *The Times* of 18 May 1964; and in *The Impact of Statute Law*, p. 261; Allen, *Law in the Making*, pp. 488–9, 500–501, 509, 520, 525, 527.

16. Allen, *Law in the Making*, pp. 298–9, 303–4; H. L. A. Hart, *The Concept of Law*, pp. 121 ff., 200; Fifoot, *English Law*, 258–9.

17. Hart, *Concept of Law*, pp. 140, 150; Cross, *Precedent*, pp. 121–30, 133–40; Allen, *Law in the Making*, pp. 340–41.

18. Cross, *Precedent*, pp. 106, 248–9, 256; Denning, *Precedent to Precedent*, pp. 22, 34; Allen, *Law in the Making*, pp. 311, 352–3.

19. Holdsworth, *Essays*, pp. 100–127; Wade on land charge registration in *C.L.J.* (1956).

20. For these paragraphs see Thompson, *Landed Society in the Nineteenth Century*; and F. H. Lawson, *Introduction to the Law of Property*; Fifoot, *English Law*, p. 121.

21. Friedmann, *Law and Social Change*, pp. 10, 16; Ginsberg, *Law and Opinion*, pp. 119, 124–6, 138; *B.P.P. 1917–39*, p. 549.

22. Lawson, *The Rational Strength of English Law*, pp. 100–106.

23. Ginsberg, *Law and Opinion*, pp. 288–93; and Hine, *Confessions*, p. 50, for the effects of the Inheritance Act.

24. Peter Hays, *New Horizons in Psychiatry* (Pelican Books), p. 282; R. Egerton on legal aid in *L.Q.R.* (1945).

25. See generally, Gray, *Civil Injuries*; Friedmann, *Law and Social Change*, pp. 75–84, 87–92, 97–100; an up-to-date textbook on tort is Harry Street, *The Law of Torts*.

26. Fifoot, *English Law*, p. 246; Allen, *Law in the Making*, p. 331; C. A. Wright in *C.L.J.* (1961); Goodhart on damages for shock in *Law in Action*, Vol. I.

27. Friedmann, *Law and Social Change*, pp. 84, 93–6; Fifoot, *English*

Law, p. 272; *Hedley Byrne & Co., Ltd* v. *Heller & Partners, Ltd*, [1963] 2 All E. R., pp. 575–618.

28. Fifoot, *English Law*, p. 225; *B.P.P. 1940–54*, pp. 494–5; J. Winocour in *Encounter* (August 1964) on Dering trial.

29. Richard Du Cann, *The Art of the Advocate* (Pelican Books).

30. C. H. Rolph, *All those in favour. The E.T.U. Trial*; Diamond in *L.Q.R.* (1959–60); I. H. Jacob in *Archives* (1964); M. Amos in *C.L.J.* (1924–6).

31. Egerton in *L.Q.R.* (1945); letter to *The Times* of 18 January 1964.

32. *B.P.P. 1940–54*, pp. 494–5; [1964] 1 All E. R., pp. 918–22; [1965] 1 All E. R., pp. 563–76; letter to *The Times* of 30 January 1965.

33. Friedmann. *Law and Social Change*, Wedderburn, *The Worker and the Law*, and Ginsberg, *Law and Opinion*, are the basis of what follows; see also Fifoot, *English Law*, pp. 173–4, 210.

34. See also H. A. Clegg, A. Fox and A. F. Thompson, *A History of British Trade Unions since 1889*, I, 305–25; Heuston, *Lord Chancellors*, p. 76; Maitland, *Collected Papers*, III, 305; Costin and Watson, II, 333; Dicey, *Law and Public Opinion*, pp. xlv ff.

35. See the T.U.C. debate reported in *The Times* of 11 September 1964; *B.P.P. 1900–16*, p. 205; *B.P.P. 1917–39*, p. 319.

36. In addition to Friedmann and Ginsberg, see Hornby, *Company Law*.

37. *B.P.P. 1900–16*, p. 123; *B.P.P. 1917–39*, pp. 183–4; *B.P.P. 1940–54*, p. 164; L. C. B. Gower on 'Company Directors and Take-over Bids' in *Law in Action*, II; Atiyah in *The Lawyer* (Hilary 1965).

38. See also Fifoot, *English Law*, pp. 173–4; Jeremy Lever, *The Law of Restrictive Practices and Resale Price Maintenance*.

39. Borrie and Diamond, *The Consumer, Society and the Law*; *B.P.P. 1900–16*, p. 186; *B.P.P. 1940–54*, p. 154; G. Gardiner, 'Freedom of Contract' in *Law in Action*, II.

40. Heuston, *Lord Chancellors*, p. 45; Fifoot, *English Law*, pp. 239–40; Ginsberg, *Law and Opinion*, pp. 166–9.

41. See generally, Fitzgerald, *Criminal Law*; Radzinowicz and J. W. C. Turner (ed.), *The Modern Approach to Criminal Law* (1945); C. Hibbert, *The Roots of Evil*; J. B. Mays, *Crime and the Social Structure*. On criminal statistics, see Radzinowicz, as reported in *The Times* of 4 June 1964; Central Statistical Office, *Annual Abstract of Statistics*; F. H. McClintock and Evelyn Gibson, *Robbery in London* (1961); McClintock, *Crimes of Violence* (1963); the issue of *Twentieth Century* on Crime (Winter 1962.)

42. Burn, *Age of Equipoise*, p. 139; Lord Devlin, *The Enforcement of Morals* (1959); E. V. Rostow in *C.L.J.* (1960); H. L. A. Hart, *Law, Liberty and Morality*; J. E. Hall Williams in *L.Q.R.* (1958).

43. G. Williams, *The Sanctity of Life and the Criminal Law*; Aleck Bourne, *A Doctor's Creed*; *B.P.P. 1917–39*, p. 539; A. C. Armitage in *C.L.J.* (1957); Lady Wootton of Abinger, 'Diminished Responsibility: A Layman's View', in *L.Q.R.* (1960); for a balanced view of the present relationship of law and psychiatry, see Hays, *New Horizons in Psychiatry*, chapter 14.

44. Friedmann, *Law and Social Change*, p. 107; C. Howard, *Strict Responsibility*.

45. Kennedy, *Ward Trial*, pp. 90, 95, 99, 132, 144; C. H. Hoffman in *The Lawyer* (Trinity 1964).

46. Lee, *Social Leaders and Public Persons*, pp. 16, 54–5, 183; Chapman, *British Government Observed*, pp. 51–4; Glanville Williams, *The Proof of Guilt*, pp. 274–8, 281–5, 289–93; *B.P.P. 1900–16*, p. 357; *B.P.P. 1917–39*, p. 521; *B.P.P. 1940–54*, p. 455; Kennedy, *Ward Trial*, p. 233; report of the Bassett inquest in *The Times* of 1 May 1964.

47. Cross in *L.Q.R.* (1960); Williams, *Proof of Guilt*, pp. 43–76, 148 ff., 165; Kennedy, *Ward Trial*, pp. 35, 194, 201.

48. Williams, *The Proof of Guilt*, pp. 22–6, 128, 190–272; L. Blom-Cooper, *The A6 Trial*; Kennedy, *Ward Trial*, pp. 28, 68, 75, 83, 205, 218, 234, 236; *The Twentieth Century* (Winter 1962), pp. 102–3; Heuston, *Lord Chancellors*, p. 55; Devlin, *The Enforcement of Morals*.

49. Chapman, *British Government Observed*, p. 52; Williams, *The Proof of Guilt*; Kennedy, *Ward Trial*, p. 227; C. J. Hampson and T. F. T. Plucknett, *The English Trial and Comparative Law*, pp. 16, 27; Giles, *Magistrates' Courts*, for offences triable summarily; C. H. Rolph, *All Those in Favour?*

50. Williams, *The Proof of Guilt*, pp. 86–95, 222, 259–64; parliamentary debates reported in *The Times*, 28 January and 14 February 1964; *B.P.P.* passim, for inquiries ordered by the Home Secretary.

51. R. S. E. Hinde, *The British Penal System*, 1773–1950; M. Grunhut, *Penal Reform*; Howard Jones, *Crime and the Penal System*; D. L. Howard, *The English Prisons*; Wootton in *L.Q.R.* (1960); *B.P.P. 1917–39*, p. 539; *The Twentieth Century* (Winter 1962), pp. 14, 43–9, 68–70; Nigel Walker, *Crime and Punishment in Britain*.

52. *B.P.P. 1900–16*, p. 370; *B.P.P. 1940–54*, p. 479; Armitage in *C.L.J.* (1957); Williams, *The Proof of Guilt*, pp. 88–94; *The*

Twentieth Century (Winter 1962), pp. 7–19, 50–57; T. Parker and R. Allerton, *The Courage of His Convictions*; T. C. N. Gibbens, *Psychiatric Studies of Borstal Boys*; Evans, *Government*, plates 166–7; Hays, *New Horizons in Psychiatry*, pp. 297–303.

53. See generally, E. C. S. Wade and G. G. Phillips, *Constitutional Law*; G. H. Le May, *British Government 1914–53: Select Documents*; G. Marshall and G. C. Moodie, *Some Problems of the Constitution*; Wade, *Administrative Law*.

54. See also, Ginsberg, *Law and Opinion*, p. 203; Chapman, *British Government Observed*.

55. Friedmann, *Law and Social Change*, p. 104.

56. G. W. Keeton, *Trial by Tribunal*.

57. [1963] 2 All E. R., pp. 66–120; Friedmann, *Law and Social Change*, pp. 143–8; Ginsberg, *Law and Opinion*, pp. 109, 114–15, 225; D. Lloyd on 'Disciplinary Powers of Professional Bodies' in *Modern Law Review* (1950). See Wade's inaugural lecture at Oxford in 1962, *Law, Opinion and Administration*, for the present condition of administrative law; but cf. Professor J. D. B. Mitchell's review of Wade, *Administrative Law*, in *L.Q.R.* (1962) for a less optimistic view.

58. Ginsberg, *Law and Opinion*, pp. 105–15, 232; Friedmann, *Law and Social Change*, pp. 129, 145; T. C. Thomas, 'Trade Unions and their Members' in *C.L.J.* (1956).

59. Costin and Watson, II, 320; Wade, *Administrative Law*, p. 194; J. Ll. J. Edwards, *The Law Officers of the Crown*, caps. 10–11; Chapman, *British Government Observed*, p. 56.

60. See [1963] 3 All E. R., p. 544, for a case in which the Privy Council had to interpret the Nigerian constitution.

61. D. H. N. Johnson in *International and Comparative Law Quarterly* (1962); Schwarzenberger, *Frontiers of International Law*, pp. xviii–xx; Brierly, *Law of Nations*, p. 98; A. H. Robertson, *Human Rights in Europe; Times Law Report*, 13 September 1963; remarks of Lord Shawcross, *The Times*, 2 July 1963.

62. Birks, *Gentlemen of the Law*, p. 26; Squibb, *Court of Chivalry*, p. 123; report of a charge of embracery at Leeds in *The Times* of 21 January 1965; Pritchard in *C.L.J.* (1960); Hornby, *Company Law*, pp. 100 ff.

63. Friedmann, *Law and Social Change*, pp. 74, 81, 87; Dicey, *Law and Public Opinion*, pp. xxxvii–xxxviii.

64. Chapman, *British Government Observed*, p. 57; Friedmann, *Law and Social Change*, p. 260.

65. Ginsberg, *Law and Public Opinion*, pp. 213, 261–3.

TABLE OF CASES

TABLE OF CASES

TABLE OF STATUTES

TABLE OF STATUTES

INDEX

figures in italics represent the main references

Abbott, Charles, 338
Abjuring the realm, 120
Abortion, 415
Abridgements, 198, 286
 Fitzherbert's *Grand Abridgement*,
  198
Absolute monarchy, 254
Accessories to crime, 65, 272
Account, action of, 310
Accountants, encroach on
 lawyers' preserve, 351, 392
Accumulations Act, 373
Acquittals, statistics of, in eight-
 eenth century, 276
Actions, *See* Forms of action
Acton Burnell, Statute of, 316
Acts of Parliament, *See* Statutes
Actuaries, 322, 408
Actus reus, 416
Administrative courts, 423
 in England in sixteenth century,
  158
Administrative law, 66, *243*, 295,
 *384*ff., *422*ff.
Admiralty, *See* Courts
Adoption Acts, 403
Adulteration of Food Act, 378
Adultery, in jurisdiction of Church
 courts, 160
Advocacy, 211, 290
 and juries, 406
Affidavits, 294, 406
Affray, 81
Agency, 305, *311*
Alabama case, and the international
 court, 382
Alderman, the, 23, *27*
Alderson v. *Temple*, 317
Alfred, King, 17, 19, 21, 29
Allen v. *Allen*, 403

Almoner, the King's, 155
Amalgamated Society of Railway
 Servants, 409
Amercements, *See* Fines
American colonies, 295
 law of, *302*ff.
 See also United States of America
American Law Review, 351
Angevin kings, 3off., 130
Anson, William, *Law of Contract*
 by, 349
Anstey, Richard of, 122ff., 140, 331
Anthropology and law, 239, 287
Appeals, 52, 138, 340, 357
 none in Anglo-Saxon times, 21
 from lord to overlord, 36
 in criminal cases, 75, 139, 347
 to Rome, 122, 161, 255
 from Chancery, 257
 Lord Mansfield's development of,
  284
 from Scotland and Ireland, 299
 to Privy Council from colonies,
  301, 303
 from commonwealth, 429
 in equity, 339
 See also Courts
Appeals of felony, 40, 51, 60, *62*ff.,
  66, 76, 119
 and trespass, 97
 in Court of Chivalry, 163
 abolished, 363
Appeals of treason, 164
Appellate Jurisdiction Act, 342
Apprentice and Servant Act, 333,
  360
Apprentices at law, 135, 169, *174*,
  188, 197
 inns of, 187
Approvers, 84, 126, 181

479

Barristers, 171, *175*ff., 188, 197, 207, 287, 354
  and solicitors, 177, 352, 391
  as king's counsel, law officers and judges, 182
  dress of, 206
  in twentieth century, 389ff.
Bate's Case, 254
Bastardy, 85
Battle, trial by, *See* Trial
Beccaria, 334, 359
Beck, Adolf, 420
Becket, Thomas, 36, 144
Bellingham, Richard, 302
Bentham, Jeremy, 203, 236, 297, 332, *334*ff., 357, 359
Bereford, William, Chief Justice, 134
Bevan, on duties of care, 370
Bigamy, 300, 360, 372
Bill of Rights, 292, 296, 387
Bills, 57, 141, 154, 157, 197
  in Parliament, 57, 194, 212, 226, 338
  in eyre, 67, 76
  of indictment, 77
  of Middlesex, 119ff., 123, 220, 367
  of exceptions, 138
  alleging crimes, 158
  See also Petitions
Bills of Exchange Act, 394
Binding over, to keep the peace, 72
  to good behaviour, 85
Bindoff, S. T., on Statute of Artificers, 233
Blackburn, Lord, 336, 353, 356
Blackmail, 156
Blackstone, William, 289, 290, 297, 299, 318, 332, 334, 350, 370
  Commentaries on the laws of England, by, 286, 303
Blasphemy, 255
Board of Trade,
  and company law, 376, 395

and Monopolies Commission, 413
Bologna, teaching of Roman Law at, 192, 240
Bombay, grant of, in socage, 299
Bonsor v. *Musicians Union*, 426
Bookland, 25ff.
Books of Entries, 199
'Bootless wrongs', 17
  and felonies, 63
Boroughs, 20, 218, 244, 295, 307, 345
  customs of, 216, 218
  incorporation of, 248
Boson v. *Sandford*, 307
Boswell, James, 291, 367
Bourchier, Robert, chancellor, 191
Bow Street
  magistrates, 270
  'runners', 271, 346
Bracton, Henry of, 169, 201, 350
  and case law, 200, 221
  on kingship, 202, 253
'Bracton's Note Book', 198, 350
Bramwell, Lord, 336
Breach of close, as trespass, 83
Breach of promise, 406
Breaking bulk, felony of, 310
Breaking on the wheel, 276
Brevia Placitata, 134, 198
Brewster Sessions, 268
Bridewell, 85
Bristol, founds own law society, 288
British Academy, jurists and foundation of, 355
Broadmoor asylum, 366
Brok, Lawrence del, king's attorney and judge, 169, 180
Brougham, Lord Chancellor, 331, *335*ff., 366
  creates Judicial Committee of Privy Council, 341
'Brougham's Act' on the drafting of statutes, 338
Bryce, James, 349

standard form, 413
public, 425
See also Consideration, Privity
Conveyancing and conveyancers, *25*, 46, 53, *89*, 113, *178*ff., 189, 196, 201, 286, 352, *373*ff., 390, 400, 414
Cooper v. *Wandsworth Board of Works*, 386
Copyhold, 95–6, 184, 216, 400
Coroners, 49, 59, 120, 127, 167, 346, 418
Corporations, 187, 229, 230, *248*ff., 261, 295, 301, 315, 380, *408*ff.
public, *381*ff., 423
See also Companies
Correction, houses of, 85
Costs, 179, 208, 211, 244, 351, 369, 391, 407
Councils of the magnates, 157, 167, 172
Counsel,
allowed to accused of treason, 274
allowed to accused of felony, 365
County and Borough Police Act, 345
County councils, 345
Counties, the, 20, 35, 345, 429
lawyers in, *183*ff.
governed by J.P.s, 268, 292
in America, 304
See also Courts, Sheriff
Courts, the,
conflicts between, 256
reform of the civil courts, *339*ff.
consolidation of, in nineteenth century, 340ff.
move out of Westminster Hall, 343
modern criminal, *344*ff.
Courts
folk-moots, 14ff.
village, 17
manorial, 18, 33, 70, 172

seignorial, 18, 35, 49, 114, 184, 268
in the United States of America, 303
hundred, 20ff., 33, 35, 114
shire, 22ff., 29, 35, 39, 41, 48, 51, 114, 194, 343
honour, 33, 36, 44, 114
assizes, 43, 68, 74, 138, 183, 268–9, 273, 274, 297, 346
the eyre, 42ff., 48, 49, 51, *59*ff., 176, 181, 251
articles of, 48, 60, 66
breakdown of, 67, 70
of the forest, 256
King's Bench (*coram rege*), 50ff., 71, 74–5, 105, 111, 114, 119ff., 138, 146, 152, 168, 170, 176, 180, 214, 243, 244, 257, *282*ff., 291, 295, 317, 332, 343, 387, 388
Common Pleas, 51, 55, 105, 111, 114, 120, 122, 134, 140, 141, 152, 171ff., 179, 209, 213, 219, 344
Exchequer, 50, *159*, 168, 172, 181, 254, 310
gaol delivery, 67, 74, 86
oyer and terminer, 68, 86, 114, 122, 176, 177, 219, 300
trailbaston, 68
nisi prius hearings, 68, 74–5, 122, 137, 143, 146, 176, 184
Star Chamber, 75, 79, 81, 112, 120, 132, 149, *152*ff., 157, 158, 197, 199, 211, 242, 256, 294
Court of Chivalry, 78, *162*ff., 244, 245, 267, 301, 340, 429
Court of Wards, 89, 150, 160, 266
Exchequer Chamber, 105, 222, 319, 340, 397
'conciliar courts', 140, *149*ff., 161, 190ff., 200, 220, 246, 261, 294, 303
Court of Admiralty, 131, 141, 163, 166, 203, 301, *307*ff., 321, 340, 346
Court of Requests, 154ff.

Land Market – *contd*
in twentieth century, 401
Land registration, 109, 266, 281, 332, 374, 390, 400
Landlord and tenant law, modern, 402
Langdale v. *Mason and Others*, 323
Larceny, 65, 82, 275, 363
Latilla v. *Inland Revenue*, 398
Law books, *194*ff., 350
Law Commissioners, 396, 431
Law officers of the Crown, 175, *179*ff., 353, 383, 393
See also Attorney-general, Solicitor-general, Director of Public Prosecutions
Land Transfer Act, 373
Larceny Act, 377
Law Amendment Society, 351, 356
Law of Property Act, 373
Law reform, 320ff., 389, 394
Law Reform Committee, 394
Law Reform (Personal Injuries) Act, 404
Law of the land, *lex terrae*, 56
Law reports, 133, *199*ff., *221*ff., 286, 293, 350, 356–7
The English Reports, 200
Law Revision Committee, 395
Law Society, 347, 390, 403, 407
Law terms, *122*ff., 249
Laws,
old English, 13ff., 195, 224
written, 194
Lawrance, Mr Justice, 413
Lawmen, lawfinders, old English, 28, 39, 50
Lawyers,
in society, *206*ff.
wealth and income of, 208, 290, 391
hostility to, 211
in politics, 211ff., 393
in eighteenth-century society, 285ff.

in twentieth-century society, 392
Leasehold, 25, 46, *92*ff., 99, 400
Leasehold Enfranchisement Bill, 402
Lease and release, conveyancing device of, 109
Lee, Rowland, bishop of Coventry and president of the Council in the Marches of Wales, 156
Legal aid, 244, 372, 392, 403, 407, 418, 430
Legal Aid and Advice Act, 407
Legal argument, *132*ff., 198, 235
Legal concepts, 234ff., 363
Legal dress, 206
Legal education, 8, 189, 347ff., 389
Legal history, 9, 202ff.
Legal fictions, 53, 75, 89, 94, 97, 120, 219, 248, 309, 337, 368
Legal profession, 57, *167*ff., *351*ff., *389*ff.
See also Attorneys, Judges, etc.
Legal records, 7, 51, 125, 171, 194, 197
pipe rolls, 37, 59
plea rolls, 52, 62, 129, 140, *142*, 180, 343
eyre rolls, 59
Legislation, 194, *224*ff., *291*ff., 336
Magna Carta as, 57
retrospective, 234
nineteenth-century reformers' faith in, 334, 336
programmes of, 337
penal, and nineteenth-century social reform, 361
private members' bills, 395, 396
See also Statutes, Subordinate legislation
Legislators, *232*ff.
Legitimacy Acts, 403
Liability, strict, in modern tort, 382, 405, 407
Lewis, David, master of requests, 155

St Paul's, serjeants consult clients
  in, 173–4
St Bartholomews, Smithfield, store
  for legal records, 172, 180
St Germain, Christopher, writer
  on equity, 204, 237
Sale, law of, 16, 103, 309, 321, 337,
  413
Sale of Food and Drugs Act, 378
Sale of Goods Act, 394
Salkeld, Charles, solicitor, 289
Salomon v. *Salomon*, 411
Savigny, 349
Sanctuaries, 120, 250
Scriptoria, 29, 178
Scandalum magnatum, 80
Scotland,
  Reception in, 241
  English writs in, 298
Scroggs, Chief Justice, 274
Scrope, Archbishop, 79, 165
Scrope v. *Grosvenor*, 163
Sedition, 79ff., 85
Seditious libel, 272
Seisin, 41, *45*ff., 90, 92, 112
  livery of, 46, 54, 108
Self-help, 21, 33, 41, 119
Selborne, Lord Chancellor, 341,
  348ff., 354, 383
Selden, John, legal writer, 203, 204
Selden Society, the, 350
Seals, *29*
  the great seal of England, 37, 50
Sentencing, 129, 154, 367, 420
Serjeants-at-law, 84, 140, 172, 188,
  198, 206, 352
  inns of, 175, 182, 332, 347, 352
Settled Land Act, 323
Settlements, *See* Family settlements
Settlement, Act of, 294
Seven Bishops' Case, 272
Shares, 313, 376ff., 411
Shaw v. *D.P.P.*, 415
Shelley's Case, 92, 200, 283
Sheriffs, 21, 27ff., 35, 37, 39, 48,
  268

Shires, *See* Counties, Courts
Sheppard, William, *A Touchstone
  of Common Assurances* by, 179,
  286
Sherman, Gilbert, attorney, 211
Simpson v. *Wells*, 218
Slade's Case, 104ff.
Slander, 80, 106, 294, 406
Smith, Sir Thomas, legal writer,
  131, 142, 203
Solicitor-general, 175, 182, 190
  206, 353, 393
Solicitors, 140, *175*ff., 287ff., 290,
  347, *351*ff., 390ff.
Smith v. *Bromley*, 285
Somers, Lord Chancellor, 289
Sommersett's Case, 295
South Sea Bubble, 314
Specific performance, 55, 147
Spelman, Sir Henry, 259
Stamp Act, 303
Stampe, Thomas, recorder of
  Wallingford, 208
Staple, merchants of the, 153, 312,
  316
Stare decisis, *See* Precedent
State trials, 71
Status, 23, 247ff.
Statute Law Committee, the,
  338
Statute Law Revision Acts, 338
Statute-law, *225*
Statute-rolls, 194, 205
Statutes, 48, 58, 158, 194, 230,
  *338*ff.
  penal, 77, 158
  judicial interpretation or con-
    struction of, 79, *220*ff., 227ff.,
    230, 232, 260, 293, 355, 387,
    398
  consolidating, 226, 337, 338, 377,
    394
  private acts, 227, 384
  local acts, 292, 316
  Public General Acts, 339, 395
  temporary acts, 422

Statutes of the Realm, 195, 234, 338, 350
Statutes Revised, 350
Statutes-merchant and statutes-staple, 316
Statutory duties, 370
Statutory Rules and Orders, 384
Stephen, Serjeant, on pleading, 332, 368
Stephen, Sir James Fitzjames, 300, 336, 337, 348, 352, 354–5, 361
Stockdale v. *Hansard*, 388
Story, Professor Joseph, 304
Stow, John, on the sixteenth-century courts, 84, 152, 185
Stowell, Lord, judge of the Admiralty Court, 308, 331, 353, 383
Strafford, Earl of, attainder of, 258
Stratford v. *Lindley*, 410
Strode's Case, 257
Subordinate legislation, 229, 384ff.
Sugden, Lord Chancellor, 200
Suicide, 60, 64, 421
  attempted, no longer a crime, 415
Suicide Act, 395, 416
Summary Jurisdiction Act, 364
Summary offences, 419
Surety, 16, 19, 21ff., 170
  See also Bail
Suspending power of the King, 292

Taff Vale Case, 409
Tailors of Ipswich, Case of the, 223
Taltarum's Case, 91
Tanistry Case, 218
Taxation, 20, 37
  derived from feudal incidents, 88
Taxation Acts, 397, 398
Taxing masters, 351, 369
Tenures, 26
  feudal, 30ff.
  in chief, 31, 34, 36, 45, 89
  in serjeanty, 32

'freehold', 32
  in fee-farm, 32
  socage, 32, 89, 279
  in fee simple, 90, 92, 110
  and estates, 91
  for life, 94
  feudal, abolition of, 279
  See also Copyhold
Theft, 17, 40, 61
  quasi-, 310
  See also Larceny
Thellusson, Peter, will of, 373, 375
Textus Roffensis, 195
Tiptoft, John, earl of Worcester, judge in Court of Chivalry, 165
Thorne v. *the Motor Trade Association*, 412
Thornton, Gilbert of, judge, 169
Thorpe, Chief Justice, 135
Thurlow, Lord Chancellor, 295
Tolpuddle martyrs, 380
Tort, 98ff., 357, 369ff.
  outlawry in, 121
  and insurance, 404
  modern law of, 405ff.
Trade, law and, 324–5
Trade Disputes Act, 329, 409ff.
Trade unions, 327ff., 355, 379ff., 408ff., 426
Trade Union Act, 408
Transportation of convicts, 271, 277, 365
Treason, 17, 65, 79, 151, 266
  constructive, 80
  See also Appeals of treason
Treason Felony Act, 360
Treasons, Statute of, 78
Trespass, civil action of, 64, 94, 95, 97ff., 114, 332, 379
Trespass, criminal, 65ff., 76, 82, 97
Trespass on the case, civil actions of, 100ff., 303, 319, 332, 379
Trial,
  old English, 22
  by ordeal, 24, 40, 61, 129
  by battle, 40, 62, 84, 129